To my parents, to whom I owe everything and more.

Latin: A New Grammar

Latin grammar taught and explained, with examples

Juan Coderch

Latin: A New Grammar

Latin grammar taught and explained, with examples

First Edition

ISBN: **978-0-9571387-2-8**

Printed by CreateSpace (South Carolina, United States)

Latin: A New Grammar

Latin grammar taught and explained, with examples

Index of contents

The numbers make reference to the numbered paragraphs, not to the pages.

Preface

ALPHABET AND WRITING

a) The alphabet [1]
b) Pronunciation [2]
c) Accentuation [3]

THE NOMINAL SYSTEM

a) Definition of basic grammatical concepts: *case, declension* and *gender*

1. Concepts of *syntactical function, endings* and *case* [4]
2. Main syntactical functions and correspondence to cases [6]
3. Concept of *declension* [8]
4. Concept of *gender* [9]
5. Lack of definite article [10]

b) Declensions

General observations [11]
1. 1st declension [12]
2. 2nd declension [14]
3. 3rd declension [18]
4. 4th declension [26]
5. 5th declension [28]

c) Adjectives

General observations [29]
1. 1st class of adjectives [30]
2. 2nd class of adjectives [32]
3. Position of the adjective [36]
4. Use of the adjective as a noun [37]

d) Numeral adjectives

1. Cardinals [38]
2. Ordinals [40]
3. Multiplicatives [41]
4. Distributives [42]

e) Comparative and superlative

1. General observations [43]
2. Accidence [44]
3. Syntax [48]

f) Pronouns

1. Demonstrative pronouns [55]
2. Personal pronouns [61]
3. Possessive pronouns [63]
4. Anaphoric pronoun [64]
5. Identity pronouns [65]
6. Reflexive pronouns [67]
7. Interrogative pronoun and adjective [70]
8. Other interrogative pronouns [72]
9. Relative pronoun [75]
10. Indefinite relative pronoun [76]
11. Other indefinite pronouns [77]
12. Negative pronouns [94]

g) Adverbs and prepositional adverbs

1. General observations [100]
2. Modal adverbs [101]
3. Comparative and superlative of modal adverbs [103]
4. Quantitative adverbs [105]
5. Adverbs of time [106]
6. Adverbs of place [108]
7. Interrogative adverbs [111]
8. Indefinite adverbs [112]
9. Affirmative and negative adverbs [114]
10. Prepositional adverbs [116]

h) The correlatives

1. Correlative adverbs [118]
2. Correlative adjectives [125]

THE VERBAL SYSTEM

a) General observations

1. Mechanic of the Latin verbs [130]
2. The tenses [131]
3. The moods [132]
4. The voices [133]
5. Formation of tenses [134]
6. Formation of moods [136]
7. Types of verbs [137]
8. Principal parts [138]

b) The four regular conjugations

1. The 1st conjugation [140]
2. The 2nd conjugation [150]
3. The 3rd conjugation [158]
4. The 4th conjugation [166]
5. The mixed conjugation [174]

c) The passive voice

1. Present-stem tenses [182]
2. Perfect-stem tenses [188]

d) Deponent and semi-deponent verbs

1. Deponent verbs [192]
2. Nominal forms in deponent verbs [194]
3. Semi-deponent verbs [197]
4. Passive deponent verbs [198]

e) Verb sum and its compounds

1. Verb **sum** [199]
2. Compounds of **sum** [200]
3. Verb **possum** [202]
4. Verb **prosum** [203]

f) Irregular verbs

1. Verb **volo** [204]
2. Verb **nolo** [205]
3. Verb **malo** [206]
4. Verb **eo** and its compounds [207]
5. Verb **fero** and its compounds [209]
6. Verb **edo** [211]
7. Verb **fio** [212]
8. Defective verbs [213]

g) Overview of peculiar constructions

1. Previous notes [215]
2. List of verbs: peculiar constructions [216]

h) Compound verbs

1. General remarks [217]
2. Meaning of the preposition [218]
3. Regime of the verb [219]
4. Main compound verbs [220]

SYNTAX OF CASES

a) Use of cases

1. General observations [221]
2. Nominative [222]
3. Vocative [223]
4. Accusative [224]
5. Genitive [229]
6. Dative [233]
7. Ablative [237]

b) Prepositions

1. General observations [243]
2. Prepositions of one case [244]
3. Prepositions of two cases [259]

c) Expressions of time and place

1. Expressions of time [262]
2. Expressions of place [266]

d) Regime of verbs and adjectives

1. General observations [271]
2. Verbs that rule a given case [272]
3. Adjectives followed by a given case [275]

SYNTAX OF CLAUSES

a) Simple clauses

1. Describing real actions [278]
2. Expressing potential actions [279]
3. Expressing commands and prohibitions [283]
4. Expressing wishes [288]
5. Asking questions [291]
6. Impersonal verbs [295]

b) Subordinate clauses

1. The concept of *consecutio temporum* [305]
2. Causal clauses [311]
3. Purpose clauses [313]
4. Temporal clauses [316]
5. Concessive clauses [322]
6. Result clauses [324]
7. Conditional clauses [328]
8. Relative clauses [336]
9. Comparative clauses [348]
10. Fear clauses [352]
11. Indefinite clauses [354]
12. Proviso clauses [358]
13. **Quominus** and **quin** clauses [359]
14. Summary of the uses of **cum** [363]
15. Summary of the uses of **ut** [366]
16. Completive **quod** clauses [368]

c) Infinitive clauses

1. General principles [369]
2. Which tense of infinitive? [374]
3. Where there is no change of subject [376]
4. Historical infinitive [377]
5. Exclamatory infinitive [378]

d) Participle clauses

1. General principles [379]
2. The participle is impersonal [381]
3. The temporal correlation [382]
4. Participle as a verb [386]
5. Participle as a noun [391]
6. The ablative absolute [393]

e) Indirect speech

1. General remarks [402]
2. Indirect statement clauses [404]
3. Indirect command clauses [409]
4. Indirect question clauses [415]
5. Subordinate clauses in indirect speech [422]
6. A special technique: *Oratio Obliqua* [426]

f) Uses of the gerund and gerundive

1. Definition and forms [436]
2. Uses of the gerund [438]
3. Gerundive replacing the gerund [442]
4. Exceptions to the replacement [444]

g) The periphrastic conjugation and the supine

1. The active periphrastic [445]
2. The passive periphrastic [446]
3. The supine in -um [447]
4. The supine in -u [448]

h) Combination of negatives

1. Tendencies in the use of negatives [449]
2. Negatives cancelling or reinforcing each other? [450]

ALIA

a) Peculiarities and idioms

1. General remarks [452]
2. Non-verbal expressions [453]
3. Verbal expressions [460]

b) Words that are easily confused

1. Non-verbal forms [461]
2. Verbal forms [462]

Index of grammatical terms

Index of Latin words

Preface

Characteristics of this new grammar

My purpose in writing this new grammar has been to offer a complete and explained grammar, one that, while still being a handy grammar, user-friendly and simple, covers as much as possible. I have tried to write it in a teaching- and learning-oriented way, as practical as possible, positioning myself in the place of the usual university and college student (or a sixth-former) and thinking which kind of grammar I would like to have: one that helps me to learn the language, with explanations, with examples, etc., avoiding very advanced stages but at the same time without falling too short.

In the course of time I have observed that a lot of instructors like teaching the language directly from the grammar. Although my personal preference is using a textbook and using the grammar only as reference tool rather than using it as only teaching material, I have taken this practice into account and I have written this grammar also with it in mind, so that instructors that follow this practice may find it and its corresponding book of exercises a useful tool.

I would like to make some more comprehensive comments about its characteristics:

a) All the needed grammar: As mentioned above, without falling too short and without making the student have to go to a larger grammar to find what they need after the initial stages, but at the same time avoiding a phone book, as students want something reduced but that offers all they need to read the classical authors.

b) Teaching skills: Offering students very clear explanations of what is being presented, not just the presentation of tables and a couple of examples. I also include the same comments I make when teaching *in situ* in front of the students, for instance calling the students' attention to avoid some common mistakes, to make them realise this or that similarity, this or that difference, etc. We could say that at some points it may sound as if somebody had recorded the teachers' voice when explaining each item on the whiteboard and then had typed the explanations.

c) Clear structure: A clear division of accidence, syntax, etc. (the Index of Contents is very illustrative about this point). This helps students to learn things in an ordered way and to find each item easily. I distinguish different blocks for the nominal system, the verbal system, syntax of clauses, etc., and inside each of these blocks the classification into different sub-sections makes finding each grammatical item easy.

d) A good amount of exercises (in an additional book): Ideal for students who not only need to study Latin grammar but who want to be able to practise each one of the presented aspects. These exercises will be published as an additional book; this has the advantage of leaving the grammar on its own in a much more reduced size (and cheaper), ideal for those who want only the grammar for consultation and do not want to buy an immense amount of exercises that they will not use.

e) Basic vocabulary: This grammar offers a reduced list of the most useful terms that follow a given scheme (a declension, a verbal system, etc.) after that scheme has been presented. For instance, after deponent verbs have been presented, I offer a list of the most frequent verbs of this kind. This helps students to realize that the scheme they have learnt has not been studied just for itself, but for a given purpose: there they have the most usual terms that follow it.

Use of original authors

An important point is the use of classical authors to illustrate what has been explained. A lot of the very initial examples are made up, which has allowed me to adapt any sentence to the level of a student who is beginning to learn this or that construction, but it would be nonsense not to offer at the same time original sentences taken from classical authors, so I have considered it convenient to include, side by side with the made-up ones, real original sentences.

I have tried to be careful in this procedure of including sentences from original authors: there is nothing easier than typing a preposition in the searcher for a database of Latin texts and finding sentences in which this or that preposition is used, but I would not see much sense in offering as an example a long sentence with a relative clause in subjunctive or any other difficult structure just to show an example of this or that preposition, so that my tendency has been to choose easy sentences that illustrate what I want the student to see, avoiding unnecessary complications.

Note about the translation of Latin examples

In a few cases, the translation of Latin sentences may not sound as fluent as an English speaker would expect and they may sound somehow "forced", but we have preferred to remain as faithful to the Latin as possible, to the detriment of English fluency, in order to help show the specific grammatical point being discussed.

Feedback

It would be a pleasure to receive comments from colleagues about any mistake they may spot or any suggestion. The way in which this book is published (Print On Demand) allows to modify the original pdf in 24-48 hours, so that any copy ordered after the new version has been modified and e-mailed to the printer will already be printed with the modification in it.

E-mail: **jc210@st-andrews.ac.uk**

Acknowledgments

As for my Classical Greek grammar, I would like to express my gratitude to several people who have helped me: Dan Batovici, for teaching me how to do the technical formatting of the book in order both to meet the technicalities requested by the printer and to make it more user-friendly and pleasant to the readers; Patrick Tsitsaros, who has made the final reading of the text to make sure it was presented in the way a student would like to find it and has corrected several typos, and Andrew Pickin, who has designed the cover (produced by the Reprographics Unit at the University of St Andrews).

And, above all, a great *Thank you* to Geoffrey Steadman, from Tennessee, without whose help and guidance in the procedures of POD both these grammars would not have seen the light.

Juan Coderch

St Andrews, May 2013 **http://coderch-greek-latin-grammar.weebly.com**

Alphabet and writing

a) The alphabet [1]

1/ The Latin alphabet is the same we use for English except for some letters that did not exist in Latin: **w, x, y** and **z**; the classical alphabet was this one:

a, b, c, d, e, f, g, h, i, l, m, n, o, p, q, r, s, t, u

Further ahead, they adopted the letters x, y and z to transcribe words of Greek origin.

> **Note**
>
> Originally, Latin had only capital letters, but Latin texts are usually published in lower case, with capital letters for proper names, first vowel after a full stop, etc.

2/ It will be observed that the -**j**- and the -**v**- are missing; the explanation is that there was a vocalic -**i**- and a consonantal -**i**- (before a vowel), and a vocalic -**u**- and a consonantal -**u**- (also before a vowel). Some texts display the consonantal -**i**- as a -j-, so we can find **iuventus** and **juventus**, **iam** and **jam**, etc.

With respect to the -**v**-, it was used as the capital letter for any -**u**-, either vocalic or consonantal, so that it was normal to find **uestis** in lower case and **VESTIS** in capital letters; nevertheless, it became normal to use the -**v**- also in lower case to replace the consonantal -**u**-, so that we can also find **vestis**.

> **Note**
>
> Some publishers prefer to keep -**u**- in lower case for both the vocalic and the consonantal -**u**-, which may produce for instance **uulnus** instead of **vulnus**, while keeping the -**v**- as capital letter also for both, which may produce for instance **VVLNUS**.

b) Pronunciation [2]

1/ Latin letters are pronounced as expected for an English speaker, but we should note the following:

a/ With respect to vowels:

a	as *a* in *father*
e	as *e* in *met*
i	as *i* in *police*
o	as *o* in *lock*
u	as *o* in *today*

b/ With respect to consonants:

c	as *k* in *kilometre*	
g	as *g* in *good*	✧ Never as *g* in *giant.*
ch	as *k* in *kilometre*	✧ So, as if the *h* did not have any effect.
ph	as *ph* in *philosophy*	
ll	as two consecutive (but separate) *l*	
h	in English-speaking countries it is pronounced, as *h* in *have*, although it is also very normal to silence it, as *h* in *honest.*	

2/ There is no general agreement about how Latin was pronounced, the rules we have given so far are general guidelines, but it is normal to find that in some countries other pronunciation rules are followed, or even within the same country according to the educational background of the instructor; for instance, the Italian pronunciation of Latin makes the letter **c** be pronounced like the *ch* of *chocolate, China,* etc. if it precedes an **e** or an i.

Another point in which there is a lack of agreement is about how to pronounce the very frequent diphthong **ae**: as an *a* followed by an *e*, or as an *a* followed by an *i* (so, as the *y* of *my*), although the most general tendency is the first option.

c) Accentuation [3]

There are no graphic accents in Latin as for instance there are in French; we offer here some very basic guidelines.

1/ Most Latin words of two or more syllables stress the pronunciation (as we do with the *pro* of *property*) of their penult syllable (we have written in capital letters the syllable that should be stressed): **aMIcus, ROsa, DOmus, cogNOSco**; but words of three syllables or more that have a short penult syllable stress the antepenult syllable: **DOminus, reCIprocus** (what makes a syllable long or short is the nature of the vowel in it, and what makes it difficult to know is that any vowel can be short or long; for instance, **a** is long in **irritatio**, but short in **agilis**).

2/ Not all Latin words will have an accent on one of their syllables; for instance, the preposition **inter** has none: **inter** stresses equally the syllables **in-** and **-ter**.

THE NOMINAL SYSTEM

a) Definition of basic grammatical concepts: *case, declension* and *gender*

1. Concepts of *syntactical function, endings* and *case*
2. Main syntactical functions and correspondence to cases
3. Concept of *declension*
4. Concept of *gender*
5. Lack of definite article

b) Declensions

General observations
1. 1st declension
2. 2nd declension
3. 3rd declension
4. 4th declension
5. 5th declension

c) Adjectives

General observations
1. 1st class of adjectives
2. 2nd class of adjectives
3. Position of the adjective
4. Use of the adjective as a noun

d) Numeral adjectives

1. Cardinals
2. Ordinals
3. Multiplicatives
4. Distributives

e) Comparative and superlative

1. General observations
2. Accidence
3. Syntax

f) Pronouns

1. Demonstrative pronouns
2. Personal pronouns
3. Possessive pronouns
4. Anaphoric pronoun
5. Identity pronouns
6. Reflexive pronouns
7. Interrogative pronoun and adjective
8. Other interrogative pronouns
9. Relative pronoun
10. Indefinite relative pronoun
11. Other indefinite pronouns
12. Negative pronouns

g) Adverbs and prepositional adverbs

1. General observations
2. Modal adverbs
3. Comparative and superlative of modal adverbs
4. Quantitative adverbs
5. Adverbs of time
6. Adverbs of place
7. Interrogative adverbs
8. Indefinite adverbs
9. Affirmative and negative adverbs
10. Prepositional adverbs

h) The correlatives

1. Correlative adverbs
2. Correlative adjectives

a) Definition of basic grammatical concepts: *case, declension* and *gender*

1. Concepts of *syntactical function, endings* and *case*

a) Concepts of *syntactical function* and *endings* [4]

1/ In comparison to Modern English, the Latin language works in a very peculiar way: like Classical Greek, Russian and other languages, Latin is a highly inflected language, which means that the words of a sentence change their ending according to the grammatical function they implement, verbal forms change according to their person, etc. While Old English was a highly inflected language, Modern English is classified as a weakly inflected language, as only some characteristics of inflection are still present in English nowadays, such as plurals, the use of pronouns, some inflected verbal forms and the possessive indicator ('s, which derives from the Old English genitive case).

2/ Back to Modern English and Latin, observe these two sentences:

THE SLAVE SEES THE MASTER. THE MASTER SEES THE SLAVE.

In English, word order is crucial to indicate the role (or grammatical function) of a word in a sentence. In the first example given above, THE SLAVE is the subject (i.e. the one who performs the action), while in the second one it is the direct object (i.e. the one who is acted upon). The opposite happens with THE MASTER: it is the direct object in the first sentence, but is the subject in the second one.

3/ Observe now both sentences translated into Latin: (**servus** THE SLAVE; **dominus** THE MASTER; **videt** SEES)

- **Servus videt dominum** THE SLAVE SEES THE MASTER.
- **Dominus videt servum** THE MASTER SEES THE SLAVE.

As we can see, noun endings are different according to the function they perform in the sentence: **servus**, which is the subject in the first sentence, becomes **servum** in the second sentence, because here it is the direct object. The opposite happens with **dominum**: from being the direct object in the first sentence, it becomes **dominus** in the second one because here it is the subject of the action. Moreover, word order is very variable in Latin, as it can change on the basis of which element of the sentence you want to emphasize; for instance, the second sentence could have been presented as **dominum videt servus** or even as **videt dominum servus**.

Both of them mean THE SLAVE SEES THE MASTER: the endings -**us** and -**um** respectively are what indicates who the subject is and who the direct object is, not their position in the sentence. The sentence **Servum videt dominus** could NEVER mean THE SLAVE SEES THE MASTER just because the word SLAVE appears first in the sentence and the word MASTER appears later: the *endings* of the words is what determines who is seeing whom, not the position of the words in the sentence.

b) Concept of *case* [5]

1/ The grammatical function of a noun in a Latin sentence (subject, direct object, etc.) is indicated by its form, not by its position in the sentence. In Latin a noun can take six different forms, according to the role it performs, and each of these forms is called a *case*. For instance, considering the two words employed in the former examples, we observed that the ending -**us** was used when the noun represented the role of subject: this is an example of *nominative case* (i.e. the case of the subject of a sentence). We also noted the employment of the ending -**um** associated with the role of direct object: this is an example of *accusative case* (i.e. the case of the direct object of a sentence). So, according to the function they must play, nouns change their form following different patterns, known as *declensions* (it must be noted that singular and plural endings of the same cases are different).

2/ There are six cases in Latin. Their names (and usual abbreviations) are as follows:

- ❑ Nominative — Nom. or N.
- ❑ Vocative — Voc. or V.
- ❑ Accusative — Acc.
- ❑ Genitive — Gen. or G.
- ❑ Dative — Dat. or D.
- ❑ Ablative — Abl.

✧ The order in which the cases are listed here is common in the UK and many other English-speaking countries, but Latin grammars in other countries can present them in a different order.

2. Main syntactical functions and correspondence to cases

a) Main syntactical functions [6]

1/ The next necessary step is to acquire a sound understanding of the main syntactical functions. We will offer two examples for each of these functions in English:

❑ The **subject** is the noun or pronoun that performs the action described in the sentence:

- *THE HORSE* HAS GOOD TEETH. — *THE HORSE* is the *subject* of this sentence.
- *THE CHILDREN* CAME LATE. — *THE CHILDREN* is the *subject* of this sentence.

❑ The **predicative object** indicates how or what something or somebody is:

- YOUR BIRTHDAY PRESENT IS *NICE*. — *NICE* is the *predicative object* of this sentence.
- PETER IS *OUR LEADER*. — *OUR LEADER* is the *predicative object* of this sentence.

❑ The ***addressed object*** is the person (or abstract entity) that is addressed directly by somebody:

- "*FATHER*, COME HERE", SAID THE BOY. — *FATHER* is the *addressed object*.
- WHAT ARE YOU DOING, *CHILDREN*? — *CHILDREN* is the *addressed object*.

❑ The **direct object** is the person (or entity, thing, etc.) who is acted upon by the subject:

- I HAVE *A BOOK*. — *A BOOK* is the *direct object*.
- I SEE *THE CITY*. — *THE CITY* is the *direct object*.

❑ The **possessive object** is the person (or entity, thing, etc.) to whom something belongs or is related:

- I SEE THE GATE *OF THE HOUSE.* — *OF THE HOUSE* is the *possessive object* of this sentence.
- I SEE *PETER'S* FATHER. — *PETER'S* is the *possessive object* of this sentence.
  ✧ In the sense that it means *OF PETER*.

❑ The **indirect object** is the person (or thing) for whom or to whom something is done:

- I GIVE THIS *TO PETER.* — *TO PETER* is the *indirect object* of this sentence.
- I GIVE *PETER* THIS. — *PETER* is the *indirect object* of this sentence.
  ✧ In the sense that it means *TO PETER*.
- I HAVE BROUGHT THIS *FOR PETER* — *FOR PETER* is the *indirect object* of this sentence.

❑ The **circumstantial object** is the person (or entity, thing, etc.) related to the action in some aspect:

- I FIGHT *WITH A SWORD.* — *WITH A SWORD* is the *circumstantial object* of this sentence.
  ✧ In this case, it expresses the instrument.
- I AM *IN ITALY.* — *IN ITALY* is the *circumstantial object* of this sentence.
  ✧ In this case, it expresses the location.
- I HAVE DONE THIS *FOR MONEY.* — *FOR MONEY* is the *circumstantial object* of this sentence.
  ✧ In this case, it expresses the reason.

Important

Students tend to confuse *direct object* and *indirect object* when nouns or personal pronouns are presented with the function of indirect object without the preposition TO. Observe these examples:

I SEE *HIM*:	*HIM* is the **direct object**	
I TELL *HIM* THIS:	*HIM* is the **indirect object**	✧ Because it means *TO HIM*. The direct object is THIS.

2/ Prepositions are used in Latin as well, but not so frequently as in English, because in some situations the meaning is implicitly expressed by the choice of specific cases. For instance, in the former example I SEE THE GATE *OF THE HOUSE*, the phrase *OF THE HOUSE* will be translated by putting *THE HOUSE* in the correct case (therefore adding the necessary ending to the noun); for this reason the preposition *OF* is not literally translated, as the meaning of the preposition is expressed by the corresponding case. Something similar would happen in translating the sentence I GIVE THIS *TO PETER*: the sense of the preposition *TO* would be expressed by the grammatical case of the word *PETER*, reflected by its ending; in this kind of sentence, the English preposition *TO* would not be translated.

3/ Other questions may come to mind now; for instance, in the sentences above there was no example featuring the prepositions IN or WITH. Then, how will we translate IN THE FIELD, WITH MY FRIENDS, or DURING THE SUMMER? As will be explained in detail in the corresponding sections, these complements can be expressed by combinations of prepositions and specific cases, or by the choice of a particular case.

b) Correspondences between functions and cases [7]

So, depending on the function of a word in a sentence, we will put it in a specific case, which implies a definite ending to be added to the word. The correspondences are as follows:

- ❑ **Nominative:** Used for *subjects* and *predicative objects*. So, in the sentence *THE TEACHER* SEES THE HOUSE, the subject *THE TEACHER* would be expressed by the nominative case. In the sentence THE TEACHER IS *TALL*, the predicative object *TALL* would also be in nominative.

- ❑ **Vocative:** Used to address or call someone (*addressed object*). So, in the sentence *PETER*, COME HERE!, *PETER* would be expressed by the vocative case.

- ❑ **Accusative:** Used for *direct objects*. So, in the sentence THE STUDENTS SEE *THE TABLE*, the direct object *THE TABLE* would be expressed by the accusative case. ✧ With some prepositions, the accusative can also be used to express *circumstantial objects*.

- ❑ **Genitive:** Used for *possessive objects*. So, in the sentence I LIKE THE PEOPLE *OF THIS CITY*, the possessive object *OF THIS CITY* would be expressed by the genitive case.

- ❑ **Dative:** Used for *indirect objects*. So, in the sentence I HAVE BROUGHT THIS *FOR YOU*, the indirect object *FOR YOU* would be expressed by the dative case.

- ❑ **Ablative:** Used for *circumstantial objects*. So, in the sentence I WRITE WITH A PEN, the circumstantial object *WITH A PEN* would be expressed by the ablative case.

Remember that questions on how to translate expressions like AT MIDDAY, IN THAT CITY, etc. will be dealt with in the corresponding sections; they will be expressed sometimes employing combinations of prepositions and cases, sometimes with a specific case.

3. Concept of *declension* [8]

To *decline* a noun means to go through all its possible endings (six in singular and six in plural). Leaving adjectives to later analysis, Latin nouns can be classified in five groups, called *declensions*, and the words belonging to the same declension are declined following the same pattern, i.e. they adopt the same ending for each case. For instance, both the nouns we met in the previous examples (**servus** SLAVE and **dominus** MASTER) belong to the same declension, therefore they change their endings in the same way according to the function they must perform.

There are five declensions in Latin. The first declension is relatively easy to learn. The second one has three sub-variants (with some internal variations), but it is not very difficult. The third declension is the most complex one, as both of its main sub-variants present several different forms, or sub-categories. The fourth declension is relatively easy, just two sub-variants, and the fifth declension is again like the first one.

4. Concept of *gender* [9]

There are three genders in Latin: *masculine, feminine* and *neuter.* Although in some cases the correspondence between name and gender seems to be logical (for instance, the Latin words for MOTHER and SISTER are feminine, as expected, and those for FATHER and BROTHER are masculine, as expected), in other cases this logic does not seem to be apparent (for instance, the word for DIGNITY is feminine, and the word for LIMIT is masculine, while in English both would be considered neuter and we would use the pronoun *IT* when referring to them).

The following list of nine English nouns and the gender of the corresponding Latin word shows that the gender of nouns is unpredictable and, for this reason, it must be learnt together with the noun (in the same way as a student of German must learn that in German *Messer* KNIFE is neuter, *Löffel* SPOON is masculine, and *Gabel* FORK is feminine):

- RIVER **flumen** neuter
- WISDOM **sapientia** feminine
- FIELD **ager** masculine
- HEAD **caput** neuter
- FEAR **timor** masculine
- GATE **porta** feminine
- EYE **oculus** masculine
- HATRED **odium** neuter
- SUMMER **aestas** feminine

How to know whether a noun is masculine, feminine or neuter will be explained in the chapter devoted to declensions.

5. Lack of definite article [10]

It will have been observed in the examples that there is no definite article in Latin equivalent to the English THE.

Therefore, the word **dominus** could mean:

- MASTER
- THE MASTER
- A MASTER

The word **dea** could mean:

- GODDESS
- THE GODDESS
- A GODDESS

b) declensions

General observations [11]

1/ There are five declensions in Latin. The degree of difficulty between them can be represented by this simple pyramidal structure, with the bottom representing the easiest degree and the top representing the most difficult one:

most difficult			3		
medium		2		4	
easiest	1				5

To learn the declensions properly, it is convenient to have their scheme clear from the very beginning, which could be called the "map of declensions", the way in which they are grammatically structured. Therefore, we offer here a schematic table of the declensions and their sub-types, in the same way as they will be found in this chapter:

1. 1st declension	2. 2nd declension	3. 3rd declension	4. 4th declension	5. 5th declension
(no sub-variants)	a) 1st sub-variant	a) Consonant stems	a) 1st sub-variant	(no sub-variants)
	b) 2nd sub-variant	b) -i stems	b) 2nd sub-variant	
	c) 3rd sub-variant			

2/ For each declension, we will highlight the case endings by writing them in bold type and by separating them from the stem of the word with a hyphen, to make it easier for the student to memorise them (our advice is not to memorise as a paradigm the whole declined word, but to memorise only the endings: -a, -a, -am, -ae, -ae, -a etc.).

3/ Latin nouns are usually presented by their *singular nominative and genitive forms.* Even though adjectives also use inflectional models based on declensions, they will be presented in another way, introduced in the corresponding chapter.

1. 1st declension [12]

a/ The 1st declension has no sub-types, which makes it extremely simple and easy to memorise. It is used for nouns and adjectives.

	singular	plural
Nom.	puell-a	puell-ae
Voc.	puell-a	puell-ae
Acc.	puell-am	puell-as
Gen.	puell-ae	puell-arum
Dat.	puell-ae	puell-is
Abl.	puell-a	puell-is

Example: **puella, -ae** GIRL

✧ We highlight the endings in bold, in order to help with their memorisation.

Notes

1/ Almost all nouns of the 1st declension are feminine, but some of them are masculine (**nauta, -ae** SAILOR, for instance).

2/ Some words may have **-abus** instead of **-is** for the dative and ablative plural, to avoid confusion with their corresponding masculine counterparts of the 2nd declension: **dea, -ae** GODDESS may have **deabus** instead of **deis**, for instance, in order to avoid the coincidence with **deis**, dative and ablative plural of **deus, -i** GOD (2nd declension).

3/ The expressions **pater familias** and **mater familias** keep an ancient genitive in **-as** instead of **-ae**.

The following list presents some of the most frequent nouns belonging to this sub-variant. Keeping with the conventional practice mentioned above, here are listed the singular nominative and genitive forms of each noun, and, except those indicated with an *m.* of *masculine*, all of them are feminine:

agricola, -ae (m.)	FARMER
amica, -ae	FRIEND
amicitia, -ae	FRIENDSHIP
ancilla, -ae	SLAVE GIRL
aqua, -ae	WATER
causa, -ae	CAUSE
cena, -ae	DINNER
cura, -ae	CARE
dea, -ae	GODDESS
fama, -ae	FAME
familia, -ae	FAMILY
femina, -ae	WOMAN
filia, -ae	DAUGHTER
fortuna, -ae	FORTUNE
gloria, -ae	GLORY
hasta, -ae	SPEAR
hora, -ae	HOUR, TIME
ianua, -ae	DOOR
incola, -ae (m.)	INHABITANT
iniuria, -ae	INJUSTICE
insula, -ae	ISLAND
invidia, -ae	ENVY
ira, -ae	ANGER
lingua, -ae	LANGUAGE
magistra, -ae	TEACHER
mensa, -ae	TABLE
mora, -ae	DELAY
natura, -ae	NATURE
nauta, -ae (m.)	SAILOR
patria, -ae	HOMELAND
pecunia, -ae	MONEY
poena, -ae	PENALTY
poeta, -ae (m.)	POET
puella, -ae	GIRL
regina, -ae	QUEEN
sapientia, -ae	WISDOM
scientia, -ae	KNOWLEDGE
terra, -ae	LAND
turba, -ae	CROWD
unda, -ae	WAVE
via, -ae	WAY
victoria, -ae	VICTORY
vita, -ae	LIFE

b/ Some words have only a plural: [13]

✧ Note that we introduce them by saying their Nom. and Gen. plural.

divitiae, -arum	WEALTH	Athenae, -arum	ATHENS
insidiae, -arum	AMBUSH, PLOT	nuptiae, -arum	WEDDING

Others have one meaning in the singular and another one in the plural:

copia, -ae	ABUNDANCY	/	copiae, -arum	TROOPS
littera, -ae	LETTER (a, b, c, ...)	/	litterae, -arum	LETTER (written message)
vigilia, -ae	WATCH	/	vigiliae, -arum	SENTINELS

2. 2nd declension [14]

The 2nd declension, like the 1st one, is also used for nouns and adjectives. It has three sub-variants:

- ⇨ The type -us, -i
- ⇨ The type -ø, -i
- ⇨ The type -um, -i

a) First sub-variant: the type -us, -i

Example: **dominus, -i** MASTER

	singular	plural
Nom.	domin-us	domin-i
Voc.	domin-e	domin-i
Acc.	domin-um	domin-os
Gen.	domin-i	domin-orum
Dat.	domin-o	domin-is
Abl.	domin-o	domin-is

The noun deus, -i GOD has some alternative forms:

	singular	plural
Nom.	deus / divus	dei / dii / di
Voc.	deus / dive	dei / dii / di
Acc.	deum / divum	deos
Gen.	dei / divi	deorum / deum
Dat.	deo / divo	deis / diis / dis
Abl.	deo / divo	deis / diis / dis

✧ Given its importance, it is worth keeping in mind all the possible forms that this word may adopt.

Notes

1/ Almost all nouns of this sub-type are masculine, but some of them are feminine.

2/ Nouns ending in -**ius** make their Voc. sing. by deleting the -**us** but without adding the usual -**e**: **filius**, Voc. **fili**; **Antonius**, Voc. **Antoni**. In fact what happened is that the -**e** became an -i because of phonetic assimilation with the -i of the end of the stem, and later both -ii merged into one, leaving a result that makes it look as if no ending -**e** had been added. These nouns also may contract the two -ii of the Gen. sing. (one of the stem, one of the ending) into one: filii > fili.

3/ Now that we see the coincidence in -**is** of the endings for the Dat./Abl. plural in the 1st and the 2nd declensions, we see why we can use -**abus** in the 1st declension for pairs of words that have their feminine version in the 1st decl. and their masculine version in the 2nd decl.: **filia, -ae** Abl. pl. **filiis**, and **filius, -i** Abl. pl. also **filiis**; to avoid this coincidence, we can use -**abus** for the feminine word (1st declension): **filiabus**.

The following list presents some of the most frequent nouns belonging to this sub-variant:

amicus, -i	FRIEND	filius, -i	SON	nuntius, -i	MESSENGER
animus, -i	SOUL	gladius, -i	SWORD	oculus, -i	EYE
annus, -i	YEAR	locus, -i	PLACE	populus, -i	PEOPLE
cibus, -i	FOOD	ludus, -i	GAME, SCHOOL	servus, -i	SLAVE
deus, -i	GOD	modus, -i	MANNER	socius, -i	ALLY
discipulus, -i	STUDENT	morbus, -i	DISEASE	somnus, -i	SLEEP
dominus, -i	MASTER	murus, -i	WALL	tyrannus, -i	TYRANT
equus, -i	HORSE	numerus, -i	NUMBER	vulgus, -i	MOB

✧ The word **locus, -i**, in its usual meaning of PLACE, has a neuter plural: **loca, -orum**. But if it means PLACE IN A BOOK, PASSAGE, it goes on being masculine also in plural: **loci, -orum**.

b) Second sub-variant: the type -ø, -i [15]

This sub-variant presents the characteristic of having a stem ending in -**er** and not having any ending (which we represent by -ø) for the nom. and voc. singular. Most of the nouns that belong to this sub-variant lose the -**e**- of -**er** as soon as an ending is added to the stem (which in fact means always except in nom. and voc. singular), but some others keep it.

We will use the noun **puer, -i** BOY to illustrate the declension of the nouns that keep the -**e**-:

	singular	plural
Nom.	puer-ø	puer-i
Voc.	puer-ø	puer-i
Acc.	puer-um	puer-os
Gen.	puer-i	puer-orum
Dat.	puer-o	puer-is
Abl.	puer-o	puer-is

Example: **puer, -i** BOY

✧ Observe: For the genitive, we show only -i

And **magister, -tri** TEACHER is an example of nouns that lose the -**e**; note that showing -**i** for the genitive is not enough in these words: we must show enough letters to make clear that the -**e** has been lost.

	singular	plural
Nom.	magister-ø	magistr-i
Voc.	magister-ø	magistr-i
Acc.	magistr-um	magistr-os
Gen.	magistr-i	magistr-orum
Dat.	magistr-o	magistr-is
Abl.	magistr-o	magistr-is

Example: **magister, -tri** TEACHER

✧ Observe: to show the genitive, we must give (in this example) **-tri**, instead of only **-i**

Notes

1/ All nouns of this sub-type are masculine.

2/ There is one word, MAN, that has a stem ending in -**ir** instead of -**er**: **vir, -i**; it would belong to the group that keep the -**e** (the -i, in this case): singular **vir, vir, virum, viri, viro, viro**; plural **viri, viri, viros, virorum, viris, viris**.

3/ Sometimes this sub-type is called "sub-type in -**er**" instead of "sub-type in -**ø**", just because the stem always finishes in -**er** and, no ending being attached in the Nom. sing., the word will end in -**er**, but we must see clearly that -**er** is not an ending.

Some common nouns that follow this sub-type are:

ager, agri	FIELD	magister, -tri	TEACHER
liber, libri	BOOK	puer, pueri	BOY

c) Third sub-variant: the type -um, -i [16]

	singular	plural
Nom.	templ-um	templ-a
Voc.	templ-um	templ-a
Acc.	templ-um	templ-a
Gen.	templ-i	templ-orum
Dat.	templ-o	templ-is
Abl.	templ-o	templ-is

Example: **templum, -i** TEMPLE

✧ The order of cases may be different in some countries, but this order helps because of the rule of the first three cases for neuters.

Notes

1/ All nouns of this sub-type are neuter.

2/ The double golden rule for neuters is: the three first cases are identical, and in plural they end in -**a**.

The most common nouns that follow this sub-type are:

aurum, -i	GOLD	imperium, -i	COMMAND	principium, -i	BEGINNING
auxilium, -i	HELP	initium, -i	BEGINNING	proelium, -i	BATTLE
bellum, -i	WAR	iudicium, -i	JUDGEMENT	signum, -i	SIGNAL
beneficium, -i	BENEFIT	odium, -i	HATRED	studium, -i	ZEAL
caelum, -i	SKY	officium, -i	DUTY	telum, -i	MISSILE
consilium, -i	PLAN	oppidum, -i	TOWN	templum, -i	TEMPLE
donum, -i	GIFT	otium, -i	LEISURE	verbum, -i	WORD
exitium, -i	DESTRUCTION	perfugium, -i	REFUGE	vitium, -i	VICE
factum, -i	DEED	periculum, -i	DANGER		
ferrum, -i	SWORD	praemium, -i	REWARD		

✧ Observe the amount of neuter words in -**ium**: it should be noted that the genitive must keep both -**ii**: **initii**, **iudicii**, **consilii**, etc.

As in the 1st declension, here are words that have only plural: [17]

fasti, -orum	FASTI (sacred days)
inferi, -orum	GODS OF THE UNDERWORLD
liberi, -orum	CHILDREN (meaning sons and daughters)
superi, -orum	GODS
Delphi, -orum	DELPHI
arma, -orum	WEAPONS

And other nouns have a different meaning in each number:

auxilium, -i	HELP	/	auxilia, -orum	AUXILIARY TROOPS
impedimentum, -i	OBSTACLE	/	impedimenta, -orum	BAGGAGE
castrum, -i	CASTLE	/	castra, -orum	MILITARY CAMP

3. 3rd declension [18]

The 3rd declension is the most difficult one, and it is used for masculine, feminine and neuter nouns and adjectives. It has two sub-types: consonant stems and -i stems.

a) Consonant stems

1/ The main characteristic of the consonant stems is that the main stem, the stem on which we will apply the case endings, has suffered some alterations in the Nom. and Voc. singular (and also acc. sing., if the word is neuter). Sometimes the ending for these two cases will be **-s** and this consonant will produce some changes in the stem, sometimes there is no ending and then the stem has suffered some alteration precisely because of the lack of ending. The final result is that the Nom. / Voc. (and Acc., if neuter) sing. may look quite different from the stem to be used for the other cases, and this compels dictionaries to give almost the whole word of the genitive to make its form clear.

So, if in the 1st declension it was enough with knowing one stem (**puell-**, for instance) to apply the case endings on it, and it was enough also in the 2nd declension (with the exception of -**er** nouns that lose the -**e**-), in the 3rd declension we must know BOTH stems very clearly: the one for the Nom. / Voc. singular (and Acc., if neuter) and the other one (which in fact is the original one) on which we will apply the endings for the other cases (a typical mistake among beginners is to apply the endings for the other cases on the stem of the Nom. sing.).

In a summary: we must accept the Nom. sing. as it is given to us by the dictionary and then we must apply the endings for the other cases on the stem given to us by the genitive singular (after removing the genitive ending).

The consonant stems are also called *imparisyllabic* because the number of syllables in Nom. and Gen. is almost always different (for instance, **tempus** has 2 syllables and **temporis** has 3 syllables).

2/ Let's start with the declension of masculine or feminine nouns: [19]

	singular	plural
Nom.	miles	milit-es
Voc.	miles	milit-es
Acc.	milit-em	milit-es
Gen.	milit-is	milit-um
Dat.	milit-i	milit-ibus
Abl.	milit-e	milit-ibus

Example: **miles, -itis** SOLDIER

✧ Observe that there is no proper ending in Nom. / Voc. singular.

Observe that we must use the Nom. sing. given to us (**miles**) ONLY for the Nom. and Voc. sing. (and acc., if the word is neuter), and the stem given by the genitive (**milit-**) to form all the other cases by adding the corresponding endings. The most common mistake in the declension of a word of this type is to write Nom. **miles**, Voc. **miles**, Acc. **milesem**, Gen. **milesis**, Dat. **milesi**, etc., applying the endings to the nominative.

¤ To repeat it in other words: to decline this word, we use the first form given to us, **miles**, for the Nom. / Voc. sing., and then, from the Acc. sing. onwards and all of the plural, we must forget about **miles**, we can not use it any more, and we must use the stem given by the genitive after removing the ending -**is**: **milit-**.

The most common masculine or feminine nouns that follow this sub-type are:

aestas, -atis (f.)	SUMMER	dolor, -oris (m.)	PAIN	miles, -litis (m.)	SOLDIER
aetas, -atis (f.)	LIFE, AGE	dux, ducis (m.)	GENERAL	mos, moris (m.)	CUSTOM
amor, -oris (m.)	LOVE	homo, -minis (m.)	HUMAN BEING	mulier, -eris (f.)	WOMAN
arbor, -oris (f.)	TREE	honor, -oris (m.)	HONOUR,	oratio, -onis (f.)	SPEECH
auctor, -oris (m.)	AUTHOR	imperator, -oris (m.)	COMMANDER	orator, -oris (m.)	SPEAKER
civitas, -atis (f.)	STATE	iudex, iudicis (m.)	JUDGE	paupertas, -atis (f.)	POVERTY
comes, -itis (m.)	COMPANION	labor, -oris (m.)	WORK	pax, pacis (f.)	PEACE
consul, -ulis (m.)	CONSUL	laus, laudis (f.)	PRAISE	pes, pedis (m.)	FOOT
custos, -odis (m.)	GUARD	lex, legis (f.)	LAW	plebs, plebis (f.)	COMMON PEOPLE
cupiditas, -atis (f.)	DESIRE	libertas, -atis (f.)	FREEDOM	princeps, -cipis (m.)	EMPEROR
dignitas, -atis (f.)	DIGNITY	lux, lucis (f.)	LIGHT	probitas, -atis (f.)	HONESTY

ratio, -onis (f.)	JUDGEMENT	servitus, -utis (f.)	SLAVERY	uxor, -oris (f.)	WIFE
rex, regis (m.)	KING	sol, solis (m.)	SUN	veritas, -atis (f.)	TRUTH
sacerdos, -otis (m.)	PRIEST	soror, -oris (f.)	SISTER	virtus, -utis (f.)	COURAGE
salus, -utis (f.)	SAFETY	tempestas, -atis (f.)	STORM	vox, vocis (f.)	VOICE
senectus, -utis (f.)	OLD AGE	timor, -oris (m.)	FEAR		

3/ Let's see now the declension of neuter nouns: [20]

	singular	plural
Nom.	tempus	tempor-a
Voc.	tempus	tempor-a
Acc.	tempus	tempor-a
Gen.	tempor-is	tempor-um
Dat.	tempor-i	tempor-ibus
Abl.	tempor-e	tempor-ibus

Example: **tempus, -oris** TIME

✧ Observe that there is no proper ending in Nom./Voc./Acc. singular.

The only difference is that, following the golden rule of neuters, the three first cases are identical (so, we will use the nominative given to us for one case more) and they end in -**a** in the plural.

The most common neuter nouns that follow this sub-type are:

caput, -itis	HEAD	iter, itineris	WAY	os, oris	MOUTH
carmen, -minis	SONG	ius, iuris	LAW, RIGHT	pectus, -oris	CHEST
corpus, -oris	BODY	litus, -oris	SHORE	scelus, -leris	CRIME
flumen, -minis	RIVER	nomen, -minis	NAME	tempus, -oris	TIME
genus, -neris	TYPE, CLASS	opus, operis	DEED	vulnus, -neris	WOUND

b) -i stems [21]

1/ The -i stems do not experience this difference between the nominative and the other cases so frequently, as the most frequent is that both stems are identical. For masculine and feminine nouns, the nominative sing. endings are -**is**, -**es**, or -**er**. As the variation of so many different endings for the nom. sing. does not apply in the -i stems, it is customary to present their declension with the corresponding ending for that case separated by a hyphen as any other case instead of giving it as a single unit as we did for the consonant stems.

Another characteristic of the -i stems is that their ending for the genitive plural is -**ium** instead of -**um**. The other endings are the same as for the consonant stems.

The -i stems are also called "parisyllabic" because the number of syllables in Nom. and Gen. is almost always the same one (**mare**: 2 syllables / **maris**: 2 syllables, for instance).

2/ Let's see the declension of **nubes, -is** (fem.) CLOUD : [22]

	singular	plural
Nom.	nub-es	nub-es
Voc.	nub-es	nub-es
Acc.	nub-em	nub-es/is
Gen.	nub-is	nub-ium
Dat.	nub-i	nub-ibus
Abl.	nub-e	nub-ibus

Example: **nubes, -is** CLOUD

The most common masculine or feminine nouns that follow this sub-type are:

civis, -is (m./f.)	CITIZEN	caedes, -is (f.)	SLAUGHTER	ignis, -is (m.)	FIRE
navis, -is (f.)	SHIP	classis, -is (f.)	FLEET	piscis, -is (m.)	FISH
auris, -is (f.)	EAR	collis, -is (m.)	HILL	vallis, -is (f.)	VALLEY
avis, -is (f.)	BIRD				

3/ For neuter nouns, the usual nom. sing. endings are **-e**, **-al**, or **-ar**. Moreover, they present two further characteristics: the three first cases in plural end in -**ia** instead of -**a**, and the ablative sing. is **-i** instead of -**e** (neuter -i stems are very conservative in the sense of keeping the characteristic -i as much as possible), although sometimes -**e** can be found. [23]

Let's see the declension of **mare, -is** SEA :

	singular	plural
Nom.	mar-e	mar-ia
Voc.	mar-e	mar-ia
Acc.	mar-e	mar-ia
Gen.	mar-is	mar-ium
Dat.	mar-i	mar-ibus
Abl.	mar-i/e	mar-ibus

Example: **mare, -is** SEA

✧ The plural **maria** should be pronounced **mária** and not **maría**, which is a first name.

Apart from **mare**, the most common neuter noun that follows this sub-type is **rete, -is** NET. In fact hardly any noun follows it, but it is much used (like the masc./fem. sub-type) for adjectives.

c) Consonant stems or -i stems? [24]

The rule about the number of syllables almost always works, but there are several exceptions:

1/ These nouns are imparisyllabic, but they are declined through the -**i** stem sub-type (which means that they will have -**ium** in the gen. plural (and -**ia** in the neuter plural for the neuter **animalia**). Observe that, except **animal**, all of them have a nominative ending with two consonants: in fact there was an -i- between these two consonants and they were parisyllabics, but the -i- was lost and, losing one syllable, they became apparently imparisyllabics:

animal, -alis (n.)	ANIMAL	pars, partis (f.)	PART
urbs, urbis (f.)	CITY	arx, arcis (f.)	CITADEL
mons, montis (m.)	MOUNTAIN	gens, gentis (f.)	RACE, PEOPLE
mens, mentis (f.)	MIND	nox, noctis (f.)	NIGHT
mors, mortis (f.)	DEATH	ars, artis (f.)	ART

2/ On the opposite, these nouns are parisyllabic, but they are declined through the consonant stem sub-type:

mater, matris (f.)	MOTHER
pater, patris (m.)	FATHER
frater, fratris (m.)	BROTHER
senex, -nis (m.)	OLD MAN

✧ Observe that FATHER, MOTHER and BROTHER form part of this group, but SISTER is not included.

d) Further observations [25]

1/ There are some very archaic nouns, like **turris, -is** TOWER, that have an acc. sing. in -**im** instead of **-em: turrim**. Another well-known example is the acc. **Tiberim** TIBER (river).

2/ Another similar case is **vis** STRENGTH, but moreover it lacks genitive and dative sing. (although some grammars quote **vis** as a supposed genitive), and its plural is based on the stem **vir**-:

	singular	plural
Nom.	vis	vires
Voc.	vis	vires
Acc.	vim	vires
Gen.	---	virium
Dat.	---	viribus
Abl.	vi	viribus

✧ Confusing forms of this word with forms of **vir, -i** (2nd declension) is a typical mistake.

3/ As in other declensions, there are words with a different meaning in each number:

aedis, -is	TEMPLE	/	aedes, -ium	HOUSE
sors, sortis	LUCK	/	sortes, -ium	ORACLE
finis, -is	BOUNDARY	/	fines, -ium	TERRITORY
ops, opis (f.)	HELP	/	opes, opum	WEALTH, RESOURCES

4/ And, as usual, some words have only plural:

moenia, -ium WALLS (of a city)

4. 4th declension [26]

The 4th declension has two sub-types: one for masculine and feminine words, and one for neuters. As many of its endings are -**us**, it is very common to confuse it with words of the 2nd declension.

a) First sub-type: the type in -us, -us

	singular	plural
Nom.	senat-us	senat-us
Voc.	senat-us	senat-us
Acc.	senat-um	senat-us
Gen.	senat-us	senat-uum
Dat.	senat-ui	senat-ibus
Abl.	senat-u	senat-ibus

Example: **senatus, -us** SENATE

✧ Observe that the ending **-us** occurs six times, half of the twelve possibilities.

The word **domus, -us** HOUSE developed some forms of the 2nd declension. Putting together all the possibilities, we have these forms:

	singular	plural
Nom.	domus	domus
Voc.	domus	domus
Acc.	domum	domus / domos
Gen.	domus / domi	domuum / domorum
Dat.	domui / domo	domibus
Abl.	domu / domo	domibus

✧ Given the frequency of this word, it is worth remembering all its possible forms.

Notes

1/ Almost all nouns that follow this sub-type are masculine, but for instance **domus** and **manus, -us** HAND, BAND (of people) are feminine.

2/ In former times, the original ending -**ibus** was in fact -**ubus**, it moved to -**ibus** because of influence of the 3rd declension. But some archaic words may keep it.

The most common masculine or feminine nouns that follow this sub-type are:

cursus, -us (m.)	RACE, COURSE
exercitus, -us (m.)	ARMY
fructus, -us (m.)	FRUIT
manus, -us (f.)	HAND
metus, -us (m.)	FEAR
sensus, -us (m.)	FEELING
vultus, -us (m.)	FACE

b) Second sub-type: the type in -u, -us [27]

	singular	plural
Nom.	gen-u	gen-ua
Voc.	gen-u	gen-ua
Acc.	gen-u	gen-ua
Gen.	gen-us	gen-uum
Dat.	gen-ui/u	gen-ibus
Abl.	gen -u	gen-ibus

Example: **genu, -us** KNEE

✧ All of them are neuter.

Observe the possibility of either **-ui** or **-u** for the dative sing. neuter. This alternation may also be found in the first sub-type for masc./fem. (**-us, -us**), but it is more frequent in neuters (**-u, -us**).

Apart from **genu**, another common noun that follows this sub-type is **cornu, -us** HORN.
✧ Usually, **cornu** is used in the sense of WING or FLANK of an army: **dextrum/sinistrum cornu** RIGHT/LEFT FLANK.

5. 5th declension [28]

The 5th declension, like the 1st one, has only one type.

	singular	plural
Nom.	di-es	di-es
Voc.	di-es	di-es
Acc.	di-em	di-es
Gen.	di-ei	di-erum
Dat.	di-ei	di-ebus
Abl.	di-e	di-ebus

Example: **dies, -ei** DAY

Notes

a/ All words of the 5th decl. are feminine, except **dies, -ei**, which can be masculine when it means a specific day as date rather than unit of length of time.

b/ The word **res, rei** THING will be found a lot of times in conjunction with adjectives, forming a concept that may be written as a single word (but each half must be declined independently): **respublica** THE STATE, **reipublicae** OF THE STATE, etc.

Other nouns of this declension are:

fides, -ei FAITH
spes, -ei HOPE

c) Adjectives

General observations [29]

a/ An adjective has gender: In Latin, as in many other languages, if an adjective accompanies a masculine noun, it must be masculine; the adjective must be feminine if it accompanies a feminine noun, neuter if the noun is neuter. On the basis of the different classes adjectives belong to, gender will be expressed by means of different declensions.

b/ Classes of adjectives: There are two classes of adjectives in Latin, and each adjective belongs to one of these classes: please note that we are talking about *classes*, not *declensions*. For instance, the Latin adjective that means GOOD belongs to the first class, and the adjective that means EASY belongs to the second one.

1. 1st class of adjectives [30]

a/ The first class makes use of the 1st and 2nd declensions. They are the so-called "2-1-2 adjectives", as they inflect as follows:

- ⇨ If the adjective is *masculine,* it follows the 2nd declension (first or second sub-variant).
- ⇨ If the adjective is *feminine,* it follows the 1st declension.
- ⇨ If the adjective is *neuter,* it follows the 2nd declension (third sub-variant).

The dictionary form shows the three nominative sing. forms (masc./fem./neuter). For instance,

bonus, -a, -um	GOOD
malus, -a, -um	BAD
miser, -a, -um	WRETCHED
pulcher, -chra, -chrum	NICE

In the cases in which the masculine follows the second sub-variant, like **miser** or **pulcher**, there is the possibility that in the rest of the masculine and in all the feminine and neuter the adjective loses the -**e**- (like in **magister, -tri**) or keeps it (like in **puer, pueri**). In case that it loses the -**e**-, the same is done as with a noun: for the feminine and neuter, enough letters must be given to show that the -**e**- has disappeared. For instance, it would be wrong to write **pulcher, -a, -um**, as this would mean **pulcher, pulchera, pulcherum**, which are wrong forms: the dictionary must say **pulcher, -chra, -chrum** to show the disappearance of the -**e**-.

The most frequent adjectives following the *2-1-2 scheme* are:

adversus, -a, -um	OPPOSITE	**antiquus, -a, -um**	ANCIENT	**bonus, -a, -um**	GOOD
aequus, -a, -um	EQUAL	**avarus, -a, -um**	GREEDY	**carus, -a, -um**	DEAR
altus, -a, -um	HIGH, TALL	**beatus, -a, -um**	HAPPY	**certus, -a, -um**	CERTAIN
amicus, -a, -um	FRIENDLY	**bellus, -a, -um**	NICE	**clarus, -a, -um**	FAMOUS

cupidus, -a, -um	DESIROUS	liber, -a, -um	FREE	Romanus, -a, -um	ROMAN
dexter, -tra, -trum	RIGHT (SIDE)	longus, -a, -um	LONG	sacer, sacra, sacrum	SACRED
dignus, a, -um	WORTHY	magnus, -a, -um	BIG, LARGE	saevus, -a, -um	SAVAGE
doctus, -a, -um	WISE, LEARNED	malus, -a, -um	BAD	salvus, -a, -um	SAFE
Gallus, -a, -um	GAUL / GALLIC	medius, -a, -um	MIDDLE	sinister, -tra, -trum	LEFT (SIDE), ILL-OMENED
Graecus, -a, -um	GREEK	miser, -a, -um	WRETCHED		
gratus, -a, -um	PLEASING	mortuus, -a, -um	DEAD	superbus, -a, -um	ARROGANT
humanus, -a, -um	HUMAN	multus, -a, -um	MUCH	tutus, -a, -um	SAFE
incertus, -a, -um	UNCERTAIN	novus, -a, -um	NEW	verus, -a, -um	TRUE
infirmus, -a, -um	WEAK	parvus, -a, -um	SMALL	vivus, -a, -um	ALIVE
iratus, -a, -um	ANGRY	plenus, -a, -um	FULL		
laetus, -a, -um	HAPPY	pulcher, -chra, -chrum	NICE		

Do not confuse the adjective **bellus, -a, -um** NICE with the neuter noun **bellum, -i** WAR.

b/ Two common mistakes: [31]

– There are some indefinite adjectives (the indefinite adjectives is a grammatical category to be dealt with in another chapter) that have the nominatives in **-us, -a, -um**, but in fact they present some peculiarities in their declension. For instance, **nullus, -a, -um** NONE, NO ONE: it may seem that its declension is identical to that of the former adjectives, but in fact it is not.

– Another common mistake is to make noun and adjective agree in declension rather than in gender, just because it sounds better: **Video *altam* nautam** instead of **Video *altum* nautam**. Adjective and noun must agree in case, number and gender (in this example, accusative masculine singular), but do not necessarily follow the same declension; **nauta** SAILOR is masculine in Latin, so the adjective must be masculine as well, therefore it will follow the 2nd declension. The fact that the noun SAILOR itself belongs to the 1st declension must not affect the choice of the declension used to inflect the adjective: the choice must be based on the gender of the noun, NOT on the declension followed by the noun.

2. 2nd class of adjectives [32]

This class of adjectives uses only the 3rd declension to inflect all genders. This class is usually subdivided into adjectives of one, of two or of three endings, but in fact it would be more accurate to say one, two or three nominatives singular.

We will start by the adjectives of two nominatives; the type of three nominatives is a small derivation from them, and those of one nominative will be explained at the end as they present some strange characteristic.

a) Adjectives of two nominatives

They are declined by the 3rd declension -**i** stem, and they follow this pattern:

	singular		plural	
	masc./fem.	*neuter*	*masc./fem.*	*neuter*
Nom.	fortis	forte	fortes	fortia
Voc.	fortis	forte	fortes	fortia
Acc.	fortem	forte	fortes	fortia
Gen.	← fortis →		← fortium →	
Dat.	← forti →		← fortibus →	
Abl.	← forti →		← fortibus →	

Example: **fortis, -e** STRONG

✧ Observe that the three last cases are common for the three genders.

Notes

1/ The masculine and feminine have identical forms.

2/ The three genders have identical forms for the last three cases.

3/ The ablative singular is -**i** even if the adjective is masculine or feminine.

4/ All adjectives belonging to this type will be presented as -is, -e: fortis, -e.

Other frequent adjectives that follow this scheme are:

brevis, -e BRIEF
communis, -e COMMON
crudelis, -e CRUEL
difficilis, -e DIFFICULT
dissimilis, -e DIFFERENT
dulcis, -e SWEET
facilis, -e EASY
fidelis, -e FAITHFUL
gravis, -e SERIOUS
immortalis, -e IMMORTAL
levis, -e LIGHT
mirabilis, -e AMAZING
mortalis, -e MORTAL
nobilis, -e NOBLE
omnis, -e ALL
similis, -e SIMILAR
talis, -e SUCH
tristis, -e SAD
turpis, -e SHAMEFUL
utilis, -e USEFUL

b) Adjectives of three nominatives [33]

A derivation from the former type; the difference is that they have a special form for Nom. and Voc. sing. masculine:

	singular			plural	
	masc.	*fem.*	*neuter*	*masc./fem.*	*neuter*
Nom.	acer	acris	acre	acres	acria
Voc.	acer	acris	acre	acres	acria
Acc.	acrem	acrem	acre	acres	acria
Gen.	← acris →			← acrium →	
Dat.	← acri →			← acribus →	
Abl.	← acri →			← acribus →	

Example: **acer, acris, acre** HARSH, SHARP

✧ As with **fortis, -e**, the three last cases are common for the three genders.

Notes

1/ Except for the two **acer** in Nom. and Voc. singular, the rest of the declension is identical to adjectives of two nominatives.

2/ Therefore, **acris** is valid only for feminine, not for both.

Apart from acer, the only frequent adjective of this type is **celer, celeris, celere** SWIFT, QUICK.

c) Adjectives of one nominative [34]

1/ Most of them follow the -**i** stem declension, but some of them follow the consonant stem declension (later we will indicate which ones).

They have only one nominative for the three genders, and they follow this pattern:

	singular		plural	
	masc./fem.	*neuter*	*masc./fem.*	*neuter*
Nom.	← felix →		felices	felicia
Voc.	← felix →		felices	felicia
Acc.	felicem	felix	felices	felicia
Gen.	← felicis →		← felicium →	
Dat.	← felici →		← felicibus →	
Abl.	← felici →		← felicibus →	

Example: **felix, -icis** HAPPY

✧ In some cases, the Abl. sing. can be **-e** instead of **-i**.

Notes

a/ As they have only one Nom. sing., the way of introducing them is by saying the Nom. and Gen. sing., as if it were a noun: **felix, -icis** HAPPY.

b/ Observe that the Acc. sing. must have two options: if the adjective accompanies a neuter noun, it must be equal to the nominative. So, except for the Acc., the singular would have only one column.

c/ Observe that the plural is identical to that of the former types.

The most frequent ones are:

audax, -acis	BOLD	imprudens, -entis	IMPRUDENT	prudens, -entis	PRUDENT
clemens, -entis	CLEMENT	ingens, -entis	HUGE	sapiens, -entis	WISE
diligens, -entis	DILIGENT	mendax, -acis	LIAR, FALSE	velox, -ocis	SWIFT, QUICK
ferox, -ocis	FIERCE	potens, -entis	POWERFUL		

2/ As we have said, some adjectives of one nominative are declined through the consonant stem scheme, like this one: [35]

	singular		plural	
	masc./fem.	*neuter*	*masc./fem.*	*neuter*
Nom.	← vetus →		veteres	vetera
Voc.	← vetus →		veteres	vetera
Acc.	veterem	vetus	veteres	vetera
Gen.	← veteris →		← veterum →	
Dat.	← veteri →		← veteribus →	
Abl.	← vetere →		← veteribus →	

Example: **vetus, -eris** ANCIENT

✧ Note the consonant stem endings.

Adjectives of one ending that follow the consonantal declension are those whose nominative does NOT finish in any of these combinations:

-ns, -ax, -ix, -ox ✧ Observe that the adjectives of the former list, those following the **-i** stem pattern, have a nominative finishing in any of these endings.

The most frequent adjectives that follow this consonant stem pattern are:

dives, divitis RICH
inops, -opis (x) POOR, NEEDY
memor, -oris (x) MINDFUL
particeps, -cipis PARTAKING
pauper, -eris POOR
princeps, -cipis FIRST, CHIEFTAIN
pubes, -eris ADULT
sospes, -itis SAFE AND SOUND
superstes, -stitis SURVIVING
supplex, -licis (x) SUPPLIANT
✧ Observe: -ex, not -ix, -ax or -ox
vetus, -eris OLD

(x) These three have the ablative sing. in -i: they were influenced by the -i stem type.

3. Position of the adjective [36]

a/ A small number of adjectives that convey special meanings may give a different sense to the sentence according to their position, as shown in the following examples:

- In monte *medio* sum I AM IN THE MOUNTAIN IN THE MIDDLE
  ✧ The mountain that is in the middle of a row of several mountains, for instance.
- In *medio* monte sum I AM THE MIDDLE OF THE MOUNTAIN
  ✧ The area between the base and the summit.
- In quattuor partes divisas copias educit, duas, ut *medio* monte duceret, duas ... HE TOOK HIS TROOPS OUT DIVIDED INTO FOUR PARTS: TWO IN ORDER TO TAKE THEM THROUGH THE MIDDLE OF THE MOUNTAIN, TWO ... (Livy, *Ab Urbe Condita*).
- Afranius copias educit et in *medio* colle sub castris constituit AFRANIUS TAKES OUT HIS TROOPS AND ARRANGES THEM IN THE MIDDLE OF THE HILL UNDER HIS CAMP (Caesar, *Bellum Civile*).
- Prima luce *medio* in alveo cum stationibus hostium proelium commisit AT DAWN HE JOINED BATTLE IN THE MIDDLE OF THE RIVER-BED WITH THE SENTRIES OF THE ENEMY (Livy, *Ab Urbe Condita*).

b/ In any case, this was not a golden rule. Observe this exception in Caesar:

- **Ipse interim in colle *medio* triplicem aciem instruxit** MEANWHILE, HE HIMSELF ARRANGED A TRIPLE LINE ON THE MIDDLE OF THE HILL (Caesar, *De Bello Gallico*).
  ✧ From the larger context, it can be seen that it means THE MIDDLE OF THE HILL, not THE HILL IN THE MIDDLE.

c/ A common idiom is **in mediis undis** IN THE MIDDLE OF THE WAVES, although Latin writers used to write **mediis in undis**:

- ***Mediis* sitiemus *in undis*** LET'S BE THIRSTY IN THE MIDDLE OF THE WAVES (Ovid, *Metamorphoses*).

4. Use of the adjective as a noun [37]

a/ As in many languages, adjectives can be used as nouns. We have seen the adjective **amicus, -a, -um** FRIENDLY, but formerly we had seen the nouns **amica, -ae** and **amicus, -i**, both meaning FRIEND, which obviously are nothing else than the feminine and masculine of the adjective, used as nouns.

Maybe the most common use is **Romani** THE ROMANS, **Galli** THE GAULS, **omnia** EVERYTHING, etc.:

- **Labor *omnia* vincit** HARD WORK CONQUERS ALL (Virgil, *Georgicae*).
- ***Omnia* circumspexit Quinctius, *omnia* periclitatus est** QUINCTIUS CONSIDERED EVERYTHING, TESTED EVERYTHING (Cicero, *Pro Quinctio*).

Adjectives like **boni**, if used on its own, may need some free translation in English (to translate it by THE GOOD ONES would sound strange in English, but in fact this is the way it sounded in Latin):

- **Sed sunt in illo numero multi *boni*, docti, pudentes, qui ad hoc iudicium deducti non sunt** BUT THERE ARE IN THAT BODY MANY VIRTUOUS, LEARNED AND MODEST PEOPLE WHO HAVE NOT BEEN BROUGHT TO THIS TRIAL (Cicero, *Pro Flacco*).

b/ Their use in neuter plural in abstract sense is also very common, and also in this case we may need some free translation in English:

- **Amo *bona*** I LOVE GOOD THINGS.
- **Non facio *mala*** I DO NOT DO BAD THINGS.
- **Maiorum gloria posteris quasi lumen est, neque *bona* neque *mala* eorum in occulto patitur** THE GLORY OF THE ANCESTORS IS LIKE A LIGHT FOR THE DESCENDANTS, AND IT DOES NOT LEAVE IN DARKNESS EITHER THEIR VIRTUES OR THEIR VICES (Sallust, *Bellum Iugurthinum*).

c/ The adjective **liber**, in its masculine plural form **liberi, -orum**, if used on its own, may have the meaning of CHILDREN, sons and daughters indistinctly:

- **Cari sunt parentes, cari *liberi*, propinqui, familiares** PARENTS, CHILDREN, RELATIVES AND FRIENDS ARE DEAR (Cicero, *De Officiis*).

d) Numeral adjectives

To present the whole numerical system would exceed the purpose of this grammar, so we present here those that the student is more liable to find.

1. Cardinals [38]

a/ The cardinals from *1* to *20* (after the translation, we add their representation in Roman ciphers):

1	unus, -a, -um	I	*11*	undecim	XI
2	duo, duae, duo	II	*12*	duodecim	XII
3	tres, tria	III	*13*	tredecim	XIII
4	quattuor	IV	*14*	quattuordecim	XIV
5	quinque	V	*15*	quindecim	XV
6	sex	VI	*16*	sedecim	XVI
7	septem	VII	*17*	septendecim	XVII
8	octo	VIII	*18*	duodeviginti	XVIII
9	novem	IX	*19*	undeviginti	XIX
10	decem	X	*20*	viginti	XX

Note that *18* and *19* are expressed by saying how many are left to reach 20.

From all of these, only *1, 2* and *3* are declined, the rest of them are indeclinable. We will see the declension of **unus, -a, -um** in the chapter of indefinite pronouns. **Duo** and **tres** are declined this way:

	masc.	*fem.*	*neuter*
Nom.	duo	duae	duo
Acc.	duos	duas	duo
Gen.	duorum	duarum	duorum
Dat.	duobus	duabus	duobus
Abl.	duobus	duabus	duobus

	masc./fem.		*neuter*
Nom.	tres		tria
Acc.	tres		tria
Gen.	←	trium	→
Dat.	←	tribus	→
Abl.	←	tribus	→

Obviously, both of them follow plural patterns, and **tres, tria** follows the regular plural of an **-is, -e** adjective.

b/ From here on, *20, 30*, etc. are as follows:

30	triginta	XXX	*70*	septuaginta	LXX
40	quadraginta	XL	*80*	octoginta	LXXX
50	quinquaginta	L	*90*	nonaginta	XC
60	sexaginta	LX			

c/ When we have to form a compound number, for instance TWENTY-FOUR or TWENTY-SEVEN, we form it this way: [39]

quattuor et viginti (24), septem et viginti (27)

but TWENTY-EIGHT and TWENTY-NINE would be formed this way:

duodetriginta, undetriginta (i.e., following the pattern of *18* and *19*).

The same pattern would be followed with the other compounds:

unit + et + *tenth* except for compounds ending in *8* or *9*.

d/ From 100 on, they are as follows:

100	centum	C	*600*	sescenti, -ae, -a	DC
200	ducenti, -ae, -a	CC	*700*	septingenti, -ae, -a	DCC
300	trecenti, -ae, -a	CCC	*800*	octingenti, -ae, -a	DCCC
400	quadringenti, -ae, -a	CD	*900*	nongenti, -ae, -a	CM
500	quingenti, -ae, -a	D			

Observe that from *200* on they are declined following the *2-1-2 scheme*, but *100* is indeclinable.

e/ With respect to the thousands, *1,000* **mille** is indeclinable; it is considered an adjective, but it is not declined:

- *Mille milites* vidimus WE SAW 1,000 SOLDIERS.

To say TWO THOUSAND, THREE THOUSAND, etc., we use **milia** (observe: only one -l-), which is considered a noun meaning THOUSANDS and is declined like the neuter plural of **facilis**:

Nom.	milia
Acc.	milia
Gen.	milium
Dat.	milibus
Abl	milibus

After it, we must use the *partitite genitive*:

- Tria milia *militum* vidi I SAW THREE THOUSAND SOLDIERS ("... three thousands of soldiers").

✧ Observe that we use the neuter **tria**, because **milia** is a neuter noun.

✧ In some cases, the genitive partitive can be found also after **mille**:

- Mille *militum* vidimus WE SAW ONE THOUSAND (OF) SOLDIERS.

Let's see some examples:

- Non *quinquaginta* modo, *quadringentos filios* habet HE HAS GOT NOT ONLY FIFTY CHILDREN: HE HAS GOT FOUR HUNDRED (Plautus, *Bacchides*).
- Bis ex *duorum bellorum* flamma ferroque servata est IT WAS SAVED TWICE FROM BLAZE AND DESTRUCTION OF TWO WARS (Cicero, *In Verrem*).

- *Ducentos equites* ei attribuit (Caesar, *De Bello Gallico*). HE ASSIGNED TO HIM TWO HUNDRED HORSEMEN
- Egressus cum *tribus legionibus* eum locum petit AFTER DEPARTING WITH THREE LEGIONS HE HEADS FOR THAT PLACE (Caesar, *De Bello Gallico*).
- *Mille* milites ... in praesidium cum frumento missi (sunt) ONE THOUSAND SOLDIERS WERE SENT TO THE GARRISON WITH SUPPLIES (Livy, *Ab Urbe Condita*).
- *Duas legiones Romanas* et *decem milia* sociorum peditum, *mille equites socios, sescentos Romanos* Gallia prouincia ... habuit THE PROVINCE OF GAUL RECEIVED TWO ROMAN LEGIONS, TEN THOUSAND ALLIED INFANTRY SOLDIERS, ONE THOUSAND ALLIED HORSEMEN AND SIX HUNDRED ROMAN ONES (Livy, *Ab Urbe Condita*).

2. Ordinals [40]

The ordinals corresponding to the 10 first positions are adjectives that follow the *2-1-2 scheme*:

FIRST	primus, -a, -um	SIXTH	sextus, -a, -um
SECOND	secundus, -a, um	SEVENTH	septimus, -a, -um
THIRD	tertius, -a, -um	EIGHTH	octavus, -a, -um
FOURTH	quartus, -a, -um	NINTH	nonus, -a, -um
FIFTH	quintus, -a, -um	TENTH	decimus, -a, -um

Some examples of ordinals:

- *Tertio die* Caesar vallo castra communit (Caesar, *Bellum Civile*). ON THE THIRD DAY CAESAR BARRICADED THE CAMP WITH A WALL
- *Septimus* mihi *liber* Originum est in manibus (Cicero, *Cato Maior de Senectute*). I HAVE IN MY HANDS THE SEVENTH BOOK OF THE ORIGINES

3. Multiplicatives [41]

They indicate the number of times that an amount or something is repeated. They are adjectives of one ending:

duplex, -plicis	DOUBLE
triplex, -plicis	TRIPLE
quadruplex, -plicis	QUADRUPLE

Also these multiplicative adverbs should be known:

semel	ONCE
bis	TWICE
ter	THRICE
centiens	ONE HUNDRED TIMES

✧ Adverbs are dealt with in another chapter, but it seemed logical to include these ones here.

Some examples:

- Liberare iuravisti me haud *semel*, sed *centiens* YOU SWORE TO FREE ME NOT ONCE, BUT ONE HUNDRED TIMES (Plautus, *Poenulus*).
- Rem publicam *bis* servavi I SAVED THE STATE TWICE (Cicero, *Pro Sestio*).
- Caesar ... *duplicem* eo loco fecerat vallum CAESAR HAD BUILT A DOUBLE WALL IN THAT PLACE (Caesar, *Bellum Civile*).

4. Distributives [42]

They indicate in which amount the subject (or object) is to be considered:

singuli, -ae, -a	ONE BY ONE
bini, -ae, -a	IN GROUPS OF TWO
trini, -ae, -a	IN GROUPS OF THREE

- Rex Creo *vigiles nocturnos singulos* semper locat KING CREON ALWAYS ARRANGES SEPARATE ("ONE BY ONE") NIGHT SENTRIES (Plautus, *Amphitruo*).

A very important use they have is that they are used for nouns that have no singular (or that have a different meaning in singular):

- *Bina castra* cepimus WE CAPTURED TWO CAMPS.
- *Binas* a te accepi *litteras* I RECEIVED FROM YOU TWO LETTERS (Cicero, *Epistulae ad Familiares*).

e) Comparative and superlative

1. General observations [43]

Usually, when the concept of "comparative" degree of adjectives is mentioned, the first type that springs to mind is the comparative of *superiority* (TALLER THAN...); however, both in English and in Latin, there are two additional types of comparatives, which will be introduced in this chapter: the comparative of *inferiority* (LESS TALL THAN...) and the comparative of *equality* (AS TALL AS...). First we will deal with the comparative of superiority and with the superlative (from now on, as happens in most grammars, when we mention just *comparative* we will mean *comparative of superiority*).

We must insist on the fact that a comparative or superlative is just an adjective and that therefore it will have to agree with its noun in gender, number and case.

2. Accidence [44]

a) Comparative

Adjectives form their comparative form by means of the suffixes **-ior** / **-ius** added to the stem of the adjective; the resulting adjective will be declined through the 3rd declension *consonant stem*; no matter whether the adjective in its original form (usually called "positive form") belongs to the 1st or 2nd class of adjectives: its comparative will be declined through the 3rd declension consonant stem; let's see the comparative of **altus-, -a, -um**:

	singular		plural	
	masc./fem	*neuter*	*masc./fem*	*neuter*
Nom.	alt-ior	alt-ius	alt-ior-es	alt-ior-a
Voc.	alt-ior	alt-ius	alt-ior-es	alt-ior-a
Acc.	alt-ior-em	alt-ius	alt-ior-es	alt-ior-a
Gen.	← alt-ior-is →		← alt-ior-um →	
Dat.	← alt-ior-i →		← alt-ior-ibus →	
Abl	← alt-ior-e →		← alt-ior-ibus →	

Notes

1/ The Abl. sing, is always -**e**, even if the adjective must be neuter.

2/ Observe that the suffix -**ius** is used ONLY for the three first cases of the neuter singular; the rest of the singular and ALL of the plural use -**ior**, whether it is neuter or not. There is the wrong tendency to say that -**ior** is used for masc. and fem. and -**ius** for neuter, but we can see that only three of the twelve forms in neuter use -**ius**.

b) Superlative [45]

The superlative is formed by adding the suffix -**issim**- to the stem and declining it as an adjective of the 1st class (again, no matter whether the adjective in its positive form belongs to the 1st or 2nd class of adjectives: its superlative will be declined through the **-us, -a, -um** scheme): **alt-issim-us, -a, -um.**

Some adjectives with the stem ending in -**il**- add -**limus** instead of -**issimus**:

facilis, -e	superl.	facillimus
difficilis, -e	superl.	difficillimus
similis, -e	superl.	simillimus
dissimilis, -e	superl.	dissimillimus

And some others, those that have a nom. masc, sing. ending in -**er**, add -**rimus** to this masculine form (and they do not elide the **-e-** even if the adjective in its positive form elides it):

celeber, -bris, -bre	superl.	celeberrimus
pulcher, -chra, -chrum	superl.	pulcherrimus

c) Irregular comparatives and superlatives [46]

1/ Some adjectives change their stem when forming the comparative and the superlative, and moreover the usual suffix -**issim**- of the superlative has disappeared in most of them. The four most frequent ones change the stem completely:

Positive		*Comparative*	*Superlative*
bonus, a, -um	GOOD	melior, -ius	optimus, -a, -um
malus, -a, -um	BAD	peior, peius	pessimus, -a, -um
magnus, -a, -um	BIG	maior, -ius	maximus, -a, -um
parvus, -a, -um	SMALL	minor, -us	minimus, -a, -um

Note that **minor, -us** lacks the -i- of -**ior** and -**ius**, but it goes on being declined by the 3rd declension like the other ones.

2/ Other ones, not so frequent and that do not change their stem but just modify it partially, are:

Positive		*Comparative*	*Superlative*
vetus, -teris	OLD	vetustior, -ius	veterrimus, -a, -um
dives, divitis	RICH	ditior, -ius	ditissimus, -a, -um
propinquus, -a, -um	NEAR	propior, -ius	proximus, -a, -um

- Quis me est *ditior*? — WHO IS REACHER THAN ME? (Plautus, *Aulularia*).
- Tanto deteriores sunt quanto *vetustiores* — THE OLDER THEY ARE, THE WORSE THEY ARE (Columella, *De Re Rustica*).

3/ A very important one: [47]

multus, -a, -um MUCH (MANY in plural) has a very peculiar comparative: in the *singular*, it is **plus**, which is a neuter noun; its declension is:

Nom.	plus
Acc.	plus
Gen.	pluris
Dat.	[non-existent]
Abl.	plure

If it is followed by a noun, this noun will be a *partitive genitive*:

- *Plus aquae* volo — I WANT MORE (OF) WATER.
- Cito te intelleges *plus* audire — QUICKLY YOU WILL REALISE THAT YOU HEAR MORE (Cato, *De Agri Cultura*).
  ✧ In the previous sentences, Cato has mentioned a remedy for healing people with hearing difficulties.

In the *plural*, it is an adjective, and it has a form for masculine and feminine and another one for neuter, declined like the plural of **facilis, -e** with the exception that the expected neuter ending **-ia** is just **-a** (as if it were a consonant stem):

Nom.	plures	/ plura
Acc.	plures (or pluris)	/ plura
Gen.	plurium	
Dat.	pluribus	
Abl.	pluribus	

Its use is the expected one:

- *Plures libros* habeo — I HAVE MORE BOOKS.
- Postremo vicit sententia *plurium* — FINALLY THE OPINION OF THE MAJORITY PREVAILED (Livy, *Ab Urbe Condita*).

3. Syntax

a) Comparative [48]

1/ The comparative will usually have a second term of comparison. Observe this sentence:

THE STUDENT IS TALLER *THAN THE TEACHER*.

The second term in this comparison is *THAN THE TEACHER*. There are two ways of expressing it:

➪ By using **quam** (= THAN) and putting THE TEACHER in the same case as the first term of the comparison (in this sentence, THE STUDENT, which happens to be in nominative):

Discipulus altior *quam magister* est.

➪ By putting THE TEACHER in ablative (without any word equivalent to THAN):

Discipulus altior est *magistro*.

This second system can be used only when two objects (or people) are being compared directly and when the first element to be compared is either in nominative or accusative (as in the last example); for instance, we can not use it to say GOING HOME IS BETTER THAN GOING TO THE FORUM, we must use the **quam** method:

Melius est domum ire *quam ad forum*.

✧ ad forum is a prepositional phrase, it is not a noun that we can put in ablative.

Let's see some examples:

- *Miseriorem* ego ex amore *quam te* vidi neminem (Plautus, *Casina*) — I HAVE SEEN NOBODY AS UNFORTUNATE AS YOU IN LOVE
- Neminem *me fortiorem* esse censebam (Curtius Rufus, *Historiae Alexandri Magni*). — I THOUGHT THAT THERE WAS NOBODY STRONGER THAN ME
- Qui *me* alter est *audacior* homo aut qui *confidentior*? — WHAT OTHER MAN IS BRAVER THAN ME, OR MORE SELF-CONFIDENT? (Plautus, *Amphitruo*).
- *Ferocior* etiam *quam Romulus* fuit (Livy, *Ab Urbe Condita*). — HE WAS EVEN MORE FEROCIOUS THAN ROMULUS

2/ The comparative can be used without any second term: [49]

- *Deteriores* enim iugulari cupio, *meliores* vincere — I WANT THE WEAKER ONES TO HAVE THEIR THROAT CUT AND THE BETTER ONES TO WIN (Cicero, *Philippicae*).
- Castra *altiore* vallo muniri iubet (Caesar, *De Bello Gallico*). — HE ORDERS THAT THE CAMP BE FORTIFIED WITH A HIGHER PALISADE

Or the second term can even be another verb:

- Peiores morimur *quam nascimur* — WE DIE AS WORSE PERSONS THAN WE ARE BORN (Seneca iunior, *Epistulae Morales ad Lucilium*).

b) Superlative [50]

The superlative can have two meanings:

1/ Absolute meaning:	• *Caesar sapientissimus est*	CAESAR IS VERY WISE.
2/ Relative meaning:	• *Caesar sapientissimus est*	CAESAR IS THE WISEST ... (out of whom?).

When it is used with relative meaning, the second term of the superlative expression can be expressed in three ways:

⇨ genitive:	• *Caesar sapientissimus est omnium ducum* ✧ This is the most common way.	CAESAR IS THE WISEST OF ALL GENERALS
⇨ ex + ablative:	• *Caesar sapientissimus est ex omnibus ducibus*	CAESAR IS THE WISEST OUT OF ALL GENERALS.
⇨ inter + accusative:	• *Caesar sapientissimus est inter omnes duces*	CAESAR IS THE WISEST AMONG ALL GENERALS.

Some original examples:

- Exercitus autem Caesaris, qui erat *optimus*, ... BUT CAESAR'S ARMY, THAT WAS THE BEST ONE, ... (Cicero, *Epistulae ad Brutum*).
- *Horum omnium fortissimi* sunt Belgae THE BELGAE ARE THE BRAVEST OF ALL OF THESE (Caesar, *De Bello Gallico*).
- *Peritissimos* belli navalis fecit Athenienses HE MADE THE ATHENIANS VERY EXPERT PEOPLE IN THE ART OF NAVAL WAR (Nepos, *Vitae*).
- ... transire *latissimum* flumen, ascendere *altissimas* ripas, subire *iniquissimum* locum ... TO CROSS A VERY WIDE RIVER, TO CLIMB VERY HIGH BANKS, TO GO UP TO A VERY DISADVANTAGEOUS PLACE (Caesar, *De Bello Gallico*).

c) Further observations [51]

1/ Comparative of inferiority

It is formed by means of the adverbs **minus ... quam**:

- Petrus *minus* altus est *quam* Antonius PETER IS LESS TALL THAN ANTHONY.
  ✧ Note that both elements compared must be in the same case.
- Intellectum est nostros propter gravitatem armorum ... *minus* aptos esse ad huius generis hostem IT WAS PERCEIVED THAT OUR MEN, BECAUSE OF THE WEIGHT OF THEIR ARMS, ... WERE LESS SUITED FOR AN ENEMY OF THIS KIND (Caesar, *De Bello Gallico*).
- ... quod *minus* idoneis equis utebantur ... BECAUSE THEY WERE USING HORSES LESS SUITABLE (Caesar, *De Bello Gallico*).
- Eadem equestris pugna causam *minus* mirabilem dedit THE CAVALRY FIGHT OFFERED A LESS SINGULAR PRETEXT (Livy, *Ab Urbe Condita*).

2/ Comparative of equality [52]

It is formed by means of the adverbs **tam ... quam**:

- Petrus *tam* altus est *quam* Antonius PETER IS AS TALL AS ANTHONY.
  ✧ Note that both elements compared must be in the same case.
- ... non *tam* sapiens *quam* ii qui nihil curant ... NOT AS WISE AS THOSE WHO CARE FOR NOTHING (Cicero, *De Domo Sua*).

3/ Comparative and superlative by means of adverbs

Some adjectives do not admit the suffixes **-ior**, **-ius**, like for instance **idoneus, -a, -um** SUITABLE. These adjectives form the comparative by means of the adverbs **magis/plus ... quam**:

- Librum *magis* idoneum habeo I HAVE A MORE SUITABLE BOOK.
- ... et ceteris rebus de quibus *magis* idoneo tempore loquemur ... AND IN OTHER MATTERS ABOUT WHICH WE WILL SPEAK AT A MORE APPROPRIATE TIME (Anon., *Rhetorica ad Herennium*).

And they form the superlative by means of the adverb **maxime**:

- Librum *maxime* idoneum habeo I HAVE A VERY SUITABLE BOOK.
- *Maxime* idoneum ad muniendum locum credidit esse praeter amnem Avum HE CONSIDERED A PLACE NEAR THE RIVER AVUS TO BE THE MOST SUITABLE ONE TO BE FORTIFIED (Livy, *Ab Urbe Condita*).

4/ A very common use of quam + *superlative* [53]

Quam + *superlative* means that the person (or thing) possesses the mentioned quality in the highest intensity in which it can be possessed; this implies translating it using some additional words in English to reflect this sense. Observe the difference between both examples:

- Socrates doctissimus est SOCRATES IS VERY WISE.
- Socrates *quam doctissimus* est SOCRATES IS AS WISE AS ANYBODY CAN BE.
- ... *quam clarissimi* viri qui, illa urbe pulsi, carere ingrata civitate quam manere in improba maluerunt ... MEN AS WISE AS ANBODY CAN BE, WHO, EXPELLED FROM THAT CITY, PREFERRED TO LACK OF AN UNGRATEFUL CITY THAN TO REMAIN IN A WICKED ONE (Cicero, *De Legibus*).

5/ Singular superlative with quique EACH meaning ALL [54]

Sometimes, when we want to refer to a group of people qualified by a superlative (THE BEST STUDENTS, THE FASTEST RUNNERS, THE BRAVEST SOLDIERS, etc.), we can express the collectivity by means of the indefinite pronoun **quique** EACH in singular and the superlative.

For instance, if we want to say I GAVE A BOOK TO THE BEST STUDENTS

⇨ we can translate it as **Librum dedi optimis discipulis**

⇨ but we can also translate it as **Librum dedi *cuique optimo discipulo***

✧ which in fact means I GAVE A BOOK *TO EACH BEST STUDENT*.

Some examples:

- *Ferocissimus quisque* iuvenum cum armis voluntarius adest THE BRAVEST OF THE YOUNG MEN OFFER THEMSELVES WITH THEIR WEAPONS (Livy, *Ab Urbe Condita*).

  ✧ Literally, EACH BRAVEST OF THE YOUNG MEN OFFERS HIMSELF WITH HIS WEAPONS.

- Equos dehinc *fortissimo cuique bellatori* tradit HENCE HE GIVES HORSES TO THE MOST COURAGEOUS FIGHTERS (Tacitus, *Annales*).

  ✧ Literally, ... TO EACH MOST COURAGEOUS FIGHTER.

f) Pronouns

Introductory note: Many of the pronouns presented in this chapter are adjectives in origin, but as a general rule they are referred to as "pronouns", grammatically speaking. So if they accompany a noun, they are to be treated as adjectives (for instance, **Video hanc puellam** I SEE THIS GIRL) but, if they appear alone, they are to be considered as pronouns (for instance, **Video hanc** I SEE THIS ONE). For this reason in some of the following explanations both the terms "adjective" and "pronoun" are used indistinctly. In some cases, nevertheless, they can only be pronouns, as for instance in the case of personal pronouns *I, you*, etc. Moreover, most of them lack vocative.

1. Demonstrative pronouns [55]

a) Accidence

There are three demonstrative pronouns (also called "deictic pronouns") in Latin:

- ⇨ hic, haec, hoc THIS
- ⇨ iste, ista, istud THIS / THAT
- ⇨ ille, illa, illud THAT

In keeping with the grammar of adjectives, these are declined in singular or plural, masculine, feminine or neuter forms. As usual, if the adjective accompanies a noun, they will agree with it in gender, case and number.

In general lines, it can be said that they are irregular in the singular but they follow the usual pattern **-i, -ae, -a** in the plural (with some exception). But in the singular they show a characteristic shared by a lot of other pronouns: they have **-ius** for all genders of genitive and -i for all genders of dative.

1/ hic, haec, hoc THIS [56]

	singular			plural		
	masc.	*fem.*	*neuter*	*masc.*	*fem.*	*neuter*
Nom.	hic	haec	hoc	hi	hae	haec
Acc.	hunc	hanc	hoc	hos	has	haec
Gen.	huius	huius	huius	horum	harum	horum
Dat.	huic	huic	huic	his	his	his
Abl.	hoc	hac	hoc	his	his	his

Notes

a/ The plural has the only exception of the Nom./Acc. **haec** instead of the expected **ha**; apart from this, it follows the **-i, -ae, -a** parameter.

b/ Except the genitive, all the other forms in the singular end in this characteristic **-c**.

c/ Observe the mentioned **-ius** for all Gen. sing. and -i for all Dat. sing. We will find them in most pronouns.

2/ iste, ista, istud THIS / THAT [57]

	singular			plural		
	masc.	*fem.*	*neuter*	*masc.*	*fem.*	*neuter*
Nom.	iste	ista	istud	isti	istae	ista
Acc.	istum	istam	istud	istos	istas	ista
Gen.	istius	istius	istius	istorum	istarum	istorum
Dat.	isti	isti	isti	istis	istis	istis
Abl.	isto	ista	isto	istis	istis	istis

Notes

a/ The plural is completely regular.

b/ It can be translated by THIS or THAT, but usually it conveys a pejorative meaning (iste homo THIS / THAT WICKED MAN) or a possessive meaning OF YOURS (iste liber THIS / THAT BOOK OF YOURS).

3/ ille, illa, illud THAT [58]

	singular			plural		
	masc.	*fem.*	*neuter*	*masc.*	*fem.*	*neuter*
Nom.	ille	illa	illud	illi	illae	illa
Acc.	illum	illam	illud	illos	illas	illa
Gen.	illius	illius	illius	illorum	illarum	illorum
Dat.	illi	illi	illi	illis	illis	illis
Abl.	illo	illa	illo	illis	illis	illis

It declines completely equal to iste, ista, istud.

b) Syntax [59]

1/ Normal use as adjective

We will find it accompanying a noun as any other adjective:

- *Hunc librum* non legi — I HAVE NOT READ THIS BOOK.
- Erat ob *has causas* summa difficultas (Caesar, *De Bello Gallico*). — BECAUSE OF THESE REASONS THERE WAS A HUGE DIFFICULTY

2/ Use of demonstrative adjectives as pronouns

As all adjectives, demonstratives can be used on their own (i.e. without accompanying a name). In this case, the gender of the adjectives will indicate its referent. For example:

- *Hos* video — I SEE THESE ONES ✧ Masculine direct objects, such as boys, soldiers, etc.

- *Has* video I SEE THESE ONES ✧ Feminine direct objects, such as girls, women, etc.
- At ego amo *hanc* BUT I LOVE THIS ONE (Plautus, *Poenulus*).
- *Hunc* Athenienses non solum in bello, sed etiam in pace diu desideraverunt THE ATHENIANS LONGED FOR HIM (literally, FOR THIS ONE) NOT ONLY IN WAR BUT ALSO IN PEACE (Nepos, *Vitae*).

3/ It is very common to find demonstrative pronouns in neuter forms, where they stand for abstract concepts or imply a neuter object, as in the following examples: [60]

- Caesar *haec* dixit CAESAR SAID THESE THINGS ✧ i.e. THESE WORDS or just THIS.
- *Hoc* amamus WE LOVE THIS.
  ✧ This last object can be a concept, an activity, etc., but not a person, since it is neuter; it could even refer to a proposal somebody has previously made, or to some characteristic of the discourse, which has to be clarified in the previous sentences.
- *Haec* elocutus dextram Philippo offert AFTER SAYING THESE THINGS, HE OFFERS HIS RIGHT HAND TO PHILIPPUS (Curtius, *Historiae Alexandri Magni*).

2. Personal pronouns [61]

a) Accidence

	I	YOU (sing.)	WE	YOU (plur.)
Nom.	ego	tu	nos	vos
Voc.	----	tu	----	vos
Acc.	me	te	nos	vos
Gen.	mei	tui	nostri, -um	vestri, -um
Dat.	mihi	tibi	nobis	vobis
Abl.	me	te	nobis	vobis

b) Syntax

1/ The nominative form of personal pronouns is used only to emphasise the subject of an action, for example in order to highlight a contrast with someone else's action, as in the following example:

- *Ego* laboro, sed *tu* dormis I AM WORKING, BUT YOU ARE SLEEPING.
- Audacissimus *ego* ex omnibus? Minime AM I THE BRAVEST OF ALL? NOT AT ALL (Cicero, *Pro Roscio Amerino*).
- *Tu* id semper facis, quia semper potes YOU ARE ALWAYS DOING THIS BECAUSE YOU ARE ALWAYS ABLE TO (Cicero, *Pro Quinctio*).
- Et *tu* intellegis et *nos* existimare possumus BOTH YOU UNDERSTAND IT AND WE CAN CONSIDER IT (Cicero, *In Verrem*).

2/ With respect to the other cases, they are used as we would use any noun:

- Video *mensam* — I SEE THE TABLE / Video *te* — I SEE YOU.
- *Magistro* do librum — I GIVE THE BOOK TO THE TEACHER / *Tibi* do librum — I GIVE YOU THE BOOK.
- Da *consuli* pecuniam — GIVE THE MONEY TO THE CONSUL! / Da *mihi* pecuniam — GIVE ME THE MONEY!

3/ As there is no third person pronoun in Latin, we can use the demonstrative **hic** or **ille** for the nominative and the anaphoric **is, ea, id** for any case: [62]

- Video *eam* — I SEE HER.
- *Eis* libros do — I GIVE THE BOOKS TO THEM / I GIVE THEM THE BOOKS.
- Imperator *eos* conlaudat — THE COMMANDER EXTOLS THEM (Livy, *Ab Urbe Condita*).
- Res ipsa aspera est, sed vos non timetis *eam* — THE MATTER ITSELF IS A DIFFICULT ONE, BUT YOU DO NOT FEAR IT (Sallust, *Catilinae Coniuratio*).

  ✧ Note: MATTER is feminine in Latin, so Latin must use **eam** for IT.
- Sex novae legiones erant scribendae. *Eas* ... consules scribere iussi — SIX NEW LEGIONS HAD TO BE RECRUITED. I ORDERED THE CONSULS TO RECRUIT THEM (Livy, *Ab Urbe Condita*).

3. Possessive pronouns [63]

a) Accidence

They are declined following the *2-1-2 scheme*:

⇨ meus, -a, -um	MY		⇨ noster, -tra, -trum	OUR	
⇨ tuus, -a, -um	YOUR	✧ one owner	⇨ vester, -tra, -trum	YOUR	✧ more than one owner
⇨ suus, -a, -um	HIS / HER / ITS OWN		⇨ suus, -a, -um	THEIR OWN	

b) Syntax

1/ If the subject of the sentence is also the person who owns the objects referred to, then the possessive adjective is not used explicitly.

For example, if we want to translate into Latin the sentence I GIVE BOOKS TO MY FRIENDS

a/ we would write simply **Do libros amicis**, without any Latin word meaning MY,
b/ and it would be clear that I mean my friends, not somebody else's friends.

In keeping with this principle,

– the sentence **Vides patrem** will mean YOU SEE *YOUR* FATHER because the subject is YOU,
– the sentence **Videt patrem** will mean HE SEES *HIS* FATHER because the subject is HE.

- Ego ibo ad fratrem — I'LL GO TO MY BROTHER'S PLACE (Plautus, *Captivi*).
- Patrem occidit Sex. Roscius — S. ROSCIUS KILLED HIS OWN FATHER (Cicero, *Pro Roscio Amerino*).
- Erat ea tempestate Romae Numida quidam ... qui ... profugus ex patria abierat — THERE WAS AT THAT TIME IN ROME A CERTAIN NUMIDIAN WHO HAD FLED FUGITIVE FROM HIS HOMELAND (Sallust, *Bellum Iugurthinum*).

2/ The possessive **suus, -a, -um** is always reflexive. The owner is always the subject of the sentence:

- **Caesar videt *suum exercitum*** CAESAR SEES HIS OWN ARMY
- ***Oculos* pascat uterque *suos*** LET EACH ONE FEED HIS OWN EYES (Ovid, *Amores*).
- ***Domum suam* recitantibus praebet** HE OFFERS HIS HOUSE TO THOSE WHO RECITE (Plinius Secundus, *Epistulae*).

To say POMPEIUS APPROACHES, AND CAESAR SEES HIS (POMPEIUS') ARMY we would have to use the genitive of the anaphoric pronoun (introduced further down, in Point 4) **is, ea, id**:

Pompeius appropinquat et Caesar videt *eius* exercitum

✧ In fact we are saying ... AND CAESAR SEES THE ARMY *OF HIM*.

- **Ubi de *eius* adventu Helvetii certiores facti sunt, ...** WHEN THE HELVETIANS WERE INFORMED ABOUT HIS ARRIVAL, ... (Caesar, *De Bello Gallico*).

  ✧ Note: **de *suo* adventu** would have meant that the Helvetians were informed about their own arrival, something that would make no sense.
- **Sequens annus gravi vulnere animum domumque *eius* adflixit** THE FOLLOWING YEAR AFFLICTED HIS SOUL AND HIS HOUSE WITH A GRAVE WOUND (Tacitus, *Agricola*).

  ✧ Agricola's mother died the following year.

3/ Possessive pronouns can be replaced by the genitive form of the corresponding personal pronoun, but this is not common:

- **Video matrem *tui*** I SEE YOUR MOTHER.

  ✧ **Video *tuam matrem*** would be much more common.

4. Anaphoric pronoun [64]

a) Accidence

In order to supply the missing personal pronoun in the third person, especially when used as an object, it is necessary to use the so-called anaphoric pronoun. The word "anaphoric" means that it refers to something or somebody already mentioned previously. Its declension is as follows:

	singular			plural		
	masc.	*fem.*	*neuter*	*masc.*	*fem.*	*neuter*
Nom.	is	ea	id	ei / ii	eae	ea
Acc.	eum	eam	id	eos	eas	ea
Gen.	eius	eius	eius	eorum	earum	eorum
Dat.	ei	ei	ei	eis / iis	eis / iis	eis / iis
Abl.	eo	eo	eo	eis / iis	eis / iis	eis / iis

b) Syntax

The anaphoric pronoun overtakes the function of the non-existent 3rd person pronoun (and sometimes it can also be used with a noun, as demonstrative adjective with the meaning of **ille, illa, illud** or of **hic haec, hoc**, see 3rd example):

- Cum *eis* ludo — I AM PLAYING WITH THEM.
- Omnes cives amant *eum* — ALL CITIZENS LOVE HIM.
- *Eis pueris* pecuniam do — I GIVE MONEY TO THESE BOYS. ✧ Observe: as if **eis** were **his**.
- Alfenus cum *eis* et propter *eos* periit quos diligebat — ALFENUS DIES WITH THOSE AND BECAUSE OF THOSE HE APPRECIATED (Cicero, *Pro Quinctio*).
- Ubi *eos* convenit? — WHERE DID HE MEET THEM? (Cicero, *Pro Roscio Amerino*).
- Spectat *eam* Tereus — TEREUS BEHOLDS HER (Ovid, *Metamorphoses*).

In Latin there is no need to mention the anaphoric pronoun if it can be easily understood from the context:

- Pecuniam tibi offero et tu accipis — I OFFER MONEY TO YOU AND YOU ACCEPT [IT].
- Ita credo — SO I BELIEVE [IT] (Cicero, *Pro Quinctio*).

5. Identity pronouns [65]

There are two identity pronouns:

- ➪ idem, eadem, idem — SAME
- ➪ ipse, ipsa, ipsum — I MYSELF, YOU YOURSELF, HE HIMSELF, SHE HERSELF, etc.

a) Accidence

	singular			plural		
	masc.	*fem.*	*neuter*	*masc.*	*fem.*	*neuter*
Nom.	idem	eadem	idem	eidem	eaedem	eadem
Acc.	eundem	eandem	idem	eosdem	easdem	eadem
Gen.	eiusdem	eiusdem	eiusdem	eorundem	earundem	eorundem
Dat.	eidem	eidem	eidem	eisdem	eisdem	eisdem
Abl.	eodem	eodem	eodem	eisdem	eisdem	eisdem

✧ About the plural: **eidem** and **eisdem** can become **iidem** and **iisdem**.

	singular			plural		
	masc.	*fem.*	*neuter*	*masc.*	*fem.*	*neuter*
Nom.	ipse	ipsa	ipsum	ipsi	ipsae	ipsa
Acc.	ipsum	ipsam	ipsum	ipsos	ipsas	ipsa
Gen.	ipsius	ipsius	ipsius	ipsorum	ipsarum	ipsorum
Dat.	ipsi	ipsi	ipsi	ipsis	ipsis	ipsis
Abl.	ipso	ipsa	ipso	ipsis	ipsis	ipsis

b) Syntax [66]

1/ idem, eadem, idem

It means SAME in the sense of THE SAME ONE, NOT A DIFFERENT ONE:

- Tu et ego *eundem librum* habemus — YOU AND I HAVE THE SAME BOOK.
- Iterum *eodem bello* omnes copias eorum fugavit — ONCE MORE, HE ROUTED IN THE SAME WAR ALL THEIR TROOPS (Nepos, *Vitae*).
- Aliis modis *easdem res* efferre possumus — WE CAN CARRY OUT THE SAME THINGS THROUGH DIFFERENT WAYS (Cicero, *De Fato*).
- Legem recitari iussit, qua intra decem annos *eundem consulem* refici non liceret — HE ORDERS TO READ OUT A LAW ACCORDING TO WHICH THE SAME CONSUL COULD NOT BE REAPPOINTED WITHIN TEN YEARS (Livy, *Ab Urbe Condita*).

2/ ipse, ipsa, ipsum

It implies a reinforcement of the identity of the noun it goes with:

- *Caesarem ipsum* vidi — I SAW CAESAR HIMSELF.
- Volo *vos ipsos* haec Caesari dicere — I WANT YOU YOURSELF TO SAY THIS TO CAESAR.
- *Servos ipsos*, quod ad me attinet, neque arguo neque purgo — THE SLAVES THEMSELVES, IN RESPECT TO WHAT CONCERNS ME, I NEITHER ACCUSE NOR ACQUIT (Cicero, *Pro Roscio Amerino*).
- Eam intrare haud fere quisquam praeter *ducem ipsum* audebat — HARDLY ANYBODY EXCEPT THE GENERAL HIMSELF DARED TO GO INTO IT (Livy, *Ab Urbe Condita*).
- *Senatus ipse* iudicavit — THE SENATE ITSELF WILL DECIDE (Cicero, *De Haruspicum Responso*).

6. Reflexive pronouns [67]

a) Accidence

1/ In English the reflexive pronoun *SELF* is used in order to say that the object of a sentence is the same as the subject, e.g.: HE KILLED *HIMSELF*, SHE BOUGHT *HERSELF* A BOOK, etc. Latin does not have special reflexive pronouns for the 1st and 2nd persons singular and plural, it uses the normal personal pronouns:

• Librum mihi emis	YOU BUY A BOOK FOR ME.	✧ Mihi is not reflexive.
Librum *mihi* emo	I BUY A BOOK FOR MYSELF.	✧ Mihi has here a reflexive sense.
• Te video	I SEE YOU.	✧ Te is not reflexive.
Te vides in speculo	YOU SEE YOURSELF IN THE MIRROR.	✧ Te has here a reflexive sense.

Therefore, the reflexive pronouns for the 1st and 2nd person will be the same as the personal pronouns (obviously, nominative and vocative can not be used in a reflexive sense, as the function of the reflexive is always that of an object).

2/ But Latin has a reflexive pronoun for the 3rd person both singular and plural (curiously enough, the only person that has no personal pronoun):

Acc.	se
Gen.	sui
Dat.	sibi
Abl.	se.

It is obvious that it is related to the possessive suus, -a, -um we have seen previously.

b) Syntax [68]

As said, it can be used only as object:

- Brutus *se* necat BRUTUS KILLS HIMSELF.
- Caesar *sibi* librum emit CAESAR BUYS A BOOK FOR HIMSELF.
- Ipsa *se* necavit SHE KILLED HERSELF (Hyginius, *Fabulae*).
- Locis impeditis ac silvestribus *se* occultabat HE HID HIMSELF IN DIFFICULT AND WOODY PLACES (Caesar, *De Bello Gallico*).
- Nonnumquam ... animus *sibi* falsas imagines fingit SOMETIMES THE MIND FASHIONS FALSE IMAGES FOR ITSELF (Seneca iunior, *Epistulae Morales ad Lucilium*).

c) The indirect reflexive [69]

1/ We may find any form of se used in a subordinate sentence, and then we may hesitate whether it means the subject of the main sentence or of the subject of the subordinate:

Caesar dicit Brutum *se* vulneravisse:

Is Caesar saying that Brutus has wounded him (Caesar: "BRUTUS HAS WOUNDED ME") ...
... or that Brutus has wounded himself?

Usually, if we find the reflexive pronoun on its own, it will mean the subject of the main sentence instead of the subject of the subordinate inside which the reflexive pronoun is found, so in our example it would mean *Caesar*. This use of any form of se is called *indirect reflexive*.

2/ If we want to say CAESAR SAYS THAT BRUTUS HAS WOUNDED HIMSELF, we will complement the reflexive with the necessary form of ipse:

Caesar dicit Brutum *se ipsum* vulneravisse.

3/ And, to consider all possibilities, let's remember this:

Caesar dicit Brutum *eum* vulneravisse would mean CAESAR SAYS THAT BRUTUS HAS WOUNDED HIM,

⇨ and this HIM would mean *somebody else,* not *Caesar.*

7. Interrogative pronoun and adjective [70]

a) Accidence

In this case, there is a difference between the pronoun (the interrogative on its own) and the adjective (the interrogative accompanying an adjective).

1/ The interrogative pronoun is declined in this way (observe that in singular the masculine and feminine forms are identical):

	singular		plural		
	masc./fem.	*neuter*	*masc.*	*fem.*	*neuter*
Nom.	quis	quid	qui	quae	quae
Acc.	quem	quid	quos	quas	quae
Gen.	cuius	cuius	quorum	quarum	quorum
Dat.	cui	cui	quibus	quibus	quibus
Abl.	quo	quo	quibus	quibus	quibus

2/ When it is used as an adjective, the declension is absoutely identical to that of the relative (to be seen further ahead):

	singular			plural		
	masc.	*fem.*	*neuter*	*masc.*	*fem.*	*neuter*
Nom.	qui	quae	quod	qui	quae	quae
Acc.	quem	quam	quod	quos	quas	quae
Gen.	cuius	cuius	cuius	quorum	quarum	quorum
Dat.	cui	cui	cui	quibus	quibus	quibus
Abl.	quo	qua	quo	quibus	quibus	quibus

✧ Observe that the plural is identical for both pronoun and adjective.

b) Syntax [71]

Observe that in English there are not specific plural forms for WHO, WHICH etc.; so, the sentences **Quis hic adest?** and **Qui hic adsunt?** will be both translated as WHO IS HERE?, even though in the second case clearly the question regards the identity of several people.

Some examples of its use as pronoun:

- *Quis* huius rei testis est? — WHO IS A WITNESS OF THIS? (Cicero, *Pro Quinctio*).
- Potionem istam *cui* dedisti? — TO WHOM DID YOU GIVE THIS DRINK? (Quintilianus, *Declamationes Minores*).
- Est auctor *quis* denique eorum? — WHO IS, THEN, THEIR AUTHOR? (Horace, *Sermones*).
- *Quae* tibi manet vita? — WHAT LIFE IS THERE LEFT FOR YOU? (Catullus, *Carmina*)
- *Quis* nunc te adibit? — WHO WILL COME TO YOU NOW? (Catullus, *Carmina*).

- *Quem* nunc amabis? WHOM WILL YOU LOVE NOW? (Catullus, *Carmina*).
- *Cuius* esse diceris? WHOSE WILL YOU SAY THAT YOU ARE? (Catullus, *Carmina*).
- A *quibus* auxilium petam? FROM WHOM AM I TO SEEK HELP? (Cicero, *Pro Roscio Amerino*).
- *Quid* ais? Volgo occidebantur? Per *quos* et a *quibus*? WHAT DO YOU SAY? WERE THEY BEING KILLED OPENLY? THROUGH WHOM AND BY WHOM? (Cicero, *Pro Roscio Amerino*).

Some examples of its use as adjective:

- *Quem hominem* ... condemnasti? WHAT MAN DID YOU CONDEMN? (Cicero, *In Verrem*).
- *Quae civitas* est in Asia ... ? WHAT CITY IS THERE IN ASIA ...? (Cicero, *Pro Lege Manilia*).
- *Quem locum* tuae probandae virtutis exspectas? WHAT OPPORTUNITY OF PROVING YOUR BRAVERY DO YOU EXPECT? (Caesar, *De Bello Gallico*). ✧ Note: **locum** may mean OPPORTUNITY.
- *Quibus rebus* id adsecutus es? BY WHAT MEANS DID YOU OBTAIN THAT? (Cicero, *In Verrem*).
- *Qui homo*? Adulescentulus corruptus et ab hominibus nequam inductus? WHAT (KIND OF) MAN? A CORRUPTED YOUNG MAN, MADE WRETCHED BY MEN? (Cicero, *Pro Roscio Amerino*).

8. Other interrogative pronouns [72]

In addition to the interrogative pronoun **quis, quid** (adjective **qui, quae, quod**), there are in Latin other interrogative pronouns with more specific meanings, which will be described in the following paragraphs.

a) The quantitative interrogative quantus, -a, -um HOW BIG / HOW LARGE?

1/ The accidence follows the usual *2-1-2 scheme*. With respect to the meaning, we must make clear that it asks about the size, not about the quantity:

- *Quantus* est *exercitus* Caesaris? HOW LARGE IS CAESAR'S ARMY?

A sentence like *Quantos libros* habes?
⇨ would NOT mean HOW MANY BOOKS HAVE YOU GOT?
⇨ but HOW *LARGE* BOOKS HAVE YOU GOT?
✧ As if asking whether they are small books, or large volumes, etc.

- Sed si est *tantus dolor*, quantus Philoctetae? BUT IF THE PAIN IS SO INTENSE ("LARGE"), HOW INTENSE ("LARGE") IS PHILOCTETES' PAIN? (Cicero, *Tusculanae Disputationes*).
- Paenitet te, *quanto* hic fuerit *usui* ? DO YOU REGRET WHAT A LARGE PROFIT HE HAS BEEN TO YOU? (Plautus, *Pseudolus*).
- *Quanti* eam emit? FOR HOW MUCH DID HE BUY HER? (Plautus, *Epidicus*).
- *Familiam* vero *quantam* ... habeat quid ego dicam? WHY SHOULD I MENTION HOW A LARGE FAMILY HE HAS? (Cicero, *Pro Roscio Amerino*).

2/ This interrogative can also be used in exclamatory sense:

- *Quantas res* turbo, *quantas* moveo machinas! WHAT LARGE TURMOILS I CREATE! WHAT LARGE ENGINES I SET TO WORK! (Plautus, *Miles Gloriosus*).
- Immo vero *quantus exercitus*! AND INDEED, WHAT A LARGE ARMY! (Cicero, *Pro Flacco*).

3/ To ask HOW MANY, Latin uses the indeclinable interrogative **quot**:

- *Quot discipulos* habes? HOW MANY STUDENTS DO YOU HAVE?
- *Quot* sunt? HOW MANY ARE THEY? (Plautus, *Rudens*).
- Quotiens et *quot nominibus* a Syracusanis statuas auferes? HOW OFTEN AND FOR HOW MANY INDIVIDUALS WILL YOU TAKE STATUES FROM THE SYRACUSANS? (Cicero, *In Verrem*).
- *Quot aratores* adveniente te fuerunt agri Mutycensis? HOW MANY CULTIVATORS OF THE DISTRICT OF MUTYCA WERE THERE WHEN YOU ARRIVED? (Cicero, *In Verrem*).
- Hoc mihi dedit, sed ... post *quot labores*? HE GAVE IT TO ME, BUT AFTER NOW MANY TOILS? (Seneca iunior, *De Beneficiis*).

4/ As **quantus, -a, -um**, it can be used in exclamatory sense:

- *Quot* quantasque *uirtutes* ... collegit et miscuit! HOW MANY AND HOW GREAT VIRTUES HE ACQUIRED AND MIXED! (Plinius Secundus, *Epistulae*).
- *Quot oppida* in Syria, *quot* in Macedonia devorata sunt! HOW MANY TOWNS HAVE BEEN DEVOURED IN SYRIA, HOW MANY IN MACEDONIA! (Seneca iunior, *Epistulae Morales ad Lucilium*).

> **Note**
>
> **quantus, -a, -um** can also have the meaning of the correlative AS LARGE AS, see the corresponding chapter.

b) The qualitative interrogative qualis, -e OF WHAT KIND? [73]

The declension follows the *3-3 scheme* of **facilis, -e**. This interrogative (as usual, it can also be used as exclamatory) asks about the quality of the person, thing, etc.

- *Quales amicos* habes? WHAT KIND OF FRIENDS DO YOU HAVE?
- *Qualis* est ista mens? WHAT KIND OF TOUGHT IS THIS? (Cicero, *Tusculanae Disputationes*).
- Meam uxorem, Libane, nescis *qualis* sit? MY WIFE, LIBANUS, DON'T YOU KNOW WHAT KIND OF PERSON SHE IS? (Plautus, *Asinaria*).
- Cernite sim *qualis*! BEHOLD WHAT KIND OF PERSON I AM! (Ovid, *Fasti*).

> **Note**
>
> **qualis, -e** can also have the meaning of the correlative SUCH AS, see the corresponding chapter.

c) The selective interrogative uter, utra, utrum WHICH OF THE TWO? [74]

1/ It is used to imply that the referents are exactly *two* in number:

- *Utrum librum* vis? WHICH BOOK DO YOU WANT?
  - ✧ As we use this adjective, we imply that there are only two books to choose from, so we could have translated it as WHICH ONE OF THE TWO BOOKS DO YOU WANT?
- *Uter* igitur nostrum est cupidior dicti? WHICH OF BOTH OF US IS MORE DESIROUS OF A SMART SAYING? (Cicero, *Pro Plancio*).
- *Uter* igitur est divitior? WHICH ONE OF BOTH IS RICHER? (Cicero, *Paradoxa Stoicorum*).
- *Utra lex* antiquior? WHICH LAW IS OLDER? (Quintilianus, *Declamationes Minores*).

2/ It is declined like **pulcher, -chra, -chrum**, except in the Gen. sing. **utr-ius** and Dat. sing. **utr-i** for all genders:

- *Utri puero* librum dedisti? TO WHICH BOY DID YOU GIVE THE BOOK?
- Num quid igitur aliud in iudicium venit nisi *uter utri* insidias fecerit? THEREFORE, WHAT ELSE MUST BE DEALT WITH IN THIS TRIAL IF NOT WHICH ONE OF BOTH PLANNED A PLOT AGAINST WHICH ONE? (Cicero, *Pro Milone*).

3/ In the plural it is used only for words that have no singular or to mean two groups:

- *Utra castra* cepit Caesar? WHICH CAMP DID CAESAR CAPTURE?
- *Utros milites* mavis? WHICH SOLDIERS DO YOU PREFER? (of two groups).

Note

Uter, utra, utrum can also have the indefinite meaning of EITHER OF BOTH, see further down in *Point 11 Other indefinite pronouns.*

9. Relative pronoun [75]

a) Accidence

The relative pronoun inflects as follows:

	singular			plural		
	masc.	*fem.*	*neuter*	*masc.*	*fem.*	*neuter*
Nom.	qui	quae	quod	qui	quae	quac
Acc.	quem	quam	quod	quos	quas	quae
Gen.	cuius	cuius	cuius	quorum	quarum	quorum
Dat.	cui	cui	cui	quibus	quibus	quibus
Abl.	quo	qua	quo	quibus	quibus	quibus

b) Syntax

As further detailed explanations regarding relative clauses will be given in the chapter devoted to secondary clauses, in this chapter is reported just an outline of its basic use .

Let's see an example of *relative period*, i.e. the group made of one main sentence and a relative subordinate clause:

- Video pueros *quibus* praemia dedisti I SEE THE BOYS TO WHOM YOU GAVE PRIZES.

Explanation:

Quibus TO WHOM is the *relative pronoun* that introduces the secondary clause, while **pueros** THE BOYS is the so-called *antecedent*, or the word to which the relative pronoun refers to. The relative pronoun and its antecedent must agree in gender and number, but not in case, as the case will depend on the function performed by the two terms in their respective sentence: **pueros** THE BOYS is in accusative because it is direct object of the main sentence, while **quibus** TO WHOM is in dative because it is the indirect object of the relative sentence.

Examples:

- Pueri *qui* heri in Circo aderant docti sunt THE BOYS WHO WERE IN THE CIRCUS YESTERDAY ARE CLEVER.
- In templo *quod* heri vidisti nunc cum amicis est HE IS NOW WITH HIS FRIENDS IN THE TEMPLE THAT YOU SAW YESTERDAY.
- Praefuit paucis navibus, *quas* ex Syria iussus erat in Asiam ducere HE WAS IN COMMAND OF A FEW SHIPS THAT HE HAD BEEN ORDERED TO LEAD FROM SYRIA TO ASIA (Nepos, *Vitae*).
- In senatu litteras recitavit ... in *quibus* scriptum erat C. Manlium arma cepisse IN THE SENATE HE READ A LETTER IN WHICH IT WAS WRITTEN THAT C. MANLIUS HAD TAKEN UP ARMS (Sallust, *Catilinae Coniuratio*).
- Sabinus cum iis copiis, *quas* a Caesare acceperat, in fines Unellorum pervenit SABINUS ARRIVED AT THE FRONTIER OF THE UNELLIANS WITH THOSE TROOPS THAT HE HAD DECEIVED FROM CAESAR (Caesar, *De Bello Gallico*).

10. Indefinite relative pronoun [76]

a/ There are two indefinite relative pronouns:

- ⇨ **quicumque, quaecumque, quodcumque**
- ⇨ **quisquis** (masc./fem.), **quidquid** (neuter)

The first one is declined like the relative + **cumque** added: **quibuscumque**, **quemcumque**, etc., and the second one is generally used only as subject, in nominative.

b/ The meaning of the indefinite relative pronoun is the one indicated by its own name, i.e. WHOEVER, WHATEVER, and is used in order to introduce a relative clause with a general meaning (sometimes with no antecedent):

- *Quicumque* hoc dicit, sapiens est WHOEVER SAYS THIS, IS WISE.
- *Quicumque* hoc fecit, supplicio dignus est WHOEVER DID THIS DESERVES A PUNISHMENT (Cicero, *In Verrem*).
- *Quemcumque* rogaveris, hoc respondebit WHOMEVER YOU ASK WILL ANSWER THIS (Cicero, *Pro Cluentio*).
- Iuppiter te perdat, *quisquis* es (Plautus, *Pseudolus*). MAY IUPPITER MAKE AWAY WITH YOU, WHOEVER YOU ARE!

11. Other indefinite pronouns [77]

Indefinites in Latin can be divided into two groups: those that derive from the relative and those that do not derive from it. With respect to the first group, those that derive from the relative, it will be observed that, while the adjective keeps a different form for each of the three genders, the pronoun has only one for masculine and feminine; nevertheless, in a few cases it can be found that the feminine form of the adjective is used also in pronominal sense (i.e., without any noun), so that grammars differ about whether the pronoun should have a feminine form of its own (that would be equal to that of the adjective) or not.

a) Indefinites that derive from the relative

1/ **aliquis, aliquid** (**aliqui, aliqua, aliquod** if adjective)

Accidence

It is declined like the interrogative preceded by the invariable prefix **ali-**, but the expected **aliquae** in the Nom. fem. sing. (adjectival form) and the neuter plural (in both) will be **aliqua**.

Syntax

It means SOME, ANY, SOMETHING, ANYTHING, SOMEBODY, etc.: something or somebody unknown but real:

- *Aliquem* vidi, sed nescio quem — I SAW SOMEBODY, BUT I DO NOT KNOW WHO.
- Pater expectat aut me aut *aliquem nuntium* (Plautus, *Captivi*). — MY FATHER IS EXPECTING EITHER ME OR SOME MESSENGER
- ... aut ipse occurrebat aut *aliquos* mittebat (Livy, *Ab Urbe Condita*). — EITHER HE HIMSELF CAME UP OR HE SENT SOME PEOPLE

2/ **quis, quid** (**qui, qua/quae, quod** if adjective) [78]

Accidence

It is declined like the interrogative, but the **quae** in the Nom. fem. sing. (in the adjectival forms) and the neuter plural (in both) can be **qua** (note: in the former pronoun **aliqui** etc., these forms ending in **-a** were compulsory; in this pronoun **quis** etc., these forms are optional).

Syntax

a/ It means ANY, ANYTHING, ANYBODY, etc.: something or somebody whose existence is just possible. Usually it is used after **si, nisi, ne** and **num**. The meaning is very similar to the meaning of **aliquis**, but it is more indefinite. A way of explaining it is by saying that it is in fact the former pronoun **aliquis** but that after the mentioned words **si, nisi, ne, num** the prefix **ali-** is not applied.

This pronoun has a strong visual similarity to the interrogative **quis? qui?** WHO? WHAT? The context should make the distinction clear.

- Si *quis* venit, dic mihi statim — IF ANYBODY COMES, TELL ME IMMEDIATELY.
- Puerum reddat, si *quis* eum petat — LET [HER] GIVE UP THE CHILD, IF ANYBODY ASKS FOR HIM (Plautus, *Truculentus*).
- Ne *quis* se commovere auderet, quantum terroris iniecit! — SO THAT NOBODY WOULD DARE TO STIR, WHAT AN AMOUNT OF TERROR HE STRUCK INTO THEM! (Cicero, *In Verrem*).
  ✧ Literally, SO THAT NOT ANYBODY WOULD...

b/ In the use after **num**, a frequent mistake in translation must be avoided:

- Num *quis* negat? — DOES ANYBODY DENY [IT]? (Cicero, *Pro Cluentio*).

The usual mistake is translating the former example by WHO DENIES IT? In fact, the sentence that would mean WHO DENIES IT? would be **Quis negat?** The presence of **Num** tells us that **quis** is the indefinite pronoun, not the interrogative pronoun.

Another example:

- Num *quem tribunum* pl. servi M. Tulli pulsaverunt? — DID THE SLAVES OF M. TULLIUS ATTACK ANY TRIBUNE? (Cicero, *Pro Tullio*).

The usual mistake is translating this by WHAT TRIBUNE DID THE SLAVES OF M. TULLIUS ATTACK? But in order to mean this the sentence should be **Quem tribunum...**, without the **Num**.

c/ This pronoun has a variant, with the same meaning, adding the invariable suffix **-piam**: [79]

- Vide num *quispiam* consequitur prope nos SEE WHETHER ANYBODY IS FOLLOWING US (Plautus, *Rudens*).
- Iniquum me esse *quispiam* dicet SOMEBODY WILL SAY THAT I AM UNFAIR (Cicero, *In Verrem*).

The difference between this pronoun **quispiam** and the former two **aliquis** and **quis** is that **quispiam** can be used instead of either: we can see in the first example that we can use it after num (we would not be able to use **aliquis** after **num**), and in the second example we see that we can use it even if not preceded by any of the mentioned words (**num, si,** etc.).

3/ quidam, quiddam (quidam, quaedam, quoddam if adjective) [80]

Accidence

Like the interrogative plus the invariable -**dam**, but the -**d**- makes any -**m**- change to -**n**-: **quorundam, quendam**, etc.

Syntax

It means A CERTAIN, somebody or something definite but whose specific identity is not revealed:

- *Quendam virum* vidi heri YESTERDAY I SAW A CERTAIN MAN.
  ✧ Somebody definite, but without specifying who.
- Amat *mulier quaedam quendam* A CERTAIN WOMAN LOVES A CERTAIN MAN (Plautus, *Miles Gloriosus*).
- Scribit ad *quosdam Melitensis* ut ea vasa perquirant HE WRITES TO SOME PEOPLE OF MELITA TO LOOK FOR THOSE VESSELS (Cicero, *In Verrem*).

4/ quisque, quidque/quicque (quisque, quaeque, quodque if adjective) [81]

Accidence

It is declined like the interrogative plus the invariable -**que**. Observe the double option in neuter.

Syntax

a/ It means EACH, EVERY, and usually it does not stand in the first position of a sentence:

- Suam *quisque homo* rem meminit EACH MAN REMEMBERS HIS AFFAIRS (Plautus, *Mercator*).
- Sua *cuique civitati* religio, Laeli, est, nostra nobis EACH CITY HAS ITS RELIGION, LAELIUS, WE HAVE OURS (Cicero, *Pro Flacco*).

Its use together with the adjective **unus** is very frequent (sometimes even forming a single word: **unusquisque**):

- Respondet *unus quisque* ut erat praeceptum EACH ONE ANSWERS AS IT HAD BEEN INSTRUCTED (Cicero, *In Verrem*).

b/ Its use with a superlative singular to mean a specific group that has some kind of highest quality is very common (see the chapter on superlatives for more examples):

- *Doctissimus magister quisque* aderat The wisest teachers were present
  ✧ Literally, EACH WISEST TEACHER WAS PRESENT.
- Librum dedi *optimo cuique discipulo* I GAVE A BOOK TO THE BEST STUDENTS
  ✧ Literally, ... TO EACH BEST STUDENT.

c/ With an ordinal, its use in a distributive sense is very common: **[82]**

- **Necaverunt militem *decimum quemque*** THEY KILLED ONE OF EVERY TEN SOLDIERS
  ✧ Literally, ... EACH TENTH SOLDIER.
- ***Decimum quemque* militem sorte ductum fusti percussit** HE HIT WITH A STICK ONE OF EVERY TEN SOLDIERS, TAKEN OUT BY LOT (Iulius Frontinus, *Strategemata*).
- **Igitur *tertio quoque* die cibus aegro commodissime datur** THEREFORE, EVERY THREE DAYS FOOD IS GIVEN VERY GENTLY TO THE PATIENT (Celsus, *De Medicina*).

d/ An idiomatic use:

Together with **ut** and a superlative in its own sentence and **ita** and another superlative in the other sentence, it is used to express what in English would correspond to THE MORE..., THE MORE... (observe that, while in Latin there are two superlatives, we translate them into English by using the comparative MORE, not the superlative MOST):

- **Ut *quisque acerbissime crudelissimeque* dixit, ita quam maxime ab inimicis Caesaris conlaudatur** THE MORE PASSIONATE AND CRUEL ANY ONE APPEARED, THE MORE HE WAS PRAISED BY CAESAR'S ENEMIES (Caesar, *Bellum Civile*).
- **In morbis corporis, ut *quisque* est *difficillimus*, ita medicus nobilissimus atque optimus quaeritur** ABOUT ILLNESSES OF THE BODY, THE WORSE IT IS, THE MORE RENOWNED AND BETTER DOCTOR IS REQUIRED (Cicero, *Pro Cluentio*).

5/ **quilibet, quidlibet** (**quilibet, quaelibet, quodlibet** if adjective) **[83]**

Accidence

It is declined like the interrogative plus the invariable -**libet**, and this -**libet** can be replaced by -**vis**.

Syntax

The meaning is ANYONE, ANYTHING, but the difference with **quis, quae, quod** is that **quilibet** has the meaning of ANYONE YOU MAY WANT, WHOMEVER YOU WANT:

- ***Quilibet* nautarum vectorumque tranquillo mari gubernare potest** ANYONE OF THE SAILORS OR OF THE PASSENGERS CAN STEER ON A QUIET SEA (Livy, *Ab Urbe Condita*).
- ***Quoslibet* ex his elige** CHOOSE WHOMEVER YOU WANT FROM THESE ONES (Seneca, *Epistulae Morales ad Lucilium*).

6/ **quisquam, quidquam/quicquam** (only as pronoun; the equivalent adjective is **ullus, -a, -um**) **[84]**

Accidence

It is declined like **quis, quid** (observe the double option in neuter) + the suffix -**quam**. It is considered to be used only as a pronoun, not as an adjective.

Syntax

a/ The meaning is the same one as **aliquis**, SOMEONE, ANYONE, SOMETHING, ANYTHING, but it is mainly used in negative sentences (or sentences that imply a negative sense):

- **Domum suam istum non fere *quisquam* vocabat** HARDLY ANYONE INVITED HIM TO HIS HOUSE (Cicero, *Pro Roscio Amerino*).
- **Negavit *quemquam* esse in civitate praeter se qui id efficere posset** HE DENIED THAT THERE WAS ANYBODY IN THE CITY BUT HIM WHO COULD CARRY IT OUT (*Cicero, Pro Cluentio*).

Observe this question:

- **Laudatum etiam vos *quemquam* venitis?** HAVE YOU COME TO PRAISE ANYBODY? (Cicero, *In Verrem*).

The answer is expected to be "No", and this is why, even if the sentence is not grammatically negative, **quemquam** has been used, because the sentence implies a negative sense.

b/ Given the usual Latin practice of advancing the negative word as much as possible, it is very frequent to find

neque quisquam... AND NOT ANYBODY...

to express the meaning AND NOBODY... :

- ... ***neque quisquam homo* mihi obviam venit** ... AND NOBODY COMES TO MEET ME (Plautus, *Rudens*).
- ... ***neque quisquam* est vulneratus** ... AND NOBODY WAS HURT (Nepos, *Vitae*).

b) Indefinites that do not derive from the relative [85]

All of them have the usual characteristics of Gen. sing. **-ius** and Dat. sing. **-i** for all genders. There are no morphological differences between their use as pronouns or as adjectives.

To make their study easier, we can try to group them. The very first group would be formed by **unus, solus** and **totus**. Their characteristic is that they are not related to any other pronoun, it could be said that each of these three pronouns is an individuality on its own.

1/ unus, -a, -um

a/ It means ONE in the strict sense of ONLY ONE, so that the use of the adverb ONLY in translating it is very helpful:

- ***Unum librum* habeo** I HAVE ONLY ONE BOOK.
- **Helvetii ... impedimenta in *unum locum* contulerunt** (Caesar, *De Bello Gallico*). THE HELVETIANS GATHERED THEIR BAGGAGE INTO ONE PLACE
- **Orgetorigis filia atque *unus* e filiis captus est** ORGETORIX'S DAUGHTER AND ONLY ONE OF HIS SONS WERE CAPTURED (Caesar, *De Bello Gallico*).
- **[dixerunt] sese *unis Suebis* concedere** (Caesar, *De Bello Gallico*). THEY SAID THAT THEY YIELDED ONLY IN FRONT OF THE SUEBII

b/ It has plural (let's take into account that for instance in Greek the equivalent to **unus, -a, -um** has no plural), with the meaning of THE ONLY ONES:

- **Ubii autem, qui *uni* ex Transrhenanis ad Caesarem legatos miserant, ... magnopere orabant ut ...** THE UBII, THE ONLY ONES FROM THOSE BEYOND THE RHINE WHO HAD SENT AMBASSADORS TO CAESAR, EARNESTLY ENTREATED THAT... (Caesar, *De Bello Gallico*).

2/ solus, -a, -um [86]

It means ALONE, but, just as in the former pronoun, the use of the adverb ONLY in translating it is very helpful. In this aspect, it may resemble the use of the former **unus, -a, -um**, but **solus** has rather a meaning of WITHOUT ANYBODY ELSE:

- *Soli Petro* hoc dixi — I SAID THIS ONLY TO PETER.
- Dein *Micipsa filius* regnum *solus* obtinuit — LATER MICIPSA, HIS SON, REIGNED ALONE (Sallust, *Bellum Iugurthinum*).
- Nec *solos* tangit *Atridas* iste dolor — AND THIS PAIN AFFLICTS NOT ONLY THE ATRIDAE (Vergil, *Aeneis*).

3/ totus, -a, -um [87]

It means WHOLE:

- *Totam urbem* vidi I SAW THE WHOLE CITY.
- Scipio ... per *totam urbem* omnia templa deum cum populo Romano circumiit SCIPIO, IN THE COMPANY OF THE ROMAN PEOPLE, WENT AROUND ALL THE TEMPLES OF THE GODS THROUGH THE WHOLE CITY (Livy, *Ab Urbe Condita*).
- *Totius* fere *Galliae* legati principes civitatum ad Caesarem gratulatum convenerunt THE CHIEFTAINS OF THE CITIES OF ALMOST ALL GAUL CAME AS AMBASSADORS TO CONGRATULATE CAESAR (Caesar, *De Bello Gallico*).

The second group would be formed by **alius** and **ullus**. Their common characteristic is that they refer to *more than two units* of the same concept (people, things, places, etc.). [88]

4/ alius, alia, aliud

Note on accidence: the genitive sing. is replaced by **alterius** (see next pronoun), because the nominative itself finishes in **-ius** and this would create confusion.

a/ The basic meaning is OTHER:

- Repente *alii milites* venerunt — SUDDENLY OTHER SOLDIERS CAME.
- Cur dixisti testimonium in *alios*? — WHY DID YOU DECLARE AGAINST OTHERS? (Cicero, *Pro Sulla*).
- Ipsi has *aliasque provincias* regitis — YOU YOURSELVES RULE THESE AND OTHER PROVINCES (Tacitus, *Historiae*).

b/ First special use:

It has two special uses; the first of them is its use in two consecutive sentences, with the meaning of SOME in the first one and the meaning of OTHERS in the second one:

- *Alii* laborant, *alii* dormiunt — SOME ARE WORKING, OTHERS ARE SLEEPING.
- Impellit *alios* avaritia, *alios* iracundia et temeritas (Caesar, *De Bello Gallico*). — AVARICE IMPELS SOME, WRATH AND TEMERITY IMPEL OTHERS

c/ Second special use: [89]

The second special use is the repetition of two different forms of it within the same sentence, each form meaning a different concept:

Alii alios libros legunt.

The explanation is very simple: it is the former use of a form of **alius** in two consecutive sentences, but twice (one subject and one object) and with the second sentence elided.

Imagine this double sentence:

- ***Alii alios libros* legunt, *alii alios libros* legunt** SOME READ SOME BOOKS, OTHERS READ OTHER ONES.

The two **alii** mean SOME ... OTHERS (PEOPLE), and the two **alios** mean SOME ... OTHER (BOOKS), in fact we are saying SOME READ SOME BOOKS, OTHERS READ OTHER BOOKS, but the Latin technique of repeating twice the same form of **alius** to mean SOME ... OTHER produces in fact the same sentence repeated twice, so that the only thing Latin does is elide the second sentence.

Two more examples:

- ***Aliud alios* movet** A REASON MOVES SOME MEN, ANOTHER REASON MOVES OTHER MEN / DIFFERENT REASONS MOVE DIFFERENT MEN (Plinius Secundus, *Epistulae*).
- **Sed quia divorsi redeuntes *alius* ab *alia parte* atque omnes idem significabant, consul...** BUT AS COMING FROM DIFFERENT PLACES, SOME FROM ONE PLACE AND SOME OTHERS FROM ANOTHER PLACE, ALL BROUGHT THE SAME NEWS, THE CONSUL... (Sallust, *Bellum Iugurthinum*).

d/ Indicating reciprocity:

In the following example we find again two different forms of **alius** within the same sentence, but in this case the translation by ONE ANOTHER / EACH OTHER is more adequate just because both forms of **alius** refer to the same concept (thing, person or whatever):

- **Urgent itaque *alii alios*** SO, THEY URGE EACH OTHER (Livy, *Ab Urbe Condita*)
- **In fugam versi (sunt), non agminibus, ut prius, nec *alius alium* respectantes** THEY TURNED ROUND IN ORDER TO FLEE, BUT NOT IN COLUMNS, AS BEFORE, NOR WAITING ONE ANOTHER (Tacitus, *Agricola*).

5/ ullus, -a, -um **[90]**

This is supposed to be the adjective equivalent to the pronoun **quisquam** (see above). The meaning is ANY, SOME, but used in sentences that either are negative or imply a negative sense:

- **Nec *locus* tibi *ullus* dulcior esse debet patria nec...** NEITHER ANY PLACE MUST BE DEARER FOR YOU THAN YOUR HOMELAND NOR... (Cicero, *Epistulae ad Familiares*).
- **Cui novae calamitati *locus ullus* relictus?** FOR WHAT NEW CALAMITY [COULD THERE BE] ANY SPACE LEFT? (Cicero, *Pro Sulla*).

  ✧ The answer is supposed to be NOT ONE, so that even if the sentence is not grammatically negative the question implies a negative sense.
- **Nec *ullus* tot malorum *finis* fuisset** AND THERE WOULD NOT HAVE BEEN ANY END TO SO MANY EVILS / AND THERE WOULD HAVE BEEN NO END TO SO MANY EVILS (Petronius, *Satyrica*).

The next group would be formed by **alter, uter** and **uterque**. Their common characteristic is that they refer to *groups of two.*

6/ alter, altera, alterum [91]

a/ It means THE OTHER ONE (of only two):

- ***Alteri consuli*** **de insidiis dixi** I TOLD THE OTHER CONSUL ABOUT THE PLOT.
- **Hanc me iussit Lesbonico suo gnato dare epistulam, et item *hanc alteram* suo amico Callicli iussit dare** HE ORDERED ME TO GIVE THIS LETTER TO HIS SON LESBONICUS, AND LIKEWISE THIS OTHER ONE TO HIS FRIEND CALICLES (Plautus, *Trinummus*).

b/ It may be used twice in the same sentence, or in two consecutive sentences, in the same way we have seen above (but this time meaning clearly that there are *only two options*):

- ***Alter alterum*** **facit** EACH ONE (OF BOTH) DOES A DIFFERENT THING / ONE DOES ONE THING, THE OTHER ONE DOES ANOTHER THING.
- ***Alter*** **dormit,** ***alter*** **laborat** ONE IS SLEEPING, THE OTHER ONE IS WORKING.
- ***Alteram*** **ille amat** ***sororem,*** **ego** ***alteram*** HE LOVES ONE OF THE TWO SISTERS, I LOVE THE OTHER ONE (Plautus, *Bacchides*).

c/ But this meaning of THE OTHER ONE out of only two is not a golden rule. Observe this example from Cicero, in which **alteram** is just one out of three:

- **Intellego, iudices, tris totius accusationis partis fuisse, et earum unam in ...,** ***alteram*** **in ..., tertiam in ... esse versatam** I UNDERSTAND, O JUDGES, THAT THIS ACCUSATION HAS THREE PARTS, AND THAT ONE OF THEM DEALS WITH..., ANOTHER ONE DEALS WITH..., AND THE THIRD ONE DEALS WITH... (Cicero, *Pro Murena*).

7/ uter, utra, utrum [92]

It means EITHER:

- **Si** ***uter*** **volet, recuperatores dabo** IF EITHER WANTS IT, I WILL ASSIGN JUDGES (Cicero, *In Verrem*).

Remember that **uter** is also the interrogative that means WHICH ONE OF THE TWO? Context should make it clear:

- ***Uter*** **igitur est divitior?** WHICH ONE OF BOTH IS RICHER? (Cicero, *Paradoxa Stoicorum*).

8/ uterque, utraque, utrumque [93]

Declined like **uter, utra, utrum**, it means EACH OF BOTH. It is the equivalent of **quisque, quaeque, quodque** EACH, EVERY but when it deals with *only two*:

- **Cum** ***uterque*** **utrique esset exercitui in conspectu, ...** WHEN EACH (ARMY) WAS IN SIGHT OF THE OTHER ARMY, ... (Caesar, *De Bello Gallico*).

  ✧ Note: there were only two armies involved, this is why **uterque** has been used instead of **quisque**.
- **Suas** ***uterque*** **legiones reducit in castra** EACH ONE (OF BOTH) TAKES HIS LEGIONS BACK TO THE CAMP (Caesar, *Bellum Civile*).

12. Negative pronouns [94]

There are four negative pronouns. The two first ones are related to the indefinite pronouns we have seen in the former section:

a) nullus, -a, -um

Accidence

It has singular and plural, and it declines following the *2-1-2 scheme* except for the two usual characteristics of genitive singular in -**ius** for the three genders and dative singular in -**i** also for the three genders.

Syntax

It means NO ONE, NONE, and it is obvious that it has been formed by the contraction of **non** and **ullus** (NOT ANYONE). It is related to **alius** and **ullus**: all of them refer to groups of *three or more*.

- *Nullam* video   I SEE NO ONE.
  ✧ Meaning specifically a feminine agent: no girl, no female teacher, no woman, etc.
- *Nullos* habuit *hortos, nullam suburbanam aut maritimam sumptuosam villam*   HE HAD NO GARDENS, NO SUMPTUOUS VILLA NEAR THE CITY OR ON THE COAST (Nepos, *Vitae*).
- *Nullam* ab eo *epistulam* acceperat   HE HAD RECEIVED NO LETTER FROM HIM (Curtius Rufus, *Historiae Alexandri Magni*).
- *Nullus* eripiet *deus* te mihi   NO GOD WILL SNATCH YOU AWAY FROM ME (Seneca iunior, *Hercules Furens*).

Please see the corresponding chapter on combination of negatives for the different meanings of **nullus** combined with **non**.

b) neuter, neutra, neutrum [95]

Accidence

It is declined like **uter, utra, utrum**, but with the suffix **ne**- attached to it.

Syntax

1/ It means NEITHER, and obviously it is related to the former pronouns **alter, uter** and **uterque**: all of these deal with groups of two. In nowadays grammar, its use is very evident: *neuter* means *neither masculine nor feminine*.

- *Neuter* neutri invidet   NEITHER FEELS ENVY OF THE OTHER ONE (Plautus, *Stichus*).
- *Neuter* consulum potuerat bello abesse   NEITHER OF THE CONSULS HAD BEEN ABLE TO BE ABSENT FROM THE WAR (Livy, *Ab Urbe Condita*).
  ✧ And we know that there were only two consuls.
- Diu pugna *neutro* inclinata stetit   FOR A LONG TIME THE FIGHT WAS FAVOURABLE TO NEITHER (literally, IN NEITHER [SIDE]) (Livy, *Ab Urbe Condita*).

2/ It can be used also in plural, in the sense of two groups:

- *Neutros* fefellit ... hostes adpropinquare THAT THE ENEMY WERE APPROACHING DID NOT ESCAPE THE NOTICE OF EITHER GROUP (Livy, *Ab Urbe Condita*).
  ✧ Literally, THAT THE ENEMY WERE APPROACHING ESCAPED THE NOTICE OF NEITHER GROUP.
- *Neutris* animus est ad pugnandum NO ONE OF BOTH GROUPS HAS ANY DESIRE OF FIGHTING (Livy, *Ab Urbe Condita*).

c) nihil [96]

Accidence

Nihil, that means NOTHING, is a neuter singular form. Theoretically, it has only nominative and accusative, and for the other cases a periphrasis of **nulla res** NO THING was used:

Nom.	nihil
Voc.	non-existent
Acc.	nihil
Gen.	nullius rei
Dat.	nulli rei
Abl.	nulla re

But we can find the form **nihilum, -i**, declined as a neuter of the 2nd declension. And it is also very frequent to find the contracted form **nil**.

Syntax [97]

1/ Its use does not imply any special complication, just the expected use of a pronoun with the meaning of NOTHING:

- *Nihil* facio I AM DOING NOTHING.
- Tale *nihil* timeo I FEAR NOTHING SUCH (Ovid, *Heroides*).
- Labienus ... de suo ac legionis periculo *nihil* timebat LABIENUS FEARED NOTHING ABOUT DANGER FOR HIMSELF OR FOR HIS LEGION (Caesar, *De Bello Gallico*).
- *Nihil* est iam sanctum atque sincerum in civitate THERE IS NOTHING SACRED OR SINCERE IN THE CITY ANY MORE (Cicero, *Pro Quinctio*).

In some cases, when translating into English, it may sound more natural if we shift the negative sense to the English verb:

- *Nihil* volo I DO NOT WANT ANYHTING / I WANT NOTHING.

Let's see a couple of examples with the contact form:

- *Nil* horum est, iudices IT IS NOTHING OF THIS, O JUDGES (Cicero, *Pro Roscio Amerino*).
- De domo Arpini *nil* scio I KNOW NOTHING ABOUT THE HOUSE OF ARPINUS (Cicero, *Epistulae ad Atticum*).

2/ In some cases, it may be used accompanying a noun, instead of the corresponding form of **nullus, -a, -um**, as if it were an adjective: [98]

- **Hi propter propinquitatem et celeritatem hostium *nihil* iam Caesaris imperium exspectabant** THESE, BECAUSE OF THE PROXIMITY AND THE SPEED OF THE ENEMY, DID NOT EXPECT ANY ORDER FROM CAESAR ANY MORE (Caesar, *De Bello Gallico*).

  ✧ It could be argued that in fact **imperium** is an accusative of respect: THESE, BECAUSE OF THE PROXIMITY AND THE SPEED OF THE ENEMY, EXPECTED NOTHING ANY MORE WITH RESPECT TO AN ORDER.

3/ The forms that decline from **nihilum** are almost always found after a preposition:

- **Erit aliquid, quod aut *ex nihilo* oriatur aut *in nihilum* subito occidat** THERE WILL BE SOMETHING THAT EITHER IS BORN FROM NOTHING OR SUDDENLY DIES INTO NOTHING (Cicero, *De Divinatione*).

And we can very often find its genitive **nihili** OF NOTHING in the idiomatic meaning OF NO VALUE, sometimes together with the verbs **habeo, facio** and **sum**:

- **Hoc ego *nihili* habeo** I CONSIDER THIS OF NO IMPORTANCE.
- **Etiam tu, homo *nihili*?** ALSO YOU, MAN OF NO VALUE? (Plautus, *Bacchides*).
- **At ego hercle *nihili* facio** BUT, BY HERCULES, I DO NOT CARE (Plautus, *Captivi*).
- **Non modo *nihili* et improbus, sed fatuus et amens es** NOT ONLY YOU ARE OF NO VALUE ("OF NOTHING") AND DISHONEST, BUT ALSO FOOLISH AND MAD (Cicero, *Pro Rege Deiotaro*).

Please see the corresponding chapter on combination of negatives for the different meanings of **nihil** combined with **non**.

d) nemo [99]

Accidence

It is a pronoun declined through the 3rd declension, but some forms are usually replaced by the equivalent ones of the adjective **nullus**:

Nom.	nemo	
Voc.	non-existent	
Acc.	neminem	
Gen.	neminis	✧ More frequently, **nullius**
Dat.	nemini	
Abl.	nemine	✧ More frequently, **nullo**

Syntax

1/ It is a pronoun, not an adjective, with the meaning of NOBODY.

- ***Nemo* venit heri** NOBODY CAME YESTERDAY.
- **Iudex esse bonus *nemo* potest qui suspicione certa non movetur** NOBODY WHO IS NOT MOVED BY A REAL SUSPICION CAN BE A GOOD JUDGE (Cicero, *In Verrem*).

- *Nemo* potest esse in magna familia qui neminem neque servum neque libertum improbum habeat THERE CAN BE NOBODY IN A LARGE HOUSEHOLD THAT HAS NOBODY, WHETHER SERVANT OR FREE MAN, OR WORTHLESS CHARACTER (Cicero, *Pro Roscio Amerino*).
- Utrum gravius existumet, *nemini* occultum est WHICH ONE OF BOTH MATTERS HE CONSIDERS MORE IMPORTANT IS A SECRET TO NO ONE (Sallust, *Bellum Iugurthinum*).

2/ As expected, when translating into English it may sound more natural sometimes to translate it by ANYBODY instead of by NOBODY and shift the negative sense to the verb:

- Me absente *neminem* volo intro mitti DURING MY ABSENCE, I DO NOT WANT ANYBODY TO BE ALLOWED INSIDE (Plautus, *Aulularia*).

  ✧ Literally, I WANT NOBODY...
- Dubium esse *nemini* vestrum certo scio I KNOW FOR CERTAIN THAT THIS IS NOT DOUBTFUL TO ANYONE OF YOU (Cicero, *Pro Caecina*).

  ✧ Literally, I KNOW FOR CERTAIN THAT THIS IS DOUBTFUL TO NO ONE OF YOU.

3/ In some cases, it may replace the adjective **nullus**:

- Ego certe me incerto scio hoc daturum *nemini homini* I KNOW WELL THAT I WILL NOT GIVE THIS TO ANY UNKNOWN MAN (Plautus, Asinaria).

  ✧ We would have expected **nulli homini**.

We have seen in the accidence of **nemo** that **nullus** replaces it in genitive and ablative, but here we can see that in some cases it seems to work the other way round.

⌑ Please see the corresponding chapter on combination of negatives for the different meanings of **nemo** in combination with **non**.

g) Adverbs and prepositional adverbs

1. General observations [100]

When we mention adverbs, we tend to think of some frequent English words ending in -LY, such as STRONGLY, QUICKLY, SLOWLY, etc., but this is just one of several different possible morphological forms of adverbs, which can be represented by words that appear very different from each other, such as NO, TODAY, HARDLY, ENOUGH, QUICKLY, WHEN?, WHERE?, EVERYWHERE, etc.

Adverbs are indeclinable parts of speech with variable frequency rates, as some are really common while others are hardly attested. For this reason, here we will present only the most frequent ones.

2. Modal adverbs [101]

These adverbs define the way in which an action is performed (they would respond to the question How?). While a lot of times the English equivalent form ends in -LY, other translations are possible as well.

a/ Most modal adverbs derived from an adjective of the 1st class are formed adding the ending -**e** to the stem of the adjective:

from	**doctus**	WISE	>	**docte**	WISELY
from	**altus**	TALL / DEEP	>	**alte**	DEEPLY
from	**malus**	BAD	>	**male**	BADLY

- **Ad erum veniam *docte* atque *astute*** I WILL APPROACH THE MASTER WISELY AND SAGACIOUSLY (Plautus, *Rudens*).

But some adverbs take **-o** instead of **-e**:

from	**rarus**	STRANGE	>	**raro**	STRANGELY	✧ but also **rare** and **rariter** (see below)
from	**subitus**	SUDDEN	>	**subito**	SUDDENLY	

- ***Subito* duabus portis eruptionem fieri iubet** SUDDENLY HE ORDERS TO MAKE A BREAKING OUT THROUGH THE TWO GATES (Caesar, *De Bello Gallico*).

b/ If they derive from adjectives of the 2nd class, they usually add the ending -**ter** to the stem:

from	**fortis**	STRONG	>	**fortiter**	STRONGLY
from	**acer**	HARSH	>	**acriter**	HARSHLY
from	**prudens**	PRUDENT	>	**prudenter**	PRUDENTLY

- **Eversam fortunam *fortiter* ferre debemus** WE MUST BEAR ADVERSE FORTUNE BRAVELY (Cicero, *Epistulae ad Familiares*).

c/ Sometimes the stem suffers some alteration: [102]

from **bonus** GOOD > **bene** WELL ✧ **bene**, NOT **bone**

Important expression: **bene facere** + Dat. TO DO WELL

- **Pulchrum est *bene facere* rei publicae** IT IS NOBLE TO DO WELL TO THE STATE (Sallust, *Catilinae Coniuratio*).

d/ Some adverbs come from nouns (usually the noun in ablative) or even from verbs:

from	**fors**	CHANCE	>	**forte**	BY CHANCE	✧ Do not confuse with **fortis, -e**.
from	**festino**	TO HURRY	>	**festinatim**	HURRIEDLY	

Some other common ones are:

casu	BY CHANCE	**silentio**	IN SILENCE
iure	RIGHTFULLY	**vi**	BY FORCE

The combination **si forte** IN CASE BY CHANCE is very common:

- **Nostri ... impetum classis timebant, *si forte* ventus remisisset** OUR [SOLDIERS] FEARED THE ATTACK OF THE FLEET, IN CASE BY CHANCE THE WIND WOULD STOP (Caesar, *Bellum Civile*).

3. Comparative and superlative of modal adverbs [103]

a/ Just as adjectives do, adverbs may express different degrees of intensity:

– I EXPLAINED IT *WISELY*	✧ WISELY	positive adverb
– YOU EXPLAINED IT *MORE WISELY*	✧ MORE WISELY	comparative adverb
– HE EXPLAINED IT *VERY WISELY*	✧ VERY WISELY	superlative adverb

The starting point to form different degrees of an adverb is the adjective from which the adverb derives. For instance, if we want to say I EXPLAINED THIS *WISELY*, we will say **Hoc *docte* narravi**, using the normal adverb.

But if we want to say YOU EXPLAINED THIS *MORE WISELY* (comparative adverb), we must first form the comparative of the adjective WISE, which would be **doctior, -ius**, and its neuter form **doctius** will be used as comparative adverb:

- **Tu hoc *doctius* narravisti** YOU EXPLAINED THIS MORE WISELY.

And if we want to say VERY WISELY, MOST WISELY, we will use the superlative form of its adjective, but changing its ending by **-e**:

- **Ille hoc *doctissime* narravit** HE EXPLAINED THIS VERY/MOST WISELY.

Some more examples:

- **Vulnus *altissime* penetrat** THE WOUND PENETRATES VERY DEEPLY (Quintilianus, *Declamationes Maiores*).
- **Iam ex sermone hoc gubernabunt *doctius* porro** AFTER THIS CONVERSATION, THEY WILL MANAGE THEIR AFFAIRS MORE WISELY FROM NOW ON (Plautus, *Miles Gloriosus*).

b/ If the adjective forms its comparative and superlative forms irregularly, the same will happen with the different degrees of the adverb: [104]

- Ego hoc *bene* feci — I DID THIS WELL.
- Tu hoc *melius* fecisti — YOU DID THIS BETTER.
- Ille hoc *optime* fecit — HE DID IT BEST.
- *Optime* itis, *pessime* hercle dicitis (Plautus, *Poenulus*). — YOU MOVE VERY WELL, BUT, BY HERCULES, YOU SPEAK VERY BADLY

Note that the comparative and superlative adverbs come from the respective irregular comparative and superlative adjectives.

c/ In order to convey the expression AS ... AS POSSIBLE with adverbs, we must use **quam** before the superlative form of the adverb, similarly to the construction *quam + superlative adj.* that we have already seen.

- Ego hoc *quam optime* feci — I HAVE DONE THIS AS WELL AS POSSIBLE.
- Caesar *quam celerrime* venit — CAESAR CAME AS QUICKLY AS POSSIBLE.
- Scribere ad vos *quam celerrime* volumus (Cicero, *Epistulae ad Familiares*). — WE WANTED TO WRITE TO YOU AS QUICKLY AS POSSIBLE

4. Quantitative adverbs [105]

a/ The most well-known quantitative adverbs are contained in the following sequence, which comprehends respectively the *positive – comparative – superlative* forms of the same adverb:

multum - plus - plurimum MUCH – MORE – MOST

A very common combination is **plus ... quam** MORE THAN:

- Neque enim *plus quam* tres aut quattuor reliqui sunt (Cicero, *Philippicae*). — AND NOT MORE THAN THREE OR FOUR ARE LEFT
- Dolor diuturnus habet laetitiae *plus quam* molestiae (Cicero, *Tusculanae Disputationes*). — LONG-LASTING PAIN HAS MORE OF HAPPINESS THAN OF DISTURBANCE

b/ Other quantitative adverbs are:

magnopere	MUCH	→	magis	MORE	→	maxime	IN THE HIGHEST DEGREE
parum	A LITTLE	→	minus	LESS	→	minime	IN THE LOWEST DEGREE
nimis/nimium	TOO MUCH						
satis	ENOUGH						
valde	VERY						
aliquantum	A LITTLE						

They can be followed by a partitive genitive: **satis pecuniae** ENOUGH [OF] MONEY.

- Satis *eloquentiae, sapientiae* parum (Sallust, *Catilinae Coniuratio*). — ENOUGH OF ELOQUENCE, BUT JUST A LITTLE OF WISDOM ✧ Sallust is describing Catilina's character.

5. Adverbs of time

[106]

a/ We will try to group them by related meanings, but we must take into account that some of them can have several meanings; we have put here the most usual one for each adverb:

heri	YESTERDAY
hodie	TODAY
cras	TOMORROW
pridie	THE DAY BEFORE
postridie	THE DAY AFTER
cotidie	EVERY DAY
mane	IN THE MORNING
meridie	AT MIDDAY
noctu	AT NIGHT
nunc	NOW
tunc/tum	THEN
interea	MEANWHILE
statim	IMMEDIATELY
iam	ALREADY, THEN
antea	BEFORE
postea	AFTERWARDS
deinde	LATER, AFTERWARDS
mox	SOON AFTERWARDS
numquam	NEVER
umquam	EVER
nonnumquam	SOMETIMES
semper	ALWAYS
vix	HARDLY
identidem	SOMETIMES
interdum	SOMETIMES
quotannis	EVERY YEAR
interdum	FROM TIME TO TIME
paulisper	FOR A SHORT TIME
denique	FINALLY
postremo	AT LAST
tandem	AT LENGTH
olim	SOME TIME AGO
quondam	AT ONE TIME, FORMERLY

✧ iam may mean SOON if used with a future tense.

Let's see some examples:

- *Pridie* per meridiem profecti ab Sycurio erant THEY HAD SET OUT FROM SYCURIUM AROUND MIDDAY OF THE DAY BEFORE (Livy, *Ab Urbe Condita*).
- Huc legionem *postea* transicit AFTERWARDS, HE MOVED THE LEGION HITHER (Caesar, *Bellum Civile*).
- *Nonnumquam* post magnam pugnam ... licentiam omnem passim lasciviendi permittebat SOMETIMES, AFTER A GREAT BATTLE, HE ALLOWED FULL FREEDOM OF REVELLING AT PLEASURE (Suetonius, *Vitae*).
- Carthagine *quotannis* annui bini reges creabantur AT CARTHAGE, EVERY YEAR TWO KINGS WERE APPOINTED FOR AN ANNUAL PERIOD (Nepos, *Vitae*).
- Indutiomarus ... *noctu* profugit INDUTIOMARUS FLEES AT NIGHT (Caesar, *De Bello Gallico*).

b/ There are two adverbs of time that have comparative and superlative: [107]

diu	FOR A LONG TIME	diutius	FOR LONGER	diutissime	FOR VERY LONG
saepe	OFTEN	saepius	MORE OFTEN	saepissime	VERY OFTEN

- *Diu* silentium fuit THERE WAS SILENCE FOR A LONG TIME (Livy, *Ab Urbe Condita*).

- *Diutius* nostrorum militum impetum hostes ferre non potuerunt THE ENEMY COULD NOT RESIST THE ATTACK OF OUR SOLDIERS FOR LONGER (Caesar, *De Bello Gallico*).
- *Diutissime saepissimeque* Siciliam vexatam a Carthaginiensibus esse cognorat HE KNEW THAT SICILY HAD BEEN RAVAGED BY THE CARTHAGINIANS FOR A VERY LONG TIME AND VERY OFTEN (Cicero, *In Verrem*).

  ✧ Note: cognorat = cognoverat.

This one has superlative, but no comparative:

nuper	RECENTLY	nuperrime	VERY RECENTLY

- Ego *nuperrime* in libro Theophrasti scriptum inveni VERY RECENTLY, I FOUND IT WRITTEN IN A BOOK OF THEOPHRASTUS (Gellius, *Noctes Atticae*).

6. Adverbs of place [108]

a/ Some adverbs of place state the position of an object with respect to a given point of reference. Some of these adverbs will be mentioned again in the section devoted to *Prepositional adverbs*, as they may also work as prepositions followed by a noun in a given case. The following list groups the adverbs in pairs according to their sense, in order to facilitate their memorisation:

supra	ABOVE, FURTHER UP	citra	ON THIS SIDE	iuxta	SIDE BY SIDE
infra	BELOW, FURTHER DOWN	ultra	FURTHER THERE	prope	NEAR, BY THE SIDE
intra	INSIDE	circa	AROUND	longe	FAR AWAY
extra	OUTSIDE	contra	IN FRONT	procul	FAR AWAY

- Ut *supra* diximus, ... AS WE HAVE SAID ABOVE, ...
- Onerariae duae ... paulo *infra* delatae sunt TWO SHIPS OF BURDEN WERE CARRIED A LITTLE FURTHER DOWN (Caesar, *De Bello Gallico*).
- Sed ne illos quidem, qui *procul* manserant, ... BUT NOT EVEN THOSE WHO HAD REMAINED FAR AWAY ... (Sallust, *Bellum Iugurthinum*).

These six adverbs of place are grouped into two correlative series:

hic	HERE	huc	[TOWARDS] HERE	hinc	FROM HERE
illic	THERE	illuc	[TOWARDS] THERE	illinc	FROM THERE

b/ With reference to these last forms, note that they seem to share some common characteristics according to the kind of movement:

- ➪ Both adverbs meaning *place where* end in -ic
- ➪ Both adverbs meaning *place towards* end in -uc
- ➪ Both adverbs meaning *place from* end in -inc

Unfortunately, this relationship indicating *place where, place to where* and *place from where* does not always follow the [109] same rule and they must be memorised, although it will be observed that they follow a similar rule. Apart from the two former groups, other frequent ones are:

ibi	THERE	alibi	SOMEWHERE ELSE
eo	[TOWARDS] THERE	alio	TO SOMEWHERE ELSE
inde	FROM THERE	aliunde	FROM SOMEWHERE ELSE
ubi	WHERE	ubicumque	WHEREVER
quo	TO WHERE	quocumque	TO WHEREVER
unde	FROM WHERE	undecumque	FROM WHEREVER
alicubi	SOMEWHERE	ubique	ANYWHERE / EVERYWHERE
aliquo	TO SOMEWHERE	(no corresponding directional)	
alicunde	FROM SOMEWHERE	undique	FROM ANYWHERE / FROM EVERYWHERE

Observe that (disregarding the suffixes attached to the end) all of the groups seem to share the same characteristics (obviously, some groups are just a compound of another group):

- ➪ The first adverb *place where* ends in -i
- ➪ The second adverb *place towards where* ends in -o
- ➪ The third adverb *place from where* ends in -e

- – Quamvis malam rem quaeras, *illic* reperias ALTHOUGH YOU LOOK FOR SOMETHING BAD, YOU CAN FIND IT THERE.
  – At tu hercle et *illi* et *alibi* BUT YOU, BY HERCULES, [CAN FIND IT] BOTH THERE AND SOMEWHERE ELSE
  (Plautus, *Trinummus*). ✧ illi in this sentence = illic.
- *Ubicumque* esses, ad te percurrissem WHEREVER YOU WOULD BE, I WOULD HAVE RUN TOWARDS YOU (Cicero, *Epistulae ad Familiares*).
- Magna praeterea multitudo *undique* ex Gallia ... convenerat MOREOVER, A LARGE MULTITUDE FROM EVERYWHERE FROM GAUL HAD GATHERED (Caesar, *De Bello Gallico*).

c/ There are many more adverbs of place that will be learnt by means of practice, as they do not offer any characteristic **[110]**
that helps to their memorisation. For instance, hactenus THUS FAR, usquam SOMEWHERE, foras OUT OF DOORS, etc.

Hactenus is much used in the sense of ENOUGH THUS FAR:

- Sed de Graecis *hactenus* BUT [WE HAVE SPOKEN] ENOUGH ABOUT THE GREEKS (Cicero, *Brutus*).
- De quo dicam equidem paulo post, nunc autem *hactenus* ABOUT THIS, I WILL SPEAK A LITTLE LATER, NOW IT IS ENOUGH (Cicero, *De Natura Deorum*).

d/ Some adverbs of place have a comparative and a superlative, and it can be observed that the formation follows the usual parameters of comparative and superlative of modal adverbs:

longe	FAR AWAY	prope	NEAR
longius	FURTHER AWAY	propius	NEARER
longissime	VERY FAR AWAY	proxime	VERY NEAR

- Abest *longissime*, mihi crede, Caesar IT IS VERY FAR [FROM THE TRUTH], BELIEVE ME, CAESAR (Cicero, *Pro Rege Deiotaro*).
- Sed quoniam C. Caesar abest *longissime*, ... BUT AS C. CAESAR IS VERY FAR AWAY, ... (Cicero, *Pro Balbo*).
- Accedam *propius* I WILL APPROACH NEARER (Plautus, *Mercator*).

7. Interrogative adverbs [111]

Interrogative adverbs can be classified according to their sense:

a/ In modal sense:

Quomodo? Quemadmodum? HOW?

They can be written as separate words: Quo modo? Quem ad modum?

- *Quomodo* hoc obtinuisti? HOW DID YOU OBTAIN THIS?
- *Quomodo* igitur duo genera ista dividis? (Cicero, *De Partitione Oratoria*). THEREFORE, HOW DO YOU DIVIDE THESE TWO CLASSES?

b/ In temporal sense:

Quando? WHEN? Quamdiu? FOR HOW LONG?

- *Quamdiu* autem tranquillam ... multitudinem fore? (Livy, *Ab Urbe Condita*). FOR HOW LONG WOULD THE MULTITUDE REMAIN QUIET?

c/ In local sense:

Ubi? WHERE? Unde? WHERE FROM?
Quo? WHERE TO? Qua? THROUGH WHERE?

- *Ubi* erant ceteri creditores? WHERE WERE THE REMAINING CREDITORS? (Cicero, *Pro Quinctio*).
- *Ubi* aut *unde* audivit Glaucia? WHERE OR FROM WHERE DID GLAUCIA HEAR IT? (Cicero, *Pro Roscio Amerino*).

d/ In quantitative sense:

Quantum? Quanto? HOW MUCH?

- *Quantum* dedit? HOW MUCH DID HE GIVE? (Cicero, *Pro Roscio Amerino*).

e/ In causal sense:

Cur? Quamobrem? Quare? WHY?
Quin? WHY NOT?

In fact quin never introduces a real question but just a rhetorical one that can be translated by an exhortation.

- Quid facitis? *Cur* recusatis? WHAT ARE YOU DOING? WHY DO YOU REFUSE? (Cicero, *Pro Roscio Amerino*).
- *Quin* ... conscendimus equos? (Livy, *Ab Urbe Condita*). WHY DON'T WE MOUNT ON OUR HORSES? / LET'S MOUNT OUR HORSES

8. Indefinite adverbs [112]

a/ In the section on pronouns, we have dealt with indefinite pronouns; there are also indefinite adverbs, indeclinable (as all adverbs), mostly deriving from interrogative adverbs, which become indefinite just by the addition of the prefix **ali-**. Observe these two sentences:

- *Ubi* laborat agricola? WHERE IS THE FARMER WORKING?
  Agricola laborat *alicubi* THE FARMER IS WORKING SOMEWHERE.

While **ubi** means WHERE, **alicubi** means SOMEWHERE.

- Cum paucissimis *alicubi* occultabor WITH A VERY FEW MEN I WILL HIDE SOMEWHERE (Cicero, *Epistulae ad Atticum*).

We can aply the same rule to the other interrogative adverbs **quo, unde** and **qua**:

- – *Quo* it Caesar? WHERE IS CAESAR GOING?
  – Caesar *aliquo* it CAESAR IS GOING SOMEWHERE.
- – *Unde* venit heri exercitus? WHERE DID THE ARMY COME FROM YESTERDAY?
  – Heri exercitus venit *alicunde* YESTERDAY THE ARMY CAME FROM SOMEWHERE.
- – *Qua* currunt discipuli? THROUGH WHERE ARE THE STUDENTS RUNNING?
  – Discipuli *aliqua* currunt THE STUDENTS ARE RUNNING THROUGH SOMEWHERE.
- – *Quo* te agis? WHERE ARE YOU GOING?
  – Missus sum *aliquo* I HAVE BEEN SENT SOMEWHERE (Plautus, *Miles Gloriosus*).
- – Quid faciam? WHAT AM I TO DO?
  – Rogas? *Alicunde* exora mutuom AND YOU ASK IT? GET IT FROM SOMEWHERE AS A LOAN (Plautus, *Persa*).
  ◊ They are trying to get some money.

b/ The same can be done with the interrogative adverb **quando**: [113]

- – *Quando* veniet Caesar? WHEN WILL CAESAR COME? – *Aliquando* veniet HE WILL COME AT SOME POINT.
- Possumus *aliquando* ... de re pecuniaria disceptare? CAN WE AT SOME POINT DEBATE ABOUT FINANCIAL MATTERS? (Cicero, *Pro Quinctio*).

c/ With respect to **quomodo**, the only difference is that instead of the expected word **aliquomodo** we will find **aliquo modo**, as two words. Let's take into account that the interrogative **quomodo** can also be written **quo modo**, so that in fact we are applying the **ali-** prefix to one of the two options.

- – *Quomodo* hoc fecisti? HOW DID YOU DO THIS? – Hoc *aliquo modo* feci I DID THIS SOMEHOW.
- Si id, quod ex vertebra excedit, *aliquo modo* fractum est, ... IF IT, WHAT STICKS OUT OF A VERTEBRA, IS BROKEN SOMEHOW, ... (Celsus, *De Medicina*).

A lot of times, instead of **aliquo modo** SOMEHOW, we can find the expression **nescio quo modo** I DO NOT KNOW HOW:

- Pervenit res ad istius auris *nescio quo modo* THE MATTER REACHED SOMEHOW THE EARS OF THIS MAN (Cicero, *In Verrem*).
- Sed *nescio quo modo*, dum lego, adsentior BUT SOMEHOW, WHILE I READ, I GIVE MY ASSENT (Cicero, *Tusculanae Disputationes*).

9. Affirmative and negative adverbs [114]

a) Affirmative adverbs

1/ Latin has no adverb that means YES. A very common way of answering YES to a question is by repeating the verb (with the obvious change of person):

- – **Vis hodie nobiscum venire?** DO YOU WANT TO COME WITH US TODAY?
  – **Volo** I WANT.

Other ways of answering affirmatively are:

sane	CERTAINLY	**profecto**	INDEED, TRULY
nimirum	NO DOUBT	**quidem**	ASSUREDLY
certe	CERTAINLY		

- **..., non parva res, sed *nimirum* omnium maxima** ..., NOT SOMETHING SMALL, BUT NO DOUBT THE BIGGEST OF ALL (Cicero, *Pro Murena*).
- **Huius tamen insania, quae ridicula est aliis, mihi tum molesta *sane* fuit** THE INSANITY OF THIS MAN, ALTHOUGH IT IS RIDICULOUS TO OTHER PEOPLE, THEN IT WAS CERTAINLY ANNOYING TO ME (Cicero, *In Verrem*).

2/ These adverbs express possibility: **forte, fortasse, forsitan** PERHAPS. They are not affirmative adverbs, but they have been included here.

- **At enim *forsitan* hoc tibi veniat in mentem** BUT PERHAPS THIS MAY COME TO YOUR MIND (Cicero, *Pro Roscio Comoedo*).

b) Negative adverbs [115]

1/ The main one is **non** NO, but we can also find **haud**, especially with the verb **scio** TO KNOW.

- ***Haud* scio an fieri possit** I DO NOT KNOW WHETHER IT CAN BE DONE (Cicero, *In Verrem*).

Other negatives are:

minime	IN NO WAY, NOT AT ALL	
nequaquam	IN NO WAY, NOT AT ALL	
ne ... quidem	NOT EVEN	✧ Usually, the thing referred to will be found between both words.

- **Sapientem me esse dico? *Minime*** DO I SAY THAT I AM WISE? NOT AT ALL (Seneca iunior, *Dialogi*).
- **Iugulare civem *ne* iure *quidem* quisquam bonus volt** NO GOOD MAN WANTS TO SLAUGHTER A CITIZEN, NOT EVEN BY THE LAW (Cicero, *Pro Quinctio*). ✧ **volt** = **vult**.

2/ We can replace **et non** by **nec** or **neque**, and in the same way as **et ... et** means BOTH ... AND, **nec ... nec (neque ... neque)** means NEITHER ... NOR.

- **Servos ipsos, quod ad me attinet, *neque* arguo *neque* purgo** THE SLAVES THEMSELVES, AS FAR AS I AM CONCERNED, I NEITHER ACCUSE NOR ACQUIT (Cicero, *Pro Roscio Amerino*).

10. Prepositional adverbs [116]

a/ There are a group of words in Latin that perform as if they were prepositions, as for instance **sine**, which takes the ablative and means WITHOUT:

- *Sine* te hoc facere non possum   I CAN NOT DO THIS WITHOUT YOU.

Some of them are followed by the accusative, and some of them by the ablative (this is why some grammars include them in the chapter of prepositions). But these words are not prepositions, although they look like it, and the distinguishing trait is that (with exceptions) they can not be used to form compound verbs: for example, we can say **ineo**, **transeo**, etc. (**in** and **trans** are proper prepositions), but we can not say **sineeo**.

Sometimes they can play the role of simple adverbs:

- *Infra* ibimus   WE WILL GO FURTHER DOWN.

b/ The first adverbs mentioned in *Point 6 Adverbs of place* can be used as prepositional adverbs, and they must be followed by the accusative:

supra ABOVE   infra BELOW   intra INSIDE   extra OUTSIDE   citra ON THIS SIDE   ultra FURTHER THERE   circa AROUND
contra OPPOSITE   iuxta SIDE BY SIDE   prope NEAR, BY THE SIDE

- Aquam forte ea tum sacris *extra* moenia petitum ierat   BY CHANCE, SHE HAD GONE OUTSIDE THE WALLS TO FETCH WATER FOR A SACRIFICE (Livy, *Ab Urbe Condita*).
- Nostros *intra* munitiones ingredi prohibebant   THEY PREVENTED OUR [SOLDIERS] FROM ENTERING THE WALLS (Caesar, *De Bello Gallico*).

c/ Apart from these, there are other adverbs that can be used as prepositions (some have local sense, some have another sense) followed by the accusative: [117]

secundum BEHIND   propter BECAUSE OF

- ... neque *propter* loci naturam Cirtam armis expugnare potest   ... AND HE CAN NOT CAPTURE CIRTA BY ARMS BECAUSE OF THE NATURE OF THE PLACE (Sallust, *Bellum Iugurthinum*).

d/ And some other ones must be followed by the ablative:

We give the meaning as adverb, but obviously the translation will experience some change if used as preposition (for instance, **palam** PUBLICLY should be translated by IN THE PRESENCE OF if used as preposition, and also **clam** may have to be translated differently if used as a preposition).

coram FACE TO FACE   palam PUBLICLY, IN THE PRESENCE OF   clam SECRETLY

- Hoc facere *palam* discipulis nolo   I DO NOT WANT TO DO THIS IN THE PRESENCE OF THE STUDENTS.
- Cur me *coram* populo magis interrogas?   WHY DO YOU GO ON QUESTIONING ME IN FRONT OF THE PEOPLE? (Quintilianus, *Declamationes Maiores*).

Observe the two different ways of translating **clam**:

- **Non sibi *clam* vobis salutem fuga petivit?** DID HE NOT SEEK HIS SAFETY IN FLIGHT WITHOUT YOUR KNOWLEDGE? (Caesar, *Bellum Civile*).

  ✧ Here, used as prepositional adverb.

- **Noctu *clam* sustulit signa pulcherrima atque antiquissima** BY NIGHT HE REMOVED SECRETLY THOSE VERY BEAUTIFUL AND VERY ANTIQUE STATUES (Cicero, *In Verrem*).

  ✧ Here, used as adverb.

Observe that **coram**, **palam** and **clam** end in -**am**: nothing to do with the Acc. sing of the 1st declension.

h) The correlatives

1. Correlative adverbs [118]

a) Definitions and examples

1/ There are several series of adverbs that have different forms according to the function they perform in a sentence, but linked by their common meaning; for instance, the temporal adverb **tum** THEN, in a sentence like

- Eum *tum* vidi   I SAW HIM THEN.

belongs to the same series as the also temporal adverb **quando?** WHEN? in a sentence like

- *Quando* invenies?   WHEN WILL YOU ARRIVE?

Both of them belong to the same series, both of them make reference to a point in time, with the only difference that the adverb **tum** THEN in the first sentence is a *demonstrative* temporal adverb and the adverb **quando?** WHEN? in the second sentence is an *interrogative* temporal adverb.

Let's see a double example, this time with local adverbs:

- Eum *ibi* vidi, *ubi* tu heri ludebas   I SAW HIM THERE, WHERE YOU WERE PLAYING YESTERDAY.

Ibi THERE is a *demonstrative* local adverb, while **ubi** WHERE is a *relative* local adverb.

Note

The last example must not make us think that correlatives must appear in consecutive sentences; see that in the two first examples each one of them was used on its own.

We can see that the difference from an adverb to another one of the same family may be just a small change in the word (**ibi** / **ubi**) or a completely different word (**tum** / **quando**).

2/ Taking the demonstrative local adverb **ibi**, we will show the five main roles that a family of correlatives may have: [119]

- *Demonstrative:* **ibi** THERE (there are other demonstratives: **hic** HERE, for instance)
  - *Ibi* Caesarem necaverunt   THEY KILLED CAESAR THERE.
- *Relative:* **ubi** WHERE
  - Locum *ubi* Caesarem necaverunt numquam vidi   I HAVE NEVER SEEN THE PLACE WHERE THEY KILLED CAESAR.
- *Indefinite:* **alicubi** SOMEWHERE
  - Caesarem *alicubi* necaverunt   THEY KILLED CAESAR SOMEWHERE.

➢ *Indefinite relative:* **ubicumque** WHEREVER

- ***Ubicumque* es, cives te amant** WHEREVER YOU ARE, CITIZENS LOVE YOU.

➢ *Interrogative:* **ubi?** WHERE?

- ***Ubi* Caesarem necaverunt?** WHERE DID THEY KILL CAESAR?

3/ At the sight of this, we can deduce three basic characteristics that we can apply to each family of correlatives:

⇨ The relative and the interrogative are equal.
⇨ The indefinite is formed from the interrogative, adding the prefix **ali-**.
⇨ The indefinite relative is formed by adding **-cumque** to the interrogative.

The translations offered here for each term are not unvariable; the context may require some adaptations, and moreover in some cases there may be several different Latin terms with different meanings (**ibi** THERE or **hic** HERE as local demonstrative, for instance).

Let's see some original examples:

- ***Ubi* eos convenit?** WHERE DID HE MEET WITH THEM? (Cicero, *Pro Roscio Amerino*).
- **In eundem locum reuertitur atque *ibi*, *ubi* telum erat infossum, ...** HE CAME BACK TO THE SAME PLACE AND THERE, WHERE THE WEAPON HAD BEEN BURIED, ... (Nepos, *Vitae*).
- **Utinam hic prope adesset *alicubi* atque audiret haec!** IF ONLY HE WERE SOMEWHERE NEAR AND I COULD HEAR THIS! (Terentius Afer, *Adelphoe*).
- ***Ubicumque* hoc factum est, improbe factum est** WHEREVER THIS IS DONE, IT IS DONE IN A VILE WAY (Cicero, *In Verrem*).

b) The local correlative adverbs [120]

1/ We can present now the series of correlatives for each of the four local adverbs; we must first remember that there are four main types of local expressions:

– place *where* – place *from where*
– place *to where* – place *through where*

2/ We have already seen the series of correlatives of the type *place where*; now let's see those corresponding to the type *place to where*:

➢ *Demonstrative:* **eo** TOWARDS THERE

- ***Eo* licet mihi abire?** MAY I GO THERE?

➢ *Relative:* **quo** TO WHERE

- **Profecti sunt *quo* dux iussit** THEY DEPARTED TO WHERE THE GENERAL ORDERED.

- *Indefinite:* aliquo TO SOMEWHERE
  - *Aliquo* profecti sunt THEY HAVE DEPARTED TO SOMEWHERE.
- *Indefinite relative:* quocumque TO WHEREVER
  - *Quocumque* ire placet, ferro iter aperiundum est WHEREVER WE WISH TO GO, WE MUST OPEN OUR WAY WITH A SWORD (Sallust, *Catilinae Coniuratio*).
- *Interrogative:* quo? WHERE TO?
  - *Quo* vadis? WHERE ARE YOU GOING?

3/ Those corresponding to the *place from where* type are: [121]

- *Demonstrative:* inde FROM THERE
  - *Inde* venimus WE COME FROM THERE.
- *Relative:* unde FROM WHERE
  - Locus *unde* venimus pulcher est THE PLACE FROM WHERE WE COME IS NICE.
- *Indefinite:* alicunde FROM SOMEWHERE
  - Repente *alicunde* venerunt SUDDENLY THEY CAME FROM SOMEWHERE.
- *Indefinite relative:* undecumque FROM WHEREVER
  - *Undecumque* venit, semper donum mihi fert WHEREVER HE COMES FROM, HE ALWAYS BRINGS ME A PRESENT.
- *Interrogative:* unde? WHERE FROM?
  - *Unde* venis? WHERE DO YOU COME FROM?

4/ And the last series would be the series of *place through which* (not much used, it must be said): [122]

- *Demonstrative:* ea THOUGH THERE
  - Hostes *ea* urbem intraverunt THE ENEMY ENTERED INTO THE CITY THOUGH THERE.
- *Relative:* qua THROUGH WHERE
  - Locus *qua* hostes intraverunt indefensus erat THE PLACE THOUGH WHERE THE ENEMY ENTERED WAS UNPROTECTED.
- *Indefinite:* aliqua THROUGH SOMEWHERE
  - Hostes *aliqua* intraverunt THE ENEMY ENTERED THROUGH SOMEWHERE.
- *Indefinite relative:* quacumque THROUGH WHEREVER
  - *Quacumque* iter fecit, omnes necabat THROUGH WHEREVER HE MADE HIS WAY, HE KILLED EVERYBODY.
- *Interrogative:* qua? THROUGH WHERE?
  - *Qua* intraverunt hostes? THROUGH WHERE DID THE ENEMY ENTER?

Some examples:

- *Aliquo* aufugiam et me occultabo aliquot dies I WILL FLEE SOMEWHERE AND I WILL HIDE FOR SOME DAYS (Plautus, *Miles Gloriosus*).
- Putemus pecuniam bonum esse *undecumque* sumptam LET'S CONSIDER MONEY SOMETHING GOOD FROM WHEREVER IT MAY HAVE BEEN TAKEN (Seneca iunior, *Epistulae Morales ad Lucilium*).
- *Unde* sumptum? TAKEN FROM WHERE? (Cicero, *Pro Cluentio*).
- Adsunt Athenienses, *unde* ... leges ortae atque in omnis terras distributae putantur THERE ARE THE ATHENIANS, FROM WHERE LAWS ARE SUPPOSED TO HAVE ORIGINATED AND BEEN DISTRIBUTED TO ALL LANDS (Cicero, *Pro Flacco*).
- *Quacumque* iter fecit, hoc iucundissimum spectaculum omnibus ... praebebat THROUGH WHEREVER HE MADE HIS WAY, HE OFFERED A MOST DELIGHTFUL SPECTACLE TO EVERYBODY (Cicero, *In Verrem*).

c) The temporal correlative adverbs [123]

We have seen part of them at the very beginning; the whole series would be:

➢ *Demonstrative:* tum THEN

- Octavius omnia *tum* dixit OCTAVIUS SAID EVERYTHING THEN.

➢ *Relative:* cum WHEN (quando and ubi also possible)

- Ego hoc feci *cum* dux me iussit I DID THIS WHEN THE GENERAL ORDERED ME TO.

➢ *Indefinite:* aliquando SOMETIME

- *Aliquando* hoc faciam I WILL DO THIS SOMETIME.

➢ *Indefinite relative:* quandocumque WHENEVER

- *Quandocumque* Cicero loquitur, semper attentissime audio WHENEVER CICERO SPEAKS, I ALWAYS LISTEN VERY CAREFULLY.

➢ *Interrogative:* quando? WHEN?

- *Quando* pervenisti? WHEN DID YOU ARRIVE?

Let's see some examples:

- Profectus est *aliquando* tandem in Hispaniam FINALLY, AT SOME POINT HE SET OFF FOR HISPANIA (Cicero, *Philippicae*).
- Idque *quandocumque* animaduersum est, terrere nos potest AND THIS, WHENEVER IT HAS BEEN NOTICED, CAN TERRIFY US (Celsus, *De Medicina*).
- Si *quando* non pluet, uti terra sitiat, aquam inrigato IF AT SOME POINT IT DOES NOT RAIN, AS SOON AS THE GROUND IS THIRSTY, WATER IT (Porcius Cato, *De Agri Cultura*).

✧ Important: Observe that, as happened with aliquis, the adverb aliquando also loses the prefix ali- after si.

d) The frequentative correlative adverbs [124]

They are related to the meaning of *how many times* or *how often* an action takes place; the whole series is:

- *Demonstrative:* **totiens** SO OFTEN / SO MANY TIMES
  - **Quid fecerat quod eum *totiens* per insidias interficere voluistis?** WHAT HAD HE DONE, THAT YOU WANTED SO OFTEN TO KILL HIM IN AN AMBUSH? (Cicero, *De Domo Sua*).
- *Relative:* **quotiens** AS OFTEN AS / AS MANY TIMES AS
  - **Hieme saepius fascia circumire debet, aestate *quotiens* necesse est** IN WINTER, THE BANDAGE MUST GO AROUND [THE WOUND] RATHER OFTEN, IN SUMMER AS MANY TIMES AS NECESSARY (Celsus, *De Medicina*).
- *Indefinite:* **aliquotiens** AT SEVERAL TIMES
  - ***Aliquotiens* ad socios litteras de istius iniuriis miserat** AT SEVERAL TIMES HE HAD SENT TO HIS ALLIES A LETTER ABOUT THE OFFENCES OF THIS ONE (Cicero, *In Verrem*).
- *Indefinite relative:* **quotienscumque** HOWEVER OFTEN
  - ***Quotienscumque* opus erit, facito uti aquam addas** HOWEVER OFTEN IT IS NECESSARY, MAKE SURE THAT YOU ADD WATER (Cato, *De Agri Cultura*).
- *Interrogative:* **quotiens?** HOW OFTEN? / HOW MANY TIMES?
  - ***Quotiens* dicendum est tibi?** HOW MANY TIMES DO I HAVE TO TELL YOU? (Plautus, *Amphitruo*).

2. Correlative adjectives [125]

In the first part of this chapter, we have learnt how to construct *families* of correlative adverbs; now let's do the same with adjectives. The method to be followed will be the same one, and moreover the correlative adjectives can be used in all grammatical cases.

a) The correlatives SUCH ... AS and AS LARGE ... AS

1/ We will begin with the study of the *quantitative* and the *qualitative* correlative adjectives, given their importance as they can perform some functions proper to demonstrative and relative adjectives.

talis .... qualis
tantus ... quantus

Talis is a *qualitative demonstrative*, and it can be translated as SUCH, OF SUCH A KIND. It is declined like **facilis, -e**:

Nom. talis, -e
Acc. talem, -e
etc.

Qualis is a *qualitative relative* used to establish comparisons, and it can be translated as AS, SUCH AS, although the translation may vary to show the correlation with the demonstrative adjective **talis**, which is almost always used in combination with **qualis**. **Qualis** follows also the same declension of the adjective **facilis, -e**.

Note

Remember that **qualis, quale** has also the interrogative meaning OF WHICH KIND?

- *Qualis* homo est tuus frater? WHICH KIND OF PERSON IS YOUR BROTHER?

2/ Now we will show with some examples how these qualitative demonstrative and qualitative relative adjectives are used to compare things or people:

- *Talem* urbem video *qualem* numquam antea vidisti I SEE SUCH A CITY AS YOU HAVE NEVER SEEN BEFORE.
  ✧ Literally, I SEE SUCH A CITY SUCH AS YOU HAVE NEVER SEEN, but the second SUCH is superfluous in the translation.
- Athenienses *tales* sunt *quales* vincere non possumus THE ATHENIANS ARE SUCH (literally, OF SUCH A KIND) AS WE ARE NOT ABLE TO CONQUER.
  ✧ A better translation could be THE ATHENIANS ARE THE KIND OF PEOPLE WE CAN'T CONQUER.
- In *tali* urbe habitamus in *quali* omnes habitare vellent WE LIVE IN SUCH A CITY AS (literally, IN SUCH AS) ALL WOULD LOVE TO LIVE IN.
  ✧ Or also WE LIVE IN THE KIND OF CITY IN WHICH ALL WOULD LOVE TO LIVE. The possibilities of translation are several, provided that they show the correlation between the demonstrative and the relative.

The qualitative relative can also be used without the corresponding qualitative demonstrative:

- Est omnino fortium virorum, *quales* vos esse debetis, virtutem praestare IT IS PROPER OF BRAVE MEN, SUCH AS YOU HAVE TO BE, TO DISPLAY YOUR VALOUR (Cicero, *Philippicae*).

Other examples:

- **Tempus habes *tale quale* nemo habuit umquam** YOU HAVE SUCH AN OPPORTUNITY AS NOBODY HAS EVER HAD (Cicero, *Philippicae*).
- **Est autem *tale quale* floruit Athenis** IT IS OF THE SAME KIND THAT FLOURISHED IN ATHENS (Cicero, *De Optimo Genere Oratorum*)
  ✧ Cicero is talking about oratory.
- **Habet orationem *talem* consul *qualem* numquam Catilina victor habuisset** THE CONSUL MAKES SUCH A SPEECH AS CATILINA WOULD HAVE NEVER MADE AS CONQUEROR (Cicero, *Pro Sestio*).

3/ A similar phenomenon happens with the couple **tantus ... quantus**, but in this case what is pointed out is the size, not the quality, as they are a *size-quantitative demonstrative* and a *size-quantitative relative adjective*. They are inflected through the *2-1-2 scheme*. **[126]**

Tantus and **quantus** make reference to size, NOT to quantity, this is why we call them *size-quantitative*. The correlatives making reference to quantity are presented further down, with the name of *amount-quantitative*.

Tantus can be translated as SO BIG / SO LARGE, and **quantus** as [SO BIG / SO LARGE] AS. Let's see some examples:

- **Nemo habet *tantos* libros *quantos* ego habeo** NOBODY HAS SO LARGE BOOKS AS I [HAVE].
- **Hic miles habet *tantum* gladium *quantum* numquam vidisti** THIS SOLDIER HAS SUCH A BIG SWORD AS YOU HAVE NEVER SEEN.
- **In *tanto* proelio pugnavi *quantum* Athenienses numquam fecerunt** I FOUGHT IN SUCH A BIG BATTLE AS THE ATHENIANS NEVER FOUGHT.

✧ Note that if in the former sentence we had written **In *tali* proelio pugnavi *qualem* Athenienses numquam fecerunt**, we would emphasise some particular characteristic of the battle (cruel, harsh, or maybe short, or long, etc.), not the size: I FOUGHT IN SUCH A BATTLE AS ("OF THE KIND THAT") THE ATHENIANS NEVER FOUGHT.

- **Tum meretricum numerus *tantus, quantum* in urbe omni fuit ...** THEN SUCH A LARGE NUMBER OF COURTESANS AS THERE WAS IN THE WHOLE CITY ... (Plautus, *Epidicus*).
  ✧ The use of the neuter **quantum** instead of **quantus** may respond to the concept of number as an abstract concept, although **numerus** is masculine.
- **Sed si est *tantus* dolor, *quantus* Philoctetae?** AND IF THE PAIN IS SO INTENSE (BIG) AS FOR PHILOCTETES? (Cicero, *Tusculanae Disputationes*).

> **Note**
>
> Remember that **quantus** has also the interrogative meaning HOW LARGE?
> - ***Quantam* domum habes?** HOW LARGE A HOUSE DO YOU HAVE?

The difference *qualitative-quantitative* must be clear:

- **Habito in *tali* urbe...** I LIVE IN SUCH A [NICE] CITY... ✧ Emphasis on the quality, style, etc.
- **Habito in *tanta* urbe...** I LIVE IN SUCH A [BIG] CITY... ✧ Emphasis on the size.

b) The whole series of correlative adjectives [127]

1/ Here we will report the complete family of the correlative adjectives deriving from the *qualitative* interrogative adjective **qualis, -e**, that means OF WHICH KIND?

- *Qualis* homo est tuus frater? WHAT KIND OF MAN IS YOUR BROTHER?

For the sake of brevity, in some cases only the singular masculine forms will be given in the following list:

- Direct question: **qualis? quale?** OF WHAT KIND?
- Indefinite: non-existent
- Relative: **qualis, quale** SUCH AS
- Indefinite relative: **qualiscumque** OF WHATEVER KIND
- Demonstrative: **talis, tale** OF SUCH A KIND

Some examples:

- *Qualem* esse Ciceronem ducis? WHAT KIND OF PERSON DO YOU THINK CICERO IS?
- *Qualescumque* sumus tamen haec quae passi sumus pati non debuimus WHATEVER KIND OF PEOPLE WE ARE, WE OUGHT NOT TO HAVE SUFFERED WHAT WE HAVE SUFFERED (Livy, *Ab Urbe Condita*).
- Amicos non habeo *quales* tu habes I HAVEN'T GOT FRIENDS SUCH AS YOU HAVE
  ✧ Meaning ... OF THE SAME KIND AS YOU HAVE.
- Nulla domus *tales* umquam contexit amores NO HOUSE EVER ENCLOSED SUCH LOVES (Catullus, *Carmina*).

2/ The same rule can be applied to the *size-quantitative* interrogative **quantus**:

- Direct question: **quantus, -a, -um?** HOW GREAT?
- Indefinite: **aliquantus, -a, -um** SOME (meaning *size*)
- Relative: **quantus, -a, -um** AS GREAT/LARGE AS
- Indefinite relative: **quantuscumque** HOWEVER GREAT
- Demonstrative: **tantus, -a, -um** SO GREAT

- *Tantus* fuit omnium terror, ut alii adesse copias Iubae dicerent SO GREAT WAS THEIR FEAR THAT SOME STARTED TO SAY THAT JUBA'S TROOPS WERE THERE (Caesar, *Bellum Civile*).
- Non habeo exercitum *quantum* tu habes I HAVEN'T GOT AN ARMY AS LARGE AS YOU HAVE.
- *Aliquantum* timorem habebant milites THE SOLDIERS HAD SOME FEAR.
- Omnia adhuc *quantacumque* petistis obtinuistis EVERYTHING EVEN HOWEVER GREAT YOU REQUESTED, YOU OBTAINED (Livy, *Ab Urbe Condita*).

c) The series of WHO / WHAT [128]

This series contains those adjectives (or pronouns) dealing with the identity of some element of the sentence; most of its components have already been met in the respective chapters on pronouns, but we repeat them here in order to show their mutual relationship, their correlation.

- Direct question: **quis? quid?** WHO? WHAT?
- Indefinite: **aliquis, aliquid** SOMEBODY, SOMETHING
- Relative: **qui, quae, quod** WHO, WHICH
- Indefinite relative: **quicumque** WHOEVER, WHATEVER
  ✧ There is also a less common one, **quisquis** (masc./fem.), **quidquid** (neuter), used only in nom., acc. and abl.
- Demonstrative: **is, ea, id** THIS, THAT

  - *Quemcumque* rogaveris, hoc respondebit WHOMEVER YOU ASK, HE WILL ANSWER THIS (Cicero, *Pro Cluentio*).
  - Si tibi *aliquis* ad aurem accessisset et dixisset ... IF ANYBODY HAD APPROACHED YOU TO YOUR EAR AND HAD SAID ... (Cicero, *In Verrem*).

    ✧ Observe, by the way, how **aliquis** has not lost the **ali**- now: it is not immediately after the conjunction **si** IF.
  - Ire per hanc noli, *quisquis* es DO NOT GO THROUGH THAT [WAY], WHOEVER YOU ARE (Ovid, *Fasti*).

d) The series of HOW MANY [129]

In this series, a typical mistake is to consider that the plural of **quantus** has the meaning of the English HOW MANY. In fact a question like *Quantos* libros habes? would mean HOW LARGE BOOKS HAVE YOU GOT? as if asking about the size of the books, and not HOW MANY BOOKS HAVE YOU GOT? For HOW MANY, we must use the so-called *amount-quantitative* adjective presented here (**quantus** is the *size-quantitative* adjective, presented further above).

Although they are adjectives, they can not be declined, but even so they are considered adjectives.

- Direct question: **quot** HOW MANY?
- Indefinite: **aliquot** SOME (meaning *number*)
- Relative: **quot** AS MANY AS
- Indefinite relative: **quotcumque** HOWEVER MANY
- Demonstrative: **tot / totidem** SO MANY

  - *Tot* milites habemus ut urbem facile capturi simus WE HAVE SO MANY SOLDIERS THAT WE WILL CAPTURE THE CITY EASILY.
  - Non habeo *tot* libros *quot* tu habes I HAVE NOT GOT AS MANY BOOKS AS YOU HAVE.
  - Domi *aliquot* servos reliqui I HAVE LEFT SOME SLAVES AT HOME.
  - *Quotcumque* voles, una sit ista tibi HOWEVER MANY THINGS YOU MAY WANT, MAY SHE BE THE ONE FOR YOU (Propertius, *Elegiae*).
  - *Quot* annos nata dicitur? HOW OLD IS SHE SAID TO BE? (Plautus, *Cistellaria*).
  - – *Quot* sunt? HOW MANY ARE THEY?
    – *Totidem quot* ego et tu sumus AS MANY AS YOU AND I ARE (Plautus, *Rudens*).

THE VERBAL SYSTEM

a) General observations

1. Mechanic of the Latin verbs
2. The tenses
3. The moods
4. The voices
5. Formation of tenses
6. Formation of moods
7. Types of verbs
8. Principal parts

b) The four regular conjugations

1. The 1st conjugation
2. The 2nd conjugation
3. The 3rd conjugation
4. The 4th conjugation
5. The mixed conjugation

c) The passive voice

1. Present-stem tenses
2. Perfect-stem tenses

d) Deponent and semi-deponent verbs

1. Deponent verbs
2. Nominal forms in deponent verbs
3. Semi-deponent verbs
4. Passive deponent verbs

e) Verb **sum** and its compounds

1. Verb **sum**
2. Compounds of **sum**
3. Verb **possum**
4. Verb **prosum**

f) Irregular verbs

1. Verb **volo**
2. Verb **nolo**
3. Verb **malo**
4. Verb **eo** and its compounds
5. Verb **fero** and its compounds
6. Verb **edo**
7. Verb **fio**
8. Defective verbs

g) Overview of peculiar constructions

1. Previous notes
2. List of verbs: peculiar constructions

h) Compound verbs

1. General remarks
2. Meaning of the preposition
3. Regime of the verb
4. Main compound verbs

a) General observations

1. Mechanics of the Latin verbs [130]

In comparison to other languages, the conjugation of Latin verbs does not pose any special difficulty to students, as their formation follows a very regular mechanism; even most irregular verbs are really simple to conjugate, as they tend to follow the same rules. The study of Latin verbs can be easily mastered by learning the basic principles and applying them, and its structured system will allow us to present their conjugation by means of tables from the very beginning.

The main difference with English verbs is that in Latin each verbal form (except the impersonal ones: participles, infinitives, etc.) has an ending that tells us which person is meant. In English, the same form WRITE is used for I WRITE, YOU WRITE, WE WRITE, etc., and we must make use of the personal pronouns I, YOU, WE, etc. to make it clear (only the 3rd person singular is different: WRITES). In Latin, **habeo** may only mean I HAVE, **habemus** may only mean WE HAVE, **habent** may only mean THEY HAVE, etc., because of the endings **-o**, **-mus**, **-nt**, etc.

2. The tenses [131]

The tenses in Latin are more or less equivalent to those of any other language (the translations given here as example would apply for the indicative mood only):

a/ Present tense: The expected meaning of I WRITE, I AM WRITING. Some authors used it to narrate historic events (SUDDENLY CAESAR SAYS THIS instead of SUDDENLY CAESAR SAID THIS), and in that case it is called *historic present.*

b/ Imperfect tense: Continuous action in the past, I WAS WRITING. In some verbs it can be translated as if it were a perfect tense, like for instance I LOVED LUCRETIA instead of I WAS LOVING LUCRETIA, as the last translation would not sound natural.

c/ Future tense: The expected meaning: I WILL WRITE.

d/ Perfect tense: The most important tense in Latin. It corresponds to two meanings in English: I HAVE WRITTEN and I WROTE. So, it means a completed action in the past. Obviously, the translation by I HAVE WRITTEN will carry with it a meaning of action recently finished or an action the consequences of which are still being felt, while I WROTE will just mean an action in the past. Latin will use the same verbal form to say TODAY I HAVE WRITTEN and to say YESTERDAY I WROTE.

e/ Pluperfect tense: The expected meaning, I HAD WRITTEN: an action that was already finished before another action took place.

f/ Future perfect: Not much used except in conditional clauses. It has the expected meaning: I WILL HAVE WRITTEN: an action will have been completed before another one takes place.

Given the mechanical way of producing the verbal forms in Latin, it will be very convenient that, from now on, we distribute the six verbal tenses in this way (as an example, we have included the corresponding 1st person sing. of the verb TO WRITE):

Present-stem tenses	Perfect-stem tenses
Present I WRITE I AM WRITING	*Perfect* I HAVE WRITTEN I WROTE
Imperfect I WAS WRITING	*Pluperfect* I HAD WRITTEN
Future I WILL WRITE	*Future perfect* I WILL HAVE WRITTEN

It will be observed that the tenses in the left-hand column are under the common heading of **Present-stem tenses**, while those in the right-hand column have **Perfect-stem tenses** as heading. This is related to the stem they use for their conjugation: the three tenses on the left-hand column will be formed on the same stem (the *present* stem), while the three on the right-hand column will be also formed on another common stem (the *perfect* stem).

3. The moods [132]

The moods in Latin are these:

a/ Indicative: The mood used to express real facts; all the examples given above are in indicative. It has all the six tenses: present, imperfect, future, perfect, pluperfect and future perfect.

b/ Imperative: The mood used to give orders. It has only present and future tenses (therefore, the table above will be of no use for the imperative), and moreover the use of the future imperative is just restricted to some legal documents.

c/ Subjunctive: It is used for some special meanings, like for instance expressions of the kind LET'S WRITE, and in a lot of subordinates. It lacks both future tenses, so that its table is the same one as for indicative but without the two bottom boxes.

d/ Infinitive: One of the three impersonal moods. An infinitive is a verbal noun: TO EAT, TO WRITE, etc. It is the noun of an action. There are six infinitives: present, past (or perfect) and future for the active voice, and the same three ones for the passive voice.

✧ **Important:** In spite of being a noun, infinitives do not decline.

e/ Participle: Another impersonal mood. If the infinitive is a verbal noun, the participle is a verbal adjective, and it qualifies a noun: Video *scribentem* puerum I SEE A BOY THAT WRITES. The difference with respect to the infinitive is that it lacks two of the six tenses, and it declines (remember: it is an adjective).

f/ Gerund: Another impersonal mood. It can be considered like the declension of the present active infinitive (which does not decline on itself), but it has only four cases. The similarity with the gerundive (the future passive participle is called the *gerundive*) makes the gerund very often confused with it, as the four forms of the gerund are identical to some forms of the gerundive. In fact this is why that participle is called *gerundive*: because of its similarity to the gerund.

g/ Supine: The last one of the impersonal moods. It has only two forms. It can also be considered a verbal noun, but its use is very restricted to two specific possibilities.

4. The voices [133]

There are two voices in Latin:

a/ The active voice, used to express that something or somebody executes an action, for instance CAESAR WILL WRITE A BOOK, THE CHILDREN HAVE BEEN PLAYING, THE ARMY WILL FIGHT TOMORROW, SOME SENATORS KILLED CAESAR, etc. In other words: there is a subject that performs an action. It should be noted, for further references, that if there is something or somebody that receives the action (... KILLED *CAESAR*, ... WRITE *A BOOK*), the verb is called *transitive*, while if the action just takes place but there is no object ot person receiving it (... HAVE BEEN PLAYING, ... WILL FIGHT TOMORROW), the verb is called *intransitive*.

b/ The passive voice, used to express that something or somebody receives an action performed by somebody else, for instance THE BOOK WILL BE WRITTEN BY CAESAR, THE BRIDGE WAS DESTROYED BY THE SOLDIERS.

c/ A curious characteristic of the Latin verbs is that some of them are conjugated in *passive voice* but have *active meaning*. For instance, the verb **hortor** TO ENCOURAGE has passive form, but active meaning. So, the sentence **Caesar hortatur milites** must be translated by CAESAR ENCOURAGES THE SOLDIERS, and NOT by CAESAR IS ENCOURAGED... More about this can be found in the corresponding chapter on *deponent verbs* (which is the name by which these verbs are called).

5. Formation of tenses [134]

We offer here some basic information on the formation of tenses for indicative, but peculiarities applying to each conjugation will be seen further ahead in the individual presentation of each conjugation. With respect to the subjunctive, it will also be seen further ahead.

a) Active voice

The different tenses are formed by means of adding to the main stem the corresponding characteristic, called *modal-temporal characteristic* (although not all tenses have one), which will tell us what tense that verbal form is, and the *personal ending*, which will tell us whether the subject is HE, YOU, WE, etc. Moreover, some other letters called *union vowels* will have to be inserted in some tenses in order to avoid clashes of consonants when adding these several components. For instance: **reg-e-ba-mus** means WE RULED: **reg-** is the stem that tells us the meaning of the verb, **-ba-** tells us that this is an imperfect indicative, and -**mus** is the personal ending that tells us that the subject is the 1st person plural (WE). The -**e**- is a union vowel to avoid the clash of two consonants in **reg-ba** (although it would not have been difficult to pronounce **regbamus**, the tendency in the case of clash of consonants when forming verbal tenses was to put a union vowel in the middle).

1/ Present tense: Add the personal endings to the present stem. In some conjugations, a union vowel will be needed.

2/ Imperfect tense: Add the modal-temporal characteristic -**ba**- between the present stem and the personal endings. In some conjugations, a union vowel will be needed.

3/ Future tense: This is a more complicated tense: for some verbs, we must add a **-b-** between the present stem and the personal endings and moreover a union vowel will be needed, while for other verbs the modal-temporal characteristic is **-a-** for the 1st person and **-e-** for all the other ones. A complicated tense to form.

4/ Perfect tense: Add the personal endings to the perfect stem. BUT this tense has its own set of personal endings, different from those shared by the other five tenses.

5/ Pluperfect tense: After the perfect stem, add the modal-temporal characteristic **-era-** and the personal endings.

6/ Future perfect: After the perfect stem, add the modal-temporal characteristic **-er-** and the personal endings. A union vowel will be needed.

Notes

1/ With a slight variation in the 1st person singular, all of the tenses share the same personal endings except the perfect indicative, which has its own set of endings.

2/ Observe that the two top-of-column tenses (present and perfect) do not need any modal-temporal chracteristic.

3/ Perfect and pluperfect never need any kind of union vowels. Future perfect always needs them, and the three left-hand tenses need them for some conjugations.

b) Passive voice [135]

The present-stem tenses (the three left-hand tenses in the previous table) of the passive voice will be formed as in the active but using a different set of personal endings. Example: **rege-ba-mur** WE WERE RULED instead of **rege-ba-mus** WE RULED.

The perfect-stem tenses (the three right-hand tenses in the previous table) of the passive voice will be formed by means of a combination of a *participle + a form of the verb **sum** TO BE* that would be in the tense immediately on the left of the tense we want to form. Example: **recti eramus** WE HAD BEEN RULED : it is a pluperfect, so we take the participle **recti** (further ahead we will see how we obtain this participle) and add to it the form of the verb **sum** TO BE that would be in the tense on the left of it. A quick glance at the previous table will show that on the left of the pluperfect we find the imperfect, so we add to the participle the imperfect of **sum** (which in this case will be **eramus**).

6. Formation of moods [136]

a/ Subjunctive: It will be formed using the same system as indicative, but the modal-temporal characteristics will be different from those ones used for the corresponding tenses in the indicative. Moreover, subjunctive lacks both future and future perfect, so it has only four tenses.

b/ Imperative: It has its own sets of personal endings, always based on the present stem. Imperative has two tenses: present and future, but the use of the future imperative is restricted to some legal documents.

c/ Infinitive: It is a noun, and is indeclinable. It has its own endings, and it will be observed that some of the infinitives are formed by means of a *participle + the infinitive of the verb* **sum**. Infinitives are formed from the present stem or the perfect stem, depending on which infinitive we need to form.

d/ Participle: It is an adjective, therefore it has adjectival endings, and it declines thoroughly. The model verbs conjugated in the following pages will show that most participles follow a *2-1-2 scheme*, declining the same as **bonus, -a, -um**, while one of them follows the 3rd declension and declines like **prudens, -entis**. Some participles will be formed from the present stem and the addition of a suffix + adjectival endings, while others are formed from the supine.

e/ Gerund: It is based on the present stem, to which we will add the suffix -**nd**- and some 2nd declension endings.

f/ Supine: It is in fact one of the principal parts given with the other forms of the verb (see Point 8 further down). It has only got two forms.

Notes about infinitives and participles:

1/ Participles and infinitives will be presented by means of a table, like the tenses, but using this structure:

	Present	*Past (or Perfect)*	*Future*
Active	[Present active]	[Past active]	[Future active]
Passive	[Present passive]	[Past passive]	[Future passive]

✧ Obviously, in the case of participles the two boxes of Past active and Present passive will be empty.

2/ During the presentation of the verbs, it will be observed that the participles are introduced first, as some of the infinitives are in fact formed by means of a *participle + the infinitive of the verb* **sum**; so, in order to learn how to form these infinitives we must learn first how to form the participles.

3/ Although the passive voice for the personal forms will not be introduced until the four regular conjugations have been presented in the active voice, we will introduce the active and passive participles and infinitives from the very beginning, as they way in which they are formed makes this all-at-once presentation very practical.

4/ The Past participle (or Past infinitive) is called also Perfect participle (or Perfect infinitive).

7. Types of verbs [137]

a/ Latin verbs are divided into four conjugations:

– The 1st conjugation	stem in -**a**	**amare**	TO LOVE	(stem **ama**-)
– The 2nd conjugation	stem in -**e**	**habere**	TO HAVE	(stem **habe**-)
– The 3rd conjugation	stem in consonant	**regere**	TO RULE	(stem **reg**-)
– The mixed 3rd conjugation	stem in consonant	**capere**	TO TAKE	(stem **cap**-)
– The 4th conjugation	stem in -**i**	**audire**	TO HEAR	(stem **audi**-)

The mixed 3rd conjugation (also called *conjugation in -i*) has a series of characteristics that makes its forms seem of a verb of the 4th conjugation, but in fact it is a sub-type of the 3rd one.

b/ Verbs belonging to the same conjugation will form their tenses in the same way. Moreover, differences between conjugations affect only the present-stem tenses (left-hand column): all the perfect-stem tenses (right-hand column) are formed in the same way, no matter to which conjugation the verb belongs (nevertheless, we will offer the whole forms of each conjugation for the sake of offering a whole template).

c/ Irregular verbs form a group apart, although most of them follow the parameters of the 3rd conjugation.

8. Principal parts [138]

a) What are the principal parts?

To be able to conjugate any form of a Latin verb, we must know four parts of that verb:

- The first person of the present tense indicative.
- The infinitive.
- The first person of the perfect indicative.
- The supine.

We will use the first two to identify the verb (i.e., to find out to which one of the four declensions the verb belongs) and to form any of the three present-stem tenses (the left-hand tenses in the table), and we will use the third part to form the perfect-stem tenses (the right-hand tenses in the table). The fourth form, called the *supine*, apart from being used on its own (the uses of the supine will be seen in the corresponding chapter), is also used to form participles, and let's remember that we will use one of these participles to form the right-hand tenses of the passive voice.

⇨ Example of the principal parts of the verb TO LOVE: **amo, amare, amavi, amatum**

From the two first forms **amo, amare**, we can deduce that the verb belongs to the *1st conjugation.*

⇨ Example of the principal parts of the verb TO RULE: **rego, regere, rexi, rectum**

From the two first forms **rego, regere**, we can deduce that the verb belongs to the *3rd conjugation.*

b) How are the principal parts presented?

1/ As a general rule, dictionaries will not give the four words in whole, but shortened:

amo, -are, -avi, -atum

Just seeing the **amo, -are**, it is clear that the verb belongs to the 1st conjugation, and if the other forms are presented only with the last letters it is clear that all one has to do is replace them on the same stem **ama-**.

Even some dictionaries reach the point of writing **amo 1**, which would mean "Please follow the usual parameter of the 1st conjugation", that as we have seen is **-o, -are, -avi, -atum**. Nevertheless, this can be done only with those verbs of the 1st and of the 4th conjugation that do not present irregularities in their principal parts (quite a lot of them are regular) and a few verbs of the 2nd conjugation also without alterations in their stem. A lot of verbs of the 2nd conjugation and most of the 3rd display alterations in their stems (observe for instance the unexpected **-x-** and the **-ct-** in the two last forms of **rego**).

2/ If any of the principal parts is irrregular (i.e., if the stem suffers alterations), the whole word must be given. For instance, for the verb **rego**, the dictionary will say

rego, -ere, rexi, rectum

Only the infinitive **regere** can be shortened: the two other forms, with those unexpected **-x-** and **-ct-**, must be given in full.

c) Irregular verbs [139]

With respect to irregular verbs (verbs where the changes affect not only the stem but also the endings etc.), it is clear that all the principal parts must be given in full, but even with the principal parts it will not be enough: for instance, the present indicative will have to be learnt by heart, as it is irregular in all of them.

d) Lack of supine

It must be noted that not all verbs have a supine. So, some verbs will have only three principal parts, and as a general rule dictionaries indicate this absence with one or more hyphens:

disco, -ere, didici, --- TO LEARN

Another method of indicating it is this one:

disco, -ere, didici (no supine) TO LEARN

b) The four regular conjugations

1. The 1st conjugation [140]

The study of the formation of all the forms of the 1st conjugation will be rather detailed and slow; after this, the study of the forms of the other conjugations will be just introducing some changes into the parameters of the 1st conjugation.

a) Principal parts

1/ The principal parts of a verb of the 1st conjugation will usually look like this:

amo, amare, amavi, amatum	TO LOVE
navigo, navigare, navigavi, navigatum	TO SAIL

But, as has been said in the previous chapter, dictionaries will not offer the whole words, usually they will present the verb in this way:

amo, -are, -avi, -atum	TO LOVE
navigo, -are, -avi, -atum	TO SAIL

Even sometimes a dictionary may just give amo (1), meaning that the verb belongs to the 1st conjugation and that it will follow the usual parameter -o, -are, -avi, -atum.

2/ Obviously, if there is any irregularity, the dictionary will make it clear, as for instance in the verb TO GIVE:

do, dare, dedi, datum

The third form is not the expected davi, but dedi. So, the dictionary must make it clear.

b) Indicative mood [141]

We will present in a table the forms of the six tenses of the indicative mood, and afterwards we will comment on some important matters from an analytical point of view that will apply also to the other conjugations (when they do not, it will be properly indicated when presenting the other conjugations).

We will use the verb **amo** as a paradigm: **amo, amare, amavi, amatum**.

Present-stem		**Perfect-stem**	
Present		*Perfect*	
am-o	I LOVE	amav-i	I LOVED / I HAVE LOVED
ama-s		amav-isti	
ama-t		amav-it	
ama-mus		amav-imus	
ama-tis		amav-istis	
ama-nt		amav-erunt/ere	
Imperfect		*Pluperfect*	
ama-ba-m	I WAS LOVING	amav-era-m	I HAD LOVED
ama-ba-s		amav-era-s	
ama-ba-t		amav-era-t	
ama-ba-mus		amav-era-mus	
ama-ba-tis		amav-era-tis	
ama-ba-nt		amav-era-nt	
Future		*Future perfect*	
ama-b-o	I WILL LOVE	amav-er-o	I WILL HAVE LOVED
ama-b-i-s		amav-er-i-s	
ama-b-i-t		amav-er-i-t	
ama-b-i-mus		amav-er-i-mus	
ama-b-i-tis		amav-er-i-tis	
ama-b-u-nt		amav-er-i-nt	

Present-stem tenses

(left-hand side)

Note that all of them have as stem the infinitive minus the -**re**: **amare** > **ama**-. This will apply also to subjunctive.

Perfect stem tenses

(right-hand side)

Note that all of them have, as stem, the third principal part minus the -i: **amavi** > **amav-**. This will apply also to subjunctive.

ADDITIONAL OBSERVATIONS

❑ Present: [142]

Note that the first person loses the final **-a-** of the stem. The other persons are just the *stem + personal endings.*

❑ Imperfect:

As simple as the *stem + **ba** + personal endings,* but note the ending -**m** instead of -**o** for the first person.

The *modal-temporal characteristic* is what is added between the stem and the personal endings to identify the mood and the tense; in the case of imperfect indicative, it is -**ba**-.

❑ Future:

*Stem + **b** + personal endings* (again -**o** for the first person).

The problem is that, except in the first person, in the other persons the consonant -**b**- would clash with the consonant of the personal ending, and we must add a union vowel, which is **-i-**, except for the 3rd plural, which is **-u-**.

❑ Perfect: [143]

Stem + personal endings, but this tense has a special set of personal endings (valid only for this tense and only in the indicative), and observe that the 3rd plural can also be -**ere** instead of -**erunt** (but -**erunt** is much more frequent).

In some cases we can find shortened forms, like **amasti** instead of **amavisti**: the **-vi-** has been skipped. This is valid for all conjugations.

❑ Pluperfect:

*Stem + **era** + personal endings* (observe again -**m** in the 1st person).

As in the perfect, we can find shortened forms, like **amarant** instead of **amaverant**: the **-ve-** is skipped.

❑ Future perfect:

*Stem + **er** + personal endings.*

But again, except in the 1st singular, we have the problem of consonant clashing with another consonant, so we add again a union vowel, which in this case is -i-, even for the 3rd plural.

c) Subjunctive mood [144]

In this mood we do not offer any translation, as it would depend on the use of the subjunctive in each specific sentence:

Present-stem	Perfect-stem
Present	*Perfect*
am-e-m	amav-eri-m
am-e-s	amav-eri-s
am-e-t	amav-eri-t
am-e-mus	amav-eri-mus
am-e-tis	amav-eri-tis
am-e-nt	amav-eri-nt
Imperfect	*Pluperfect*
ama-re-m	amav-isse-m
ama-re-s	amav-isse-s
ama-re-t	amav-isse-t
ama-re-mus	amav-isse-mus
ama-re-tis	amav-isse-tis
ama-re-nt	amav-isse-nt

❑ Present:

All persons lose the final -a- of the stem before attaching the modal-temporal characteristic -e- (the present subjunctive has modal-temporal characteristic, the present indicative has none).

❑ Perfect:

The modal-temporal characteristic is -eri-, which means that the final result coincides with the future perfect indicative except for the first person singular.

❑ Imperfect:

The modal-temporal characteristic is -re-, which makes the final result look like the infinitive + personal endings.

❑ Pluperfect:

The modal-temporal characteristic is -isse-.

✧ Observe the lack of the two future tenses.

✧ As in the indicative, we can find shortened forms: amassem instead of amavissem, etc.

d) Imperative mood [145]

1/ The present imperative has only two forms: 2nd person singular and 2nd person plural.

The 2nd *singular* is just the present stem, without anything else: ama

- Romam *ama* LOVE ROME!
- Audaciter *pugna* FIGHT BRAVELY!

✧ Orders given to one person.

The 2nd *plural* is the present stem + te: ama-te

- Romam *amate* LOVE ROME!
- Audaciter *pugnate* FIGHT BRAVELY!

✧ Orders given to two or more people.

2/ There is a future imperative in Latin, but its use is restricted to some formal legal documents. It will not be presented in this grammar.

e) Participles [146]

Although the passive voice for the indicative, subjunctive and imperative will be introduced further ahead, it is customary to present all the possible participles together, both the active and the passive ones. The same is done with respect to infinitives in the next section.

Of six possible participles, there are only four. The translations given here are in fact "forced" and they have been included with the mere purpose of offering an approximate idea (remember that a participle is an adjective).

	Present	*Past (or Perfect)*	*Future*
Active	**ama-ns, -ntis** LOVING, THAT LOVES	non-existent	**amat-ur-us, -a, -um** THAT IS ABOUT TO LOVE
Passive	non-existent	**amat-us, -a, -um** THAT HAS BEEN LOVED	**ama-nd-us, -a, -um** THAT MUST BE LOVED

ADDITIONAL OBSERVATIONS

❑ **Present active participle:** It is formed from the present stem. It is the only one declined through the 3rd declension, because it is in fact an adjective of one ending like **prudens, -entis**. The three other ones follow the **-us, -a, -um** scheme.

> **Note**
>
> The ablative singular ending will be **-i, amanti**, if used as simple adjective, but **-e, amante**, if it has an object or it is used as a noun.

❑ **Future active and perfect passive participles:** They are formed from the supine.

❑ **Future passive participle:** It is formed from the present stem, and is usually called *gerundive*. It has been introduced here as the future passive participle just to show its place with respect to the other participles.

A way of memorising which stem must be taken to form each of them is by realising that those that share the same stem are in opposite corners (just skip the two empty boxes): present active and future passive, in diagonally across position, are formed on the present stem, and perfect passive and future active, also diagonally across, are formed on the supine.

f) Infinitives [147]

The infinitive is a verbal noun, not an adjective. There are six (remember that, in the table of participles, two are missing), and some of them are formed by means of a *participle + the infinitive of the verb* **sum**. Again, the translations are just orientative.

	Present	*Past (or Perfect)*	*Future*
Active	ama-re TO LOVE	amav-isse TO HAVE LOVED	amat-ur-um, -am, -um esse TO BE ABOUT TO LOVE
Passive	ama-ri TO BE LOVED	amat-um, -am, -um esse TO HAVE BEEN LOVED	amat-um iri TO HAVE TO BE LOVED

ADDITIONAL OBSERVATIONS

❑ With respect to the formation, observe that two of them, the present active and present passive, are based on the present stem; one of them, the past (or perfect) active, on the perfect stem (nouns "present" and "perfect" seem to match well up to now); the future active and the perfect passive are in fact *the corresponding participles +* ***esse***; and the future passive is the *supine + iri.*

❑ The future active and the perfect passive infinitives are usually used with their participial component in accusative (syntax will later show why); this is why they have been presented as **-um, -am, -um** instead of **-us, -a, -um**. In some cases (it depends on the kind of sentence, this will be seen in the corresponding chapter) they are used in nominative with the endings **-us, -a, -um**, but their use in accusative is so much more common that it justifies introducing them in the accusative form. And obviously they have also their corresponding plural forms **-os, -as, -a +** ***esse*** (again, in the nominative **-i, -ae, -a +** ***esse*** in some cases).

❑ The perfect active has that **-isse** form that makes it resemble a pluperfect subjunctive, take care not to confuse it. And, as expected, we can find shortened forms: **amasse** instead of **amavisse**. This is valid for all conjugations.

❑ The future passive is hardly ever used.

g) Gerund and supine [148]

1/ The gerund: It can be considered the declension of the present active infinitive, and therefore it is a verbal noun. It has only four cases, and it is formed, like the gerundive, from the present stem + **nd**. As usual, the translations are just approximative, in the corresponding section on their use more accurate examples will be given.

Acc.	ama-nd-um	TO LOVE
Gen.	ama-nd-i	OF LOVING
Dat.	ama-nd-o	FOR LOVING
Abl.	ama-nd-o	(BY) LOVING

✧ Note that these forms are identical to some forms of the gerundive (future passive participle).

2/ The supine: It is another verbal noun, and it has only two possible forms:

amatum	(the fourth principal part)
amatu	(the same, but without the final **-m**)

We do not offer any translation for the supine, as they are restricted to two specific uses and a forced translation here could lead to confusion, as it would coincide with some of the translations given for the gerund.

Some common verbs of the 1st conjugation [149]

(unless it is indicated otherwise, they follow the usual scheme -o, -are, -avi, -atum)

adiuvo, -are, adiuvi, adiutum	TO HELP	habito	TO DWELL	pugno	TO FIGHT
ambulo	TO WALK	impero	TO ORDER	puto	TO RECKON
appropinquo	TO APPROACH	intro	TO ENTER	rogo	TO PRAY, TO ASK
clamo	TO SHOUT	laboro	TO WORK	servo	TO SAVE
cogito	TO THINK	laudo	TO PRAISE	specto	TO WATCH
desidero	TO DESIRE	libero	TO LIBERATE	sto, stare, steti, statum	TO STAND
do, dare, dedi, datum	TO GIVE	muto	TO CHANGE	supero	TO OVERCOME
dubito	TO HESITATE	navigo	TO SAIL	voco	TO CALL
erro	TO WANDER	neco	TO KILL	vulnero	TO WOUND
exspecto	TO AWAIT	nuntio	TO ANNOUNCE		
festino	TO HURRY	paro	TO PREPARE		

For the remaining conjugations, we will present the whole forms with an illustrative purpose, but without explaining again the formation procedure, pointing out only any differences with respect to the first conjugation.

2. The 2nd conjugation [150]

a) Principal parts

A verb of the 2nd conjugation will usually have its four principal parts looking like this:

habeo, habere, habui, habitum TO HAVE moneo, monere, monui, monitum TO WARN

Although quite regular, verbs of the 2nd conjugation are not as regular as those of the 1st one and not all of them follow this parameter -o, -ere, -ui, -itum without any alteration, so that it is very common that the dictionary shortens only the infinitive form while giving the two other ones in their whole form, as for example with the verb TO LAUGH AT : irrideo, -ere, irrisi, irrisum.

b) Indicative mood [151]

We will use the verb moneo as a paradigm: moneo, monere, monui, monitum.

Present-stem		Perfect-stem	
Present		*Perfect*	
mone-o	I WARN	monu-i	I WARNED / HAVE WARNED
mone-s		monu-isti	
mone-t		monu-it	
mone-mus		monu-imus	
mone-tis		monu-istis	
mone-nt		monu-erunt/ere	
Imperfect		*Pluperfect*	
mone-ba-m	I WAS WARNING	monu-era-m	I HAD WARNED
mone-ba-s		monu-era-s	
mone-ba-t		monu-era-t	
mone-ba-mus		monu-era-mus	
mone-ba-tis		monu-era-tis	
mone-ba-nt		monu-era-nt	
Future		*Future perfect*	
mone-b-o	I WILL WARN	monu-er-o	I WILL HAVE WARNED
mone-b-i-s		monu-er-i-s	
mone-b-i-t		monu-er-i-t	
mone-b-i-mus		monu-er-i-mus	
mone-b-i-tis		monu-er-i-tis	
mone-b-u-nt		monu-er-i-nt	

✧ In the present tense, the first person keeps the -e- of the stem (in the 1st conjugation, the -a- of the stem was lost).

c) Subjunctive mood [152]

Present-stem	Perfect-stem
Present	*Perfect*
mone-a-m	monu-eri-m
mone-a-s	monu-eri-s
mone-a-t	monu-eri-t
mone-a-mus	monu-eri-mus
mone-a-tis	monu-eri-tis
mone-a-nt	monu-eri-nt
Imperfect	*Pluperfect*
mone-re-m	monu-isse-m
mone-re-s	monu-isse-s
mone-re-t	monu-isse-t
mone-re-mus	monu-isse-mus
mone-re-tis	monu-isse-tis
mone-re-nt	monu-isse-nt

✧ The only difference with respect to the 1st conjugation is that the present tense does not lose the final vowel of the stem and the modal-temporal characteristic is -**a**- instead of -**e**-...

✧... and it will also be -**a**- for the other conjugations, in fact it is -**e**- only for the 1st conjugation.

d) Imperative mood [153]

2nd singular	mone	WARN!
2nd plural	mone-te	WARN!

✧ No formation differences with respect to the 1st conjugation.

e) Participles [154]

	Present	*Past*	*Future*
Active	mone-ns, -ntis WARNING, THAT WARNS	non-existent	monit-ur-us, -a, -um THAT IS ABOUT TO WARN
Passive	non-existent	monit-us, -a, -um THAT HAS BEEN WARNED	mone-nd-us, -a, -um THAT MUST BE WARNED

✧ No formation differences with respect to the 1st conjugation.

f) Infinitives [155]

	Present	*Past*	*Future*
Active	mone-re TO WARN	monu-isse TO HAVE WARNED	monit-ur-um, -am, -um esse TO BE ABOUT TO WARN
Passive	mone-ri TO BE WARNED	monit-um, -am, -um esse TO HAVE BEEN WARNED	monit-um iri TO HAVE TO BE WARNED

✧ No formation differences with respect to the 1st conjugation.

g) Gerund and supine [156]

Gerund

Acc.	mone-nd-um	TO WARN
Gen.	mone-nd-i	OF WARNING
Dat.	mone-nd-o	FOR WARNING
Abl.	mone-nd-o	(BY) WARNING

Supine

monitum
monitu

✧ No formation differences with respect to the 1st conjugation.

Some common verbs of the 2nd conjugation [157]

debeo, -ere, debui, debitum	TO HAVE TO, TO OWE
deleo, -ere, delevi, deletum	TO DESTROY
doceo, -ere, docui, doctum	TO TEACH
habeo, -ere, habui, habitum	TO HAVE (possession)
invideo, -ere, invidi, invisum	TO ENVY
iubeo, -ere, iussi, iussum	TO ORDER
maneo, -ere, mansi, mansum	TO REMAIN
moneo, -ere, monui, monitum	TO WARN
moveo, -ere, movi, motum	TO MOVE
persuadeo, -ere, persuasi, persuasum	TO PERSUADE
praebeo, -ere, praebui, praebitum	TO OFFER
prohibeo, -ere, prohibui, prohibitum	TO PREVENT
respondeo, -ere, respondi, responsum	TO ANSWER
teneo, -ere, tenui, ----	TO HOLD
terreo, -ere, terrui, territum	TO FRIGHTEN
timeo, -ere, timui, ----	TO FEAR
video, -ere, vidi, visum	TO SEE

3. The 3rd conjugation [158]

a) Principal parts

1/ A verb of the 3rd conjugation will have its four principal parts looking like this:

duco, ducere, duxi, ductum TO LEAD
rego, regere, rexi, rectum TO RULE

Observe that while verbs of the 2nd conjugation have their first two forms -eo, -ere, verbs of the 3rd have them -o, -ere: observe the lack of -e- in the first person.

The third and fourth forms of verbs of the 3rd conjugation are almost always given, as almost always they have irregular and hardly predictable changes in their consonants.

2/ The main characteristic of the 3rd conjugation is that, to form the present-stem tenses, we start as usual, by taking the infinitive and removing -**re**; but verbs of the 3rd conjugation remove also the remaining -**e**-, so that in fact it is like removing the whole -**ere**: **reg-e-re** > **reg**-; this will make the stem end almost always in a consonant, with the consequent need of union vowels to avoid clashes of consonant + consonant.

b) Indicative mood [159]

We will use the verb **rego** as a paradigm: **rego, regere, rexi, rectum**.

Present-stem		**Perfect-stem**	
Present		*Perfect*	
reg-o	I RULE	rex-i	I RULED / HAVE RULED
reg-i-s		rex-isti	
reg-i-t		rex-it	
reg-i-mus		rex-imus	
reg-i-tis		rex-istis	
reg-u-nt		rex-erunt/ere	
Imperfect		*Pluperfect*	
reg-e-ba-m	I WAS RULING	rex-era-m	I HAD RULED
reg-e-ba-s		rex-era-s	
reg-e-ba-t		rex-era-t	
reg-e-ba-mus		rex-era-mus	
reg-e-ba-tis		rex-era-tis	
reg-e-ba-nt		rex-era-nt	
Future		*Future perfect*	
reg-a-m	I WILL RULE	rex-er-o	I WILL HAVE RULED
reg-e-s		rex-er-i-s	
reg-e-t		rex-er-i-t	
reg-e-mus		rex-er-i-mus	
reg-e-tis		rex-er-i-tis	
reg-e-nt		rex-er-i-nt	

❑ Present:

The union vowel (unnecessary in the 1st person sing.) is -i-, except -**u**- for the 3rd person plural.

❑ Imperfect:

The union vowel is -**e**- for all forms, which makes it look like the imperfect of the 2nd conjugation.

❑ Future:

In the 3rd (and 4th) conjugation the modal-temporal characteristic is -**a**- for the 1st person and -**e**- for all the other persons. Being itself a vowel, no union vowels are needed.

Note

From the 2nd singular on, it may look like a present of the 2nd conjugation (**habes, habet**, ...); so, we must always be sure of which conjugation the verb belongs to in order to be sure which tense we are dealing with.

c) Subjunctive mood [160]

Present-stem	**Perfect-stem**
Present	*Perfect*
reg-a-m	rex-eri-m
reg-a-s	rex-eri-s
reg-a-t	rex-eri-t
reg-a-mus	rex-eri-mus
reg-a-tis	rex-eri-tis
reg-a-nt	rex-eri-nt
Imperfect	*Pluperfect*
reg-e-re-m	rex-isse-m
reg-e-re-s	rex-isse-s
reg-e-re-t	rex-isse-t
reg-e-re-mus	rex-isse-mus
reg-e-re-tis	rex-isse-tis
reg-e-re-nt	rex-isse-nt

❑ Present:

The 1st person coincides with the future indicative.

❑ Imperfect:

The union vowel is -**e**-, which makes it look like a verb of the 2nd conjugation.

d) Imperative mood [161]

2nd singular present stem + **e**: reg-e RULE!
✧ The addition of this -**e**- makes it look like an imperative of the 2nd conjugation.

2nd plural present stem + **i-te**: reg-i-te RULE!
✧ The -i- is a union vowel.

e) Participles [162]

	Present	*Past*	*Future*
Active	reg-e-ns, -ntis RULING, THAT RULES	non-existent	rect-ur-us, -a, -um THAT IS ABOUT TO RULE
Passive	non-existent	rect-us, -a, -um THAT HAS BEEN RULED	reg-e-nd-us, -a, -um THAT MUST BE RULED

✧ Observe that the present active and the future passive add an -**e**- as the union vowel after the stem, which makes them look like their equivalents of the 2nd conjugation.

f) Infinitives [163]

	Present	*Past*	*Future*
Active	reg-e-re TO RULE	rex-isse TO HAVE RULED	rect-ur-um, -am, -um esse TO BE ABOUT TO RULE
Passive	reg-i TO BE RULED	rect-um, -am, -um esse TO HAVE BEEN RULED	rect-um iri TO HAVE TO BE RULED

✧ Observe that the present passive is really special: while verbs of the 1st and 2nd conjugation modified their -**re** into -**ri**, verbs of the 3rd conjugation replace the whole -**ere** ending by only an -**i**; this makes them difficult to recognise.

g) Gerund and supine [164]

Gerund

Acc.	reg-e-nd-um	TO RULE
Gen.	reg-e-nd-i	OF RULING
Dat.	reg-e-nd-o	FOR RULING
Abl.	reg-e-nd-o	(BY) RULING

Supine

rectum
rectu

✧ Observe the union vowel -**e**-: again, it makes it look as if it were of the 2nd conjugation.

Some common verbs of the 3rd conjugation [165]

ago, -ere, egi, actum	TO LEAD, TO DO
cado, -ere, cecidi, ----	TO FALL
cognosco, -ere, cognovi, cognitum	TO BECOME ACQUAINTED
credo, -ere, credidi, creditum	TO BELIEVE
curro, -ere, cucurri, cursum	TO RUN
defendo, -ere, defendi, defensum	TO DEFEND
dico, -ere, dixi, dictum	TO SAY
discedo, -ere, discessi, discessum	TO DEPART
disco, -ere, didici, ----	TO LEARN
duco, -ere, duxi, ductum	TO LEAD
gero, -ere, gessi, gestum	TO DO
lego, -ere, legi, lectum	TO READ
ludo, -ere, lusi, lusum	TO PLAY
mitto, -ere, misi, missum	TO SEND
occido, -ere, occidi, occisum	TO KILL
ostendo, -ere, ostendi, ostentum	TO SHOW
✧ There is also the verb ostento, -are with more or less the same meaning.	
pello, -ere, pepuli, pulsum	TO PUSH
peto, -ere, petivi, petitum	TO STRIVE TO, TO ASK FOR
pono, -ere, posui, positum	TO PUT
relinquo, -ere, reliqui, relictum	TO LEAVE BEHIND
scribo, -ere, scripsi, scriptum	TO WRITE
vinco, -ere, vici, victum	TO CONQUER

4. The 4th conjugation [166]

a) Principal parts

A verb of the 4th conjugation will have its four principal parts looking like this:

audio, audire, audivi, auditum TO HEAR, TO LISTEN
dormio, dormire, dormivi, dormitum TO SLEEP

This conjugation is rather regular, and this parameter **-io, -ire, -ivi, -itum** is kept by most of its verbs. As usual, any irregular form will have to be given complete when giving the main parts:

venio, -ire, veni, ventum TO COME

b) Indicative mood [167]

We will use the verb **audio** as a paradigm: **audio, -ire, -ivi, -itum**.

Present-stem		Perfect-stem	
Present		*Perfect*	
audi-o	I HEAR	audiv-i	I HEARD / HAVE HEARD
audi-s		audiv-isti	
audi-t		audiv-it	
audi-mus		audiv-imus	
audi-tis		audiv-istis	
audi-u-nt		audiv-erunt/ere	
Imperfect		*Pluperfect*	
audi-e-ba-m	I WAS HEARING	audiv-era-m	I HAD HEARD
audi-e-ba-s		audiv-era-s	
audi-e-ba-t		audiv-era-t	
audi-e-ba-mus		audiv-era-mus	
audi-e-ba-tis		audiv-era-tis	
audi-e-ba-nt		audiv-era-nt	
Future		*Future perfect*	
audi-a-m	I WILL HEAR	audiv-er-o	I WILL HAVE HEARD
audi-e-s		audiv-er-i-s	
audi-e-t		audiv-er-i-t	
audi-e-mus		audiv-er-i-mus	
audi-e-tis		audiv-er-i-tis	
audi-e-nt		audiv-er-i-nt	

❑ Present:

The union vowel -**u**- for the last form is compulsory, although in fact there is no clash between consonants.

❑ Imperfect:

The same with the union vowel -**e**- for all forms: it is phonetically unnecessary but compulsory.

❑ Future:

As in the 3rd conjugation, the modal-temporal characteristic is -**a**- for the 1st person and -**e**- for the other persons. Being itself a vowel, no union vowels are needed.

c) Subjunctive mood [168]

Present-stem	**Perfect-stem**
Present	*Perfect*
audi-a-m	audiv-eri-m
audi-a-s	audiv-eri-s
audi-a-t	audiv-eri-t
audi-a-mus	audiv-eri-mus
audi-a-tis	audiv-eri-tis
audi-a-nt	audiv-eri-nt
Imperfect	*Pluperfect*
audi-re-m	audiv-isse-m
audi-re-s	audiv-isse-s
audi-re-t	audiv-isse-t
audi-re-mus	audiv-isse-mus
audi-re-tis	audiv-isse-tis
audi-re-nt	audiv-isse-nt

d) Imperative mood [169]

2nd singular	audi	HEAR!
2nd plural	audi-te	HEAR!

e) Participles [170]

	Present	*Past*	*Future*
Active	audi-e-ns, -ntis HEARING, THAT HEARS	non-existent	audit-ur-us, -a, -um THAT IS ABOUT TO HEAR
Passive	non-existent	audit-us, -a, -um THAT HAS BEEN HEARD	audi-e-nd-us, -a, -um THAT MUST BE HEARD

✧ Observe that, although phonetically it wouldn't be necessary, the present active and the future passive add an -**e**- as the union vowel after the stem.

f) Infinitives [171]

	Present	*Past*	*Future*
Active	audi-re TO HEAR	audiv-isse TO HAVE HEARD	audit-ur-um, -am, -um esse TO BE ABOUT TO HEAR
Passive	audi-ri TO BE HEARD	audit-um, -am, -um esse TO HAVE BEEN HEARD	audit-um iri TO HAVE TO BE HEARD

g) Gerund and supine [172]

Gerund

Acc.	audi-e-nd-um	TO HEAR
Gen.	audi-e-nd-i	OF HEARING
Dat.	audi-e-nd-o	FOR HEARING
Abl.	audi-e-nd-o	(BY) HEARING

Supine

auditum
auditu

✧ Observe the phonetically unnecessary union vowel -e- again.

Some common verbs of the 4th conjugation [173]

dormio, -ire, dormivi, dormitum	TO SLEEP	punio, -ire, punivi, punitum	TO PUNISH
invenio, -ire, inveni, inventum	TO FIND	scio, -ire, scivi, scitum	TO KNOW
nescio, -ire, nescivi, nescitum	NOT TO KNOW	sentio, -ire, sensi, sensum	TO PERCEIVE
pervenio, -ire, perveni, perventum	TO ARRIVE	venio, -ire, veni, ventum	TO COME

5. The mixed conjugation [174]

The mixed conjugation is a sub-group of the 3rd conjugation, but the attachment of an -i- at the end of the present stem makes most of its forms look like those of the 4th.

a) Principal parts

1/ A verb of the mixed conjugation will have its four principal parts looking like this:

capio, capere, cepi, captum TO CAPTURE
facio, facere, feci, factum TO MAKE, TO DO

As any verb of the 3rd conjugation (of which this is a sub-group), the 3rd and 4th principal parts will usually be irregular and difficult to predict and will have to be supplied by the dictionary (observe for instance the change of -a- into -e- in these two examples).

2/ The main characteristic of the mixed conjugation is that, after removing the -**ere** from the infinitive to form the present-stem tenses, we add an **-i-** (except in the imperfect subjunctive), which makes this verb look like a verb of the 4th conjugation: **capere** > **cap-i-**, like **audire** > **audi-**. The only difference is that the **-i-** of the 4th conjugation belongs to the stem, while that of the 3rd conjugation has been added (and in fact it is phonetically shorter).

b) Indicative mood [175]

We will use the verb **capio** as a paradigm: **capio, -ere, cepi, captum**.

Present-stem		**Perfect-stem**	
Present		*Perfect*	
cap-i-o	I CAPTURE	cep-i	I CAPTURED / HAVE CAPTURED
cap-i-s		cep-isti	
cap-i-t		cep-it	
cap-i-mus		cep-imus	
cap-i-tis		cep-istis	
cap-i-u-nt		cep-erunt, -ere	
Imperfect		*Pluperfect*	
cap-i-e-ba-m	I WAS CAPTURING	cep-era-m	I HAD CAPTURED
cap-i-e-ba-s		cep-era-s	
cap-i-e-ba-t		cep-era-t	
cap-i-e-ba-mus		cep-era-mus	
cap-i-e-ba-tis		cep-era-tis	
cap-i-e-ba-nt		cep-era-nt	
Future		*Future perfect*	
cap-i-a-m	I WILL CAPTURE	cep-er-o	I WILL HAVE CAPTURED
cap-i-e-s		cep-er-i-s	
cap-i-e-t		cep-er-i-t	
cap-i-e-mus		cep-er-i-mus	
cap-i-e-tis		cep-er-i-tis	
cap-i-e-nt		cep-er-i-nt	

❑ **Present:**

As in the 4th conjugation, the union vowel -**u**- for the last form is compulsory, although there is no clash between consonants.

❑ **Imperfect:**

The same with the union vowel -**e**- for all forms: it is phonetically unnecessary but it must be included.

c) Subjunctive mood [176]

Present-stem	**Perfect-stem**
Present	*Perfect*
cap-i-a-m	cep-eri-m
cap-i-a-s	cep-eri-s
cap-i-a-t	cep-eri-t
cap-i-a-mus	cep-eri-mus
cap-i-a-tis	cep-eri-tis
cap-i-a-nt	cep-eri-nt
Imperfect	*Pluperfect*
cap-e-re-m	cep-isse-m
cap-e-re-s	cep-isse-s
cap-e-re-t	cep-isse-t
cap-e-re-mus	cep-isse-mus
cap-e-re-tis	cep-isse-tis
cap-e-re-nt	cep-isse-nt

✧ Note that the imperfect subjunctive replaces the -i- by an -**e**-, and with this we go on with the rule of the imperfect subjunctive being like the infinitive + personal endings.

d) Imperative mood [177]

Like the imperative of the normal 3rd conjugation:

2nd singular present stem + **e**: **cap-e** CAPTURE!
✧ Observe that in the imperative singular we do not add the -i-

2nd plural present stem + **i-te**: **cap-i-te** CAPTURE!

e) Participles [178]

	Present	*Past*	*Future*
Active	cap-i-e-ns, -ntis CAPTURING, THAT CAPTURES	non-existent	capt-ur-us, -a, -um THAT IS ABOUT TO CAPTURE
Passive	non-existent	capt-us, -a, -um THAT HAS BEEN CAPTURED	cap-i-e-nd-us, -a, -um THAT MUST BE CAPTURED

✧ Observe that, although phonetically it would not be necessary, the present active and the future passive add an -**e**- as the union vowel after the stem, apart from the expected **-i-** in this sub-group.

f) Infinitives [179]

	Present	*Past*	*Future*
Active	cap-e-re TO CAPTURE	cep-isse TO HAVE CAPTURED	capt-ur-um, -am, -um esse TO BE ABOUT TO CAPTURE
Passive	cap-i TO BE CAPTURED	capt-um, -am, -um esse TO HAVE BEEN CAPTURED	capt-um iri TO HAVE TO BE CAPTURED

g) Gerund and supine [180]

Gerund

Acc.	cap-i-e-nd-um	TO CAPTURE
Gen.	cap-i-e-nd-i	OF CAPTURING
Dat.	cap-i-e-nd-o	FOR CAPTURING
Abl.	cap-i-e-nd-o	(BY) CAPTURING

Supine

captum
captu

✧ Observe the phonetically unnecessary union vowel -e- again, apart from the expected -i- in this sub-group.

Some common verbs of the mixed conjugation [181]

accipio, -ere, accepi, acceptum	TO RECEIVE
conspicio, -ere, conspexi, conspectum	TO LOOK AT
cupio, -ere, cupivi, cupitum	TO DESIRE
facio, -ere, feci, factum	TO DO, TO MAKE
fugio, -ere, fugi, ----	TO FLEE
iacio, -ere, ieci, iactum	TO THROW
incipio, -ere, incepi, inceptum	TO BEGIN
interficio, -ere, interfeci, interfectum	TO KILL
suscipio, -ere, suscepi, susceptum	TO UNDERTAKE

c) The passive voice

1. Present-stem tenses [182]

a) Main characteristics

The present-stem tenses of the passive voice are formed by using a different set of endings:

➩ instead of the usual -o/-m, -s, -t, -mus, -tis, -nt ...
... we will use -(o)r, -ris/-re, -tur, -mur, -mini, -ntur ✧ 2nd singular: -ris is more frequent than -re.

The modal-temporal characteristics etc. are identical to those of the active voice.

b) 1st conjugation [183]

Indicative		Subjunctive	Imperative	
Present		*Present*		
am-or	I AM LOVED	am-e-r	ama-re (sing.)	BE LOVED!
ama-ris		am-e-ris		
ama-tur		am-e-tur	ama-mini (plural)	BE LOVED!
ama-mur		am-e-mur		
ama-mini		am-e-mini		
ama-ntur		am-e-ntur		
Imperfect		*Imperfect*		
ama-ba-r	I WAS BEING LOVED	ama-re-r		
ama-ba-ris		ama-re-ris		
ama-ba-tur		ama-re-tur		
ama-ba-mur		ama-re-mur		
ama-ba-mini		ama-re-mini		
ama-ba-ntur		ama-re-ntur		
Future				
ama-b-or	I WILL BE LOVED			
ama-b-e-ris				
ama-b-i-tur				
ama-b-i-mur				
ama-b-i-mini				
ama-b-u-ntur				

Additional observations

1/ For reasons of space, we introduce the present-stem tenses of both indicative and subjunctive side by side, but bear in mind that both columns are in fact "left-hand columns" in their respective whole tables.]

2/ Remember that passive participles and infinitives have already been introduced together with the active ones.

3/ Note the alternation **-or/-r** in the 1st singular, depending on whether there is already a previous vowel or not.

4/ Difference with respect to the active voice: the union vowel in the 2nd singular of the future is **-e-**, not **-i-** (**ama-b-e-ris**, NOT **ama-b-i-ris**).

5/ With respect to the imperative, it should be noted that the singular form is identical to the present active infinitive (remember that, in the active voice, singular does not use any ending), and that the plural form is identical to the 2nd plural of the present indicative.

c) 2nd conjugation [184]

Indicative		Subjunctive	Imperative	
Present		*Present*		
mone-or	I AM WARNED	mone-a-r	mone-re (sing.)	BE WARNED!
mone-ris		mone-a-ris		
mone-tur		mone-a-tur	mone-mini (plural)	BE WARNED!
mone-mur		mone-a-mur		
mone-mini		mone-a-mini		
mone-ntur		mone-a-ntur		
Imperfect		*Imperfect*		
mone-ba-r	I WAS BEING WARNED	mone-re-r		
mone-ba-ris		mone-re-ris		
mone-ba-tur		mone-re-tur		
mone-ba-mur		mone-re-mur		
mone-ba-mini		mone-re-mini		
mone-ba-ntur		mone-re-ntur		
Future				
mone-b-or	I WILL BE WARNED			
mone-b-e-ris				
mone-b-i-tur				
mone-b-i-mur				
mone-b-i-mini				
mone-b-u-ntur				

✧ Observe again that the union vowel in the 2nd singular of the future is -**e**-, not -i-.

d) 3rd conjugation [185]

Indicative		Subjunctive	Imperative	
Present		*Present*		
reg-or	I AM RULED	reg-a-r	reg-e-re (sing.)	BE RULED!
reg-e-ris		reg-a-ris	reg-i-mini (plural)	BE RULED!
reg-i-tur		reg-a-tur		
reg-i-mur		reg-a-mur		
reg-i-mini		reg-a-mini		
reg-u-ntur		reg-a-ntur		
Imperfect		*Imperfect*		
reg-e-ba-r	I WAS BEING RULED	reg-e-re-r		
reg-e-ba-ris		reg-e-re-ris		
reg-e-ba-tur		reg-e-re-tur		
reg-e-ba-mur		reg-e-re-mur		
reg-e-ba-mini		reg-e-re-mini		
reg-e-ba-ntur		reg-e-re-ntur		
Future				
reg-a-r	I WILL BE RULED			
reg-e-ris				
reg-e-tur				
reg-e-mur				
reg-e-mini				
reg-e-ntur				

✧ Observe that, in the 3rd conjugation, the 2nd person union vowel that moves from **-i-** to **-e-** is in the present indicative (**reg-e-ris**, NOT **reg-i-ris**), not in the future. This makes both 2nd singular present and future look equal.

e) 4th conjugation [186]

Indicative		Subjunctive	Imperative	
Present		*Present*		
audi-or	I AM HEARD	audi-a-r	audi-re (sing.)	BE HEARD!
audi-ris		audi-a-ris		
audi-tur		audi-a-tur	audi-mini (plural)	BE HEARD!
audi-mur		audi-a-mur		
audi-mini		audi-a-mini		
audi-u-ntur		audi-a-ntur		
Imperfect		*Imperfect*		
audi-e-ba-r	I WAS BEING HEARD	audi-re-r		
audi-e-ba-ris		audi-re-ris		
audi-e-ba-tur		audi-re-tur		
audi-e-ba-mur		audi-re-mur		
audi-e-ba-mini		audi-re-mini		
audi-e-ba-ntur		audi-re-ntur		
Future				
audi-a-r	I WILL BE HEARD			
audi-e-ris				
audi-e-tur				
audi-e-mur				
audi-e-mini				
audi-e-ntur				

f) The mixed conjugation [187]

Indicative		Subjunctive	Imperative	
Present		*Present*		
cap-i-or	I AM CAPTURED	cap-i-a-r	cap-e-re (sing.)	BE CAPTURED!
cap-e-ris		cap-i-a-ris		
cap-i-tur		cap-i-a-tur	cap-i-mini (plural)	BE CAPTURED!
cap-i-mur		cap-i-a-mur		
cap-i-mini		cap-i-a-mini		
cap-i-u-ntur		cap-i-a-ntur		
Imperfect		*Imperfect*		
cap-i-e-ba-r	I WAS BEING CAPTURED	cap-e-re-r		
cap-i-e-ba-ris		cap-e-re-ris		
cap-i-e-ba-tur		cap-e-re-tur		
cap-i-e-ba-mur		cap-e-re-mur		
cap-i-e-ba-mini		cap-e-re-mini		
cap-i-e-ba-ntur		cap-e-re-ntur		
Future				
cap-i-a-r	I WILL BE CAPTURED			
cap-i-e-ris				
cap-i-e-tur				
cap-i-e-mur				
cap-i-e-mini				
cap-i-e-ntur				

✧ Observe again that, like in the 3rd conjugation, in the 2nd person singular of the present indicative the union vowel **-i-** moves to **-e-**, but in this case it does not look equal to the 2nd singular of the future (**caperis** / **capieris**).

2. Perfect-stem tenses [188]

a) Formation procedure

As happens in the active voice, all the conjugations form these tenses in the same way. The way of forming these tenses is as follows:

1/ We need the perfect participle of the verb in its three singular and its three plural forms, all of them in nominative, without declining; for instance,

sing. amatus, -a, -um pl. amati, -ae, -a

2/ Any of these participles (the choice will depend, of course on the subject; for instance, for a plural feminine subject we will choose **amatae**) must be accompanied by a form of the verb **sum** (the choice of person will depend on the person of the subject); this form will be the form that would be found in the box immediately to the left in the usual table.

- For perfect tense, use the verbal forms of the present of **sum**.
- For pluperfect tense, use the verbal forms of the imperfect of **sum**.
- For future perfect tense, use the verbal forms of the future of **sum**.

Note

The forms of the verb **sum** are displayed in Chapter e).

b) Developed example for the 3rd conjugation [189]

Indicative			Subjunctive		
Perfect			*Perfect*		
rectus, -a, -um	+	sum, es, est	rectus, -a, -um	+	sim, sis, sit
recti, -ae, -a	+	sumus, estis, sunt	recti, -ae, -a	+	simus, sitis, sint
Pluperfect			*Pluperfect*		
rectus, -a, -um	+	eram, eras, erat	rectus, -a, -um	+	essem, esses, esset
recti, -ae, -a	+	eramus, eratis, erant	recti, -ae, -a	+	essemus, essetis, essent
Future perfect					
rectus, -a, -um	+	ero, eris, erit			
recti, -ae, -a	+	erimus, eritis, erunt			

For instance,

– to say GREEK MEN HAVE BEEN RULED BY ROMANS, we would choose **recti sunt** for HAVE BEEN RULED;
– to say GREEK WOMEN HAD BEEN RULED BY ROMANS, we would choose **rectae erant** for HAD BEEN RULED;
– to say YOU (A MAN) WILL HAVE BEEN RULED BY ROMANS, we would choose **rectus eris** for WILL HAVE BEEN RULED.

c) Translation [190]

1/ Do not translate these compound verbal forms word by word, as the final result would be deceptive; for instance, do not translate **rectus sum** by I AM (**sum**) RULED (**rectus**), as I AM RULED would in fact have a *present tense* meaning, not a *perfect tense* meaning. We must take into account that the combination of a participle and a form of the verb **sum** will mean that we are in fact in front of the verbal tense which is the one at the right of the box to which that form of **sum** belongs; for instance, **sum** is a present form, but its combination with the participle **rectus** means that the combination **rectus sum** is in fact a *perfect tense* (as the perfect tense is the tense which is immediately at the right of the present tense box).

- Postero die porta Iovis ... iussu proconsulum *aperta est* THE FOLLOWING DAY THE DOOR OF JUPITER WAS OPENED BY ORDER OF THE PROCONSUL (Livy, *Ab Urbe Condita*).

2/ Nevertheless, in some cases we must translate literally if the combination of *participle + verb* **sum** indicates a state rather than a passive action. For instance, **Ianua aperta est** can mean THE DOOR HAS BEEN OPENED, but if we translate it literally it will mean THE DOOR IS OPEN, indicating the state of something (IS OPEN) rather than a process (HAS BEEN OPENED). Context will make it clear.

- Si *aperta* ianua *fuisset*, funus meum parares hoc tempore, pater IF MY DOOR HAD BEEN OPEN, YOU WOULD BE PREPARING MY FUNERAL NOW, FATHER (Livy, *Ab Urbe Condita*).
  ✧ Perseus is claiming that some people came to kill him, but fortunately the door was closed.

d) Other conjugations [191]

The same would happen with any other verb, to whichever conjugation it belongs: all we must change is the participial form; we offer here the conjugation in these tenses for the verbs we have been using as patterns:

1st conjugation

Indicative			Subjunctive		
Perfect			*Perfect*		
amatus, -a, -um	+	sum, es, est	amatus, -a, -um	+	sim, sis, sit
amati, -ae, -a	+	sumus, estis, sunt	amati, -ae, -a	+	simus, sitis, sint
Pluperfect			*Pluperfect*		
amatus, -a, -um	+	eram, eras, erat	amatus, -a, -um	+	essem, esses, esset
amati, -ae, -a	+	eramus, eratis, erant	amati, -ae, -a	+	essemus, essetis,, essent
Future perfect					
amatus, -a, -um	+	ero, eris, erit			
amati, -ae, -a	+	erimus,, eritis, erunt			

2nd conjugation

Indicative			Subjunctive		
Perfect			*Perfect*		
monitus, -a, -um	+	sum, es, est	monitus, -a, -um	+	sim, sis, sit
moniti, -ae, -a	+	sumus, estis, sunt	moniti, -ae, -a	+	simus, sitis, sint
Pluperfect			*Pluperfect*		
monitus, -a, -um	+	eram, eras, erat	monitus, -a, -um	+	essem, esses, esset
moniti, -ae, -a	+	eramus, eratis, erant	moniti, -ae, -a	+	essemus, essetis, essent
Future perfect					
monitus, -a, -um	+	ero, eris, erit			
moniti, -ae, -a	+	erimus, eritis, erunt			

4th conjugation

Indicative			Subjunctive		
Perfect			*Perfect*		
auditus, -a, -um	+	sum, es, est	auditus, -a, -um	+	sim, sis, sit
auditi, -ae, -a	+	sumus, estis, sunt	auditi, -ae, -a	+	simus, sitis, sint
Pluperfect			*Pluperfect*		
auditus, -a, -um	+	eram, eras, erat	auditus, -a, -um	+	essem, esses, esset
auditi, -ae, -a	+	eramus, eratis, erant	auditi, -ae, -a	+	essemus, essetis, essent
Future perfect					
auditus, -a, -um	+	ero, eris, erit			
auditi, -ae, -a	+	erimus, eritis, erunt			

Mixed conjugation

Indicative			Subjunctive		
Perfect			*Perfect*		
captus, -a, -um	+	sum, es, est	captus, -a, -um	+	sim, sis, sit
capti, -ae, -a	+	sumus, estis, sunt	capti, -ae, -a	+	simus, sitis, sint
Pluperfect			*Pluperfect*		
captus, -a, -um	+	eram, eras, erat	captus, -a, -um	+	essem, esses, esset
capti, -ae, -a	+	eramus, eratis, erant	capti, -ae, -a	+	essemus, essetis, essent
Future perfect					
captus, -a, -um	+	ero, eris, erit			
capti, -ae, -a	+	erimus, eritis, erunt			

Some examples:

- Veneno *necatus est* HE WAS KILLED WITH POISON (Anon., *Rhetorica ad Herennium*).
- *Auditus est* magno silentio HE WAS LISTENED TO WITH GREAT SILENCE (Cicero, *Epistulae ad Quintum Fratrem*).
- Vox subito *audita est* SUDDENLY, A VOICE WAS HEARD (Ovid, *Metamorphoses*).
- Cum domos redissent, iterum *capti sunt* WHEN THEY HAD RETURNED HOME, THEY WERE CAPTURED AGAIN (Livy, *Ab Urbe Condita*).
- *Servatus est* a procuratore summa cum diligentia HE WAS PROTECTED BY THE DEPUTY WITH GREAT DILIGENCE (Cicero, *Pro Quinctio*).
- *Conservatae sunt* Syracusae SYRACUSE WAS SAVED (Cicero, *In Verrem*).
- Cupiditas belli gerendi *iniecta est* THE DESIRE OF MAKING WAR WAS THROWN IN (Caesar, *De Bello Gallico*).
  ✧ Obviously, this is an extremely literal translation, but the sense of "Everybody felt the desire of making war" is quite evident.

d) Deponent and semi-deponent verbs

1. Deponent verbs [192]

a) Definition of *deponent verb*

Some Latin verbs present an interesting characteristic: while they conjugate their tenses using a passive form, they are active in meaning. These verbs are called *deponent verbs.*

As their morphology comprehends only passive forms (except for some participles), the dictionary entry form will be passive as well; e.g. for the verb TO LOVE we find **amo, -are, -avi, -atum**, for the verb TO URGE, which is deponent, the dictionary will give us **hortor, -ari, -atus sum**, featuring the usual parts of the verb (1st person of the present, infinitive and 1st person of the perfect) but in passive voice. Observe that with deponent verbs only three forms are given in the dictionary entry, because the fourth one, the supine, is already shown in the 1st person of the perfect (**hortatus sum**). Remember that the supine is sometimes used to construct participles.

Compare and contrast these examples:

- *Hortor* — I URGE (NOT I AM URGED).
- Milites *hortati sunt* eum — THE SOLDIERS URGED HIM (NOT THE SOLDIERS WERE URGED ...).
- *Caesar eos hortabatur* — CAESAR WAS URGING THEM (NOT CAESAR WAS BEING URGED ...).
- Miltiades *hortatus est* pontis custodes — MILTIADES ENCOURAGED THOSE GUARDING THE BRIDGE (Nepos, *Vitae*).

b) How can they be identified?

There are many deponent verbs and their frequent use makes them easy to remember and then identify. Anyway, some pieces of advice will follow with regard to the identification of such verbs.

1/ If we find a sentence like **Milites hortati sunt eum** and we remember that this verb means TO URGE but we do not know whether it is deponent or not, the presence of **eum**, a direct object, will tell us that the verb cannot have a passive meaning, as this would make the sentence mean THE SOLDIERS WERE URGED... and we would not know how to translate **eum**; therefore, it must be deponent, and the translation THE SOLDIERS URGED HIM makes perfect sense.

2/ If, on the other hand, we do not know the meaning of the verb and we look it up in the dictionary, we will not find **horto**, but **hortor**, which means that the verb is deponent and that the meaning will be active.

3/ If we find the sentence **Gladiatores necantur in Circo** and we remember the meaning of the verb but do not remember whether it is deponent or not (and therefore we do not know whether the sentence means THE GLADIATORS KILL IN THE CIRCUS or THE GLADIATORS ARE KILLED IN THE CIRCUS), we should look it up in the dictionary where we would find that the dictionary shows the form **neco**: this means that it is a "normal" verb and that, therefore, the passive form used in that sentence actually expresses a passive action, so that the correct translation is THE GLADIATORS ARE KILLED IN THE CIRCUS. The choice would have been immediate if the phrase featured a personal agent in ablative (e.g. **a militibus** BY THE SOLDIERS).

c) Most frequent deponent verbs [193]

In this section, the most frequent deponent verbs are introduced in a way that may help you to remember them.

1/ First of all the verbs TO BE BORN and TO DIE:

nascor, nasci, natus sum	TO BE BORN
morior, mori, mortuus sum	TO DIE

2/ The following pairs feature verbs with the same meaning:

fateor, fateri, fassus sum	TO CONFESS	
confiteor, confiteri, confessus sum	TO CONFESS	
potior, potiri, potitus sum	TO ACQUIRE (+ Abl.)	
adipiscor, adipisci, adeptus sum	TO ACQUIRE	
conor, conari, conatus sum	TO TRY	✧ in the sense of attempt
experior, experiri, expertus sum	TO TRY	✧ in the sense of experiencing

3/ This pair comprehends verbs with opposite meaning:

fruor, frui, fructus sum	TO ENJOY
irascor, irasci, iratus sum	TO BE ANGRY

4/ Verbs of movement:

proficiscor, proficisci, profectus sum	TO SET OUT
revertor, reverti, reversus sum	TO RETURN
comitor, comitari, comitatus sum	TO ACCOMPANY
(ex)sequor, sequi, secutus sum	TO FOLLOW
gradior, gradi, gressus sum	TO STEP

5/ Compound forms of **sequor**:

consequor, consequi, consecutus sum	TO FOLLOW, TO OBTAIN
persequor, persequi, persecutus sum	TO PERSECUTE
prosequor, prosequi, prosecutus sum	TO CONTINUE
insequor, insequi, insecutus sum	TO FOLLOW FROM A SHORT DISTANCE

6/ Compound forms of **gradior**:

aggredior, aggredi, aggressus sum	TO APPROACH, TO ATTACK	✧ Also found in the form **adgre-**
egredior, egredi, egressus sum	TO GO OUT	
ingredior, ingredi, ingressus sum	TO ENTER	
progredior, progredi, progressus sum	TO ADVANCE	
regredior, regredi, regressus sum	TO RETURN	

7/ Verbs expressing feelings, activities of the mind, etc.:

miror, mirari, miratus sum — TO ADMIRE
vereor, vereri, veritus sum — TO FEAR
obliviscor, oblivisci, oblitus sum — TO FORGET (+ Gen.)
reor, reri, ratus sum — TO THINK
queror, queri, questus sum — TO COMPLAIN
precor, precari, precatus sum — TO BEG
patior, pati, passus sum — TO SUFFER, TO TOLERATE
arbitror, arbitrari, arbitratus sum — TO JUDGE

8/ Other deponent verbs:

orior, oriri, ortus sum — TO RISE
ulciscor, ulcisci, ultus sum — TO AVENGE
minor, minari, minatus sum — TO THREATEN
polliceor, polliceri, pollicitus sum — TO PROMISE
utor, uti, usus sum — TO USE (+ Abl.)
hortor, hortari, hortatus sum — TO URGE
molior, moliri, molitus sum — TO WORK
loquor, loqui, locutus sum — TO SPEAK
mereor, mereri, meritus sum — TO DESERVE

Some examples:

- Eadem Galli *fatentur* THE GAULS CONFESSED THE SAME THINGS (Sallust, *Bellum Catilinae*).
- Suum fatum *querebantur* THEY COMPLAINED ABOUT THEIR FATE (Caesar, *De Bello Gallico*).
- Quae ... *locutus sum*, ea, iudices, a vobis spero esse in bonam partem accepta THE THINGS I HAVE SAID, JUDGES, I HOPE HAVE BEEN WELL RECEIVED BY YOU IN GOOD PART (Cicero, *Pro Archia*).
- Quod ... idoneum videbatur, cum summo studio domi *exsequebantur* WHATEVER SEEMED TO BE ADEQUATE, THEY FOLLOWED IT AT HOME WITH GREAT DILIGENCE (Sallust, *Bellum Catilinae*).
- Cassius semet eo brevi venturum *pollicetur* CASSIUS PROMISES TO GO THERE SHORTLY (Sallust, *Bellum Catilinae*).
- Ex urbe *proficiscitur* HE LEAVES THE CITY (Sallust, *Bellum Catilinae*).

2. Nominal forms in deponent verbs [194]

a) Infinitives

The rule of "passive form but active meaning" works for *present* and *perfect* infinitives as well: their active forms do not exist, and the passive forms replace them:

Present: conari — TO TRY
Past: conatum esse — TO HAVE TRIED

Instead, the *future* infinitive is active in form, not passive, and of course is as well active in meaning:

Future: conaturum esse — TO BE ABOUT TO TRY

So only three out of the six forms possible forms of the infinitives (three active and three passive ones) exist in deponent verbs: the present and perfect passive and the future active, all with an active meaning. Let's see it exemplified in the verb **conor**:

	Present	*Past (or Perfect)*	*Future*
Active	non-existent; replaced by the passive form below	non-existent; replaced by the passive form below	**conaturum, -am, -um esse** TO BE ABOUT TO TRY
Passive	**conari** ↑ TO TRY ✧ Active meaning, as if above	**conatum, -am, -um esse** ↑ TO HAVE TRIED ✧ Active meaning, as if above	non-existent

Some examples:

- **Glorians maria montesque *polliceri* coepit** BOASTING, HE BEGAN TO PROMISE SEAS AND MOUNTAINS (Sallust, *Bellum Catilinae*). ✧ It is the Latin idiom that means TO PROMISE THE MOON.
- **Caesari cum id nuntiatum esset, eos per provinciam nostram iter facere *conari*, maturat ab urbe *proficisci*** WHEN IT WAS ANNOUNCED TO CAESAR THAT THEY WERE TRYING TO MAKE THEIR WAY THROUGH OUR PROVINCE, HE HASTENS TO SET OUT FROM THE CITY (Caesar, *De Bello Gallico*).

b) Participles [195]

With respect to participles, the situation is a little more complicated, as the rule "passive form but active meaning" is followed *only in one participle*; moreover, one of the passive participial forms does actually have a passive meaning.

Like in normal verbs, four participial forms (out of the possible six) exist also in deponent verbs, but remember that:

- ➩ The past passive participle will usually have active meaning (only deponent verbs, therefore, can have a perfect "active" participle).
- ➩ The future passive participle will indeed have a passive meaning, so it is the *only* form of a deponent verb that always has a passive meaning (although in some cases the perfect passive participle will keep its passive meaning as well).

The final table will look as follows (let's use the verb **hortor** as model):

	Present	*Past*	*Future*
Active	**hortans, -ntis** URGING, THAT URGES	non-existent; replaced by the passive form below ✧ Only deponent verbs can do this	**hortaturus, -a, -um** THAT IS ABOUT TO URGE
Passive	non-existent	**hortatus, -a, -um** ↑ THAT HAS URGED ✧ Almost always active meaning, as if above	**hortand-us, -a, -um** THAT MUST BE URGED ✧ It keeps its passive meaning

Further observations

1/ In some deponent verbs, the perfect passive participle will keep its passive meaning, like in the case of **emetior** TO MEASURE OUT: **emensus** means MEASURED OUT, it does not mean HAVING MEASURED OUT.

- **Ad Aratthum inde flumen itinere ingenti *emenso* retentus altitudine amnis mansit** HAVING MADE FROM THERE A LONG MARCH TO THE RIVER ARATTHUS, BEING HELD BY THE DEPTH OF THE RIVER HE HALTED (Livy, *Ab Urbe Condita*).
  - ✧ Theoretically, **itinere ingenti emenso** means A LARGE MARCH HAVING BEEN MEASURED OUT, as if somebody had measured the distance between the starting and the finishing point of the march.

Sometimes a verb can even have *both passive and active* meanings:

adeptus	(from **adipiscor**)	may either mean	ACQUIRED	or	HAVING ACQUIRED;
comitatus	(from **comitor**)	may either mean	ACCOMPANIED	or	HAVING ACCOMPANIED;
pollicitus	(from **polliceor**)	may either mean	PROMISED	or	HAVING PROMISED.

2/ In some cases the perfect participle may also convey a *present* meaning:

ratus	THINKING	rather than	HAVING THOUGHT,
usus	USING	rather than	HAVING USED,
veritus	FEARING	rather than	HAVING FEARED.

3/ The main characteristic of deponent verbs is possibly the fact that they have a perfect participle with active meaning. For example, we can say CAESAR, HAVING SAID THIS, WENT TO ROME using a participle agreeing with Caesar, because the verb **loquor** is deponent and it has a participial form that means HAVING SAID:

Caesar, haec *locutus*, Romam profectus est.

But we cannot do the same with regular verbs; for example, the sentence CAESAR, HAVING WRITTEN THE LETTER, WENT TO ROME, cannot be translated using a past participle because the verb **scribo** has no participle that means HAVING WRITTEN; for this reason, we have to change the structure and use an ablative absolute:

Caesar, *litteris scriptis*, Romam profectus est
✧ Literally, CAESAR, THE LETTER HAVING BEEN WRITTEN, WENT TO ROME.

Further examples:

- **Cum eum in itinere convenissent ... suppliciterque *locuti* flentes pacem petissent...** WHEN THEY MET HIM ON THE WAY ... AND SPEAKING IN A SUPPLIANT TONE AND CRYING, THEY ASKED FOR PEACE... (Caesar, *De Bello Gallico*).
- **Eius rei quae causa esset *miratus* ex ipsis quaesivit** WONDERING WHAT WAS THE REASON FOR THIS, HE ASKED THEM IN PERSON (Caesar, *De Bello Gallico*).
- **Caesar ex castris utrisque copias suas eduxit paulumque a maioribus castris *progressus* aciem instruxit** CAESAR LED OUT HIS ARMY FROM BOTH CAMPS AND, HAVING ADVANCED A LITTLE FROM THE LARGER ONE, HE ARRANGED THE BATTLE LINE (Caesar, *De Bello Gallico*).
- **E castris Helvetiorum *egressi* ad Rhenum finesque Germanorum contenderunt** HAVING GONE OUT OF THE CAMP OF THE HELVETII, THEY HEADED FOR THE RHINE AND THE BORDER OF THE GERMANS (Caesar, *De Bello Gallico*).
- ***Conantes* dicere prohibuit** WHEN THEY TRIED TO TALK, HE PREVENTED THEM (Caesar, *De Bello Gallico*).

c) Gerund and supine [196]

Gerund and supine are formed in deponent verbs following the same rules as those for normal verbs:

Gerund: loquendum, hortandum, etc.
Supine: locutum, hortatum, etc.

- Caesar *loquendi* finem fecit — CAESAR STOPPED SPEAKING (Caesar, *De Bello Gallico*).
- Praesumpta spes *hortandi* causas exemerat — CONFIDENT HOPE HAD REMOVED ANY REASON FOR ENCOURAGEMENT (Tacitus, *Annales*).

3. Semi-deponent verbs [197]

a/ Semi-deponent verbs feature the main characteristic of deponent verbs, i.e. they have a passive form but active meaning, but this rule applies *only* to tenses formed on the perfect-stem (the right-hand side column of tenses in our usual chart); tenses formed on the present-stem (the left-hand side column of tenses in our usual chart) present normal active forms. Therefore, the main parts of the verb given by dictionaries are a combination of active and passive forms, as in the following example:

audeo, -ere, ausus sum TO DARE

Observe that only the perfect tense form is passive (but with active meaning), as it is the only one that belongs to the column of tenses with passive form.

Other semi-deponent verbs are:

soleo, -ere, solitus sum — TO BE ACCUSTOMED TO
gaudeo, -ere, gavisus sum — TO REJOICE
(con)fido, fidere, fisus sum — TO TRUST (+ Dat.)
diffido, diffidere, diffisus sum — TO DISTRUST (+ Dat.)

Some examples:

- Ibi perpauci ... viribus *confisi* tranare contenderunt — THERE A FEW MEN, RELYING ON THEIR STRENGTH, ENDEAVOURED TO SWIM ACROSS (Caesar, *De Bello Gallico*).
- Etiam ad me venire *ausus es* — YOU EVEN DARED TO COME TO ME (Cicero, *In Catilinam*).
- Platonis libros *solitus est* divulgare — HE USED TO POPULARISE PLATO'S BOOKS (Cicero, *Epistulae ad Atticum*).

b/ The verb fio, fieri, factus sum could be considered as a semi-deponent verb, but given its peculiar morphology, deriving from the fact that it is a combination of two different verbs, it will be the object of a specific section of the chapter on Irregular Verbs.

4. Passive deponent verbs [198]

Passive deponent verbs curiously experience the inverse phenomenon of regular deponent verbs: they are active in form, but passive in meaning:

vapulo, -are, -avi (no supine) TO BE FLOGGED
exulo, -are, -avi, -atum TO BE BANISHED, TO BE SENT INTO EXILE
✧ But its use with active meaning TO BANISH is also found.

Example:

- **Mori atque *exulare* nobilissimos viros honoratissimosque passi sumus** WE PERMITTED THE MOST NOBLE AND MOST DISTINGUISHED MEN TO SUFFER DEATH AND TO BE SENT INTO EXILE (Livy, *Ab Urbe Condita*).

Final notes on deponent verbs

While the main points regarding deponent, semi-deponent and passive deponent verbs have been treated above, there is a number of additional little details that affect individual verbs specifically:

a/ Some passive deponent verbs derive from active verbs that have been transformed by phenomena of contractions. E.g.: **veneo, venire, venii** (no supine) TO BE SOLD < **venum eo** TO GO ON SALE.

- **Oppidum dirutum [est], ager *veniit*** THE CITY WAS DESTROYED, THE FIELD WAS SOLD (Livy, *Ab Urbe Condita*).

b/ Some deponent verbs can have both active and passive meanings, like **complector** TO EMBRACE or TO BE EMBRACED.

c/ Others can have either active or passive form conveying the same meaning, like **fluctuo** or **fluctuor** TO FLUCTUATE.

- **Quid si mi [mihi] animus *fluctuat*?** WHAT IF MY HEART FLUCTUATES? (Plautus, *Mercator*).
- **Haud aliter meum cor *fluctuatur*** NOT IN ANOTHER WAY MY HEART FLUCTUATES (Seneca iunior, *Medea*).

d/ Moreover, the effort of some grammarians to achieve purity in the language imposed concrete choices between active and passive: for instance, in specific cases we can find **loquis** YOU SPEAK, which has been derived from the formerly deponent **loquor**, etc.

e) Verb sum and its compounds

1. Verb sum [199]

As in almost all languages, the verb that means TO BE is irregular; nevertheless, the irregularities affect only the present-stem tenses, as the perfect-stem tenses are formed in the usual way: take the third principal part, remove the final -i, and form them following the usual procedure.

Of the three present-stem tenses, the irregularities concentrate especially in the present tense; this is a pattern that applies also to the other irregular verbs.

The principal parts of the verb are: **sum, esse, fui** (no supine).

Indicative

Present-stem		Perfect-stem	
Present		*Perfect*	
sum	I AM	fui	I WAS / HAVE BEEN
es		fuisti	
est		fuit	
sumus		fuimus	
estis		fuistis	
sunt		fuerunt / -ere	
Imperfect		*Pluperfect*	
eram	I WAS	fueram	I HAD BEEN
eras		fueras	
erat		fuerat	
eramus		fueramus	
eratis		fueratis	
erant		fuerant	
Future		*Future perfect*	
ero	I WILL BE	fuero	I WILL HAVE BEEN
eris		fueris	
erit		fuerit	
erimus		fuerimus	
eritis		fueritis	
erunt		fuerint	

Subjunctive

Present-stem	Perfect-stem
Present	*Perfect*
sim	fuerim
sis	fueris
sit	fuerit
simus	fuerimus
sitis	fueritis
sint	fuerint
Imperfect	*Pluperfect*
essem	fuissem
esses	fuisses
esset	fuisset
essemus	fuissemus
essetis	fuissetis
essent	fuissent

✧ *In the indicative,* note that, apart from the absence of the usual modal-temporal characteristics, the imperfect and the future are relatively regular; it is in the present tense where we find alternations of stem.

✧ *In the subjunctive*, note that the imperfect goes on following the rule of *infinitive + personal endings.*

Imperative

2nd *singular*	**es**	BE!
2nd *plural*	**este**	BE!

Participles

Obviously, the verb TO BE does not have passive forms. This applies also to the infinitives.

	Present	*Past*	*Future*
Active	non-existent	non-existent	**futurus, -a, -um** THAT IS ABOUT TO BE

Infinitives

	Present	*Past*	*Future*
Active	**esse** TO BE	**fuisse** TO HAVE BEEN	**futurum, -am, -um esse** TO BE ABOUT TO BE

Note

The compound infinitive **futurum (-am / -um / -os / -as / -a) esse** can be replaced by the single word **fore.**

Gerund and supine

non-existent

2. Compounds of sum [200]

a) Their meaning

There are several verbs, of very frequent use, that are formed by adding a prepositional prefix to the verb **sum**. Their meaning is always related to the concept of "being", and the prepositional prefix gives the verb its specific meaning.

These are the main compounds of **sum**; each one of them may have several translations in English, especially because of their use in idiomatic expressions, we offer here the basic one:

absum, abesse, afui	TO BE ABSENT, TO BE FAR AWAY
adsum, adesse, adfui	TO BE PRESENT, TO SUPPORT
desum, deesse, defui	TO BE LACKING

insum, inesse, infui	TO BE INSIDE
intersum, interesse, interfui	TO BE IN THE MIDDLE, TO INTERVENE
obsum, obesse, offui	TO BE AGAINST
praesum, praeesse, praefui	TO BE AT THE FRONT
supersum, superesse, superfui	TO REMAIN, TO SURVIVE.

b) Their irregularities

1/ We can see that, in some cases, the contact between the final consonant of the preposition and the **f-** of **fui** etc. produces some changes in the preposition:

abfui > afui
adfui > affui

Moreover, in some cases we can find more than one possible form.

2/ A curious irregularity is that, although the verb **sum** has no present participle, its compound **absum** has produced the present participle **absens, -entis** ABSENT:

- Et illam ducere cupiebat et metuebat *absentem patrem* HE BOTH WANTED TO TAKE THE GIRL AND WAS AFRAID OF THE ABSENT FATHER (Terentius Afer, *Phormio*).

c) Their regime [201]

1/ Some of them can be used without any kind of object, like for instance **adsum**, just in the sense of TO BE PRESENT:

- *Adsum*, impera, si quid vis HERE I AM, GIVE AN ORDER, IF YOU WANT ANYTHING (Plautus, *Miles Gloriosus*).

But they may require an object, like for instance **adsum** in the sense of TO SUPPORT:

- Quis nostrum *adfuit* Vargunteio? WHO OF US SUPPORTED VARGUNTEIUS? (Cicero, *Pro Sulla*).

2/ When they need an object to complete their meaning, almost always it will be in dative (as in the example above):

- Caesar legioni *praeerat* CAESAR WAS AT THE FRONT OF (IN COMMAND OF) THE LEGION.
- Messius III cohortibus praeerat MESSIUS WAS IN COMMAND ("AT THE FRONT") OF THREE COHORTS (Anon., *Bellum Africum*).
- Tibi semper *adero* I WILL ALWAYS SUPPORT YOU.
- Mihi *desunt* tres libri I AM MISSING THREE BOOKS ✧ Literally, THREE BOOKS ARE LACKING TO ME.
- Proelio *interfui* I WAS IN THE MIDDLE OF THE BATTLE, I INTERVENED IN THE BATTLE.
- ... Antonium, qui ei legioni *praeerat*... ANTHONY, WHO WAS IN COMMAND OF THAT LEGION (Caesar, *Bellum Civile*).
- Tota Metelli cohors hominum non ingratorum *aderat* Apronio THE WHOLE COHORT OF METELLUS, A COHORT OF NOT UNGRATEFUL MEN, SUPPORTED APRONIUS (Cicero, *In Verrem*).
- Non *deest* rei publicae consilium neque auctoritas huius ordinis THE STATE DOES NOT LACK DECISION POWER NOR AUTHORITY OF THIS BODY [THE SENATE] (Cicero, *In Catilinam*).

3/ **Absum** is a special case, as it will usually be followed by **ab** + *ablative* when distances are referred to:

- Tarentum multum *abest* a Roma — TARENTUM IS VERY FAR AWAY FROM ROME.
- Hic locus *abest* a Clupeis passuum XXII milia (Caesar, *Bellum Civile*). — THIS PLACE IS 22 MILES AWAY FROM CLUPEAE

4/ We must take into account that compounds of **sum** produce a lot of idiomatic expressions, which will affect the way in which they must be translated and their regime.

3. Verb possum [202]

[From now on, translations are not included any more.]

This compound of **sum** deserves special attention, as it presents some irregularities. Its principal parts are: **possum, posse, potui** (no supine), and it means TO BE ABLE.

Indicative

Present-stem	Perfect-stem
Present	*Perfect*
possum	potui
potes	potuisti
potest	potuit
possumus	potuimus
potestis	potuistis
possunt	potuerunt / -ere
Imperfect	*Pluperfect*
poteram	potueram
poteras	potueras
poterat	potuerat
poteramus	potueramus
poteratis	potueratis
poterant	potuerant
Future	*Future perfect*
potero	potuero
poteris	potueris
poterit	potuerit
poterimus	potuerimus
poteritis	potueritis
poterunt	potuerint

✧ In the present tense, **pot-** becomes **pos-** in front of those forms starting with **s-**. This is due to phonetic assimilation (**potsum** > **possum** etc.). This will apply also to the present subjunctive.

✧ Note that in the perfect-stem tenses it is not just adding **pot-** to the corresponding forms of **sum**: the **f-** of **fui** etc. has disappeared. This will apply also to the subjunctive.

Subjunctive

Present-stem	**Perfect-stem**
Present	*Perfect*
possim	potuerim
possis	potueris
possit	potuerit
possimus	potuerimus
possitis	potueritis
possint	potuerint
Imperfect	*Pluperfect*
possem	potuissem
posses	potuisses
posset	potuisset
possemus	potuissemus
possetis	potuissetis
possent	potuissent

✧ Note that the imperfect goes on following the rule of *infinitive + personal endings.*

Imperative, gerund and supine

non-existent

Participles

	Present	*Past*	*Future*
Active	potens, -entis	non-existent	non-existent

The same curious phenomenon as with the compound **absum**: although the verb **sum** on its own lacks present participle, the compound **possum** has one: **potens, -entis**. Nevertheless, this participle is rather used as an adjective (although a participle is obviously an adjective) with the meaning of POWERFUL.

Infinitives

	Present	*Past*	*Future*
Active	posse	potuisse	non-existent

Some examples of its use:

- Hoc toto proelio ... aversum hostem videre nemo *potuit* IN THIS WHOLE BATTLE NOBODY COULD SEE AN ENEMY TURNED IN FLIGHT (Caesar, *De Bello Gallico*).
- *Possumus* hoc quoque ex te audire? CAN WE HEAR THIS ALSO FROM YOU? (Cicero, *Pro Quinctio*).

- Quod *poterant*, id audebant WHAT THEY COULD, THEY DARED TO DO IT (Cicero, *Pro Quinctio*).
- Ego contra ostendo non modo nihil eorum fecisse Sex. Roscium sed ne *potuisse* quidem facere ON THE CONTRARY: I PROVE THAT S. ROSCIUS NOT ONLY HAS DONE NOTHING OF THESE THINGS BUT WOULD NOT EVEN HAVE BEEN ABLE TO DO THEM (Cicero, *Pro Roscio Amerino*).

4. **Verb** prosum [203]

Another compound of **sum** that deserves special attention: the suffix **pro-** becomes **prod-** (which was in fact the original prefix) in front of forms that begin with a vowel. Its principal parts are: **prosum, prodesse, profui** (no supine). It means TO BE OF USE.

Indicative

Present-stem	**Perfect-stem**
Present	*Perfect*
prosum	profui
prodes	profuisti
prodest	profuit
prosumus	profuimus
prodestis	profuistis
prosunt	profuerunt/-ere
Imperfect	*Pluperfect*
proderam	profueram
proderas	profueras
proderat	profuerat
proderamus	profueramus
proderatis	profueratis
proderant	profuerant
Future	*Future perfect*
prodero	profuero
proderis	profueris
proderit	profuerit
proderimus	profuerimus
proderitis	profueristis
proderunt	profuerint

Subjunctive

Present-stem	**Perfect-stem**
Present	*Perfect*
prosim	profuerim
prosis	profueris
prosit	profuerit
prosimus	profuerimus
prositis	profueritis
prosint	profuerint
Imperfect	*Pluperfect*
prodessem	profuissem
prodesses	profuisses
prodesset	profuisset
prodessemus	profuissemus
prodessetis	profuissetis
prodessent	profuissent

Imperative

2nd singular	prodes
2nd plural	prodeste

Participles

	Present	*Past*	*Future*
Active	non-existent	non-existent	profuturus, -a, -um

Infinitives

	Present	*Past*	*Future*
Active	prodesse	profuisse	profuturum, -am, -um esse

Gerund and supine

non-existent

Some examples of its use:

- Flacco vero quid *profuit*? BUT WHAT PROFIT WAS THIS FOR FLACCUS? (Cicero, *Pro Flacco*).
- Non, si tibi antea profuit, semper *proderit* NOT ALWAYS WILL IT BE PROFITABLE FOR YOU, EVEN IF PREVIOUSLY IT HAS BEEN (Cicero, *Philippicae*).
- Multum illam *profuturam* puto I CONSIDER IT VERY BENEFICIAL (Cicero, *De Divinatione*).
- ... si *profutura* est rei publicae, ... IF IT IS PROFITABLE TO THE STATE, ... (Cicero, *Epistula ad Octavianum*).
- Hoc mihi *profuit* THIS WAS OF USE TO ME.

  ✧ Like almost all compounds of **sum**, it rules a dative.
- Quid enim potest ... rei publicae *prodesse* nostra legatio? IN WHAT RESPECT CAN OUR LEGATION BE OF USE TO THE STATE? (Cicero, *Philippicae*).
- Non modo igitur nihil *prodest* sed obest etiam Clodi mors Miloni THEREFORE, CLODIUS' DEATH NOT ONLY IS OF NO PROFIT FOR MILO BUT EVEN IS A HINDRANCE (Cicero, *Pro Milone*).

f) Irregular verbs

1. Verb volo [204]

This verb means TO WANT, and its principal parts are **volo, velle, volui** (no supine).

Indicative

Present-stem	Perfect-stem
Present	*Perfect*
volo	volui
vis	voluisti
vult	voluit
volumus	voluimus
vultis	voluistis
volunt	voluerunt / -ere
Imperfect	*Pluperfect*
volebam	volueram
volebas	volueras
volebat	voluerat
volebamus	volueramus
volebatis	volueratis
volebant	voluerant
Future	*Future perfect*
volam	voluero
voles	volueris
volet	voluerit
volemus	voluerimus
voletis	volueritis
volent	voluerint

Subjunctive

Present-stem	Perfect-stem
Present	*Perfect*
velim	voluerim
velis	volueris
velit	voluerit
velimus	voluerimus
velitis	volueritis
velint	voluerint
Imperfect	*Pluperfect*
vellem	voluissem
velles	voluisses
vellet	voluisset
vellemus	voluissemus
velletis	voluissetis
vellent	voluissent

✧ Note that the future is formed as if the verb belonged to the 3rd conjugation.

✧ As usual, the irregularities concentrate on the present tense.

Imperative, gerund and supine

non-existent

Participles

	Present	*Past*	*Future*
Active	volens, -ntis	non-existent	non-existent

Infinitives

	Present	*Past*	*Future*
Active	velle	voluisse	non-existent

Some examples:

- Debetis *velle* quae *velimus* — YOU SHOULD WANT WHAT WE MAY WANT (Plautus, *Amphitruo*).
- Nunc iam illa non *vult* — SHE DOES NOT WANT ANY MORE (Catullus, *Carmina*).
- Hic respondere *voluit*, non lacessere — HE WANTED TO ANSWER, NOT TO IRRITATE (Terentius Afer, *Phormio*).

2. Verb nolo [205]

This verb means NOT TO WANT, and its principal parts are **nolo, nolle, nolui** (no supine). It is a contraction of **non + volo** etc., and it will be observed that some of the forms in the present indicative remain without contracting.

Indicative

Present-stem	Perfect-stem
Present	*Perfect*
nolo	nolui
non vis	noluisti
non vult	noluit
nolumus	noluimus
non vultis	noluistis
nolunt	noluerunt / -ere
Imperfect	*Pluperfect*
nolebam	nolueram
nolebas	nolueras
nolebat	noluerat
nolebamus	nolueramus
nolebatis	nolueratis
nolebant	noluerant
Future	*Future perfect*
nolam	noluero
noles	nolueris
nolet	noluerit
nolemus	noluerimus
noletis	nolueritis
nolent	noluerint

Subjunctive

Present-stem	Perfect-stem
Present	*Perfect*
nolim	noluerim
nolis	nolueris
nolit	noluerit
nolimus	noluerimus
nolitis	nolueritis
nolint	noluerint
Imperfect	*Pluperfect*
nollem	noluissem
nolles	noluisses
nollet	noluisset
nollemus	noluissemus
nolletis	noluissetis
nollent	noluissent

Imperative

2nd *singular*	noli
2nd *plural*	nolite

Notes

1/ Observe that **volo** does not have an imperative, but its compound **nolo** does have one.

2/ Remember that the imperative of **nolo** is used to express prohibitions: • **Noli hoc facere** DO NOT DO THIS!

Participles

	Present	*Past*	*Future*
Active	nolens, -ntis	non-existent	non-existent

Infinitives

	Present	*Past*	*Future*
Active	nolle	noluisse	non-existent

Gerund and supine

non-existent

Some examples:

- Si Carpinatius mihi tum respondere *noluit*, responde tu mihi nunc, Verres IF CARPINATIUS DID NOT WANT TO ANSWER TO ME THEN, YOU ANSWER TO ME NOW, VERRES (Cicero, *In Verrem*).
- Num *non vis* me obviam his ire? DON'T YOU WANT ME TO GO TO MEET THESE PEOPLE? (Plautus, *Mostellaria*).
- ... quendam, quem dicere *nolo* nomine ... SOMEONE, WHOM I DO NOT WANT TO MENTION BY NAME (Catullus, *Carmina*).
- *Noli* haec contemnere DO NOT DESPISE THESE MATTERS (Cicero, *Divinatio in Q. Caecilium*).
  ✧ Literally, DO NOT WANT TO DESPISE THESE MATTERS.
- *Nolunt* discere qui numquam didicerunt THOSE WHO NEVER LEARNT DO NOT WANT TO LEARN (Seneca iunior, *Dialogi*).

3. Verb malo [206]

This verb means TO PREFER, and its principal parts are **malo, malle, malui** (no supine). It is a contraction of **magis + volo** etc.

Indicative

Present-stem	Perfect-stem
Present	*Perfect*
malo	malui
mavis	maluisti
mavult	maluit
malumus	maluimus
mavultis	maluistis
malunt	maluerunt / -ere
Imperfect	*Pluperfect*
malebam	malueram
malebas	malueras
malebat	maluerat
malebamus	malueramus
malebatis	malueratis
malebant	maluerant
Future	*Future perfect*
malam	maluero
males	malueris
malet	maluerit
malemus	maluerimus
maletis	malueritis
malent	maluerint

Subjunctive

Present-stem	Perfect-stem
Present	*Perfect*
malim	maluerim
malis	malueris
malit	maluerit
malimus	maluerimus
malitis	malueritis
malint	maluerint
Imperfect	*Pluperfect*
mallem	maluissem
malles	maluisses
mallet	maluisset
mallemus	maluissemus
malletis	maluissetis
mallent	maluissent

✧ Note that the imperfect subjunctive goes on following the rule of *infinitive + personal endings.*

Imperative, participles, gerund and supine

non-existent

Infinitives

	Present	*Past*	*Future*
Active	malle	maluisse	non-existent

Some examples:

- Cato enim ipse iam servire quam pugnare *mavult* CATO HIMSELF PREFERS TO BE A SLAVE RATHER THAN TO FIGHT (Cicero, *Epistulae ad Atticum*).
- Inimicus quam amicus esse *maluit* HE PREFERRED TO BE AN ENEMY RATHER THAN A FRIEND (Cicero, *Philippicae*).
- Iam timent terram rates et maria *malunt* RAFTS FEAR LAND NOW AND THEY PREFER THE SEA (Seneca iunior, *Agamemnon*).

4. Verb *eo* and its compounds [207]

This verb means TO GO, and its principal parts are **eo, ire, ivi, itum**.

Indicative

Present-stem	**Perfect-stem**	
Present	*Perfect*	*(more frequent forms)*
eo	ivi	ii
is	ivisti	isti
it	ivit	iit
imus	ivimus	iimus
itis	ivistis	istis
eunt	iverunt	ierunt / -ere
Imperfect	*Pluperfect*	*(more frequent forms)*
ibam	iveram	ieram
ibas	iveras	ieras
ibat	iverat	ierat
ibamus	iveramus	ieramus
ibatis	iveratis	ieratis
ibant	iverant	ierant
Future	*Future perfect*	*(more frequent forms)*
ibo	ivero	iero
ibis	iveris	ieris
ibit	iverit	ierit
ibimus	iverimus	ierimus
ibitis	iveritis	ieritis
ibunt	iverint	ierint

Notes

a/ The future is formed as if the verb belonged to the 1st or 2nd conjugation.

b/ In the perfect-stem tenses, the forms with **-v-** are very unusual, even some of them are not found (but we have put all of them for the sake of uniformity).

c/ Moreover, in the perfect tense, **iisti** > **isti**, and **iistis** > **istis**, because **ii** > **i** before **-s-**. So, in fact it is a two-step change: **ivisti(s)** > **iisti(s)** > **isti(s)**.

d/ The alternative form **ivere** (for **iverunt**) can be considered non-existent.

Subjunctive

Present-stem	**Perfect-stem**	
Present	*Perfect*	*(more frequent forms)*
eam	iverim	ierim
eas	iveris	ieris
eat	iverit	ierit
eamus	iverimus	ierimus
eatis	iveritis	ieritis
eant	iverint	ierint
Imperfect	*Pluperfect*	*(more frequent forms)*
irem	ivissem	issem
ires	ivisses	isses
iret	ivisset	isset
iremus	ivissemus	issemus
iretis	ivissetis	issetis
irent	ivissent	issent

✧ With respect to perfect and pluperfect, see notes b/ and c/ above.

Imperative

2nd singular: i 2nd plural: ite

⌑ As a curiosity: the 2nd singular imperative is the shortest possible sentence in Latin: I! Go!

Participles

	Present	*Past*	*Future*
Active	iens, euntis	non-existent	iturus, -a, -um
Passive	non-existent	non-existent	eundus, -a, -um

✧ Observe the internal change of stem in the present participle.

✧ The use of the future passive participle will be explained in the section on Impersonal verbs.

Infinitives

	Present	*Past*		*Future*
Active	ire	isse	✧ ivisse is hardly used	iturum, -am, -um esse

Gerund and supine

Gerund

Acc.	eundum
Gen.	eundi
Dat.	eundo
Abl.	eundo

Supine

itum

✧ The supine itu is unusual.

Some examples:

- Non *it*, negat se *ituram [esse]* SHE IS NOT GOING, SHE SAYS SHE WILL NOT GO (Plautus, *Bacchides*).
- Turba miratur matrum et prospectat *euntem* THE CROWD OF MOTHERS IS ASTONISHED AND LOOKS AT HER AS SHE PASSES BY (Vergil, *Aeneis*).

  ✧ Literally, "LOOKS AT THE PASSER-BY".
- Nunc ad conloquium *eundo* temptavi pacem NOW, BY GOING TO A MEETING, I TRIED TO ACHIEVE PEACE (Livy, *Ab Urbe Condita*).
- Si *itura sit* Athenas, ... IF SHE IS ABOUT TO GO TO ATHENS, ... (Plautus, *Miles Gloriosus*).
- *Ibo* ad forum I WILL GO TO THE FORUM (Statius, *Palliatae*).
- Obviam hosti consules *eunt* THE CONSULS GO TO CONFRONT THE ENEMY (Livy, *Ab Urbe Condita*).

Compounds of eo [208]

This verb has several compounds, the main ones of which are these (as usual, each one of them may have several translations into English, we offer here the basic one):

abeo	TO GO AWAY	obeo	TO GO TO MEET, TO OPPOSE
adeo	TO APPROACH	pereo	TO DIE
circumeo	TO GO AROUND	praeeo	TO GO IN THE FIRST POSITION
exeo	TO GO OUT	redeo	TO GO BACK
ineo	TO ENTER	transeo	TO CROSS

A very important characteristic is that the perfect-tense stem loses the -v- in a lot of these verbs (although both forms can be found): transii / transivi, circumii / circumivi, etc.

Some examples:

- Quo illae *abeunt*? WHERE ARE THOSE WOMEN GOING TO? (Plautus, *Bacchides*).
- *Exeuntem* me puer secutus est WHEN I WENT OUT, THE BOY FOLLOWED ME (Seneca senior, *Controversiae*).
- Posteaquam Verres magistratum *iniit*, ... AFTER VERRES BECAME MAGISTRATE (Cicero, *In Verrem*).

  ✧ Literally, AFTER VERRES ENTERED THE MAGISTRACY, ...
- Legati gentium regem *adibant* AMBASSADORS OF PEOPLES WENT TO THE KING (Curtius Rufus, *Historiae Alexandri Magni*).
- Ceteri qui in legatione mortem *obierunt* ... THE OTHER ONES WHO, IN THE LEGATION, WENT TO MEET DEATH ... (Cicero, *Philippicae*).
- *Redeuntes* equites quos possunt consectantur atque occidunt THEY PURSUE THE HORSEMEN THEY CAN AND THEY KILL THEM ON THEIR WAY BACK (Caesar, *De Bello Gallico*).

5. Verb fero and its compounds [209]

The verb means TO BEAR, TO CARRY, and its principal parts are fero, ferre, tuli, latum.

Indicative

Present-stem	Perfect-stem
Present	*Perfect*
fero	tuli
fers	tulisti
fert	tulit
ferimus	tulimus
fertis	tulistis
ferunt	tulerunt / -ere
Imperfect	*Pluperfect*
ferebam	tuleram
ferebas	tuleras
ferebat	tulerat
ferebamus	tuleramus
ferebatis	tuleratis
ferebant	tulerant
Future	*Future perfect*
feram	tulero
feres	tuleris
feret	tulerit
feremus	tulerimus
feretis	tuleritis
ferent	tulerint

Subjunctive

Present-stem	Perfect-stem
Present	*Perfect*
feram	tulerim
feras	tuleris
ferat	tulerit
feramus	tulerimus
feratis	tuleritis
ferant	tulerint
Imperfect	*Pluperfect*
ferrem	tulissem
ferres	tulisses
ferret	tulisset
ferremus	tulissemus
ferretis	tulissetis
ferrent	tulissent

✧ As usual, the irregularities concentrate on the present tense. Note also that the future is formed as if the verb belonged to the 3rd conjugation.

Imperative

2nd *singular* fer 2nd *plural* ferte

Note

There are three other verbs that also drop the final **-e** in the imperative singular:

facio: fac
duco: duc
dico: dic

Participles

	Present	*Past*	*Future*
Active	ferens, -ntis	non-existent	laturus, -a, -um
Passive	non-existent	latus, -a, -um	ferendus, -a, -um

Infinitives

	Present	*Past*	*Future*
Active	ferre	tulisse	laturum, -am, -um esse
Passive	ferri	latum, -am, -um esse	latum iri

Gerund and supine

Gerund

Acc.	ferendum
Gen.	ferendi
Dat.	ferendo
Abl.	ferendo

Supine

latum

✧ The supine **latu** is unusual.

Some examples:

- Timeo Danaos et dona *ferentis* — I FEAR THE GREEKS, EVEN WHEN THEY BRING GIFTS (Virgil, *Aeneis*).
- Quid iste *fert* tumultus? — WHAT DOES THIS BUSTLE BRING? (Horace, *Epodi*).
- Nihil *erat latum* de me — NOTHING HAD BEEN BROUGHT (NO REQUIREMENT HAD BEEN MADE) ABOUT ME (Cicero, *De Domo Sua*).
- Hoc *ferendum* nullo modo est — THIS DOES NOT HAVE TO BE TOLERATED IN ANY WAY (Cicero, *In Verrem*).

¤ A very common use of this verb is its 3rd person **fertur**, in the meaning of IT IS SAID, as if it were **dicitur**:

- *Fertur* Caesarem vicisse — IT IS SAID THAT CAESAR HAS CONQUERED.

Compounds of fero [210]

This verb has several compounds, and the fact that its main parts begin with different consonants produces some changes in the prepositional prefixes; the main ones of these compounds are these (as usual, each one of them may have several translations into English, we offer here the basic one):

aufero, auferre, abstuli, ablatum — TO REMOVE
confero, conferre, contuli, collatum — TO PUT TOGETHER, TO SUMMARISE
effero, efferre, extuli, elatum — TO TAKE OUT, TO MAKE PUBLIC

infero, inferre, intuli, illatum — TO INFER, TO TAKE INTO
offero, offerre, obtuli, oblatum — TO OFFER, TO PUT FORWARD
praefero, praeferre, praetuli, praelatum — TO PRESENT
profero, proferre, protuli, prolatum — TO PUT FORWARD
refero, referre, rettuli, relatum — TO BRING BACK, TO RELATE
suffero, sufferre, sustuli, sublatum — TO BEAR, TO SUFFER, TO TAKE AWAY

Some examples:

- Neminem huic *praefero* I PREFER NOBODY TO THIS ONE (Nepos, *Vitae*).
- Cum Romam profectus sum, zonas, quas plenas argenti *extuli*, eas ex provincia inanes *retuli* WHEN I SET OUT TO ROME, THE MONEY-BELTS THAT I TOOK OUT FULL OF SILVER, I BROUGHT THEM BACK FROM THE PROVINCE EMPTY (Sempronius Gracchus, *Orationes*).
- Signum Apollinis pulcherrimum ex Aesculapi religiosissimo fano *sustulisti*? DID YOU TAKE AWAY FROM THE MOST HOLY TEMPLE OF AESCULAPIUS A VERY NICE STATUE OF APOLLO (Cicero, *In Verrem*).
- In pauca, ut occupatus nunc sum, *confer* quid velis SUMMARISE IN FEW WORDS WHAT YOU WANT, BECAUSE I AM BUSY (Plautus, *Pseudolus*).
- At hic nihil domum suam *intulit* praeter memoriam nominis sempiternam BUT THIS ONE BROUGHT NOTHING INTO HIS HOUSE BUT AN ETERNAL MEMORY OF HIS NAME (Cicero, *De Officiis*).
- Cum bellum civitas aut inlatum defendit aut *infert* ... WHEN A STATE REPELS A WAR WAGED AGAINST IT OR WAGES IT ... (Caesar, *De Bello Gallico*).

6. Verb *edo* [211]

The verb means TO EAT, and its principal parts are **edo, esse, edi, esum**. As can be seen, the infinitive is identical to that of the verb **sum**, and also some forms in the present indicative.

✧ There is another verb, **edo, edere, edidi, editum** TO GIVE OUT. Do not confuse them.

Indicative

Present-stem	Perfect-stem
Present	*Perfect*
edo	edi
edis / es	edisti
edit / est	edit
edimus	edimus
editis / estis	edistis
edunt	ederunt / -ere
Imperfect	*Pluperfect*
edebam	ederam
edebas	ederas
edebat	ederat
edebamus	ederamus
edebatis	ederatis
edebant	ederant
Future	*Future perfect*
edam	edero
edes	ederis
edet	ederit
edemus	ederimus
edetis	ederitis
edent	ederint

Subjunctive

Present-stem		Perfect-stem
Present	*(alternative forms)*	*Perfect*
edam	edim	ederim
edas	edis	ederis
edat	edit	ederit
edamus	edimus	ederimus
edatis	editis	ederitis
edant	edint	ederint
Imperfect	*(alternative forms)*	*Pluperfect*
ederem	----	edissem
ederes	esses	edisses
ederet	esset	edisset
ederemus	essemus	edissemus
ederetis	essetis	edissetis
ederent	essent	edissent

✧ Note that the future is formed as if the verb belonged to the 1st or 2nd conjugation.

Imperative

2nd singular	ede / es
2nd plural	edite / este

Participles

	Present	*Past*	*Future*
Active	edens, -ntis	non-existent	esurus, -a, -um

Infinitives

	Present	*Past*	*Future*
Active	edere / esse	edisse	esurum, -am, -um esse

Gerund and supine

Gerund

Acc.	edendum
Gen.	edendi
Dat.	edendo
Abl.	edendo

Supine

esum
esu

Some examples:

- Me magnus *edebat* amor A GREAT LOVE WAS CONSUMING ME (Catullus, *Carmina*).
- Non ut *edam* vivo, sed ut vivam *edo* I DO NOT LIVE IN ORDER TO EAT, BUT EAT IN ORDER TO LIVE (Fabius Quintilianus, *Institutio Oratoria*).
- Carnes vero lupi *edisse* parituris prodest aut si incipientibus parturire sit iuxta qui ederit TO EAT WOLF FLESH IS BENEFICIAL FOR WOMEN NEAR TO GIVE BIRTH OR IF, WHEN THEY BEGIN TO GIVE BIRTH, SOMEONE WHO HAS EATEN IT IS NEXT TO THEM (Pliny, *Historia Naturalis*). ✧ In fact, **edisse** means TO HAVE EATEN, it is a perfect infinitive.

7. Verb fio

[212]

This verb is a special case of semi-deponent. It means TO BECOME, TO HAPPEN, TO BE DONE, TO TAKE PLACE (observe that some of the translations sound passive in English, while others sound active). The present-stem tenses are conjugated in active voice, and the perfect-stem tenses in passive voice, but like the passive of **facio, -ere, feci, factum** (TO HAPPEN, TO TAKE PLACE, etc. mean in fact TO BE DONE).

Its principal parts are **fio, fieri, factus sum**. Observe that the infinitive itself is passive, while normal semi-deponent verbs have it active.

Indicative

Present-stem	Perfect-stem
Present	*Perfect*
fio	factus, -a, -um
fis	+ sum, es, est
fit	
fimus	facti, -ae, -a
fitis	+ sumus, estis, sunt
fiunt	
Imperfect	*Pluperfect*
fiebam	factus, -a, -um
fiebas	+ eram, eras, erat
fiebat	
fiebamus	facti, -ae, -a
fiebatis	+ eramus, eratis, erant
fiebant	
Future	*Future perfect*
fiam	factus, -a, -um
fies	+ ero, eris, erit
fiet	
fiemus	facti, -ae, -a
fietis	+ erimus, eritis, erunt
fient	

Subjunctive

Present-stem	Perfect-stem
Present	*Perfect*
fiam	factus, -a, -um
fias	+ sim, sis, sit
fiat	
fiamus	facti, -ae, -a
fiatis	+ simus, sitis, sint
fiant	
Imperfect	*Pluperfect*
fierem	factus, -a, -um
fieres	+ essem, esses, esset
fieret	
fieremus	facti, -ae, -a
fieretis	+ essemus, essetis, essent
fierent	

Notes

a/ The future is formed as if the verb belonged to the 3rd conjugation.

b/ The imperfect subjunctive is formed as if on an imaginary active infinitive **fiere** + personal endings.

Imperative

2nd singular	fi
2nd plural	fite

Participles

[It is obvious that these forms correspond to those of the verb **facio**.]

	Present	*Past*	*Future*
Passive	non-existent	factus, -a, -um	faciendus, -a, -um

✧ Whether the perfect participle has active or passive meaning, it will depend on the translation we use according to the sentence: DONE, MADE, will obviously have a passive meaning in English, while for instance HAPPENED will have an active one.

Infinitives

[It is obvious that, except **fieri**, these forms correspond to those of the verb **facio**.]

	Present	*Past*	*Future*
Passive	fieri	factum, -am, -um esse	factum iri

Gerund

non-existent

In the examples we can see the variety of meanings:

- *Fit* in hostis impetus AN ATTACK AGAINST THE ENEMY TAKES PLACE (Caesar, *Bellum Civile*).
- Cur iste *fit* consul? WHY DOES THIS MAN BECOME CONSUL? (Cassius Longinus, *Oratio*).
- Quid deinde *fit*? WHAT HAPPENS THEN? (Cicero, *Pro Quinctio*).
- *Fit* sermo inter eos A CONVERSATION AMONG THEM TAKES PLACE (Cicero, *In Verrem*).
- Quid vis *fieri*? WHAT DO YOU WANT TO HAPPEN / TO BE DONE? (Plautus, *Amphitruo*).
- Id *fieri* non potest THIS CAN NOT HAPPEN (Cicero, *De Fato*).
- Quid enim *factum est*? WHAT HAPPENED? (Cicero, *Pro Roscio Comoedo*).
- Hoc Verre praetore *factum est* solum? Non, sed etiam quaestore Caecilio DID THIS TAKE PLACE ONLY WHEN VERRES WAS PRAETOR? NO, BUT ALSO WHEN CAECILIUS WAS QUAESTOR (Cicero, *In Q. Caecilium*).
- Pater conscriptus repente *factus est* SUDDENLY, HE WAS APPOINTED SENATOR (Cicero, *Philippicae*).
- *Factus est* a nostris impetus AN ATTACK WAS MADE BY OUR PEOPLE (Cicero, *Epistulae ad Quintum Fratrem*).

8. Defective verbs [213]

Defective verbs are those that do not have a complete conjugation.

a) The most frequent ones

❑ Odi TO HATE

This verb is used only in the perfect (right-hand side) tenses, but each of the three tenses has the meaning of the corresponding one found on the left-hand side:

– The perfect	**odi**	means	I HATE,	NOT	I HATED.
– The pluperfect	**oderam**	means	I HATED,	NOT	I HAD HATED.
– The future perfect	**odero**	means	I WILL HATE,	NOT	I WILL HAVE HATED.

- ***Odi* et amo** I HATE AND I LOVE (Catullus, *Carmina*).
- ***Oderam* hominem** I HATED THAT MAN (Cicero, *Epistulae ad Atticum*).

❑ Coepi TO BEGIN

The same as before: it has only perfect tenses, but with the difference that in this verb these tenses keep their proper meaning: the perfect does mean perfect, etc.:

– The perfect	**coepi**	means	I BEGAN.
– The pluperfect	**coeperam**	means	I HAD BEGUN.
– The future perfect	**coepero**	means	I WILL HAVE BEGUN.

- **Eo se recipere *coeperunt*** THEY BEGAN TO RETREAT THERE (Caesar, *De Bello Gallico*).
- **Interim miris modis odisse *coepit* Sostratam** MEANWHILE HE BEGAN TO HATE SOSTRATA IN AN INCREDIBLE WAY (Terentius Afer, *Hecyra*).

✧ In case the present-stem tenses are needed, we can make use of the verb **incipio**

❑ Memini TO REMEMBER

The same case as **odi**: perfect-stem tenses only, but with present-stem meaning:

– The perfect	**memini**	means	I REMEMBER,	NOT	I REMEMBERED.
– The pluperfect	**memineram**	means	I REMEMBERED,	NOT	I HAD REMEMBERED.
– The future perfect	**meminero**	means	I WILL REMEMBER,	NOT	I WILL HAVE REMEMBERED.

- **Nunc uxorem me esse *meministi* tuam?** NOW DO YOU REMEMBER THAT I AM YOUR WIFE? (Plautus, *Asinaria*).

This is one of the few verbs that we can find conjugated in the future imperative, in the forms **memento** (sing.) / **mementote** (pl.):

- **Illud semper *memento*** ALWAYS REMEMBER THAT (Cicero, *Epistulae ad Familiares*).
- **– *Mementote* illud, advocati** REMEMBER THAT, COUNSELLORS.
  – Meminimus WE REMEMBER IT (Plautus, *Poenulus*).

❑ **Novi** TO KNOW

The same case as **odi**: perfect-stem tenses only, but with present-stem meaning:

– The perfect	**novi**	means	I KNOW,	NOT I KNEW.
– The pluperfect	**noveram**	means	I KNEW,	NOT I HAD KNOWN.
– The future perfect	**novero**	means	I WILL KNOW,	NOT I WILL HAVE KNOWN.

- **Sed, si ego hos bene *novi*, ...** BUT, IF I KNOW THESE PEOPLE WELL, ... (Cicero, *Pro Roscio Amerino*).
- **– Qui sunt in lecto illo altero?** WHO ARE THERE IN THAT OTHER BED?
  – Interii, miser POOR ME, I AM LOST.
  – Hominem *novisti*? DO YOU KNOW THE MAN?
  – *Novi* I KNOW HIM (Plautus, *Bacchides*).

In fact, this verb is the perfect tense of **nosco** TO GET TO KNOW, but the perfect developed a present meaning, in the sense of I HAVE GOT TO KNOW therefore I KNOW.

b) Other defective verbs [214]

❑ Verbs of saying: **aio, inquam** and **fatur**

1/ **Aio** and **inquam**, both meaning TO SAY, have only some forms, but not the same ones. For instance, **aio** has some forms of the present (**aio, ais, ait, aiunt**), all of the imperfect (**aiebam, aiebas**, etc.) and one perfect form (**ait**), while **inquam** has present (**inquam, inquis, inquit, inquiunt**), no imperfect, but it has some future forms (**inquies, inquiet**), and also a perfect (**inquit**).

- **Narra, quid est? Quid *ait*?** TELL ME, WHAT IS IT? WHAT IS HE SAYING? (Plautus, *Poenulus*).
- **"Inimicum ego", *inquis*, "accuso meum"** YOU SAY "I ACCUSE MY ENEMY" (Cicero, *Pro Sulla*).
  ✧ Observe that **inquam** is usually placed in the middle of the reproduced words.

2/ With respect to **fatur** TO SPEAK, it is deponent, and apart from **fatur** itself hardly any other personal forms are found:

- **Sic *fatur* lacrimans** SO HE SPEAKS IN TEARS (Vergil, *Aeneis*).

Its gerund **fando** can be found often, but more than SAYING it means rather BY WORD:

- **... scelera nefaria, quae neque *fando* neque legendo audivimus** .... ABOMINABLE CRIMES THAT WE HAVE HEARD NEITHER BY WORD NOR BY READING (Porcius Cato, *Orationes*).

❑ **Queo** TO BE ABLE and **nequeo** NOT TO BE ABLE

Only some forms of different tenses are used.

- **Non *queo* iam plura scribere** I CAN NOT WRITE ANY MORE (Cicero, *Epistulae ad Familiares*).
- **Durare *nequeo* in aedibus** I CAN NOT REMAIN IN THE HOUSE (Plautus, *Amphitruo*).

❑ **Quaeso** TO PRAY

Only the present tense is used. This verb is used to soften a requirement, we could say that it is the equivalent to the English word PLEASE:

- **Dic, *quaeso*, quo modo?** TELL ME, PLEASE: IN WHAT WAY? (Cicero, *In Verrem*).
- **Attendite, *quaeso*, diligenter** PAY CLOSE ATTENTION, PLEASE (Cicero, *Pro Caecina*).

✧ This verb must not be confused with the verb **quaero, -ere, quaesivi, quaesitum** TO SEEK.

g) Overview of peculiar constructions

1. Previous notes [215]

Many verbs present some peculiarities in the way they are used, and not only in the case they use (as for instance **utor** uses the ablative: **utor gladio** I USE A SWORD) but also in other respects: whether they are followed by a subordinate clause or by an infinitive clause, etc.

This is not an exhaustive list of all possible usages, but we will try to offer a summary of the most frequent ones, presented by alphabetical order of the verbs. In any case, let's take into account that this is a field in which exceptions can be found, especially in poetry, where the use of the language is much more free.

Some of the usages may appear also in other parts of this grammar; for instance, the regime of **impero** is presented also in the chapter of indirect commands, **utor** followed by an ablative is presented also in the chapter of regime of verbs, etc.

2. List of verbs: peculiar constructions [216]

❑ abdico, -are, -avi, -atum TO ABDICATE

This verb is reflexive in Latin: you abdicate "yourself" from something:

- Magistratu *se abdicavit* HE ABDICATED FROM THE MAGISTRACY (Cicero, *In Catilinam*).

✧ Do not confuse this verb with **abdico, -ere, -dixi, -dictum** TO REFUSE.

❑ accedo, -ere, -cessi, -cessum TO APPROACH

1/ This verb usually rules a prepositional object of direction:

- Caesar *ad castra* accessit CAESAR APPROACHED THE CAMP.

2/ When use with an acusative of person, without preposition, it may mean TO APPROACH in a sense of "trying to obtain their friendship":

- *Caesarem* accedo I TRY TO OBTAIN CAESAR'S FRIENDSHIP.

But this is not always so, it may also mean TO APPROACH SOMEBODY in the sense of TO ACCOST.

3/ When used with a dative, it means TO AGREE WITH:

- *Caesari* accedo I AGREE WITH CAESAR.

But it may also mean TO FALL UPON:

- *Caesari* semper multae curae accedunt MANY WORRIES ARE ALWAYS FALLING UPON CAESAR.

❑ **appello, -are, -avi, -atum** TO CALL

As many other verbs, it can rule two accusatives (a direct object and a predicative object):

- *Te* appellant *sapientem* THEY CALL YOU WISE.
- *Beatiorem hanc* appello I CALL (CONSIDER) THIS WOMAN HAPPIER (Cicero, *De Finibus*).

✧ Do not confuse this verb with **appello, -ere, -puli, -pulsum** TO PUSH

❑ **arbitror, -ari, -atus sum** TO CONSIDER

This deponent verb can rule two accusatives:

- *Me* arbitror *civem Romanum* I CONSIDER MYSELF A ROMAN CITIZEN.
  ✧ It could be argued that in fact it rules an infinitive clause, with the infinitive **esse** to be supplied:
  Me arbitror civem Romanum *esse*.

❑ **cado, -ere, cecidi, casum** TO FALL

1/ The place from which we fall can be expressed either with **de** or with **ex**:

- Cado *de/ex equo* I FALL OFF THE HORSE.

2/ Or even in ablative without preposition:

caelo cadere TO FALL FROM HEAVEN

3/ But the ablative may also be used as agent when the verb has the meaning of TO DIE:

- In proelio cecidit *manu* Caesaris HE FELL IN THE BATTLE AT THE HANDS OF CAESAR.

❑ **careo, -ere, carui** (no supine) TO LACK

1/ The thing that we lack can be either in genitive or in ablative:

- Careo *pecunia/pecuniae* I LACK MONEY.
- In hac solitudine careo omnium *colloquio* IN THIS SOLITUDE I LACK CONVERSATION WITH EVERYBODY (Cicero, *Epistulae ad Atticum*).

2/ But if it is represented by a pronoun, it can be in accusative:

- Quia *id* quod amo careo BECAUSE I LACK WHAT I LOVE (Plautus, *Curculio*).

❑ **cogito, -are, -avi, -atum** TO THINK

1/ It may rule an accusative:

- *Res novas* cogito I PLAN TO MAKE A REVOLT.
- *Quid* cogitas? WHAT DO YOU THINK?

2/ But it may also rule **de** + Abl.:

- *De meo patre* cogito I THINK ABOUT MY FATHER.

❑ **committo, -ere, -misi, -missum** TO COMMIT, TO ENTRUST

1/ When used with a dative, it has the meaning of TO ENTRUST:

- Quod si te committere *nobis* times, ... BUT IF YOU ARE AFRAID OF ENTRUSTING YOURSELF TO US, ... (Curtius Rufus, *Historiae Alexandri Magni*).

2/ Otherwise it will mean TO COMMIT:

- Sacrilegium a se *commissum esse* dixit HE SAID THAT THE SACRILEGE HAD BEEN COMMITTED BY HIMSELF (Quintilian, *Declamationes Minores*).

❑ **concedo, -ere, -cessi, -cessum** TO YIELD

1/ With a dative it keeps its original meaning of *yielding*:

- *Hostibus* concessimus WE YIELDED TO THE ENEMY.

2/ With an accusative, it means TO CONCEDE, TO GIVE:

- *Libertatem* praedonibus concedit dux THE GENERAL GIVES THE FREEDOM TO THE PIRATES.
- Sed concedo *id* quoque BUT I ALSO CONCEDE THIS (Cicero, *Pro Flacco*).

But it may also have the meaning of TO LEAVE BEHIND:

- *Meum dolorem* concedo I LEAVE MY PAIN BEHIND.

❑ **credo, -ere, credidi, creditum** TO TRUST

Although the normal regime of this verb is with an object in the dative, we can find it also with an accusative in the meaning of *entrusting* something (and the person to whom we entrust it will be in the dative):

- Tibi credo *meos filios* I ENTRUST MY CHILDREN TO YOU.

❑ **disco, -ere, didici** (no supine) TO LEARN

1/ With an accusative, it has the meaning of *learning*:

- *Litteras* disco I LEARN LITERATURE.

2/ but with an ablative it has the meaning of *getting instructed in*:

- *Armis* disco I LEARN HOW TO HANDLE THE WEAPONS / HOW TO FIGHT.
  ✧ Obviously, the verb has here the intransitive meaning of TO LEARN and **armis** is just an instrumental ablative: I LEARN WITH THE WEAPONS.
- Gladiatores *gravioribus armis* discunt quam pugnant GLADIATORS GET INSTRUCTED WITH WEAPONS HEAVIER THAN THOSE WITH WHICH THEY FIGHT (Seneca senior, *Controversiae*).

❑ **doleo, -ere, -ui, -itum** TO FEEL PAIN

1/ If it is a temporary pain, it is constructed with **a** + Abl.:

- **Doleo *ab oculis*** I FEEL PAIN IN MY EYES (Plautus, *Cistellaria*).
  ✧ I feel this pain now, in this moment.

2/ But if it is a permanent pain due to for instance age, it is constructed with an accusative of respect:

- **Doleo *oculos*** I HAVE SIGHT PROBLEMS.

3/ If we feel emotional sorrow for somebody's hard circumstances, it is constructed with **ex** or **de** + Abl., or just ablative without preposition:

- ***De Caesare* doleo** I FEEL SORROW FOR CAESAR.
- **Doleo *tanta calamitate* miseriaque sociorum** (Cicero, *In Verrem*). I FEEL SORROW FOR SO MUCH DISGRACE AND MISERY OF THE ALLIES

4/ But we can mention only the person, in the Acc. In that case, although obviously there must be some painful circumstances affecting that person, the sense is that we feel sorry for that person rather than for his/her circumstances (a difference more grammatical than otherwise):

- ***Caesarem* doleo** I FEEL SORRY FOR CAESAR.

❑ **dono, -are, -avi, -atum** TO PRESENT, TO REWARD

While **do, dare** means just TO GIVE, **dono, donare** means TO PRESENT, TO REWARD. It can be used in two ways:

1/ With an accusative of the rewarded person and an ablative of the thing with which we reward this person:

- **Dono *milites pecunia*** I REWARD THE SOLDIERS WITH MONEY.
- **... pateram ... *qua* hodie meus vir donavit *me* ...** (Plautus, *Amphitruo*). THE BOWL WITH WHICH MY HUSBAND HAS PRESENTED ME TODAY

2/ With an accusative of the given reward and a dative of the person we reward (in this aspect, like the verb **do, dare**):

- **Dono *pecuniam militibus*** I GIVE MONEY TO THE SOLDIERS AS A REWARD.

❑ **dubito, -are, -avi, -atum** TO DOUBT, TO HESITATE

1/ When accompanied by an infinitive, it should be translated by TO HESITATE:

- **Dubito *pugnare*** I HESITATE TO FIGHT.

2/ But if it is accompanied by a subordinate clause, it should be translated by TO DOUBT:

- **Dubito *num Caesar venerit*** I DOUBT WHETHER CAESAR HAS COME.

3/ If accompanied by an object, this object will usually be expressed by **de** + Abl.:

- **Sed *de hoc* non dubito** BUT I HAVE NO DOUBTS ABOUT THIS (Cicero, *In Pisonem*).

✧ About further constructions with this verb, please check also Point 13 *Quominus and quin clauses* in the chapter on Subordinate clauses.

❑ **fugio, -ere, fugi, fugitum** TO FLEE

1/ Although the most frequent use of this verb is intransitive, it can also rule an accusative, in which case it should be translated by TO FLEE AWAY FROM, TO AVOID:

- *Vinum* fugio — I REFRAIN FROM WINE.
- *Hostes* fugio — I FLEE FROM THE ENEMY.
- Odi enim celebritatem, fugio *homines* — I HATE CROWDS, I AVOID PEOPLE (Cicero, *Epistulae ad Atticum*).

2/ In this transitive use, it can also mean TO REJECT:

- *Ciceronem iudicem* fugio — I REJECT CICERO AS JUDGE.

3/ Or even TO MISS SOMEBODY'S ATTENTION...

- Hoc *me* non fugit — I REALISED THIS / THIS DID NOT ESCAPE MY ATTENTION.

... or TO MISS SOMEBODY'S MEMORY:

- Fugit *me* hoc facere — I FORGOT TO DO THIS.

❑ **gaudeo, -ere, gavisus sum** TO REJOICE

1/ This semi-deponent verb can rule either **in** + Abl. or ablative alone:

- Gaudeo *in tua victoria* / Gaudeo *tua victoria* — I AM GLAD BECAUSE OF YOUR VICTORY.

2/ We can find it also with an accusative.

- Gaudeo *tuam victoriam* — I REJOICE IN YOUR VICTORY.

✧ But in this case it may have more the sense of enjoying a specific event: the celebration for the victory, for instance.

3/ And, as expected, it can also be used with a completive sentence:

- Gaudeo *quod vicisti* — I AM GLAD BECAUSE YOU HAVE WON.
- *Salvom (= salvum) te advenire* gaudeo — I AM GLAD THAT YOU HAVE ARRIVED SAFE AND SOUND (Plautus, *Bacchides*).

❑ **habeo, -ere, habui, habitum** TO HAVE

1/ Apart from the usual meaning of TO HAVE, when used with two accusatives it has the meaning of TO CONSIDER:

- *Te amicum* habeo — I CONSIDER YOU A FRIEND.

And the same meaning can be achieved using **pro** + Abl.:

- *Te pro amico* habeo (same meaning).

2/ With a gerundive, it may have the meaning of MUST, OUGHT:

- *dicendum* habeo — I MUST SAY.

❑ impero, -are, -avi, -atum TO ORDER, TO COMMAND

It rules an **ut** clause, not an infinitive:

- Impero tibi *ut maneas* I ORDER YOU TO REMAIN.

❑ invideo, -ere, -vidi, -visum TO ENVY, TO DEPRIVE OF

The possible constructions that this verb may have are several:

1/ Its most usual construction is with a dative of the person who is envied:

- *Ciceroni* invidebant THEY ENVIED CICERO.

2/ If we want to mention also the reason for the envy, we can express it by means of **in** + Abl.:

- Ciceroni *in fama* invidebant THEY ENVIED CICERO'S FAME.

3/ Or in dative if only the reason is mentioned:

- Nemo tum *novitati* invidebat NOBODY THEN ENVIED HIS CHARACTERISTIC OF BEING A NEW MAN (Cicero, *Philippicae*).
- Huius igitur Habitus *vitae* invidebat? DID HABITUS THEREFORE ENVY THE LIFE OF THIS MAN? (Cicero, *Pro Cluentio*).

4/ But the same construction without the preposition will mean TO DEPRIVE OF:

- Ciceroni *fama* invidebant THEY DEPRIVED CICERO OF FAME.

5/ The same sense of depriving somebody of something can be expressed by putting the deprived thing in accusative:

- Ciceroni *famam* invidebant (same meaning).

6/ And, as expected, this verb can also rule a subordinate clause:

- Invideo Ciceronem *quod praeclaram famam habet* I ENVY CICERO BECAUSE OF THE GOOD FAME HE HAS.

❑ iubeo, -ere, iussi, iussum TO ORDER

Although the normal construction of this verb is *accusative + infinitive* ...

- Senatus iussit *Caesarem pugnare* THE SENATE ORDERED CAESAR TO FIGHT

... we can also find it with **ut** + subjunctive:

- Senatus iussit *ut Caesar pugnaret* THE SENATE ORDERED THAT CAESAR SHOULD FIGHT.

The difference is that in the infinitive construction it is a very direct order given to Caesar (even if not present), while in the **ut** construction it is more a decision that further ahead will be communicated to him.

- Iussit *ut invicem se occiderent* HE ORDERED THAT THEY SHOULD KILL EACH OTHER (Quintilian, *Declamationes Minores*).

❑ libero, -are, -avi, -atum TO FREE

It rules an accusative of the person we free and an ablative from the person/thing etc. from which we free it:

- *Me* liberaverunt *servitute* THEY FREED ME FROM SERVITUDE.

❑ maneo, -ere, mansi, mansum TO REMAIN, TO EXPECT

1/ This verb is usually intransitive, with the meaning of TO REMAIN:

- In urbe mansit HE REMAINED IN THE CITY.

2/ But it can also be transitive, and then it has the meaning of TO EXPECT:

- Mala mors *te* manet A BAD DEATH EXPECTS YOU.
  ✧ In the sense of something that destiny has reserved for you.

❑ metuo, -ere, metui (no supine) TO FEAR

Although the normal construction of this verb is the usual one dealt with in the chapter of Fear Clauses, we should point out also this option: ab aliquo metuere TO BE AFRAID OF SOMEONE

- Cumas se propere recepit, *ab Hannibale* metuens HE WITHDREW TO CUMAE IN HASTE, AFRAID OF HANNIBAL (Livy, *Ab Urbe Condita*).

❑ minor, -ari, minatus sum TO THREATEN

There are two possible constructions:

1/ You threaten somebody (in Dat.) with something (in Abl.):

- Magister *discipulo* minatur *poena* THE TEACHER THREATENS THE STUDENT WITH A PUNISHMENT.

2/ You threaten something (in Acc.) to somebody (in Dat.):

- Magister *discipulo* minatur *poenam* (same meaning)
  ✧ Literally, THE TEACHER THREATENS A PUNISHMENT TO THE STUDENT.
- *Numquid mihi* minatur? WITH WHAT DOES HE THREATEN ME? (Plautus, *Casina*).

In a summary: the person you threaten is always in dative, but the thing with which you threaten them can be either in accusative or in ablative.

❑ mitto, -ere, misi, missum TO SEND

Apart from its normal use with a direct and an indirect object, the use of this verb with a supine with purpose sense is very frequent:

- Legatos ad Caesarem mittunt *rogatum* auxilium THEY SEND AMBASSADORS TO CAESAR TO ASK FOR HELP (Caesar, *De Bello Gallico*).

❑ **muto, -are, -avi, -atum** TO CHANGE

1/ In its transitive meaning of TO SWAP, the object by which we swap something can be expressed either with **cum** or with **pro** (both followed by an ablative):

- **Mutavi meos libros** ***cum/pro pecunia*** I CHANGED MY BOOKS FOR MONEY.

2/ It can also be used intransitively:

- **Leges semper mutant** LAWS ARE ALWAYS CHANGING.

❑ **nego, -are, -avi, -atum** TO DENY

1/ Apart from its basic meaning of TO DENY SOMETHING, this verb is also used when we want to make a negative statement. A sentence like I SAY THAT CAESAR HAS NOT BEEN IN GAUL should be written as

Nego Caesarem in Gallia fuisse ✧ Literally, I DENY THAT CAESAR HAS BEEN IN GAUL.

2/ A typical mistake is to write *Dico* **Caesarem in Gallia** *non* **fuisse**.

So, instead of **dico** ... **non** we must use **nego**:

- ***Negavit*** **quemquam esse in civitate praeter se qui id efficere posset** HE SAID THAT THERE WAS NO ONE IN THE CITY EXCEPT HIM WHO COULD CARRY IT OUT (Cicero, *Pro Cluentio*).
  ✧ Literally, HE DENIED THAT THERE WAS ANYBODY IN THE CITY WHO...

❑ **nubo, -ere, nupsi, nuptum** TO MARRY

This verb is used when talking about *a woman marrying a man* (the expression of *a man marrying a woman* is **uxorem duco**), and it has these two possible constructions:

1/ *cum aliquo* **nubere** ✧ Literally, TO MARRY WITH SOMEBODY.

2/ *alicui* **nubere** ✧ Literally, TO MARRY TO SOMEBODY.

- **Brevi tempore post patris mortem nupsit** *A. Aurio Melino* A SHORT TIME AFTER HER FATHER'S DEATH, SHE MARRIED A. AULIUS MERINUS (Cicero, *Pro Cluentio*).

❑ **obligo, -are, -avi, -atum** TO TIE, TO COMPEL

This verb has a peculiar construction when used reflexively and with an ablative:

- ***Me*** **obligavi** ***scelere*** I TIED MYSELF TO A CRIME / I COMMITTED A CRIME.
  ✧ Literally, I TIED MYSELF WITH A CRIME, and of course this is due to the image of the subject tying himself to legal responsibilities.

❑ **pereo, -ire, -ivi, -itum** TO PERISH

Although it is an active verb, it can have an agent object: the person at whose hands the subject dies. If one dies at somebody's hands, it can be considered that TO PERISH = TO BE KILLED, so that the presence of an agent object makes more sense:

- ***A Gallis* periit** HE DIED AT THE HANDS OF THE GAULS.

Obviously, the other verbs that mean TO DIE (**morior, cado**) can also use an agent object. And this passive sense can be found also in expressions like **calescere *a sole*** TO GET WARMER BY THE SUN (literal translation).

❑ **persuadeo, -ere, -suasi, suasum** TO PERSUADE

We can find this verb used impersonally (and let's remember that this verb rules a dative):

- **Caesari autem *persuasum est* se salvum esse non posse** CAESAR WAS SURE THAT HE COULD NOT BE SAFE (Cicero, *Epistulae ad Familiares*).

❑ **peto, -ere, petivi, petitum** TO ASK FOR, TO REQUEST

The person from whom we request something is expressed by the preposition **a** + Abl.:

- ***A te* hoc peto** I REQUEST THIS FROM YOU.

❑ **placeo, -ere, placui** (no supine) TO PLEASE

1/ Although this verb has no proper supine, we can find its passive past participle in the expression **placitum est** IT SEEMED WELL:

- ***Placitum est* mihi ut postularem ...** IT SEEMED WELL TO ME (I DECIDED) TO DEMAND ... (Cicero, *Epistulae ad Familiares*).

2/ But the two most frequent ways of expressing this would have been

- **Mihi placuit postulare ...** AND **Mihi placuit ut postularem** ...

❑ **praeficio, -ere, -feci, -fectum** TO PLACE SOMEBODY IN COMMAND OF SOMETHING

1/ This verb rules an Acc. for the person we place in front and a Dat. for the institution/thing etc. in front of which we place that person:

- **Caesar *Marcum legioni* praefecit** CAESAR PLACED MARCUS IN COMMAND OF THE LEGION.

It could be said that the accusative depends on the verb **facio** (**ficio** here) and the dative depends on the **prae** (something not very orthodox to say, because in fact **prae** is not a preposition in itself and moreover, even if it were, there is no preposition in Latin that rules a dative).

❑ **praesto, -are, -stiti, -atum** TO STAY FORWARD, TO EXCEL

In its sense of TO BE AHEAD, it is constructed with a dative of the person ahead of whom you are and an ablative of the field in which you are ahead:

- Marcus praestat *aliis discipulis* (Dat.) *litteris* (Abl.) MARCUS IS AHEAD OF THE OTHER STUDENTS IN LITERATURE.

❑ **prohibeo, -ere, -bui, -bitum** TO HINDER, TO RESTRAIN

1/ The place (person, activity, etc.) away from which we keep someone can be expressed either by ablative alone or preceded by the preposition **a**:

- Te prohibeo *civitate / a civitate* I KEEP YOU AWAY FROM THE CITY.
- ... ut ... exercitum *itinere* prohiberent (Caesar, *Bellum Civile*). ...SO THAT THEY MIGHT PREVENT THE ARMY FROM MOVING FORWARD

2/ For the uses of **prohibeo** with **quominus** and **quin**, please see the corresponding section in the chapter on Subordinate Clauses.

❑ **respondeo, -ere, respondi, responsum** TO ANSWER

1/ As a general rule, the person whom we answer will be in accusative:

- *Me* statim respondit HE ANSWERED ME IMMEDIATELY.

2/ But if we mention also the content of the answer, not only the receiver, the content is what is put in accusative, and the receiver of the answer is put in dative:

- *Hoc mihi* respondit HE ANSWERED ME THIS.
- *Aliud* ergo nunc *tibi* respondeo SO, I ANSWER YOU SOMETHING ELSE (Plautus, *Mostellaria*).

3/ And if we mention only the thing to which somebody answers, we can put it either in dative or with **ad** + Acc.:

- Respondit *litteris* / Respondit *ad litteras* HE ANSWERED THE LETTER.

It is also possible to find it with **adversus** + Acc.:

- Respondit *adversus litteras* (same meaning).

❑ **rideo, -ere, risi, risum** TO LAUGH, TO SMILE

1/ When it has the meaning of TO SMILE, the person to whom the subject smiles can be either in dative or with **ad** + Acc.:

- Puer *parentibus* ridebat / Puer *ad parentes* ridebat THE CHILD WAS SMILING AT HIS PARENTS.

2/ When it has the meaning of TO LAUGH, the thing about which the subject laughs is expressed with **in** + Abl.:

- *In* eius *clade* ridebat HE WAS LAUGHING AT HIS DEFEAT.

3/ But we can also find it in accusative:

- Eius *cladem* ridebat (same meaning).

And we can find in accusative also the person whom the subject mocks:

- *Eum* ridebat HE WAS MOCKING HIM.

❑ **sentio, -ire, sensi, sensum** TO FEEL, TO REALISE

This verb has several possibilities of construction:

1/ With an accusative:

- *Famem* sentio I AM HUNGRY.
- Sentio *sonitum* I HEAR A SOUND (Plautus, *Curculio*).

2/ With **de** + Abl.:

- *De hoc* statim sensi I REALISED THIS IMMEDIATELY.

In this second construction, the meaning is rather a meaning of *realising*, rather than of physical perception. For instance, we would not say **De fame sentio** unless we mean that we realise that somebody else is hungry.

❑ **sequor, -i, secutus sum** TO FOLLOW

In its meaning of TO FOLLOW AS A CONSEQUENCE, it can have these constructions:

1/ With an infinitive clause:

- Sequitur *Caesarem iam in Italia esse* IT MUST BE DEDUCED THAT CAESAR IS ALREADY IN ITALY.

2/ With **ut** + subj.:

- Sequitur *ut Caesar iam in Italia sit* (same meaning).

❑ **sto, -are, steti, statum** TO STAND

1/ When used with an ablative, it has the meaning of TO BE TRUTHFUL TO, TO KEEP (a promise, etc.):

- *Pacto* sto I KEEP THE TREATY.
- Si qui ... eorum *decreto* non stetit, sacrificiis interdicunt IF ANYBODY HAS NOT SUBMITTED TO THEIR DECISION, THEY BAN HIM FROM THE SACRIFICES (Caesar, *De Bello Gallico*).

2/ Apart from its normal meaning of TO STAND, when used with **quominus** and with **per**+ Acc. it may have this meaning:

- Per Caesarem stat *quominus hoc fiat* IT DEPENDS ON CAESAR THAT THIS DOES NOT HAPPEN.

Observe that there is no negative adverb in the **quominus** clause, but we must add it in English.

❑ **studeo, -ere, studui,** --- TO BE EAGER FOR

1/ As a general rule, this verb rules a dative, not an accusative, and its initial meaning is TO DEVOTE ONESELF TO SOMETHING, TO BE EAGER FOR SOMETHING, TO SUPPORT (the meaning TO STUDY is rather a meaning of the late period of Latin):

- *Graecis litteris* studuit HE DEVOTED HIMSELF TO GREEK LITERATURE (Cicero, *Brutus*).
- Studuit *Catilinae* iterum *petenti* HE SUPPORTED CATILINA WHEN HE MADE A SECOND ATTEMPT (Cicero, *Pro Caelio*).

A typical mistake is to translate for instance I STUDY GREEK LITERATURE by **Studeo Graecas litteras** instead of **Studeo Graecis litteris**.

2/ But if the object of our zeal is expressed by means of a neuter pronoun, it can be expressed in accusative:

- *Hoc unum* studeo — I DEVOTE MYSELF TO ONLY THIS ONE THING.
- Non equidem *hoc* studeo — INDEED I DO NOT DESIRE THIS (Persius Flaccus, *Saturae*).

❑ **teneo, -ere, tenui, tentum** TO HOLD

1/ That the thing we hold is in accusative is quite clear:

- *Librum* teneo — I HOLD THE BOOK

2/ To express with what we hold it we can say either **manu** or **in manu**:

With the ablative alone we should consider it as an *instrumental object*:

- Librum teneo *manu* — I HOLD THE BOOK WITH MY HAND
- Teneo *dextera* genium meum — I HOLD MY GENIUS IN MY RIGHT HAND (Plautus, *Menaechmi*).

and if we use **in** + Abl. we must consider it a *place object*:

- Librum teneo *in manu* — I HOLD THE BOOK IN MY HAND.

❑ **timeo, -ere, timui** (no supine) TO FEAR

Apart from the usual construction dealt with in the section of Fear clauses (in the chapter on Subordinate clauses), we should point out how to express that we are worried about something or somebody:

1/ With a dative:

- Timeo *Caesari* — I AM WORRIED ABOUT CAESAR.
- Timeo *victoriae* — I AM WORRIED ABOUT THE VICTORY.

2/ With **de** + Abl.:

- Timeo *de Caesare* (same meaning).

❑ **venio, -ire, veni, ventum** TO COME

Although the most common construction of this verb is a directional object, we must also take into account these two options:

1/ This verb is frequently found with a dative of purpose and another dative of person:

- *Auxilio Caesari* venerunt copiae — THE TROOPS CAME TO HELP CAESAR.

2/ We can often find it also with a supine:

- *Pugnatum* venit — HE CAME TO FIGHT.
- Legatio de victoria *gratulatum* venit (Livy, *Ab Urbe Condita*). — AN EMBASSY CAME TO CONGRATULATE [HIM] ON HIS VICTORY

❑ **vereor, -eri, veritus sum** TO FEAR, TO SHOW RESPECT FOR

1/ In the usual meaning of TO FEAR, it will rule an accusative:

- Vereor *deos* I FEAR / SHOW RESPECT FOR THE GODS.

2/ But it can also rule **de** + Abl. with respect to what we feel fear that something bad may happen to it/him/her etc.:

- Vereor *de patria* I AM AFRAID ABOUT MY HOMELAND.

3/ We can find it also without the preposition **de**, just in Abl.:

- Vereor *patria* (same meaning).

In this case, this ablative could be considered an *ablative of cause*.

4/ Of course, when it rules a subordinate, it follows the usual rules presented in the point on Fear clauses in the chapter of Subordinate clauses:

- Vereor *ne aut molestus sim vobis*, iudices, aut ... I AM AFRAID THAT I MAY BE TROUBLESOME TO YOU, JUDGES, OR ... (Cicero, *Pro Roscio Amerino*).

h) Compound verbs

1. General remarks [217]

Latin verbs are sometimes found in compound forms with prepositions. For instance:

fero	TO CARRY, TO BRING	+	the preposition	**ad**	TOWARDS	=	**affero**	TO PRESENT
fero	TO CARRY, TO BRING	+	the preposition	**cum**	WITH	=	**confero**	TO BRING TOGETHER
fero	TO CARRY, TO BRING	+	the preposition	**in**	INTO	=	**infero**	TO BRING INTO
eo	TO GO	+	the preposition	**ex**	OUT OF	=	**exeo**	TO GO OUT

Take into account that sometimes the preposition may undergo some changes, especially depending on the first consonant of the verb. For instance, when the preposition **sub** is compounded with the verb **fero**, the resulting compound form is **suffero** rather than the expected **subfero**. But when the initial consonant of the verbal form changes, then the preposition may revert to its original spelling (depending on what consonant it is): the supine of **suffero** is **sublatum**, because while the **f-** of **fero** makes the **-b** become assimilated to another **f-** the **l-** of **latum** does not produce any change in the **-b**.

2. Meaning of the preposition [218]

a/ Sometimes the meaning can be interpreted, as for instance:

- **intervenio** TO COME *BETWEEN*
- **circumspecto** TO LOOK *AROUND*

b/ Prepositions may sometimes give the compound verb a certain nuance that can be difficult to be deduced from the basic meaning of the preposition. Let's see some examples:

The preposition **cum** = WITH, but **conficio** = TO ACCOMPLISH.
✧ It could be considered that **cum** adds here a sense of *putting different parts together* and therefore *finishing* something.

The preposition **per** = THROUGH, but **perficio** = TO COMPLETE.
✧ In some cases **per** conveys the sense of *completely* or *utterly*.

The preposition **inter** = BETWEEN, but **intellego** = TO UNDERSTAND.
✧ In the sense of *reading between lines, getting the sense of a text.*

c/ And in some cases the sense seems even to be disconnected from the main sense of the verb and of the preposition:

The preposition **sub** = UNDER, but **succurro** = TO HELP.
✧ The sense of **curro** = TO RUN is clear in the sense of running towards somebody, but the meaning of **sub** must be related in the sense of supporting that person.

The preposition **per** = THROUGH, but **pereo** = TO DIE.

✧ A combination of the sense of *going*, a sense provided by the verb, and the sense of *passing from one state to another one*, a sense provided by the preposition.

3. Regime of the verb [219]

a/ An important detail to note is that the regime of various compound verbs may sometimes be due to the preposition attached to them. For instance, if the preposition **de**, which is followed by an ablative, is compounded with **sisto**, the resulting verb, **desisto** TO RENOUNCE, must be followed by an ablative:

- Petrus *consulatu* destitit   PETER RENOUNCED THE CONSULATE.

By the way, we can also find, with the same meaning,

- Petrus *de consulatu* destitit.   ✧ Observe that the preposition is the same as the one of the verb.
- Petrus *a consulatu* destitit.   ✧ In this case, the preposition is another one.

b/ But sometimes the preposition will count for nothing with respect to the regime of the verb. For instance, **cum** needs an ablative, but **conficio** (**cum** + **facio**) goes on ruling an accusative as **facio** does, do not expect it to rule an ablative because of the prefix **cum**:

- Iam *omnia* confeci   I HAVE ALREADY FINISHED EVERYTHING.   ✧ A normal accusative.

4. Main compound verbs [220]

Here we offer a list of the most common compound verbs that a student will encounter in a text and is likely to need when reading or composing Latin, focusing especially on verbs that have a meaning which cannot be deduced easily from the *preposition-verb combination*. The regime of the verb is also provided when it is not as expected.

Previous observations:

a/ In some cases, although the verb exists in all of its forms, its impersonal use is more common, so we have introduced it as such.

b/ Some verbs may have several translations. We have provided the most frequent one.

c/ Some of these verbs can also be found in the section entitled *Peculiarities and idioms* and in other parts of the book, according to which grammatical aspect is being considered.

❑ With a/ab

As expected, this preposition will give verbs a meaning of *separation*, very visible in physical sense for instance in **amitto** TO SEND AWAY, but more symbolic for instance in **abrogo** TO ABROGATE.

abdico, -are, -avi, -atum   TO ABDICATE
abdico, -ere, -dixi (no supine)   TO REJECT BECAUSE OF AN UNFAVOURABLE OMEN
abdo, -ere, -didi, -ditum   TO CONCEAL, TO REMOVE

abduco, -ere, -duxi, -ductum	TO LEAD AWAY
abeo, -ire, -ii, -itum	TO DEPART
aberro, -are, -avi (no supine)	TO GO ASTRAY
abripio, -ere, -ripui, -reptum	TO TAKE AWAY
abrogo, -are, -avi, -atum	TO ABROGATE
abscindo, -ere, -scidi, -scissum	TO TEAR OFF
abscondo, -ere, -condi, -conditum	TO HIDE
absolvo, -ere, absolvi, absolutum	TO SET FREE
abstineo, -ere, abstinui, abstentum	TO REFRAIN FROM
absum, abesse, afui (no supine)	TO BE ABSENT
absumo, -ere, -sumpsi, -sumptum	TO DIMINISH, TO DESTROY
amitto, -ere, -misi, -missum	TO SEND AWAY
amoveo, -ere, -movi, -motum	TO REMOVE, TO GET RID OF
aufero, -ferre, abstuli, ablatum	TO REMOVE, TO KILL
averto, -ere, averti, aversum	TO TURN AWAY

❑ With ad

It will give its compounds a sense of *approximation*, like in **accedo** TO APPROACH, other times this sense will be more symbolic, as in **accido** TO HAPPEN.

As expected, the preposition **ad** will change its final consonant according to the initial consonant of the verb stem.

accedo, -ere, -cessi, -cessum	TO APPROACH
accido, -ere, -cidi, -cisum	TO HAPPEN ✧ In the sense of something that falls towards us.
accipio, -ere, -cepi, -ceptum	TO RECEIVE, TO ACCEPT
addo, -ere, addidi, additum	TO ATTACH
adeo, -ire, -ii, -itum	TO GO TO
adimo, -ere, ademi, ademptum	TO TAKE AWAY
adipiscor, -i, adeptus sum	TO ACHIEVE
adiungo, -ere, -iunxi, -iunctum	TO JOIN, TO ADD
adiuvo, -are, -iuvi, -iutum	TO HELP
admiror, -ari, -miratus sum	TO ADMIRE
admitto, -ere, -misi, -missum	TO ADMIT, TO SEND
admoneo, -ere, -monui, -monitum	TO WARN, TO SUGGEST
adolesco, -ere, adolevi, adultum	TO COME TO MATURITY
adsum, adesse, adfui (no supine)	TO BE PRESENT, TO SUPPORT
advenio, -ire, -veni, -ventum	TO ARRIVE
aggredior, -i, -gressus sum	TO APPROACH, TO ATTACK
agnosco, -ere, -novi, -nitum	TO RECOGNIZE ✧ Because of the presence of the letter **a**- (which in fact is the preposition **ad** shortened), thinking that this verb means NOT TO KNOW is a typical mistake.
alloquor, -i, -locutus sum	TO ADDRESS
appello, -ere, -puli, -pulsum	TO BRING IN, TO LAND
appello, -are, -avi, -atum	TO ADDRESS, TO ENTREAT

appeto, -ere, -ivi, -itum — TO STRIVE FOR
approbo, -are, -avi, -atum — TO APPROVE, TO ASSENT
appropinquo, -are, -avi, -atum — TO APPROACH
attendo, -ere, -tendi, -tentum — TO TEND TOWARDS, TO PAY ATTENTION
attineo, -ere, -ui (no supine) — TO DETAIN, TO REACH, TO CONCERN
attingo, -ere, -tigi, -tactum — TO TOUCH, TO REACH
attribuo, -ere, -ui, -utum — TO ASSIGN

❑ With ante

There are not many verbs compound with **ante**, and the meaning of *before* is obvious in all of them.

antecedo, -cedere, -cessi (no supine) — TO GO BEFORE
anteeo, -ire, -ii, -itum — TO PRECEDE
antefero, -ferre, -tuli, -latum — TO BEAR IN FRONT
antepono, -ere, -posui, -positum — TO SET BEFORE, TO PREFER
anticipo, -are, -avi, -atum — TO TAKE BEFORE

❑ With circum

Almost all of the verbs compound with **circum** carry a very strong physical meaning, as in **circumeo** TO GO AROUND.

circumdo, -dare, -dedi, -datum — TO PLACE AROUND
circumago, -agere, -egi, -actum — TO TURN ROUND, TO CARRY AROUND
circumeo, -ire, -ivi, -itum — TO SURROUND, TO GO AROUND
circumfero, -ferre, -tull, -latum — TO BEAR ROUND
circumflecto, -ere, -flexi, -flectum — TO BEND
circumfundo, -ere, -fudi, -fusum — TO POUR AROUND
circumscribo, -ere, scripsi, scriptum — TO ENCIRCLE, TO ENCOMPASS
circumspecto, -are, -avi, -atum — TO LOOK AROUND
circumspicio, -ere, -exi, -ectum — TO LOOK AROUND
circumsto, -stare, -steti (no supine) — TO STAND AROUND
circumvenio, -ire, -veni, -ventum — TO ENCIRCLE, TO SURROUND

❑ With cum (com- /con-)

The verbs compound with **cum** have usually one of these two meanings (or both):

a/ The intransitive meaning: to undertake some action together with somebody else, like **colloquor** TO TALK.
b/ To act on several objects or people simultaneously, like **compono** TO JOIN.

In other cases, they will have neither of these meanings, and the function of the prepositional prefix **cum** in the meaning of the verb will be really unnoticed, like **contemno** TO CONTEMPT, TO DESPISE.

coalesco, -ere, -alui, -alitum — TO BECOME STRONG, TO UNITE
coeo, -ire, -ii, -itum — TO GO TOGETHER
coerceo, -ere, -cui, -citum — TO HOLD TOGETHER

cogito, -are, -avi, -atum	TO THINK
cognosco, -ere, -novi, -nitum	TO BECOME ACQUAINTED WITH
cohibeo, -ere, -bui, -bitum	TO CONFINE, TO RESTRAIN
colligo, -ere, -legi, -lectum	TO GATHER, TO INFER ✧ In the sense of putting together different pieces of information.
colloco, -are, -avi, -atum	TO PLACE, TO ARRANGE, TO GIVE IN MARRIAGE
colloquor, -i, collocutus sum	TO TALK
commendo, -are, -avi, -atum	TO CONFIDE, TO COMMEND
comminor, -ari, -atus sum	TO THREATEN
committo, -ere, -misi, -missum	TO BRING TOGETHER, TO PERPETRATE
commoror, -ari, -atus sum	TO TARRY
commoveo, -ere, -movi, -motum	TO PUT IN MOTION, TO STIR
commuto, -are, -avi, -atum	TO CHANGE COMPLETELY
compareo, -ere, -parui (no supine)	TO APPEAR
comparo, -are, -avi, -atum	TO PREPARE, TO ESTABLISH ✧ There is another verb **comparo, -are, -avi, -atum** TO PUT TOGETHER, TO COMPARE.
compello, -ere, -puli, -pulsum	TO ASSEMBLE ✧ There is another verb **compello, -are, -avi, -atum** TO ADDRESS, TO REPROACH.
comperio, -ire, -peri, -pertum	TO FIND OUT ✧ This verb has also got a deponent variant: **comperior, -iri, -pertus sum,** with the same meaning.
complector, -i, -plexus sum	TO EMBRACE, TO ENCIRCLE
compleo, -ere, -evi, -etum	TO FILL UP
compono, -ere, -posui, -positum	TO BRING TOGETHER, TO JOIN
comprehendo, -ere, -di, -sum	TO CATCH, TO APPREHEND
comprimo, -ere, -pressi, -pressum	TO COMPRESS
comprobo, -are, -avi, -atum	TO ACKNOWLEDGE
concedo, -ere, -cessi, -cessum	TO WITHDRAW, TO YIELD
concido, -ere, -cidi (no supine)	TO FALL, TO PERISH ✧ It is a compound of **cado, -ere.**
concido, -ere, -cidi, -cisum	TO CUT UP, TO DESTROY ✧ It is a compound of **caedo, -ere.**
concludo, -ere, -usi, -usum	TO ENCLOSE, TO RESTRAIN, TO CONCLUDE
concurro, -ere, -curri, -cursum	TO ASSEMBLE (intransitive meaning)
condo, -ere, -didi, -ditum	TO FOUND ✧ In the sense of putting together several factors.
conficio, -ere, -feci, -fectum	TO COMPLETE, TO DESTROY, TO KILL
confido, -ere, confisus sum	TO TRUST
confirmo, -are, -avi, -atum	TO STRENGTHEN, TO ASSERT
confiteor, -eri, -fessus sum	TO CONFESS
confligo, -ere, -flixi, -flictum	TO DASH TOGETHER, TO FIGHT
confundo, -ere, -fudi, -fusus	TO POUR TOGETHER, TO DISORDER ✧ This verb is much used in the sense of disordering the ranks of the enemy, of causing confusion among them.
congredior, -i, congressus sum	TO COME TOGETHER, TO ENGAGE

conicio, -ere, -ieci, -iectum — This verb, theoretically meaning TO THROW TOGETHER, is one of the compound verbs that has a wider variety of meanings: TO UNITE (in the sense of putting things into the same place), TO FORETELL (in the sense of putting together all the different pieces of information), TO URGE (in the sense of throwing somebody towards an action), TO CAST, etc.

consentio, -ire, -sensi, -sensum — TO AGREE

consequor, -i, consecutus sum — TO FOLLOW, TO RESULT

conservo, -are, -avi, -atum — TO KEEP SAFE

consisto, -ere, -stiti, -stitum — TO STAND STILL, TO ENDURE

conspicio, -ere, -pexi, -pectum — TO OBSERVE ✧ This verb has a deponent option: **conspicor, -ari, -atus sum,** with the same meaning.

conspiro, -are, -avi, -atum — TO SOUND TOGETHER, TO CONSPIRE ✧ In the sense of people who "breathe" the same ideas.

constituo, -ere, constitui, constitutum — TO ESTABLISH, TO DRAW UP, TO DECIDE

consto, -are, constiti (no supine) — TO AGREE, TO STAND FIRM, TO CONSIST OF ✧ We can find it frequently in the sense of TO BE WELL KNOWN: • **Ipsum talem esse inter omnes *constat*** IT IS WELL KNOWN AMONG EVERYBODY THAT HE IS SUCH A MAN (Livy, *Ab Urbe Condita*).

consuesco, -ere, -suevi, -suetum — TO ACCUSTOM ONESELF

consulo, -ere, -ului, -ultum — TO DELIBERATE

consumo, -ere, -sumpsi, sumptum — TO USE UP

contemno, -ere, -tempsi, temptum — TO DESPISE

contendo, -ere, -tendi, -tentum — TO STRAIN, TO JOURNEY, TO AIM ✧ In a summary: TO HAVE A TENDENCY TOWARDS SOMETHING, whether the *action* of going there physically or a *desire*.

contineo, -ere, -tinui, -tentum — TO HOLD TOGETHER, TO CONTAIN, TO REPRESS

conveho, -ere, -vexi, -vectum — TO COLLECT

convenio, -ire, -veni, -ventum — TO COME TOGETHER, TO ASSEMBLE

converto, -ere, -verti, -versum — TO TURN ROUND, TO TRANSFORM

convinco, -ere, -vici, -victum — TO OVERCOME, TO EXPOSE

convoco, -are, -avi, -atum — TO CONVOKE

❑ With de

This preposition will usually confer its compound verbs a sense of:

a/ separation (similar to **a/ab** in some aspects), like **decedo** TO WITHDRAW
b/ movement from upwards downwards, like **demitto** TO DROP
c/ exteriorization, like **demonstro** TO INDICATE

decedo, -ere, decessi, -decessum — TO DEPART, TO WITHDRAW

decerno, -ere, -crevi, -cretum — TO DECIDE ✧ In the sense of taking a decision from what you see.

declamo, -are, -avi, -atum — TO DECLAIM

decurro, -ere, -curri, -cursum — TO RUN DOWN, TO TRAVERSE

dedico, -are, -avi, -atum — TO DEDICATE

dedo, -ere, -didi, -ditum — TO GIVE UP, TO SURRENDER

deduco, -ere, -duxi, -ductum TO LEAD AWAY, TO BRING INTO PORT

deficio, -ere, -feci, -fectum TO REVOLT, TO WITHDRAW, TO ABANDON, TO BE ABSENT • **Numquam in hac urbe qui a re publica *defecerunt* civium iura tenuerunt** NEVER IN THIS CITY HELD THOSE WHO ABANDONED THE STATE THEIR RIGHTS AS CITIZENS (Cicero, *In Catilinam*).

defigo, -ere, -fixi, -fictum TO FASTEN, TO ASTONISH ✧ In the sense of leaving people *fixed, without motion*.

deicio, -ere, deieci, deiectum TO THROW DOWN, TO KILL

delabor, -i, delapsus sum TO FALL DOWN, TO CONDESCEND

delinquo, -ere, -liqui, -lictum TO FAIL, TO COMMIT A CRIME

demitto, -ere, -misi, -missum TO DROP, TO SEND DOWN

demo, -ere, dempsi, demptum TO TAKE AWAY, TO REMOVE

demonstro, -are, -avi, -atum TO INDICATE

demoveo, -ere, -movi, -motum TO REMOVE

denego, -are, -avi, -atum TO REJECT

denuntio, -are, -avi, -atum TO DECLARE, TO MENACE, TO DENOUNCE

depello, -ere, -puli, -pulsum TO DRIVE OUT, TO EXPEL

depono, -ere, -posui, -positum TO PUT DOWN, TO CONFIDE

deprehendo, -ere, -ehendi, -ehensum TO SNATCH, TO OVERTAKE, TO UNDERSTAND

deripio, -ere, -ripui, -reptum TO TEAR OFF, TO REMOVE

descendo, -ere, -endi, -ensum TO DESCEND

designo, -are, -avi, -atum TO MARK OUT

desilio, -ere, desilui, desultum TO LEAP DOWN

desino, -ere, destiti, desitum TO DESIST, TO ALLOW ✧ In the sense of giving up any resistance.

desisto, -ere, destiti, destitum TO STAND OFF, TO DESIST ✧ In fact this is the verb that "lends" its perfect tense to **desino**.

despero, -are, -avi, -atum TO DESPAIR

despicio,-ere, -exi, -ectum TO LOOK DOWN ON, TO BE INATTENTIVE

destituo, -ere, -tui, -tutum TO ABANDON, TO SET DOWN

desum, deesse, defui (no supine) TO BE MISSING

deterreo, -ere, -ui, -itum TO DETER

devinco, -ere, devinxi, devinctum TO DEFEAT COMPLETELY

❑ With e(x)

The sense given by **e(x)** will usually be:

a/ The physical sense of *from inside to outside*, even in abstract sense as in **expono** TO EXPOSE.
b/ A sense of *completeness*, as in **efficio** TO COMPLETE. In this sense, the effect can be similar to that produced by the prefix **per**.

educo, -ere, -duxi, -ductum TO LEAD OUT • **Legiones ex castris *eduxit*** HE LED HIS LEGIONS OUT OF THE CAMP (Caesar, *De Bello Gallico*). ✧ Do not confuse with the verb **educo, -are, -avi, -atum** TO EDUCATE, although **educo, -ere** can sometimes have this meaning, in the sense of taking a child out of childhood into the world of adults.

efficio, -ere, -feci, -fectum TO EFFECT, TO PRODUCE, TO COMPLETE

effugio, -ere, -fugi (no supine) TO ESCAPE

effundo, -ere, -fudi, -fusum	TO POUR OUT, TO SPREAD ABROAD
egredior, -i, egressus sum	TO GO OUT
eicio, -ere, eieci, eiectum	TO CAST OUT, TO EXPEL
elabor, -i, elapsus sum	TO FALL OUT, TO SLIP AWAY, TO ESCAPE
eloquor, -i, elocutus sum	TO SPEAK PLAINLY
ementior, -iri, ementitus sum	TO LIE
emergo, -ere, emersi, emersum	TO RAISE UP (trans.), TO ARISE (intrans.)
emitto, -ere, emisi, emissum	TO SEND OUT, TO PUBLISH
eripio, -ere, eripui, ereptum	TO SNATCH AWAY, TO REMOVE
erumpo, -ere, erupi, eruptum	TO BREAK THROUGH, TO BREAK OUT
evado, -ere, evasi, evasum	TO GO OUT, TO ESCAPE
eveho, -ere, evexi, evectum	TO CARRY OUT ✧ In passive, very frequently it means TO PROCEED, TO MOVE FORWARD, although the passive meaning of TO BE CARRIED OUT is perfectly acceptable: • **Ipsas prope portas** ***evecti sunt*** THEY PROCEEDED [TO A LOCATION] NEAR THE GATES THEMSELVES (Livy, *Ab Urbe Condita*).
everto, -ere, everti, eversum	TO OVERTURN, TO SUBVERT, TO DESTROY ✧ In the sense of putting everything upside down.
evoco, -are, -avi, -atum	TO CALL FORTH, TO EVOKE
excido, -ere, -cidi (no supine)	TO FALL OUT, TO ESCAPE, TO DIE ✧ This verb is a compound of **cado, -ere** TO FALL.
excido, -ere, -cidi, -cisum	TO MAKE FALL, TO KILL ✧ This verb is a compound of **caedo, -ere** TO MAKE FALL.
excipio, -ere, -cepi, -ceptum	TO TAKE OUT, TO CAPTURE
exclamo, -are, -avi, -atum	TO CALL OUT, TO EXCLAIM
excludo, -ere, -clusi, -clusum	TO SHUT OUT, TO EXCLUDE
exeo, -ire, -ii, -itum	TO GO OUT
exerceo, -ere, -cui, -citum	TO WORK, TO TRAIN, TO CARRY INTO EFFECT
exhortor, -ari, -atus sum	TO EXHORT
exigo, -ere, -egi, -actum	TO THRUST OUT, TO DEMAND
existimo, -are, -avi, -atum	TO VALUE, TO RECKON
exorior, -iri, -ortus sum	TO RISE, TO ARISE, TO PRODUCE
expedio, -ire, -ivi, -itum	TO EXTRICATE, TO BRING FORWARD, TO PREPARE
expello, -ere, -puli, -pulsum	TO EXPEL ✧ It should be noted that the reduplication in the perfect in the original verb **pello, -ere, pepuli, pulsum** is lost in the compound form: **expuli**, not **expepuli**.
experior, -iri, expertus sum	TO TRY, TO EXPERIENCE
exploro, -are, -avi, -atum	TO EXAMINE
expono, -ere, -posui, -positum	TO TENDER, TO EXPOSE
exsequor, -i, -secutus sum	TO FOLLOW, TO INVESTIGATE, TO ACCOMPLISH ✧ In the sense of following something to the very end.
exsisto, -ere, -stiti (no supine)	TO STEP OUT, TO APPEAR
exsolvo, -ere, -solvi, -solutum	TO RELEASE, TO SOLVE
exspecto -are, -avi, -atum	TO EXPECT, TO AWAIT
extraho, -ere, -axi, -actum	TO DRAW OUT, TO DRAG

❑ With in

Both senses of **in** can be felt in these verbs:

a/ The sense of *direction, place towards which*, as in **incido** TO ASSAULT
b/ The sense of *interiority*, like in **incolo** TO DWELL

immisceo, -ere, -miscui, -mixtum TO INTERMINGLE
impedio, -ire, -ivi, -itum TO HINDER, TO OBSTRUCT
impello, -ere, -puli, -pulsum TO STRIKE AGAINST, TO DRIVE FORWARD ✧ See note in **expello** with respect to the perfect tense.
impendeo, -ere (no perfect, no supine) TO HANG OVER, TO BE IMMINENT
impendo, -ere, -pendi, -pensum TO EXPEND, TO LAY OUT
impingo, -ere, -pegi, -pactum TO DASH AGAINST
impleo, -ere, -plevi, -pletum TO FILL UP, TO COMPLETE
implico, -are, -avi, -atum TO INVOLVE, TO CONNECT
imploro, -are, -avi, -atum TO IMPLORE
impono, -ere, -posui, -positum TO IMPOSE, TO ESTABLISH
imprimo, -ere, -pressi, -pressum TO PRESS UPON, TO ENGRAVE
incido, -ere, -cidi (no supine) TO FALL IN, TO ASSAULT, TO HAPPEN ✧ This verb is a compound of **cado, -ere** TO FALL.
incido, -ere, -cidi, -cisum TO CUT THROUGH, TO PUT AN END TO ✧ This verb is a compound of **caedo, -ere** TO MAKE FALL
incipio, -ere, -cepi, -ceptum TO BEGIN
incito, -are, -avi, -atum TO HASTEN, TO EXCITE
includo, -ere, -usi, -usum TO CONFINE, TO INCLUDE
incolo, -ere, -lui (no supine) TO DWELL
indico, -dixi, -dictum TO PROCLAIM, TO IMPOSE ✧ Do not confuse with the verb **indico, -are, -avi, -atum**, with a very similar meaning: TO DECLARE, TO REVEAL, **etc.**
induco, -ere, -duxi, -ductum TO LEAD IN, TO PERSUADE
ineo, -ire, -ii, -itum TO ENTER, TO GO IN
infero, -ferre, -tuli, -latum TO INTRODUCE ✧ If used with a reflexive pronoun, it means TO GO:

- **Imperator in urbem *se intulit*** THE COMMANDER WENT INTO THE CITY (Cicero, *In Pisonem*).

inflamo, -are, -avi, -atum TO SET ON FIRE, TO KINDLE
ingredior, -i, -gressus sum TO ENTER, TO ENGAGE IN
inhibeo, -ere, -ui, -itum TO RESTRAIN
inicio, -ere, -ieci, -iectum TO THROW IN, TO INSPIRE ✧ There is a certain tendency to confuse this verb with **initio, -are** TO START.
inrumpo, -ere, -rupi, -ruptum TO BREAK IN, TO FALL UPON ✧ Sometimes written also **irrumpo** etc.
inruo, -ere, -rui (no supine) TO RUSH IN, TO ATTACK ✧ Sometimes written also **irruo** etc.
insero, -ere, -serui, -sertum TO INTRODUCE, TO ENROL ✧ Do not confuse with **insero, -ere, -sevi, -situm** TO IMPLANT.
inspicio, -ere, -pexi, -spectum TO INSPECT, TO EXAMINE

instituo, -ere, -ui, -utum TO SET UP, TO ARRANGE
insto, -are, -stiti, -statum TO APPROACH, TO URGE
instruo, -ere, -uxi, -uctum TO DRAW UP
insurgo, -ere, -surrexi, -surrectum TO RISE UP
intendo, -ere, -di, -tentum TO STRETCH OUT, TO AIM TO
intueor, -eri, -tuitus sum TO GAZE AT, TO CONSIDER
invado, -ere, -vasi, -vasum TO INVADE
invenio, -ire, -veni, -ventum TO FIND, TO DISCOVER
inverto, -ere, -verti, -versum TO REVERSE, TO INVERT
invideo, -ere, -vidi, -visum TO ENVY

❑ With inter

The sense of an action taking place in the middle of something else is quite perceptible, as in **intervenio** TO INTERVENE, in the sense of going into the middle of another action.

intellego, -ere, -lexi, -lectum TO PERCEIVE, TO UNDERSTAND ✧ In the sense of "reading between lines".
intercedo, -ere, -cessi, -cessum TO INTERVENE, TO INTERCEDE, TO HAPPEN ✧ In the sense of something that comes up between two other events.
intercido, -ere, -idi (no supine) TO FALL, TO HAPPEN ✧ This verb is a compound of **cado, -ere** TO FALL.
intercido, -ere, -idi, -isum TO DIVIDE, TO CUT THROUGH. ✧ This verb is a compound of **caedo, -ere** TO MAKE FALL.
intercipio, -ere, cepi, -ceptum TO INTERCEPT, TO INTERRUPT
intercludo, -ere, -usi, -usum TO SHUT OFF, TO PREVENT
interdico, -ere, -dixi, -dictum TO FORBID
intereo, -ire, -ii, -itum TO BE LOST, TO DIE • **Omnis noster equitatus, omnis nobilitas *interiit*** ALL OUR CAVALRY, ALL OUR NOBILITY DIED (Caesar, *De Bello Gallico*).
interficio, -ere, -feci, -fectum TO KILL
intermitto, -ere, -misi, -missum TO INTERMIT, TO OMIT, TO INTERRUPT
interpono, -ere, -posui, -positum TO INTERPOSE, TO INSERT, TO PLEDGE
interrogo, -are, -avi, -atum TO ASK
interrumpo, -ere, -rupi, -ruptum TO INTERRUPT, TO BREAK TO PIECES
intersum, -esse, -fui (no supine) TO BE BETWEEN, TO TAKE PART IN, TO DIFFER
intervenio, -ire, -veni, -ventum TO INTERVENE, TO HAPPEN

✧ It should also be noted that the perfect tense of the verb **lego, -ere,** from which **intellego** is a compound, is **legi**, while the perfect tense of **intellego** is **intellexi**; students have the tendency to think that the perfect of **lego** is **lexi** because of this natural influence.

❑ With ob

The most direct meaning that **ob** will give is that of opposition, as in **obsisto** TO RESIST.

obeo, -ire, -ii, -itum TO GO TO MEET
obicio, -ere, -ieci, -iectum TO THROW, TO OFFER
oblecto, -are, -avi, -atum TO DELIGHT

obligo, -are, -avi, -atum	TO BIND, TO COMPEL
obruo, -ere, -ui, -utum	TO OVERWHELM, TO COVER
obsecro, -are, -avi, -atum	TO ENTREAT
obsequor, -i, -secutus sum	TO GRATIFY, TO COMPLY
obsideo, -ere, -edi, -essum	TO BESIEGE, TO STAY
obsisto, -ere, -stiti, -stitum	TO OPPOSE, TO RESIST
obsto, -are, -stiti (no supine)	TO HINDER
obstruo, -ere, -uxi, -uctum	TO BLOCK, TO OBSTRUCT
obsum -esse, -fui (no supine)	TO BE AGAINST
obvenio, -ire, -veni, -ventum	TO GO TO MEET
obverto, -ere, -verti, -versum	TO TURN AGAINST
occido, -ere, occidi, occasum	TO FALL, TO DIE ✧ This verb is a compound of **cado, -ere** TO FALL.
occido, -ere, occidi, occisum	TO KILL ✧ This verb is a compound of **caedo, -ere** TO MAKE FALL.
occupo, -are, -avi, -atum	TO OCCUPY
occurro, -ere, -curri, -cursum	TO RUN TO MEET
offendo, -ere, -fendi, -fensum	TO HIT, TO COMMIT A FAULT AGAINST
offero, -ferre, obtuli, oblatum	TO PRESENT, TO OFFER
officio, -ere, -eci, -ectum	TO HINDER, TO OBSTRUCT
offundo, -ere, -udi, -usum	TO POUR OUT
oppeto, -ere, -ivi, -itum	TO ENCOUNTER
oppono, -ere, -posui, -positum	TO PLACE AGAINST, TO OPPOSE
opprimo, -ere, -pressi, -pressum	TO PRESS DOWN, TO SUBDUE
oppugno, -are, -avi, -atum	TO BESIEGE

❑ With per

The preposition **per** gives usually one of these two meanings to the verb:

a/ the sense of *passing from one stage to another one.*
b/ the sense of *completeness.*

For instance, **permuto, -are** has both meanings:

a/ TO EXCHANGE ✧ In the sense of something that goes from one hand to another one.
b/ TO CHANGE COMPLETELY

perago, -ere, -egi, -actum	TO TRANSFIX, TO DISTURB, TO COMPLETE
percipio, -ere, -cepi, -ceptum	TO SEIZE COMPLETELY, TO UNDERSTAND
perdo, -ere, -didi, -ditum	TO RUIN, TO WASTE
pereo, -ire, -ii, -itum	TO DISAPPEAR, TO DIE
perficio, -ere, -feci, -fectum	TO COMPLETE
permaneo, -ere, -mansi, -mansum	TO RESIST
permitto, -ere, -misi, -missum	TO LET PASS, TO ALLOW
permoveo, -ere, -movi, -motum	TO ROUSE, TO MOVE DEEPLY
permuto, -are, -avi, -atum	TO CHANGE COMPLETELY, TO EXCHANGE

persequor, -i, -secutus sum TO PURSUE
persisto, -ere, -stiti (no supine) TO PERSIST
persolvo, -ere, -solvi, -solutum TO SOLVE, TO PAY ✧ In the sense of paying off a debt completely.
perspicio, -ere, -spexi, -spectum TO LOOK THROUGH, TO REALISE
persto, -are, -stiti, -statum TO STAND, TO PERSEVERE
persuadeo, -ere, -suasi, -suasum TO PERSUADE
pertineo, -ere, -tinui (no supine) TO BELONG, TO PERTAIN
pertracto, -are, -avi, -atum TO HANDLE
perturbo, -are, -avi, -atum TO DISTURB
pervado, -ere, -vasi (no supine) TO CROSS, TO PERVADE
pervenio, -ire, -veni, -ventum TO ARRIVE
perverto, -ere, -verti, -versum TO OVERTURN, TO DESTROY
pervideo, -ere, -vidi, -visum TO LOOK OVER, TO DISCERN
pervigilo, -are, -avi, -atum TO REMAIN AWAKE WATCHING
pervolo, -velle, -volui (no supine) TO DESIRE VERY MUCH

❑ With post

Hardly any verb uses **post** to form a compound verb. It gives a meaning of *putting something behind*. It produces the opposite meaning from the one produced by **prae**.

posthabeo, -ere, -habui, -habitum TO NEGLECT
postpono, -ere, -posui, -positum TO POSTPONE, TO DISREGARD

❑ With prae

It gives a meaning of *putting something before something else*, as in **praebeo** TO OFFER. It produces the opposite meaning from the one produced by **post**.

praebeo, -ere, -ui, -itum TO OFFER
praecipio, -ere, -cepi, -ceptum TO TAKE IN ADVANCE, TO INSTRUCT
praecludo, -ere, -si, -sum TO SHUT OFF
praedico, -ere, -dixi, -dictum TO FORETELL, TO PREDICT
praedico, -are, -avi, -atum TO PROCLAIM
praeeo, -ire, -ii, -itum TO PRECEDE
praefero, -ferre, -tuli, -latum TO BEAR BEFORE, TO PREFER
praeficio, -ere, -feci, -fectum TO PUT IN COMMAND OF
praemitto, -ere, -misi, -missum TO SEND FORWARD
praemoneo, -ere, -nui, -nitum TO FOREWARN
praemunio, -ire, -ivi, -itum TO FORTIFY
praeparo, -are, -avi, -atum TO PREPARE
praepono, -ere, -posui, -positum TO PUT IN FRONT
praeripio, -ere, -ripui, -reptum TO SNATCH AWAY
praesto, -are, -stiti, -stitum TO STAND OUT, TO EXCEL

praesum, -esse, -fui (no supine) TO BE IN CHARGE OF
praetendo, -ere, -tendi, -tentum TO REACH OUT, TO SPREAD
praevideo, -ere, -vidi, -visum TO FORESEE

❑ With praeter

There are hardly any verbs compound with **praeter**, with this meaning of *along, beyond.*

praetereo, -ire, -ii, -itum TO GO BY, TO DISREGARD ✧ In the sense of passing by something without taking it.
praetermitto, -ere, -misi, -missum TO LET PASS, TO DISREGARD

❑ With pro

It produces a very similar sense to that produced by **prae**, but **pro** has a stronger sense of *movement* rather than *position.*

procedo, -ere, -cessi (no supine) TO PROCEED
proclamo, -are, -avi, -atum TO PROCLAIM, TO SAY LOUDLY
procreo, -are, -avi, -atum TO PRODUCE, TO CAUSE
prodo, -ere, -didi, -ditum TO PUT FORTH, TO APPOINT
produco, -ere, -duxi, -ductum TO LEAD FORWARD, TO DISCLOSE
profero, -ferre, -tuli, -latum TO BRING FORTH, TO MAKE KNOWN
profiteor, -eri, -fessus sum TO ACKNOWLEDGE PUBLICLY, TO CONFESS
progredior, -i, -gressus sum TO GO FORTH, TO ADVANCE
prohibeo, -ere, -ui, -itum TO FORBID, TO HINDER ✧ In the sense of holding something in front of something else
proicio, -ere, -ieci, -iectum TO THROW FORTH, TO THROW DOWN
promitto, -ere, -misi, -missum TO SEND FORTH, TO PROMISE
pronuntio, -are, -avi, -atum TO PROCLAIM
propono, -ere, -posui, -positum TO PUT FORTH, TO PROPOSE
proscribo, -ere, -scripsi, -scriptum TO ANNOUNCE IN WRITING, TO PROSCRIBE ✧ In the sense of criminals whose names were publicly written as people who had lost their properties.
prosequor, -i, -secutus sum TO FOLLOW
prospicio, -ere, -pexi, -pectum TO LOOK FORWARD
prosum, -esse, -fui (no supine) TO BENEFIT (+ Dat.)
protego, -ere, -texi, -tectum TO PROTECT
proveho, -ere, -vexi, -vectum TO CARRY FORWARD ✧ Its use in the passive meaning TO PROCEED, TO MOVE FORWARD is very common.
provideo, -ere, -vidi, -visum TO FORESEE
provoco, -are, -avi, -atum TO SUMMON, TO STIR UP

❑ With sub

Although the meaning of *under* or *from under* is quite clear, as in **submitto** TO SEND SECRETLY, in other cases it may even seem that it has the opposite meaning, *over*, as in **suggero** TO IMPOSE.

subdo, -ere, -didi, -ditum TO APPLY, TO REPLACE
subduco, -ere, -duxi, -ductum TO REMOVE SECRETLY, TO RAISE
subeo, -ire, -ii, -itum TO GO UNDER, TO APPROACH

subigo, -ere, -egi, -actum — TO SUBMIT
sublevo, -are, -avi, -atum — TO RAISE UP
submitto, -ere, -misi, -missum — TO PUT DOWN, TO SEND SECRETLY
subsequor, -i, -secutus sum — TO FOLLOW UP, TO COMPLY WITH
subsisto, -ere, -stiti (no supine) — TO STAND STILL, TO RESIST
subsum, -esse, -fui (no supine) — TO BE UNDERNEATH
subvenio, -ire, -veni, -ventum — TO COME TO HELP
subverto, -ere, -verti, -versum — TO OVERTURN
succedo, -ere, -cessi, -cessum — TO SUCCEED, TO FOLLOW AFTER
succurro, -ere, -curri, -cursum — TO (RUN TO) HELP
sufficio, -ere, -feci, -fectum — TO SUFFICE, TO APPOINT AS A REPLACEMENT
suffodio, -ere, -fodi, -fossum — TO UNDERMINE
suggero, -ere, -gessi, -gestum — TO ASSIGN, TO IMPOSE
suscipio, -ere, -cepi, -ceptum — TO TAKE UP
suspicio, -ere, -pexi, -pectum — TO ADMIRE ✧ In the sense of looking at somebody from an inferior position upwards.
sustineo, -ere, -tinui, -tentum — TO SUPPORT, TO TOLERATE

❑ With subter

In fact there is only one verb that is usually found with **subter**, that produces a sense of *from below*:

subterfugio, -ere, -fugi (no supine) — TO ESCAPE

❑ With super

Not many verbs are compounded with **super**, but all of them get a sense of *above, over* :

superiacio, -ere, -ieci, -iectum — TO THROW OVER, TO EXCEED
supersto, -are, -steti (no supine) — TO STAND OVER
supersum, superesse — TO BE LEFT OVER, TO SURVIVE, TO ABOUND

❑ With trans

The meaning of *from one side to the other* is very visible in these compounds.

traduco, -ere, -duxi, -ductum — TO LEAD ACROSS, TO TRANSLATE
traicio, -ere, -ieci, -iectum — TO TRANSPORT ACROSS, TO STRIKE THROUGH
transcurro, -ere, -curri, -cursum — TO RUN ACCROSS, TO GO BY
transeo, -ire, -ii, -itum — TO CROSS OVER, TO PERVADE
transfero, -ferre, -tuli, -latum — TO CONVEY OVER, TO POSTPONE
transfigo, -ere, -fixi, -fictum — TO PIERCE THROUGH
transgredior, -i, -gressus sum — TO STEP OVER, TO TRESSPASS
transmitto, -ere, -misi, -missum — TO SEND OVER
transporto, -are, -avi, -atum — TO CARRY OVER
transveho, -ere, -vexi, -vectum — TO CARRY OVER, TO RIDE IN PROCESSION

SYNTAX OF CASES

a) Use of cases

1. General observations
2. Nominative
3. Vocative
4. Accusative
5. Genitive
6. Dative
7. Ablative

b) Prepositions

1. General observations
2. Prepositions of one case
3. Prepositions of two cases

c) Expressions of time and place

1. Expressions of time
2. Expressions of place

d) Regime of verbs and adjectives

1. General observations
2. Verbs that rule a given case
3. Adjectives followed by a given case

a) Use of cases

1. General observations [221]

We have seen in the introductory chapter on syntactical functions a quick general view of the main functions and the case associated with each one. In this chapter we will try to give a more complete view.

Except for the nominative and vocative, each one of the other cases has a wide variety of functions, one or two of them the most common ones, and a large spectrum of derivative functions, and the way of classifying their several functions is an open choice. How many to include and how to subdivide them has always been very subjective, so we will include here the functions that we consider that are worth knowing and we will group them trying to follow a logic system, avoiding unnecessary theoretical complications.

We will deal here only with the uses that cases can express on their own, not those uses that are expressed by means of prepositions (with accusative or ablative) or special uses in specific syntactical constructions that will be dealt with in their respective chapter of peculiar constructions.

2. Nominative [222]

a/ Its main function is that of subject:

- *Cicero* in Catilinam orationem fecit   CICERO MADE A SPEECH AGAINST CATILINE.

b/ Another of its functions is of predicative object (also called *attribute*); the predicative object is usually an adjective, but it can also be a noun:

- Hic magister *altus* est   THIS TEACHER IS TALL.
- Cicero *spes* reipublicae est   CICERO IS THE HOPE OF THE STATE.

c/ It will be used also with some passive expressions of *being considered, become, happen*, etc.:

- Cicero *doctissimus homo* iudicatur   CICERO IS CONSIDERED A VERY WISE MAN.
- Octavius *dux* factus est   OCTAVIUS WAS APPOINTED GENERAL.
- Post paucos annos *pontifex maximus* factus est   AFTER A FEW YEARS HE WAS APPOINTED PONTIFEX MAXIMUS (Livy, *Ab Urbe Condita*).
- Posteaquam *reus* factus est...   AFTER HE WAS MADE PRISONER... (Cicero, *In Verrem*).
- *Tantus* in curia *clamor* factus est ut populus concurreret   THERE WAS SUCH AN UPROAR IN THE SENATE THAT THE PEOPLE CAME RUNNING (Cicero, *In Verrem*).

3. Vocative [223]

It is used to address somebody directly; remember that only in the first subtype of the 2nd declension it has an ending different from that of the nominative, and that the Voc. of meus is mi:

- Quid debeo nunc facere, *mi domine?*   WHAT MUST I DO NOW, MY MASTER?

4. Accusative [224]

a) Main function: direct object

1/ Plain direct object

The person or object receiving the direct action of a transitive verb:

- *Filium* amo — I LOVE MY SON.
- Hostes *urbem* deleverunt — THE ENEMY DESTROYED THE CITY.
- Legimus *librum* Clitomachi — WE READ CLITOMACHUS' BOOK (Cicero, *Tusculanae Disputationes*).

⌑ The two uses described further down are in fact extensions of this function of direct object.

2/ Internal accusative

Also called *cognate accusative*, it is a direct object that comes from the same stem as the verb of the sentence:

- Longam *pugnam pugnavimus* — WE FOUGHT A LONG FIGHT.
  ✧ Observe that we have kept this "internality" also in English, although it sounds awkward, but it is the way it sounded in Latin.
- Prius quam istam *pugnam pugnabo, ...* — BEFORE I FIGHT THIS FIGHT, ... (Plautus, *Pseudolus*).

3/ Double accusative [225]

a/ Some verbs have two accusatives: one for the direct object and another one for the person involved in the action (apart from the subject):

- Doceo *pueros linguam Latinam* — I TEACH THE STUDENTS LATIN LANGUAGE.
  ✧ The tendency in English would be to expect THE STUDENTS to be in dative.
- *Librum Caesarem* celavit — HE HID THE BOOK FROM CAESAR.
- *Hoc* ipsus magister *me* docuit — THE TEACHER HIMSELF TAUGHT ME THIS (Plautus, *Aulularia*).

Other verbs that use the same construction and some examples with them:

flagito, -are — TO REQUEST SOMETHING FROM SOMEBODY
posco, -ere — TO ASK SOMETHING FROM SOMEBODY
rogo, -are — TO ASK SOMETHING FROM SOMEBODY

- Cotidie Caesar *Haeduos frumentum* ... flagitare — EVERYDAY CAESAR REQUESTED CORN FROM THE HAEDUI (Caesar, *De Bello Gallico*).
- *Sagmina* inquit *te* rex posco — I ASK FROM YOU, O KING, THE SACRED HERBS (Livy, *Ab Urbe Condita*).
- *Aliud te* rogo — I ASK SOMETHING ELSE FROM YOU (Plautus, *Mostellaria*).

b/ The other kind of verbs that have double accusative are verbs that, apart from having a direct object, have also a *predicative object* that attributes some quality or status to the direct one (and a predicative must always be in the same case as the word of which it is a predicative, so it will also be in the Acc.):

- *Te amicum* ducebam — I CONSIDERED YOU A FRIEND.
  ✧ Both, whom I consider and what I consider him to be, must be in the accusative.
- Senatus *Ciceronem consulem* creavit — THE SENATE APPOINTED CICERO CONSUL.
- Ex consularibus *te* creavit *potissimum* (Cicero, *Pro Milone*). — HE APPOINTED YOU AS THE BEST ONE OF THE MEN OF CONSULAR RANK

Other verbs that use the same construction and some examples with them:

dico, -ere — TO CALL SOMEBODY SOMETHING
existimo, -are — TO CONSIDER SOMEBODY SOMETHING
facio, -ere — TO MAKE (in the sense of TO APPOINT) SOMEBODY SOMETHING
iudico, -are — TO JUDGE SOMEBODY AS SOMETHING
nomino, -are — TO CALL SOMEBODY SOMETHING
puto, -are — TO CONSIDER SOMEBODY SOMETHING
voco, -are — TO CALL SOMEBODY SOMETHING

- *Te bonum amicum* existimabam — I CONSIDERED YOU A GOOD FRIEND.
- Populus *Caesarem gloriam* Romae vocavit — THE PEOPLE CALLED CAESAR THE GLORY OF ROME.
- *M. Livium consulem* fecerunt — THEY APPOINTED MARCUS LIVIUS CONSUL (Livy, *Ab Urbe Condita*).

b) Other uses [226]

1/ Accusative of extension

a/ It has two uses: in time and in space, and it means the extension along which the action takes place. These first examples makes reference to the time (accusative of extension *in time*):

- Milites *tres horas* ambulaverunt — THE SOLDIERS WALKED (FOR) THREE HOURS.
- *Octoginta* regnavit *annos* — HE REIGNED FOR EIGHTY YEARS (Cicero, *Cato Maior de Senectute*).
- *Duas horas* Thyrrei fuimus — WE WERE TWO HOURS IN THYRREUM (Cicero, *Epistulae ad Familiares*)

✧ Observe that in English we can add DURING or FOR to the time expression.

And this example makes reference to the space (accusative of extension *in space*):

- Milites *tria milia* passuum ambulaverunt — THE SOLDIERS WALKED (FOR) THREE MILES.
- Ubi *paulum* ambulaverunt, ... — AFTER THEY HAVE WALKED FOR A WHILE, ... (Celsus, *De Medicina*).

✧ Again, in English we can add DURING or FOR.

b/ Do not confuse an accusative of extension with a direct object, as both will be in accusative without preposition:

- Mei discipuli semper omnes suos onerosos libros (dir. obj.) *decem milia* (acc. ext.) passuum ferre debent si laborem non fecerunt — MY STUDENTS MUST ALWAYS CARRY ALL THEIR HEAVY BOOKS FOR TEN MILES IF THEY HAVE NOT DONE THE HOMEWORK.

c/ It can also be used to indicate dimensions:

- Fossa *novem pedes* alta erat — THE DITCH WAS NINE FEET DEEP.
- Id est *decem pedes* et longitudine et latitudine quadratum (Varro, *Res Rusticae*). — IT IS A SQUARE FORM OF TEN FEET BOTH WIDE AND LONG

2/ Exclamatory accusative [227]

The examples will make clear its use:

- *Me miserum!* POOR ME!
- *O maestam cladem!* O SAD DEFEAT!
- *O me miserum, o me infelicem!* POOR ME, UNHAPPY ME! (Cicero, *Pro Milone*).

3/ Accusative of respect

Sometimes the accusative, instead of being the direct object of the verb, specifies with respect to what the action of the verb takes place. For instance:

- Hoc homo similis deo est *caput et manus* THIS MAN IS SIMILAR TO A GOD IN (WITH RESPECT TO) HIS HEAD AND HIS HANDS.
- Servilium magistrum equitum servaverat, ipse vulneratus *umerum* HE HAD SAVED SERVILIUS, THE MASTER OF THE CAVALRY, ALTHOUGH HE HIMSELF WAS WOUNDED IN HIS ARM (Plinius Secundis, *Naturalis Historia*).

In fact this is not a very common construction in Latin (except in its use as *adverbial accusative*, see further down), and it is considered a structure borrowed from Greek.

4/ Adverbial accusative [228]

The accusative neuter of some nouns and adjectives is sometimes used in an adverbial sense, and in fact all of these accusatives could be considered *accusatives of respect*:

multum	MUCH	primum	IN THE FIRST PLACE
id temporis	AT THAT POINT OF TIME	secundum	IN THE SECOND PLACE
nihil	IN NO WAY	maximam partem	FOR THE MOST PART

- Mei discipuli semper *multum* laborant MY STUDENTS ALWAYS WORK A LOT.
- *Multum* inter se distant haec facultates THESE QUALITIES DIFFER A LOT AMONG THEM (Cicero, *De Oratore*).
- ... quos ego iam ad me *id temporis* venturos esse praedixeram ... THOSE WHOM I HAD PREDICTED WOULD COME TO MY HOUSE AT THAT POINT OF THE DAY (Cicero, *In Catilinam*).
- Atqui *nihil* interest, iudices, utrum... BUT IT DOES NOT MATTER (literally, IT MATTERS IN NO WAY), JUDGES, WHETHER... (Cicero, *Pro Balbo*).
- *Maximam partem* lacte atque pecore vivunt FOR THE MOST PART THEY LIVE BY MILK AND CATTLE (Caesar, *De Bello Gallico*).

5/ Time expressions

Apart from the mentioned accusative of extension in temporal sense, this case is also used in other expressions of time that will be presented in the corresponding chapter.

5. Genitive [229]

a) Main function: possessive genitive

1/ It indicates the possessor of something

- Librum *magistri* habeo — I HAVE THE TEACHER'S BOOK.
- Arma *hostium* cepimus — WE TOOK THE WEAPONS OF THE ENEMY.
- Postridie ... cum *hostium* legionibus pugnavimus — AT THE FOLLOWING DAY WE FOUGHT WITH THE LEGIONS OF THE ENEMY (Cato, *Origines*).

Position of the genitive:

As we can see, it is very common that the genitive is positioned before the noun on which it depends, and even if it means splitting a noun from the preposition on which the noun depends. So, instead of ...cum legionibus *hostium*... we have found ...cum *hostium* legionibus... And it is also normal that this practice of placing it before the noun splits the noun from an adjective accompanying it:

- Facile est hoc cernere in primis *puerorum* aetatulis — IT IS EASY TO SEE THIS IN THE FIRST TENDER AGES OF CHILDREN (Cicero, *De Finibus*).

2/ Its use with an infinitive [230]

The infinitive indicates an activity *typical of, proper of,* etc. the person in the genitive; usually, an additional English word will have to be added to help the translation have meaning.

- Discipulos docere *magistri* est — IT IS (THE DUTY, for instance) OF A TEACHER TO TEACH STUDENTS.
- Hoc dicere *Caesaris* est — SAYING THIS IS (TYPICAL, for instance) OF CAESAR.
- *Summi ducis* est Galbam occidere — IT IS THE DUTY OF A HIGH-RANK GENERAL TO KILL GALBA (Iuvenalis, *Saturae*).

3/ Subjective and objective genitive

In some cases, the usual translation by OF can be confusing; observe this example:

Timor *hostium* magnus erat.

Does it mean the fear that somebody felt for the enemy, or the fear that the enemy felt in front of somebody else? Usually the context will help to solve it. If it means the fear that somebody felt in front of the enemy, it is called *objective genitive*, because in fact *the enemy* is the object that somebody fears; if it means the fear that the enemy are feeling, it is called *subjective genitive*, because *the enemy* is the subject that experiences the feeling.

Let's see an example of objective genitive:

- Aliis timor *hostium* audaciam ingrediendi flumen fecit — THE FEAR OF THE ENEMY (THE FEAR THEY FEEL FOR THE ENEMY) MADE OTHERS ENTER THE RIVER (Livy, *Ab Urbe Condita*).
  ✧ Literally, ... PRODUCED TO OTHERS THE BOLDNESS TO ENTER THE RIVER.

And now an example of subjective genitive:

- Induratur praeter spem resistendo hostium timor — THE FEAR OF THE ENEMY (THE FEAR THAT THE ENEMY FEELS) HAS HARDENED, RESISTING BEYOND EXPECTATION (Livy, *Ab Urbe Condita*).

b) Other uses [231]

1/ Genitive of characteristic

Also called *genitive of description*, it describes a characteristic of something or somebody:

- Homo *magni corporis* venit heri — YESTERDAY CAME A MAN OF BIG CORPULENCE.
- Ego et Calvisius, homo *magni iudicii*... (Cicero, *Epistulae ad Familiares*). — I AND CALVISIUS, A MAN OF GREAT JUDGEMENT, ...

It is also used to describe a quantity:

- Eos vicit exercitu *trium legionum* — HE CONQUERED THEM WITH AN ARMY OF THREE LEGIONS.

2/ Judicial genitive

The blame, the accusation, is put in the genitive:

- Verres accusatus est *multorum scelerum* — VERRES WAS ACCUSED OF MANY CRIMES.
- Accusatus est *repetundarum* — HE WAS ACCUSED OF EXTORTION (Asconius Pedianus, *In Toga Candida*).

Two things must be noted about this matter of judicial verbs:

– The *person* whom we accuse is put in the accusative, as expected:

- *Quem* ego accuso? — WHOM DO I ACCUSE? (Cicero, *In Verrem*).

– And the *blame* can also be expressed with **de** + Abl.:

- Accusavi *de pecuniis repetundis* — I ACCUSED (THEM) OF EXTORTION (Cicero, *Pro Rabirio Postumo*).

3/ Genitive of value

It is used for expressing an approximate or general value. The most common verbs that are used with the meaning of *considering* are **puto**, **facio**, **aestimo** and **duco**, and the most common words that we will find in genitive are:

maximi	OF MUCH (VALUE)	magni	OF GREAT (VALUE)
minimi	OF HARDLY ANYTHING	quanti?	OF HOW MUCH (VALUE)?
parvi	OF LITTLE (VALUE)		

- Tuam amicitiam *maximi* puto — I HAVE YOUR FRIENDSHIP IN HIGH ESTEEM.
- Hanc victoriam *parvi* aestimo — I VALUE THIS VICTORY AT VERY LITTLE.
- *Quanti* debemus amorem ducere? — AT HOW MUCH MUST WE VALUE LOVE?
- Non ego illud *parvi* aestimo — I DO NOT VALUE THAT AT VERY LITTLE (Livy, *Ab Urbe Condita*).

Note

The exact price of something is expressed by the *ablative of price* (see further down), but when asking about the price we can use the genitive:

- *Quanti* eam emit? — FOR HOW MUCH DID HE BUY HER? (Plautus, *Epidicus*).

4/ Partitive genitive [232]

It is used to express the total from which a part is meant:

- Plerique *civium* pugnare volebant MOST OF THE CITIZENS WANTED TO FIGHT.
- Nemo *militum* fugit NO ONE OF THE SOLDIERS FLED.
- Sicuti plerique *vestrum* sciunt, ... AS MOST OF YOU KNOW, ... (Cicero, *Pro Cluentio*).
- Clariore voce, ut magna pars *militum* exaudiret, ..., inquit ... WITH A LOUDER VOICE, SO THAT THE MOST PART OF THE SOLDIERS COULD HEAR, HE SAID ... (Caesar, *De Bello Gallico*).

This construction is also common with numbers, when we want to say for instance FIVE OF THE SOLDIERS instead of FIVE SOLDIERS:

quinque milites FIVE SOLDIERS ≠ quinque militum FIVE OF THE SOLDIERS (from a larger group).

5/ With quantitative adverbs

Some adverbs of quantity can be followed by a genitive (in fact it is a derivative use of the partitive genitive):

- Satis *pecuniae* habeo I HAVE ENOUGH [OF] MONEY.
- Nimis *vini* bibis YOU ARE DRINKING TOO MUCH [OF] WINE.
- Si iam satis *aetatis ac roboris* haberet, ipse pro Sex. Roscio diceret IF HE HAD ENOUGH [OF] AGE AND [OF] STRENGTH, HE HIMSELF WOULD SPEAK IN FAVOUR OF S. ROSCIUS (Cicero, *Pro Roscio Amerino*).

6/ With some verbs and adjectives

Some verbs rule genitive: (see more complete list in the corresponding chapter)

- Meminerunt huius coniurationis Tanusius Geminus in historia, Marcus Bibulus in edictis
  T. GEMINUS IN HIS NARRATIVE [AND] M. BIBULIUS IN HIS EDICTS REMEMBER (MENTION) THIS CONSPIRACY
  (Suetonius Tranquillus, *De Vita Caesarum*).

Note

Some of these verbs can also rule an accusative:

- Memini omnino *tuas litteras* I REMEMBER YOUR LETTER COMPLETELY (Cicero, *Epistulae at Atticum*).

And also some adjectives: (see more complete list in the corresponding chapter)

- Amphoram plenam *aquae* habeo I HAVE AN AMPHORA FULL OF WATER.
- Cur semper avidi *pecuniae* estis? WHY ARE YOU ALWAYS DESIROUS OF MONEY?
- T. Quinctius plenus *lacrimarum* ad suos versus ... inquit ... T. QUINCTIUS, FULL OF TEARS, TURNING TOWARDS HIS PEOPLE, SAID ... (Livy, *Ab Urbe Condita*).

Note

Some of these adjectives can also rule an ablative:

- Ex tuis litteris plenus sum *expectatione* de Pompeio FROM YOUR LETTERS, I AM FULL OF EXPECTATION ABOUT POMPEIUS (Cicero, *Epistulae ad Atticum*).

6. Dative [233]

a) Main function: indirect object

1/ It indicates the person (object, institution, etc.) for or to whom something is done

- Dic veritatem *magistro* — TELL THE TRUTH TO THE TEACHER.
- Has ego, si vis, *tibi* dabo — I WILL GIVE THEM TO YOU, IF YOU WANT (Plautus, *Asinaria*).
- Hoc ego *tibi* dico — I TELL YOU THIS (Ennius, *Tragoediae*).

2/ Dative of interest

It expresses the person (object, institution, etc.) that may be indirectly affected (in a positive or negative way) by the action. In fact it is almost the same as an indirect object:

- Haec omnia *Romae* feci — I HAVE DONE ALL OF THIS FOR ROME.
- Statuam *Caesari* in foro ponere volo — I WANT TO PLACE A STATUE IN THE FORUM FOR CAESAR.
  ✧ Observe this last example: it says FOR CAESAR, not OF CAESAR, so in his honour, whether the statue represents Caesar himself or not.
- Hoc *mihi* aegre est — THIS IS SAD FOR ME (Plautus, *Captivi*).
- Credite hoc *mihi*, iudices — BELIEVE THIS, JUDGES (Cicero, *In Verrem*).
  ✧ The **mihi** is untranslatable here, it gives a sense of *in my benefit*.

3/ Dative of reference

It indicates the person for whom the statement is real:

- Hoc *mihi* veritas est — IN MY OPINION, THIS IS TRUE.
- Omnes milites audaces sunt *duci* — FOR THE GENERAL (IN THE GENERAL'S OPINION), ALL THE SOLDIERS ARE BRAVE.
- Hoc *mihi* non est dubium — IN MY OPINION, THIS IS NOT DOUBTFUL (Cicero, *Epistulae ad Familiares*).
  ✧ One could argue that this is a dative of interest, THIS IS NOT DOUBTFUL TO ME. Sometimes the borderline between both is very debatable.

b) Other uses [234]

1/ Possessive dative

Usually, to indicate possession, we make use of the verb **habeo**, but in combination with the verb **sum** the dative can also be used to indicate possession.

Therefore, instead of saying	Habeo multos libros	I HAVE MANY BOOKS ...
... we can say	Multi libri sunt *mihi*	MANY BOOKS ARE FOR ME = I HAVE MANY BOOKS.

So, the possessed object becomes the subject of the sentence (and therefore it must be in nominative) and the possessor is put in dative.

Another example:

Instead of saying **Dux habebat multos filios** THE GENERAL HAD MANY SONS ...
... we can say **Multi filii erant *duci*** MANY SONS WERE FOR THE GENERAL = THE GENERAL HAD MANY SONS.

- *Tibi* sunt gemini et trigemini ... filii YOU HAVE TWINS AND TRIPLETS (Plautus, *Miles Gloriosus*).

Note

Not always a dative with the verb **sum** has this meaning of possession, sometimes it can merely indicate its pure meaning of indirect object: **Hic liber est *tibi*** may just mean THIS BOOK IS FOR YOU, rather than YOU HAVE THIS BOOK.

2/ Dative of purpose [235]

Sometimes the dative can mean the purpose of an action; sometimes it can be translated by an infinitive, sometimes another option must be used:

- Caesar duas legiones *auxilio* misit CAESAR SENT TWO LEGIONS TO HELP ✧ Literally, ... FOR HELP.
- Cicero *magno exemplo* fuit CICERO WAS A GREAT EXAMPLE ✧ Literally, ... FOR A GREAT EXAMPLE.
- Quinque milites *praesidio* relinquam I WILL LEAVE FIVE SOLDIERS AS DEFENCE ✧ Literally, ... FOR DEFENCE.
- Haec clades *magno dolori* fuit THIS DEFEAT PRODUCED A BIG PAIN ✧ Literally, ... WAS FOR A BIG PAIN.
- *Exemplo* fuit ad imitandum HE WAS AN EXAMPLE TO BE IMITATED (Suetonius Tranquillus, *De Grammaticis et Rhetoribus*).
- *Exemplo* est Regulus REGULUS IS AN EXAMPLE (Plinius C. Secundus, *Epistulae*).
  ✧ Pliny means, in this case, an example of negative qualities.

3/ Double dative

In fact, it is the use of the dative of purpose combined with another dative of the person or object affected by the action; this produces a combination of two datives in the sentence, and context will make clear which one is that of purpose and which one is that of person or object affected. For instance, observe the same examples as before, but with a second dative added:

- Caesar duas legiones *auxilio nobis* misit CAESAR SENT TWO LEGIONS TO HELP US ✧ Literally, ... FOR HELP FOR US.
- Cicero *magno exemplo omnibus* fuit CICERO WAS A GREAT EXAMPLE FOR ALL.
- Quinque milites *praesidio urbi* relinquam I WILL LEAVE FIVE SOLDIERS AS DEFENCE FOR THE CITY
  ✧ Literally, ... TO DEFEND THE CITY.
- Haec clades *magno dolori mihi* fuit THIS DEFEAT GAVE ME GREAT PAIN.
- Cicero *saluti senatui* fuit CICERO WAS THE SALVATION OF THE SENATE.
- Libri sunt *curae magistro* THE TEACHER TAKES CARE OF THE BOOKS
  ✧ Literally, THE BOOKS ARE FOR CONCERN FOR THE TEACHER.
- Semper *mihi magno dolori* fuit IT WAS ALWAYS A SOURCE OF SORROW (Cicero, *Epistulae ad Familiares*).
- *Nemini* meus adventus *labori aut sumptui* neque publice neque privatim fuit MY ARRIVAL WAS NO PROBLEM NOR EXPENSE TO ANYONE, EITHER PUBLICLY OR PRIVATELY (Cicero, *In Verrem*).
- *Praesidio impedimentis* legionem quartam decimam reliquit HE LEFT THE 14TH LEGION AS PROTECTION FOR THE BAGGAGE (Caesar, *De Bello Gallico*).

4/ Agent dative [236]

In the passive periphrastic, the agent is not expressed by **a** + ablative but by a *dative*:

- **Liber** ***mihi*** **scribendus est** A BOOK MUST BE WRITTEN BY ME / I MUST WRITE A BOOK.

In any case, it is possible that this dative coincides with another dative, an indirect object, within the same sentence.

Observe the sentence **Liber** ***tibi mihi*** **scribendus est**. Does it mean I MUST WRITE A BOOK FOR YOU or YOU MUST WRITE A BOOK FOR ME?

In these cases of possible confusion, the agent can be left in the usual form of ***a*** + *ablative* even if it is in a passive periphrastic:

- **Liber tibi** ***a me*** **scribendus est** I MUST WRITE A BOOK FOR YOU.

5/ Dative with verbs and adjectives

Some verbs that in English rule a direct object rule a dative in Latin: (see more complete list in the corresponding chapter)

- Milites *duci* parent THE SOLDIERS OBEY THE GENERAL.
- *Hostibus captis* parcere volo I WANT TO SPARE THE CAPTURED ENEMIES.
- Paret *senatui*? DOES HE OBEY THE SENATE? (Cicero, *Philippicae*).

Also some adjectives rule a dative: (see more complete list in the corresponding chapter)

- Aeneas similis *deo* erat AENEAS WAS SIMILAR TO A GOD.
- Haec arma *pugnae* apta non sunt THESE WEAPONS ARE NOT ADEQUATE FOR THE FIGHT.

7. Ablative [237]

[A lot of the functions presented here can also be performed with an ablative preceded by a preposition; remember that in this section we deal only with uses without preposition.]

a) Main function: separation

In fact it is its original function, but it does not mean that it is the most frequent one; so, rather that *main function*, we should say *original function*. It has to do with expressions of separation, origin, etc.:

- Catilina *nobili genere* natus rempublicam delere volebat CATILINA, BORN FROM A NOBLE ORIGIN, WANTED TO DESTROY THE STATE.
- Postea expulsus est *patria* AFTER THIS, HE WAS EXPELLED FROM HIS FATHERLAND.
- Te libero *servitute* I FREE YOU FROM SLAVERY.

Also in expressions of depriving somebody of something, of lacking, etc.:

- Mei discipuli me privant *somno* MY STUDENTS DEPRIVE ME OF SLEEP.
- Careo *pecunia* I LACK MONEY
  ✧ The thing you lack is expressed in ablative, in the sense that you are away from it.

b) Other uses [238]

1/ Instrumental ablative

It tells us the instrument, tool, etc. with which some action is performed:

- Multos libros *calamo* scripsi I HAVE WRITTEN MANY BOOKS WITH A PEN.
- Hoc *pecunia* impetravit HE ACHIEVED THIS WITH MONEY.
- Antiochus *epistulis* bellum gerit, *calamo et atramento* militat ANTIOCHUS WAGES WAR WITH LETTERS, AND HE FIGHTS WITH PEN AND INK (Porcius Cato, *Orationes*).
- Te lex Terentia ... populi Romani *pecunia* frumentum a Siculis emere iussit? DID THE TERENTIAN LAW ORDER YOU TO BUY GRAIN FROM THE SICILIANS WITH THE MONEY OF THE ROMAN PEOPLE? (Cicero, *In Verrem*).

Let's remember that when we mean *company* rather than *instrument* we must use the preposition **cum** (this is usually called *ablative of accompaniment*):

- *Cum amicis* ludo I PLAY WITH MY FRIENDS.

2/ Ablative of characteristic

Very similar to the genitive of characteristic, with which it can alternate:

- Tuus frater vir *magno ingenio* est YOUR BROTHER IS A MAN OF A GREAT CHARACTER.
- M. Cicero homo *magna eloquentia* et Q. Roscius histrio *summa venustate* M. CICERO, A MAN OF GREAT ELOQUENCE, AND Q. ROSCIUS, AN ACTOR OF HIGHEST ELEGANCE (A. Gellius, *Noctes Atticae*).

✧ Any of the above characteristics could have been expressed in the genitive.

3/ Ablative of cause [239]

It expresses the reason or cause for some event:

- Post victoriam milites *gaudio* exultabant AFTER THE VICTORY, THE SOLDIERS WERE EXULTANT WITH HAPPINESS.
- *Metu* fugerunt THEY FLED BECAUSE OF FEAR.
- Erupit e senatu triumphans *gaudio* HE RUSHED FORTH FROM THE SENATE TRIUMPHANT WITH (BECAUSE OF) HAPPINESS (Cicero, *Pro Murena*).

4/ Ablative of price

It is used when the exact price of something is meant (the genitive is used for the general value, see above):

- Hoc emi *quinque sestertiis* I HAVE BOUGHT THIS FOR FIVE SESTERTII .
- De illo emi virginem *triginta minis* I BOUGHT A MAIDEN FROM HIM FOR THIRTY MINAE (Plautus, *Curculio*).

✧ Of course, **quinque** and **triginta** are indeclinable.

5/ Ablative of respect

It is used to indicate with respect to what an assessment is valid:

- Mei discipuli differunt inter se *lingua et moribus* MY STUDENTS DIFFER FROM EACH OTHER IN LANGUAGE AND CUSTOMS.

- Romani Gallos *divitiis* superabant THE ROMANS WERE SUPERIOR TO THE GAULS IN WEALTH.
- Hi omnes *lingua, institutis, legibus* inter se differunt ALL OF THESE DIFFER FROM EACH OTHER IN LANGUAGE IN REGULATIONS AND IN LAWS (Caesar, *De Bello Gallico*).

It may seem very similar to the *dative of reference*, but that is a matter of personal point of view and this is a matter of a real fact used as a reference.

6/ Ablative of manner [240]

a/ It indicates the way in which something takes place; it would answer to the question How?

- Pugnavimus *summa vi* WE FOUGHT WITH THE MAXIMUM STRENGTH.
- Eum *dolo* ceperunt THEY CAPTURED HIM BY MEANS OF A DECEIT.
- Si omnia *dolo* fecit, ... IF HE DID EVERYTHING BY MEANS OF A DECEIT, ... (M. Porcius Cato, *Orationes*).
- Quem locum Marius, quod ibi regis thesauri erant, *summa vi* capere intendit MARIUS TRIED TO TAKE THAT PLACE WITH THE MAXIMUM STRENGTH, AS THERE WERE THE TREASURIES OF THE KING (Sallust, *Bellum Iugurthinum*).

When the meaning concentrates more in the way of the background rather than of the means, the use of the preposition **cum** is frequent:

- Alii *cum laetitia*, alii *cum spe* recesserunt SOME WENT AWAY WITH HAPPINESS, OTHERS WITH HOPE (Plinius C. Secundus, *Panegyricus*).

It must be noted that, in the case that the noun is accompanied by an adjective, the preposition **cum** is usually positioned between the adjective and the noun, but we can find it at the beginning or even there can be no **cum** at all. For example:

- Vos oro atque obsecro, iudices, ut attente *bonaque cum venia* verba mea audiatis I ASK AND BESEECH FROM YOU, JUDGES, THAT YOU LISTEN TO MY WORDS WITH ATTENTION AND GOOD WILL (Cicero, *Pro Roscio Amerino*).
- Primum abs te hoc *bona venia* peto FIRST, I ASK THIS FROM YOU WITH GOOD WILL (Terentius Afer, *Phormio*).

b/ Connected with the ablative of manner, in fact as a derivative use of it, we can find the *ablative of intensity*, used to indicate the degree of difference in a comparative:

- Petrus est *multo* altior quam Antonius PETER IS MUCH TALLER THAN ANTHONY. ✧ Literally, TALLER *BY MUCH*.
- Nos nostris exercitibus quid pollicemur? *Multo* meliora atque maiora WHAT DO WE OFFER TO OUR ARMIES? MUCH BETTER AND LARGER ASSETS (Cicero, *Philippicae*). ✧ Literally, BETTER *BY MUCH*.
- *Paulo* longius oratio mea provecta est hac de causa BECAUSE OF THIS MY SPEECH HAS BEEN LENGTHENED A LITTLE LONGER (Cicero, *Pro Roscio Comoedo*). ✧ Literally, LONGER *BY A LITTLE*.

7/ Ablative with some verbs and adjectives [241]

Some verbs that in English seem to use a direct object use an ablative in Latin:

- In proelio *gladio* utor IN THE BATTLE I USE A SWORD.
- *Tua amicitia* semper fruimus WE ALWAYS ENJOY YOUR FRIENDSHIP.
- *Cautioribus* utitur *consiliis* (Cicero, *Philippicae*). HE TAKES RATHER PRUDENT DECISIONS ✧ Literally, HE MAKES USE OF RATHER...
- Nunc *vestro beneficio* fruor NOW I ENJOY YOUR FAVOUR (Cicero, *Post Reditum ad Populum*).

Also some verbs that in English would require a prepositional object:

- Mea patria abundat *navibus* — MY FATHERLAND IS ABUNDANT IN SHIPS.
- Abundat pectus *laetitia* meum — MY HEART IS FULL OF HAPPINESS (Plautus, *Stichus*).

Also some adjectives rule an ablative:

- Caesar dignus *laude* erat — CAESAR WAS WORTHY OF PRAISE.
- Vir certe fuit dignus *tanto cognomine* — THE MAN WAS REALLY WORTHY OF SUCH A GREAT NAME (Livy, *Ab Urbe Condita*).
- Erat in verborum splendore elegans, *compositione* aptus — HE WAS ELEGANT IN THE SPLENDOUR OF HIS WORDS, WELL PREPARED FOR WRITING (Cicero, *Brutus*).

8/ Adverbial ablative

Some ablatives have become fixed expressions:

vi	BY FORCE	una mente	BY COMMON AGREEMENT
re ipsa	IN FACT	pedibus	ON FOOT

- Ad lacum Averni per speciem sacrificandi, *re ipsa* ut temptaret Puteolos ..., descendit — HE CAME DOWN TO THE LAKE OF AVERNUS WITH THE EXCUSE OF MAKING A SACRIFICE, IN FACT TO ATTACK PUTEOLI (Livy, *Ab Urbe Condita*).
- Ex equis desiliunt ac *pedibus* proeliantur — THEY DISMOUNT FROM THE HORSES AND THEY FIGHT ON FOOT (Caesar, *De Bello Gallico*).

9/ Agent ablative [242]

In the passive voice, the agent object, the person by whom the action is performed is expressed by **a/ab** + *ablative* :

- Pons a *Romanis* deletus est — THE BRIDGE WAS DESTROYED BY THE ROMANS.
- Multa *a Caesare* in eam sententiam dicta sunt — MANY THINGS WERE SAID IN THIS SENSE BY CAESAR (Caesar, *De Bello Gallico*).

  ✧ In some cases, the translation by passive may sound too unnatural; this sentence could be translated by CAESAR SAID MANY THINGS IN THIS SENSE.

Nevertheless, if what causes the action is not a person, the preposition **a/ab** is omitted:

- Pons *tempestate* deletus est — THE BRIDGE WAS DESTROYED BY A STORM.

Please see above in the uses of the dative about the use of the dative as agent in some cases.

10/ Ablative in expressions of time

This will be dealt with in the corresponding section.

b) Prepositions

1. General observations [243]

a/ To express some concepts, sometimes it is enough with the use of the cases, like for instance the function of indirect object in I HAVE BROUGHT THIS FOR CAESAR: we use the dative, we do not need any preposition meaning *for*. But sometimes we need prepositions to express some other concepts, like for instance in the sentence THIS WAS USUAL AMONG THE GAULS: we will need a preposition for AMONG THE GAULS.

Latin prepositions can be followed by *only two cases: either accusative or ablative;* some of them can be followed only by accusative, others only by ablative, and some others by both. In this last group, the meaning of the preposition will be different depending on which case follows them.

Each preposition may correspond to more than one meaning in English, and in some cases meanings may have nothing to do with each other; for instance, the preposition **ab** may mean AWAY FROM (as in HE RAN AWAY FROM THE ENEMY) and also BY (as in HE WAS KILLED BY CAESAR).

b/ With respect to the group of prepositions themselves, it must be said that there are a series of adverbs that can behave like prepositions, i.e., they are followed either by an accusative or by an ablative, like for instance **propter** + Acc. BECAUSE OF. They are called *prepositional adverbs;* they have already been presented in the chapter of *Adverbs and prepositional adverbs.* About which ones are prepositions and which ones are prepositional adverbs, the general rule is that if they can be used to form compound verbs they are considered *prepositions*, like for instance **prae** (**praefero**, **praeduco**, etc.); prepositional adverbs do not form compound verbs. Moreover, there is a reduced group of prepositions (like **apud**) that are really prepositions, but they do not form compound verbs, but they must not be considered prepositional adverbs, as they can not be used on their own: they need to be followed by a noun.

2. Prepositions of one case [244]

a) Prepositions followed by the accusative

❑ ad

Its basic meaning is TOWARDS:

- *Ad templum eo* — I GO TOWARDS THE TEMPLE.
- Ex eo oppido pons *ad Helvetios* pertinet (Caesar, *De Bello Gallico*). — FROM THAT CITY A BRIDGE EXTENDS TO THE HELVETII

It may also have meaning of proximity: NEAR, BY, AT, NEXT TO:

- *Ad me* manet — HE STAYS WITH ME ✧ Literally, HE REMAINS BY ME (IN MY HOUSE).
- *Ad ianuam* constitit — HE STOPPED AT THE DOOR.
- Nec ulli iuvenes sunt reperti *ad ianuam* (Phaedrus, *Fabulae Aesopiae*). — AND NO YOUNGSTERS WERE FOUND AT THE DOOR

Also with temporal sense:

- *Ad noctem* laboravimus — WE WORKED UNTIL THE NIGHT.
- Illi aegre *ad noctem* oppugnationem sustinent (Caesar, *De Bello Gallico*). — THEY SUSTAIN THE ATTACK UNTIL THE NIGHT WITH DIFFICULTY

It may also have a comparative sense:

- Nihil [est] *ad Persium* HE IS NOTHING IN COMPARISON TO PERSIUS (Cicero, *De Oratore*).

⌑ Some idioms:

ad summam senectutem	UNTIL A VERY ADVANCED AGE	ad diem	ON THE AGREED DAY
ad necem	UNTIL DEATH	ad quoddam tempus	FOR SOME TIME
ad lunam	IN THE LIGHT OF THE MOON		

❑ ante [245]

It means BEFORE, IN FRONT OF, both in geographical and in temporal sense:

- *Ante Caesarem* stabat HE WAS STANDING IN FRONT OF CAESAR.
- *Ante pugnam* eum vidi I SAW HIM BEFORE THE BATTLE.
- Totam causam, iudices, explicemus atque *ante oculos* expositam consideremus LET'S PRESENT THE WHOLE PROCESS, JUDGES, AND ONCE IT HAS BEEN EXPOSED BEFORE OUR EYES LET'S CONSIDER IT (Cicero, *Pro Roscio Amerino*).

⌑ Some idioms:

paucis ante diebus	A FEW DAYS BEFORE	✧ In fact, in this expression **ante** is used as adverb.
anno ante	A YEAR BEFORE	✧ And also here it is an adverb.

❑ apud [246]

It means AMONG, BY, AT THE HOUSE OF:

- *Apud Gallos* habito — I LIVE AMONG GAULS.
- ... si iste *apud eos* quaestor non fuisset (Cicero, *Divinatio in Q. Caecilium*). — IF HE HAD NOT BEEN QUAESTOR AMONG THEM

It may also mean IN THE WORKS OF:

- *Apud Caesarem* hoc legere possumus WE CAN READ THIS IN CAESAR'S WORKS.

❑ circum [247]

It means AROUND:

- *Circum* urbem curro I RUN AROUND THE CITY.
- *Circum* se praesidia amicorum atque clientium occulte habebat HE HAD AROUND HIM, SECRETLY, A PROTECTION BODY OF FRIENDS AND CLIENTS (Sallust, *Catilinae Coniuratio*).

In some cases it may have also a directional sense:

- Quod ubi ex Publicio audivit, pueros *circum* amicos dimittit WHEN HE HEARD THIS, HE SENT SLAVES AROUND TO HIS FRIENDS (Cicero, *Pro Quinctio*).

❑ erga [248]

It means WITH RESPECT TO, TOWARDS:

- Crudelitatem eius *erga homines* odi I HATE HIS CRUELTY TOWARDS PEOPLE.
- Grata *erga tantam virtutem* civitas fuit THE CITY WAS GRATEFUL TOWARDS SO MUCH BRAVERY (Livy, *Ab Urbe Condita*).

❑ inter [249]

In geographical sense, it means IN THE MIDDLE OF, AMONG, BETWEEN:

- *Inter duos exercitus* stabamus WE WERE STANDING BETWEEN THE TWO ARMIES.
- Sunt qui Larentiam vulgato corpore lupam *inter pastores* vocatam putent THERE ARE PEOPLE WHO THINK THAT LARENTIA, A PROSTITUTE, WAS CALLED "SHE WOLF" AMONG THE SHEPHERDS (Livy, *Ab Urbe Condita*).

In temporal sense, it means IN THE MIDDLE OF, DURING:

- *Inter concilium* hoc dixit DURING THE MEETING HE SAID THIS.

⌑ Some idioms:

inter haec MEANWHILE
inter nos AMONG US ✧ With some sense of secrecy
inter omnia BEFORE EVERYTHING
inter moras MEANWHILE

❑ ob [250]

It has a causal meaning, BECAUSE OF:

- *Ob hanc victoriam* eum laudant THEY PRAISE HIM BECAUSE OF THIS VICTORY.
- *Ob eam rem* me omnes Summanum vocant BECAUSE OF THIS ALL CALL ME SUMMANUS (Plautus, *Curculio*).

⌑ An idiom: ob beneficium AS PAYMENT FOR A FAVOUR

❑ penes

It means IN POWER OF, IN THE HANDS OF:

- Post cladem, *penes Romanos* eramus AFTER THE DEFEAT, WE WERE IN THE HANDS OF THE ROMANS.
- Erat *penes principes* tota res publica ALL THE STATE WAS IN THE HANDS OF THE CHIEFTAINS (Cicero, *De Republica*).

Observe the difference in the meaning of these two very similar expressions.

- *Penes te* es? ARE YOU IN YOUR SOUND MIND?
- *Penes te* est IT IS IN YOUR HANDS (IN YOUR POWER).

❑ per [251]

Its basic meaning is THROUGH, and this may be applied in several senses: temporal, geographical, etc.:

- *Per urbem* iuvenes currebant — YOUTHS WERE RUNNING THROUGH THE CITY.
- *Per tres horas* pugnavimus — WE FOUGHT [FOR] THREE HOURS.
  ✧ This can also be expressed without the preposition per, as in English without FOR.
- *Per Ciceronem* hoc obtinui — I GOT THIS THROUGH (THANKS TO, BY MEANS OF) CICERO.
- Celeriter Petreius *per Vettones* ad Afranium pervenit — PETREIUS CAME QUICKLY TO AFRANIUS THROUGH THE VETTONES (Caesar, *Bellum Civile*).
- Arma *per Italiam* locis opportunis parare — HE MADE PREPARATION OF WEAPONS THROUGH (AROUND) ITALY IN APPROPRIATE PLACES (Sallust, *Catilinae Coniuratio*).
  ✧ The infinitive in this sentence is a Historical Infinitive.

⌑ Some idioms:

per manus — FROM HAND TO HAND
per singulos dies — EVERY DAY
per ludum — FOR FUN

❑ post [252]

The basic meaning is AFTER and BEHIND :

- *Post hoc*, Romam ire volebamus — AFTER THIS, WE WANTED TO GO TO ROME.
- *Post montem* exercitus manet — THE ARMY IS WAITING BEHIND THE MOUNTAIN.
- *Post dominationem* L.Sullae, — ... AFTER THE DICTATORSHIP OF SULLA, ... (Sallust, *Catilinae Coniuratio*).

❑ praeter

Its basic meanings are BEYOND, ALONG and IN FRONT OF, which can produce several translations in English, according to the sense:

- Omnes necaverunt *praeter duos* — THEY KILLED ALL EXCEPT TWO ✧ Literally, ... BEYOND TWO.
- *Praeter opinionem*, ego hoc non feci — AGAINST PEOPLE'S OPINION, I DIDN'T DO THIS.
- *Praeter hoc flumen* ambulavimus — WE WALKED ALONG THIS RIVER.
- *Praeter castra* Caesaris suas copias traduxit — HE TOOK HIS TROOPS PAST (IN FRONT OF) CAESAR'S CAMP (Caesar, *De Bello Gallico*).
- Repente *praeter opinionem* omnium confessus est — SUDDENLY, AGAINST EVERYBODY'S OPINION (EXPECTATION), HE CONFESSED (Cicero, *In Catilinam 3*).

⌑ An idiom: praeter modum — BEYOND MEASURE

❑ trans

The meaning is BEYOND, TO/AT THE OTHER SIDE OF:

- Exercitum *trans flumen* duxit — HE LED THE ARMY TO THE OTHER SIDE OF THE RIVER.
- Proximi sunt Germanis, qui *trans Rhenum* incolunt — THEY ARE NEAR TO THE GERMANS, WHO LIVE AT THE OTHER SIDE OF THE RHINE (Caesar, *De Bello Gallico*).

b) Prepositions followed by the ablative [253]

❑ a / ab / abs ✧ Usually, **a** before a consonant, **ab** before a vowel or some consonants, **abs** before **t-**.

The basic meanings are FROM, AWAY FROM, but its use in different senses (temporal, geographical, etc.) may produce very different translations in English:

- *Ab Italia* veni heri — I CAME FROM ITALY YESTERDAY.
- Castra multum abest *a mari* — THE CAMP IS VERY FAR FROM THE SEA.
- *Ab urbe condita* — FROM THE FOUNDATION OF THE CITY.
- Hoc obtinui *a meo amico* — I GOT THIS FROM MY FRIEND.
- Legati *ab Haeduis et a Treveris* veniebant (Caesar, *De Bello Gallico*). — AMBASSADORS CAME FROM THE HAEDUANS AND FROM THE TREVERI
- Maturat *ab urbe* proficisci (Caesar, *De Bello Gallico*). — HE HURRIES TO SET OUT FROM THE CITY
- Milia passuum tria *ab* eorum *castris* castra ponit (Caesar, *De Bello Gallico*). — HE PITCHES HIS CAMP THREE MILES AWAY FROM THEIR CAMP

A very important use is its use as agent of the passive voice:

- Pons deletus est *a militibus* — THE BRIDGE WAS DESTROYED BY THE SOLDIERS.
- *Ab equitibus* est interfecta — IT WAS KILLED BY THE CAVALRY (Caesar, *De Bello Gallico*).

⌑ Two idioms:

ab annis ACCORDING TO THE AGE **a se** BY HIMSELF/HERSELF

- Populum digessit *ab annis* Romulus — ROMULUS DISTRIBUTED THE PEOPLE ACCORDING TO THE AGE (Ovid, *Fasti*).

❑ cum [254]

It means WITH. Obviously, it must not be confused with its meaning as a conjunction (see the corresponding chapter on subordinates).

- *Cum amicis* ludo — I AM PLAYING WITH MY FRIENDS.
- *Cum amicis ducibusque* copiarum ... de bello consultabat — HE CONSULTED WITH HIS FRIENDS AND THE GENERALS OF THE ARMY ABOUT THE WAR (Curtius Rufus, *Historiae Alexandri Magni*).

We should remember that when an instrument is meant, rather than company, the ablative is used without the preposition **cum** (see the former chapter).

❑ de [255]

It has several meanings; one of them is FROM, but always meaning movement *from a superior position downwards*:

- Venio *de monte* — I COME FROM THE MOUNTAIN (meaning FROM THE TOP OF THE MOUNTAIN DOWNWARDS).
- Prometheus post XXX annos *de monte Caucaso* est solutus — PROMETHEUS, AFTER THIRTY YEARS, WAS FREED FROM THE MOUNT CAUCASUS (Hyginius, *Fabulae*).

  ✧ It is supposed he went downwards, so the preposition **de** keeps its sense.

Another meaning is ABOUT:

- Librum *de amore* legi — I READ A BOOK ABOUT LOVE.
- Nescioquid *de amore* loquitur — HE SAYS I DO NOT KNOW WHAT ABOUT LOVE (Terentius Afer, *Eunuchus*).

It may also have a causal meaning:

- *His de causis* Pompeius revenit — BECAUSE OF THESE REASONS POMPEIUS RETURNED.
- Caesar *his de causis*, quas commemoravi, Rhenum transire decreverat — CAESAR HAD DECIDED TO CROSS THE RHINE BECAUSE OF THESE REASONS THAT I HAVE REMINDED (Caesar, *De Bello Gallico*).

⌑ Some idioms:

de medio die	AFTER MIDDAY	de improviso	SUDDENLY
de nocte	BY NIGHT	de industria	ON PURPOSE

❑ e / ex [256]

The general meaning is FROM INSIDE TO THE OUTSIDE OF, but the English translation may be very different when it is taken in the sense of *departure point*:

- *E castris* exercitum duxit — HE LED THE ARMY OUT OF THE CAMP.
- Septem *ex Hispania* naves delevit — HE DESTROYED SEVEN SHIPS FROM HISPANIA
  ✧ Meaning that these ships had come originally from Hispania.
- *Ex eo tempore* eum iterum non vidi — FROM THAT TIME I HAVEN'T SEEN HIM AGAIN.
- Consul *e curia* eggressus ... domum redit — THE CONSUL, AFTER WALKING OUT OF THE SENATE, WENT HOME (Livy, *Ab Urbe Condita*).
- Invidia *ex opulentia* orta est — FROM WEALTH, ENVY AROSE (Sallust, *Catilinae Coniuratio*).
- Qui sim, *ex eo*, quem ad te misi, cognosces — WHO I AM, YOU WILL KNOW IT FROM THAT MAN THAT YOU SENT TO ME (Sallust, *Catilinae Coniuratio*).
- *Ex eo tempore* neque pax neque bellum cum Veientibus fuit — FROM THAT TIME THERE WAS NEITHER PEACE NOR WAR WITH THE VEIENTI (Livy, *Ab Urbe Condita*).

It may also have causal meaning:

- *Qua ex causa* heri quam celerrime veni — BECAUSE OF THIS REASON I CAME AS QUICKLY AS POSSIBLE YESTERDAY.

⌑ Some idioms:

ex consule	AFTER BEING CONSUL
diem ex die	DAY AFTER DAY
ex eo	FROM THEN ✧ The omission of **tempore** is evident.
ex nullius iniuria	WITHOUT HARMING ANYBODY
ex omnium sententia	ACCORDING TO EVERYBODY'S OPINION

❑ prae [257]

Its basic meaning is IN FRONT OF, BEFORE, BECAUSE OF, IN COMPARISON TO:

- *Prae me,* fortis es — IN COMPARISON TO ME, YOU ARE STRONG.
- *Prae hoc scelere* fugere debeo — I MUST FLEE BECAUSE OF THIS CRIME.
- *Prae metu* ubi sim nescio — BECAUSE OF FEAR, I DO NOT KNOW WHERE I AM (Plautus, *Casina*).

❑ pro

The basic meaning is IN FRONT OF, ON BEHALF OF, IN EXCHANGE FOR:

- *Pro patria* pugnavimus — WE FOUGHT ON BEHALF OF OUR HOMELAND.
- Omnia *pro contione* dixi — I SAID EVERYTHING IN FRONT OF THE ASSEMBLY.
- Hoc tibi *pro tua virtute* dederunt — THEY HAVE GIVEN YOU THIS IN EXCHANGE FOR YOUR BRAVERY.
- Dulce et decorum est *pro patria* mori — TO DIE FOR YOUR COUNTRY IS PLEASANT AND RIGHT (Horatius, *Carmina*).
- *Pro me* pugnabit L. Philippus — L. PHILIPPUS WILL FIGHT FOR ME (Cicero, *Pro Quinctio*).
- *Pro pudore, pro abstinentia, pro virtute* audacia largitio avaritia vigebant INSTEAD OF TEMPERANCE, ABSTINENCE AND INTEGRITY, SHAMELESSNESS, PRODIGALITY AND AVARICE WERE PREVAILING (Sallust, *Catilinae Coniuratio*).

> **Note**
>
> This preposition is used exceptionally with the accusative in the expression *Pro* deum hominumque *fidem!* OH, THE FAITH OF GODS AND MEN!

¤ Some idioms:

pro viribus	ACCORDING TO ONE'S STRENGTH
pro suffragio	AS A RESULT OF THE VOTING PROCEDURE
pro tempore et pro re	ACCORDING TO THE TIME AND THE CIRCUMSTANCES

❑ sine [258]

It means WITHOUT:

- *Sine militibus* urbem capere non possum — I CAN'T CAPTURE THE CITY WITHOUT MY SOLDIERS.
- *Sine mora* praetoribus se tradunt — WITHOUT DELAY THEY HAND THEMSELVES OVER TO THE PRAETORS (Sallust, *Catilinae Coniuratio*).

❑ tenus

It is a very unusual preposition, and it is always postponed to its noun; it means UP TO, AS FAR AS:

- *Hoc monte tenus* ibimus WE WILL GO UP TO THAT MOUNTAIN.
- Cum per aquam ferme *genu tenus* altam tres milites sequerentur, ... WHEN THREE SOLDIERS WERE FOLLOWING [HIM] THROUGH THE WATER, DEEP ALMOST UP TO THE KNEE, ... (Livy, *Ab Urbe Condita*).

3. Prepositions of two cases [259]

Almost always their use with the accusative will imply *motion towards*, and their use with the ablative will imply *state without motion.*

❑ in

a/ With acusative, it means INTO:

- *In urbem* venio — I COME INTO THE CITY.
- Consul triumphans *in urbem* redit (Livy, *Ab Urbe Condita*). — THE CONSUL RETURNS TO THE CITY CELEBRATING HIS TRIUMPH

With a noun meaning a person, it may have hostile sense:

- *In Caesarem* orationem dixi — I MADE A SPEECH AGAINST CAESAR.
- Ipse habuit graves *in Caesarem* contiones (Caesar, *Bellum Civile*). — HE HIMSELF MADE SOME STRONG DISCOURSES AGAINST CAESAR

It may also have temporal sense:

- *In multam noctem* legimus — WE WERE READING UNTIL THE DEEP NIGHT.

b/ With ablative, it means IN without any movement implied:

- *In urbe* sum — I AM IN THE CITY.
- Nostra omnis vis *in animo et corpore* sita est (Sallust, *Catilinae Coniuratio*). — ALL OUR STRENGTH IS LOCATED IN OUR SOUL AND OUR BODY

¤ Some idioms:

In any of both cases, the idioms that this preposition produces are several; first let's see some with the accusative:

in perpetuum	FOR EVER	in universum	IN GENERAL
in multam noctem	UNTIL DEEP NIGHT	in barbarum	IN A SAVAGE WAY

And now some with the ablative:

in tam multis annis	DURING SO MANY YEARS	in spe esse	TO HOPE
in armis	WITH THE WEAPONS ON		

❑ sub [260]

a/ With the accusative, it means UNDER, with an idea of movement *from above under*.

- *Sub aquam eo* — I GO UNDER THE WATER ✧ Meaning that I am outside the water and I go under it.
- *Sub montem eo* — I GO TO THE FOOT OF THE MOUNTAIN.
  ✧ In this case, it does not mean UNDER it, just AT THE BASE of it.
- *Sub montem*, in quo erat oppidum positum Ilerda, succedunt — THEY MOVE FORWARD TO THE FOOT OF THE MOUNTAIN ON WHICH ILERDA STOOD (Caesar, *De Bello Gallico*).

It may also be used in a temporal sense, with a meaning of TOWARDS:

- *Sub vesperum* Caesar pervenit CAESAR ARRIVED TOWARDS THE EVENING.
- Utrimque legati fere *sub idem tempus* ad res repetendas missi [sunt] FROM BOTH SIDES LEGATES WERE SENT AROUND THE SAME TIME TO DEMAND RESTITUTION (Liby, *Ab Urbe Condita*).

b/ With ablative, it has the same meaning of UNDER but without any sense of movement from above under:

- Pisces *sub aqua* habitant FISHES LIVE UNDER THE WATER.
- *Sub monte* habito I LIVE AT THE FOOT OF THE MOUNTAIN.
- Novam ipse aliam *sub Albano monte* condidit HE HIMSELF FOUNDED A NEW ONE (CITY) AT THE FOOT OF THE ALBANUS MOUNTAIN (Livy, *Ab Urbe Condita*).

It may be used in symbolic sense:

- *Sub Caesare* omnia meliora erant UNDER CAESAR (IN CAESAR'S TIME) EVERYTHING WAS BETTER.

¤ Some idioms:

With the ablative:

sub oculis WITHIN SIGHT
sub septentrionibus IN THE NORTH

With the accusative:

sub vesperum AT DUSK

❑ subter [261]

Its use and meaning is almost parallel to that of sub, and its use is very scarce.

- Equo citato *subter murum* hostium ad cohortes avehitur HE RODE AWAY AT FULL GALLOP UNDER THE ENEMY'S WALL TO HIS COHORTS (Livy, *Ab Urbe Condita*).

❑ super

a/ With accusative, it has a meaning of OVER, ON, usually with a sense of movement:

- *Super lectum* arma pono I PUT THE WEAPONS ON THE BED.
- Hannibal proelio abstinuit castrisque *super ripam* positis, cum ... HANNIBAL REFRAINED FROM ENGAGING AND, HAVING PITCHED THE CAMP ON THE BANK, WHEN ... (Livy, *Ab Urbe Condita*).
  - ✧ Accusative is used because in this case the verb pono implies some sense of movement: the camp was not there, and Hannibal pitches it there.

It may also have a temporal sense:

- Cum tale *super cenam* facinus narraret Ulixes Alcinoo, ... WHEN ULYSSES EXPLAINED SUCH A DEED TO ALCINOOS DURING THE DINNER, ... (Iunius Iuvenalis, *Saturae*).

And also a numerical sense:

- *Super trecentos milites* habeo I HAVE MORE THAN 300 SOLDIERS.
- Coniugibus liberisque et senioribus *super sexaginta annos* in propinquam Epirum missis, ... AFTER THEIR WIVES AND CHILDREN AND ELDERLY PEOPLE HAD BEEN SENT TO THE NEARBY EPIRUS FOR MORE THAN SIXTY YEARS, ... (Livy, *Ab Urbe Condita*).

✧ Observe the lack of sense of movement in these two last examples.

b/ With ablative, it lacks this sense of movement:

- Arma iacent *super lecto* THE WEAPONS ARE ON THE BED.

It may also be used in a symbolic sense, with different meanings:

- *Super hoc*, multa alia fecit APART (literally, ABOVE) FROM THIS, HE DID MANY OTHER THINGS.
- Percepi *super his rebus nostris* te loqui I HAVE REALISED THAT YOU WERE TALKING ABOUT THESE MATTERS OF OURS (Plautus, *Mostellaria*).

c) Expressions of time and place

1. Expressions of time [262]

[The extensive meanings that prepositions can have in their use offer more possibilities than those expressed here; in this section, we concentrate only on the standard procedures for the usual expressions of time.]

a) When?

1/ The moment of time in which something happened is expressed by the ablative without preposition:

prima vigilia	IN THE FIRST WATCH	hieme	IN WINTER
decimo die	ON THE TENTH DAY	aestate	IN SUMMER

- *Tertio die* Caesar vallo castra communit ON THE THIRD DAY CAESAR FORTIFIES THE CAMP WITH A WALL (Caesar, *Bellum Civile*).
- Magnis itineribus *hieme* aspera pervenit ad oppidum Suthul BY FORCED MARCHES HE ARRIVED AT THE CITY OF SUTHUL THROUGH A HARSH WINTER (Sallust, *Bellum Iugurthinum*).

2/ Some expressions of long periods use the preposition **in**:

in senectute IN OLD AGE

- Non sunt *in senectute* vires IN OLD AGE THERE IS NO STRENGTH (Cicero, *Cato Maior de Senectute*).

3/ There are a number of expressions which are often used in Latin to convey *time when,* and some of these have been listed below. Adverbial expressions can be found in the corresponding section:

die et nocte	DAY AND NIGHT	ineunte anno	AT THE BEGINNING OF THE YEAR
prima luce	AT DAYBREAK	exeunte anno	AT THE END OF THE YEAR
hoc noctis	AT THAT MOMENT OF NIGHT	omnibus annis	EVERY YEAR
sub noctem	AT NIGHTFALL	paucis post diebus	AFTER A FEW DAYS
uno tempore	AT THE SAME TIME	✧ In this expression, **post** is an adverb.	

b) For how long? [263]

1/ The duration in time is expressed by the accusative, with or without the preposition **per**:

- Milites *(per) tres horas* pugnaverunt THE SOLDIERS FOUGHT DURING THREE HOURS.
- *Totam noctem* hic fui I HAVE BEEN HERE FOR THE WHOLE NIGHT.
- Summa vi *totum diem* oppugnarunt THEY WERE ATTACKING FOR THE WHOLE DAY WITH ALL OF THEIR STRENGTH (Livy, *Ab Urbe Condita*).

2/ With **per**, the sense of *non-stop activity* is stressed:

- Senatus *per totum diem* saepe consulitur — OFTEN THE SENATE RECEIVES CONSULTATION DURING THE WHOLE DAY (Seneca iunior, *Dialogi*).

3/ In some cases (less frequently), also the ablative can be used:

- Romani *decem annis* Gallos pugnaverunt — THE ROMANS FOUGHT WITH THE GAULS FOR TEN YEARS.
- *Annis viginti* errans a patria afuit — HE WAS ABSENT FROM HIS HOMELAND WANDERING FOR TWENTY YEARS (Plautus, *Bacchides*).

c) Since when? [264]

The amount of *units of time* during which an action has been happening (and is still happening) is expressed with the adverb **iam** followed by an ordinal in Acc., increasing in one unit the number of periods already covered:

- Marcus *iam quintum annum* consul est — MARCUS HAS BEEN CONSUL FOR FOUR YEARS.
  ✧ He is in the fifth year of his consulship, this is why we say **quintum**.
- Ab illo tempore *annum iam tertium et vicesimum* regnat — SINCE THEN, HE HAS BEEN KING FOR TWENTY-TWO YEARS (Cicero, *Pro Lege Manilia*). ✧ So, now he is in his 23rd year as king.

d) In how much time?

The period of time needed to complete an action is expressed by the ablative:

- *Septem diebus* hoc fecero — I WILL HAVE DONE THIS IN SEVEN DAYS.
- Numidae *paucis diebus* iussa efficiunt — THE NUMIDIANS CARRY OUT THE ORDERS IN A FEW DAYS (Sallust, *Bellum Iugurthinum*).

e) How long ago? [265]

The period of time elapsed since something happened is expressed in ablative, preceded by **abhinc**:

- Hunc librum emi *abhinc tribus annis* — I BOUGHT THIS BOOK THREE YEARS AGO.
- Quo tempore? *Abhinc annis XV* — WHEN? FIFTEEN YEARS AGO (Cicero, *Pro Roscio Comoedo*).

f) Within which period?

The period of time within which something happened or will happen is expressed by the ablative; in fact this is a small derivation from the former Point d):

- *Proximis diebus* hoc tibi feram — I WILL BRING YOU THIS WITHIN THE NEXT DAYS.
- Si pluvia non incesserit, rigato *quindecim proximis diebus* — IF IT DOES NOT RAIN, WATER WITHIN THE NEXT FIFTEEN DAYS (Moderatus Columella, *De Arboribus*).

2. Expressions of place [266]

[The extensive meanings that prepositions can have in their use offer more possibilities that those expressed here; in this section, we concentrate only on the standard procedures for the usual expressions of place.]

a) Where?

1/ The place where something takes place is expressed by the preposition **in** + ablative:

- Habito *in Italia* — I LIVE IN ITALY.
- *In hac urbe* eum viderunt — THEY SAW HIM IN THIS CITY.
- Si vos *in eo loco* essetis, quid aliud fecissetis? (Porcius Cato, *Orationes*). — IF YOU WERE IN THAT PLACE, WHAT ELSE WOULD YOU HAVE DONE?

2/ In some sporadic cases we can find alternation between using the preposition or not using it; for instance:

- Nona Caesaris legio ... castra *eo loco* posuit — CAESAR'S NINTH LEGION PITCHED THE CAMP IN THAT PLACE (Caesar, *Bellum Civile*). ✧ Compare with **in eo loco** in the sentence above.

3/ Names of cities, small islands, and the nouns **domus** HOUSE, **rus** COUNTRY (as opposed to CITY) and **humus** FLOOR [267]
experience a double phenomenon: they do not use preposition and moreover the case used is not ablative but *locative* (a seventh case which had disappeared from the normal use and which had remained only for some expressions). The ending of the locative is equal to that of the genitive for nouns of the 1st and 2nd declension in singular, and is equal to ablative for the other cases (some grammars do not consider these other cases as locative, but just as ablative).

Let's see some examples of locative:

- Caesarem *Romae* necaverunt — THEY KILLED CAESAR IN ROME. ✧ **in Roma** is a typical mistake.
- Hostes manebant *Tarenti* — THE ENEMY WERE REMAINING IN TARENTUM.
- Socrates *Athenis* docet — SOCRATES TEACHES IN ATHENS.
- Hannibal *Carthagine* habitat — HANNIBAL LIVES IN CARTHAGE.
  ✧ We can find also **Carthagini**, by influence of 2nd declension locative.
- Nunc *domi* dormit — HE IS NOW SLEEPING IN THE HOUSE.
- *Ruri* habitare malo — I PREFER TO LIVE IN THE COUNTRY.
- Dum haec *Romae* geruntur, ... — WHILE THESE EVENTS TAKE PLACE AT ROME, ... (Sallust, *Catilinae Coniuratio*).
- Reliqui, qui *domi* manserunt, ... — THOSE WHO HAVE REMAINED AT HOME ... (Caesar, *De Bello Gallico*).
- Miramur *Athenis* Minervam — AT ATHENS WE ADMIRE [THE TEMPLE OF] MINERVA (Cicero, *In Verrem*).
- Verum arbitrabantur *Corinthi* et *Carthagini*, etiam si ... — BUT THEY THOUGHT THAT IN CORINTH AND CARTHAGE, EVEN IF ... (Cicero, *De Lege Agraria*).

A very common idiom that makes use of the locative is this one: **domi militaeque** AT HOME AND IN THE ARMY

✧ Apart from meaning the two kinds of activities, military and civil life, it may also mean IN PEACE AND IN WAR.

- Igitur *domi militiaeque* boni mores colebantur — SO, GOOD CUSTOMS WERE PRACTISED BOTH IN PEACE AND IN WAR (Sallust, *Catilinae Coniuratio*).

4/ Apart from the exact sense of *in* a place, other prepositions may be used to indicate proximity etc.:

- *Apud Helvetios* habito I LIVE AMONG THE HELVETIANS.
- Multi floruerunt *apud Graecos*, sed Phalereus Demetrius meo iudicio praestitit ceteris AMONG THE GREEKS, MANY FLOURISHED, BUT DEMERIUS PHALEREUS, IN MY OPINION, EXCELLED THE OTHERS (Cicero, *Orator*).

b) Where to? [268]

1/ The place towards which we go is expressed by the accusative preceded by the preposition **ad**, if we mean TOWARDS, or the preposition **in**, if we mean INTO:

- *Ad urbem* eo I GO TOWARDS THE CITY.
- Eunt agmine *ad urbem* THEY GO TOWARDS THE CITY IN COLUMN (Livy, *Ab Urbe Condita*).
- *In urbem* eo I GO INTO THE CITY.
- Eum ... *in urbem* vocant THEY CALL HIM INTO THE CITY (Livy, *Ab Urbe Condita*).

The preposition **in** followed by a name of person would imply *hostility*; behold the difference:

- *Ad Caesarem* eo I GO TO CAESAR.
- *In Caesarem* eo I GO AGAINST CAESAR.
- Antonius autem, etsi tanto odio ferebatur *in Ciceronem*, ... BUT ANTHONY, ALTHOUGH HE FELT SUCH A HATRED AGAINST CICERO, ... (Nepos, *Vitae*).

2/ In the cases formerly mentioned of names of cities and small islands, the word **domus**, etc., the same phenomenon takes place: they do not use a preposition (but they remain in accusative, there is no further change to any other case as happened if we wanted to express *place where*):

- *Romam* eo I GO TO ROME.
- *Domum* eo I GO HOME. ✧ Observe that in English we do not use a preposition either.
- *Athenas* eum misi I SENT HIM TO ATHENS.
- Adherbal tametsi *Romam* legatos miserat, ... ADHERBAL, ALTHOUGH HE HAD SENT AMBASSADORS TO ROME, ... (Sallust, *Bellum Iugurthinum*).
- Deinde se ex curia *domum* proripuit LATER HE RUSHED FROM THE SENATE TO HIS HOUSE (Sallust, *Catilinae Coniuratio*).

3/ We must take into account that a lot of times the structure of the gerundive will make us find expressions like **ad Romam** (so, **Romam** preceded by a preposition). This is not a breakage of the rule of no preposition in front of **Roma**, but the structure of the gerundive that makes the preposition be there:

- ... non *ad Romam obsidendam*, sed ... NOT IN ORDER TO BESIEGE ROME, BUT ... (Livy, *Ab Urbe Condita*).

c) Where from? [269]

1/ The place from which we come is expressed by the preposition **e/ex** if we mean the *movement from inside to outside* or by the preposition **a/ab** if we mean just the *movement of getting away from somewhere*; in this aspect, **e/ex** is the opposite to **in** + Acc., and **a/ab** is the opposite to **ad** + Acc.:

in + Acc. ⇔ e/ex + Abl.
ad + Acc. ⇔ a/ab + Abl.

- *Ex urbe* venio I COME FROM THE CITY ✧ Meaning that I was inside the city and I have gone out of it.
- Postridie in castra *ex urbe* ad nos veniunt flentes principes ON THE DAY AFTER THE CHIEFTAINS COME FROM THE CITY INTO THE CAMP TO US, CRYING (Plautus, *Amphitruo*).
- *Ab urbe* venio I COME FROM THE CITY ✧ Meaning that I was in the area of the city, not necessarily inside it, maybe just around.
- Cum paulo longius *a castris* processisset, ... WHEN HE HAD ADVANCED A LITTLE MORE AWAY FROM THE CAMP, ... (Caesar, *De Bello Gallico*).

2/ As expected, names of cities, small islands, **domus** etc. will not use a preposition:

- *Roma* venio I COME FROM ROME.
- *Domo* venio I COME FROM HOME.
- ... cum in me incurrit *Roma* veniens Curio meus ... WHEN MY FRIEND CURIO, ARRIVING FROM ROME, CAME UPON ME (Cicero, *Epistulae ad Atticum*).

3/ Exception: In Livy, the use of the preposition **ab** before **Roma** is very frequent:

- Paucos post dies decem legati *ab Roma* venerunt AFTER A FEW DAYS TEN AMBASSADORS CAME FROM ROME (Livy, *Ab Urbe Condita*).

d) Through where? [270]

1/ The place through where some action takes place is expressed with the preposition **per** + Acc.:

- *Per totam urbem* currebant THEY WERE RUNNING THROUGH THE ENTIRE CITY.
- Vulgatur fama *per urbem* THE RUMOUR SPREADS AROUND THE CITY (Vergil, *Aeneis*).
- Horatius Cocles ... iussit suos *per pontem* redire in urbem HORATIUS COCLES ORDERED HIS MEN TO GO BACK ACROSS THE BRIDGE (Iulius Frontinus, *Strategemata*).

2/ But we can use also the ablative without preposition:

- *Ponte* fugerunt THEY FLED ACROSS THE BRIDGE.
- Cum magna praeda *eodem ponte* in castra revertuntur THEY COME BACK INTO THE CAMP ACROSS THE SAME BRIDGE WITH A BIG BOOTY (Caesar, *Bellum Civile*).

d) Regime of verbs and adjectives

1. General observations [271]

a/ Most verbs that have an object, like the verb **video** TO SEE, rule the accusative case, but some rule other cases. For instance, the verb **careo** TO LACK rules the ablative case:

- *Caesarem* video — I SEE CAESAR.
- Careo *pecunia* — I LACK MONEY.

So, verbs that are transitive in English (i.e., they have a direct object) do not always use an accusative in Latin. Let's see more examples of this lack of correspondence between English and Latin:

The verb **persuadeo** TO PERSUADE rules a dative, and the verb **utor** TO USE rules an ablative:

- *Tibi* persuadeo — I PERSUADE YOU.
- *Gladio* utor — I USE A SWORD.

The unusual regime of these verbs is usually indicated in dictionaries.

b/ Moreover, some verbs may also take different constructions to express the same idea. For instance, the verb **mitto** TO SEND may be followed either by a dative or by **ad** + accusative:

- Librum mitto *tibi* / Librum mitto *ad te* — I SEND YOU A BOOK.
- Hic est quem ego *tibi* misi — THIS IS THE ONE I SENT YOU (Plautus, *Curculio*).
- Antonium ... misi *ad te* — I SENT ANTHONY TO YOU (Cicero, *Epistulae ad Familiares*).

Therefore, a verbal expression that has been taught in some given way may later be found used differently. Dictionaries may offer the most common regime, but bear in mind that the construction offered here or in any other book will not be the only possible construction.

c/ To complicate matters further, in some cases a verb, even without shifting to another construction, may use a preposition or not. For instance, the verb **libero, -are** TO FREE may be used followed by an ablative preceded by **a(b)** or by no preposition:

- Cyzicum *obsidione* liberavit — HE FREED CYZICUM FROM SIEGE (Nepos, *Vitae*).
- Sicut *a Philippo* Graeciam liberavit, ... — JUST AS HE FREED GREECE FROM PHILIPPUS, ... (Livy, *Ab Urbe Condita*).

Note

It could be argued that the use of a preposition means automatically another construction. In any case, we just wanted to note the double option of using the same case with or without preposition.

Continuous practice will teach this, and the easiest way of learning it is to try to remember the construction when you come across it. Again, it would be far too extensive to cover all the possible constructions some verbs may adopt, and, when reading, the student must have some flexibility to accept previously unknown constructions and even to deduce them from comparison with verbs of similar meaning when composing in Latin.

We provide a list of some of the most frequent verbs that do not use the usual accusative case. Although most verbs are quoted and translated, additional comments and/or examples have been supplied for some to help the student's understanding.

d/ Some adjectives also require complementing words to be in a certain case. For instance, the adjective **dignus, -a, -um** WORTHY requires that the complement (the thing of which something or somebody is worthy) be in ablative:

- **Caesar dignus *tua amicitia* est** CAESAR IS WORTHY OF YOUR FRIENDSHIP.

In the list offered here, note that several of the adjectives may be related to some verbs given in the former section. As happens in the list of verbs, some of the adjectives have additional comments aside from the translation and/or an example when it has been considered convenient.

2. Verbs that rule a given case [272]

✧ It is worth noting that several of the verbs that use cases other than accusative are deponent or semi-deponent.

a) Verbs that rule genitive

interest, interesse, interfuit / refert, referre, retulit IT IS OF INTEREST

✧ These two impersonal verbs, mentioned in the corresponding section, need the genitive of the person affected by the interest:

- **Aratoris autem interest ... se frumenta habere** THE FARMER IS INTERESTED IN HAVING CORN (Cicero, *In Verrem*). Literally, IT IS OF INTEREST OF THE FARMER TO HAVE CORN.

memini, -isse (defective) TO REMEMBER

- **Dum *matris* meminit, obliviscetur novercae** WHILE HE REMEMBERS HIS MOTHER, HE WILL FORGET HIS STEP-MOTHER (Seneca senior, *Controversiae*).

✧ Also possible with accusative, especially if the object is a thing:

- **Si *haec* memineritis, ...** IF YOU REMEMBER THESE THINGS, ... (Cicero, *Pro Quinctio*).

✧ As an additional comment, it is worth saying that this verb is one of the few verbs in which we can find the future imperative in use:

- **Sed hoc *mementote*** BUT REMEMBER THIS (Cicero, *De Oratore*).

misereor, -eri, miser(i)tus sum (deponent) TO PITY

- **Patris tui misereor** I PITY YOUR FATHER (Annaeus Seneca senior, *Controversiae*).

✧The impersonal and active form **miseret** rules an accusative of the person affected by the feeling and a genitive of the reason (see the corresponding section on Impersonal Verbs):

- **Miseret *me illius*** I FEEL SORRY FOR HIM (Plautus, *Bacchides*).

obliviscor, -i, oblitus sum (deponent) TO FORGET
- ***Duorum*** **oblitus est?** HAS HE FORGOTTEN BOTH OF THEM? (Seneca iunior, *De Beneficiis*).
- ***Mei*** **oblitus est** HE HAS FORGOTTEN ME (Gellius, *Noctes Atticae*).

✧ Also possible with accusative, especially if the object is a thing:
- **Oblitus sum** ***omnia*** I HAVE FORGOTTEN EVERYTHING (Plautus, *Bacchides*).

✧ But observe the following example, in which the object is not a person but is in genitive:
- **Memini enim, memini neque umquam obliviscar** ***noctis illius*** **cum ...** I REMEMBER INDEED, I REMEMBER AND I WILL NEVER FORGET THAT NIGHT WHEN ... (Cicero, *Pro Plancio*).

b) Verbs that rule dative [273]

adsum, adesse, affui (no supine) TO SUPPORT, TO BE PRESENT AT

✧ It is common that compounds of **sum** rule a dative; see **desum, praesum**, etc. further down.

✧ In geographical sense, it means just TO BE PRESENT, but the meaning of *supporting* derives from the concept of being side by side with somebody:
- **Aderat** ***in senatu*** **Verres** VERRES WAS PRESENT AT THE SENATE (Cicero, *In Verrem*).
- **Affuit et** ***clientibus*** HE ALSO SUPPORTED HIS CLIENTS (Suetonius, *De Vita Caesarum*).

appropinquo, -are, -avi, -atum TO APPROACH

✧ It can also be used with **ad** + Acc.

cedo, -ere, cessi, cessum TO YIELD TO
confido, -ere, confisus sum (semi-deponent) TO TRUST

credo, -ere, -didi, -ditum TO TRUST, TO BELIEVE

✧ If the object is a person, it is usually in the dative:
- **Tu** ***mihi*** **non credis** ***ipsi*** **?** DON'T YOU BELIEVE ME MYSELF? (Cicero, *De Oratore*).

✧ But if the object is not a person but a concept, it is usually in the accusative:
- ***Unum illud*** **credo** I JUST BELIEVE THAT ONE THING (Cicero, *In Q. Caecilium*).

✧ Observe this double example, in which the person is in dative and the thing to be believed is in accusative:
- **Fortasse** ***haec*** **tu nunc** ***mihi*** **non credis quae loquor** MAYBE YOU NOW DO NOT BELIEVE *TO ME* THESE THINGS THAT I AM SAYING (Plautus, *Pseudolus*).

desum, deesse, defui (no supine) TO BE MISSING TO

✧ The person to whom something is missing is what is expressed in dative:
- **Domus** ***tibi*** **deerat? At habebas** DID YOU LACK A HOUSE? BUT YOU HAD IT! (Cicero, *Pro Scauro*).

✧ But it is very normal that there is no dative, leaving just the sense that something was missing:
- **Studium ad pugnandum virtusque deerat** DESIRE FOR FIGHTING AND BRAVERY WERE MISSING (Caesar, *Bellum Civile*).

diffido, -ere, diffisus sum (semi-deponent) TO MISTRUST
displiceo, -ere, -cui, -citum TO DISPLEASE
faveo, -ere, favi, fautum TO FAVOUR
gratulor, -ari, -atus sum (deponent) TO CONGRATULATE
ignosco, -ere, -novi, -notum TO FORGIVE
immineo, -ere (no more forms) TO OVERHANG

impero, -are, -avi, -atum TO COMMAND

- **Naves longas X *Gaditanis* ut facerent imperavit** HE ORDERED THE INHABITANTS OF GADES TO BUILD TEN LONG SHIPS (Caesar, *Bellum Civile*).

✧ Of course, it is possible that the person who receives the order is not even mentioned (but if mentioned it should be in dative):

- **Praeterea imperavit frumentum ... comportare** MOREOVER HE ORDERED TO GATHER CORN (Sallust, *Bellum Iugurthinum*).

✧ We should remember that **iubeo**, with the same meaning, rules an *Acc. + infinitive* clause, not a dative:

- ***Indutiomarum* ad se cum ducentis obsidibus *venire* iussit** HE ORDERED INDUTIOMARUS TO COME TO HIM WITH TWO-HUNDRED HOSTAGES (Caesar, *De Bello Gallico*).

indulgeo, -ere, -dulsi, -dultum TO INDULGE TO

invideo, -ere, -vidi, -visum TO ENVY

- **Ego *nemini* invideo** I ENVY NO ONE (Petronius, *Satyrica*).

irascor, -i, iratus sum (deponent) TO BE ANGRY WITH
noceo, -ere, -cui, -citum TO HARM

nubo, -ere, nupsi, nuptum TO MARRY (woman as subject)

- **Neque ita multo post *A. Caecinae* nupsit** AND NOT MUCH LATER SHE MARRIED A. CAECINA (Cicero, *Pro Caecina*).

✧ If the subject is the man, the expression that means to marry is **uxorem ducere** + Acc.:

- **Foedus cum eo percussit et filiam eius *uxorem duxit*** HE MADE A TREATY WITH HIM AND MARRIED HIS DAUGHTER (Seneca senior, *Controversiae*).

obsequor, -i, obsecutus sum (deponent) TO OBEY

- ***Auspiciis* plurimum obsecutus est Romulus** FOR THE MOST PART, ROMULUS OBEYED THE AUSPICES (Cicero, *De Republica*).

✧ Note that the stem verb **sequor** TO FOLLOW rules accusative:

- **Secutus est inde *Romanos*** FROM THEN, HE FOLLOWED THE ROMANS (Livy, *Ab Urbe Condita*).

obsto, -are, -stiti (no supine) TO HINDER
occurro, -ere, occurri, occursum TO COME ACROSS
parco, -ere, peperci, parsum TO SPARE

pareo, -ere, -ui, -itum TO OBEY

✧ Do not confuse with **paro, -are, -avi, -atum** TO PREPARE or with **pario, -ere, peperi, partum** TO PRODUCE, TO GIVE BIRTH.

persuadeo, -ere, -suasi, -suasum TO PERSUADE
placeo, -ere, -cui, -citum TO PLEASE

praesum, -esse, -fui (no supine) TO BE AT THE HEAD OF

- ***His* praeerat Viridovix** VIRIDOVIX WAS AT THE HEAD OF THEM (meaning *their chief*) (Caesar, *De Bello Gallico*).

prosum, prodesse, profui (no supine) TO BENEFIT

- **Tua disciplina nec *mihi* prodest nec *tibi*** YOUR DISCIPLINE BENEFITS NEITHER ME NOR YOU (Plautus, *Bacchides*).

resisto, -ere, restiti (no supine) TO RESIST

servio, -ire, -ivi, -itum TO BE A SLAVE TO
✧ Do not confuse with **servo, -are, -avi, -atum** TO SAVE.

studeo, -ere, studui (no supine) TO DEVOTE ONESELF TO, TO FEEL A TENDENCY FOR, TO SUPPORT
- **Studuit *Catilinae* iterum *petenti*** HE SUPPORTED CATILINA WHEN THIS ONE MADE A SECOND ATTEMPT (Cicero, *Pro Caelio*).
- **... Sulpicius Galus, qui maxume omnium nobilium *Graecis litteris* studuit ...** SULPICIUS GALUS, WHO MOST OF ALL THE NOBLES DEVOTED HIMSELF TO GREEK LITERATURE (Cicero, *Brutus*).

✧ Further ahead, in late Latin, this verb developed the modern meaning of TO STUDY. A typical mistake when composing in Latin is to translate I STUDY LITERATURE by ***Litteras* studeo** instead of by ***Litteris* studeo**.

subvenio, -ire, -veni, -ventum TO HELP
succurro, -ere, -curri, -cursum TO HELP
supersum, -esse, -fui (no supine) TO OUTLIVE

c) Verbs that rule ablative [274]

careo, -ere, -ui (no supine) TO LACK
- **Quamquam abest a culpa, *suspicione* tamen non caret** ALTHOUGH HE HAS NO BLAME, NEVERTHELESS HE DOES NOT LACK SUSPICION (Cicero, *Pro Roscio Amerino*).

desisto, -ere, -stiti, -stitum TO CEASE FROM

egeo, -ere, egui (no supine) TO LACK, TO NEED
- **Nihil adpetunt, *nulla re* egent** THEY REQUIRE NOTHING, THEY LACK NOTHING (Cicero, *Paradoxa Stoicorum*).

✧ This verb can also rule genitive:
- ***Auxilii* egeo** I NEED HELP.

fruor, frui, fructus sum (deponent) TO ENJOY
fungor, fungi, functus sum (deponent) TO PERFORM

potior, -iri, potitus sum (deponent) TO OBTAIN
- ***Magno* pecoris atque hominum *numero* potitur** HE OBTAINS A LARGE NUMBER OF CATTLE AND OF MEN (Caesar, *De Bello Gallico*).

✧ Also possible with accusative and genitive:
- **Amisit animam, potitus est *gloriam*** HE LOST HIS LIFE, HE OBTAINED GLORY (Anon., *Rhetorica ad Herennium*).
- **Hic simul atque *imperii* potitus est, persuasit ...** AS SOON AS HE OBTAINED THE POWER, HE PERSUADED... (Nepos, *Vitae*).

utor, uti, usus sum (deponent) TO USE
vescor, vesci (no perfect form) TO EAT

3. Adjectives followed by a given case [275]

a) Adjectives followed by a genitive

avidus, -a, -um GREEDY FOR

cupidus, -a, -um DESIROUS OF

- Cupidus *belli* adversus Antiochum Eumenes erat EUMENES WAS DESIROUS OF WAR AGAINST ANTIOCHUS (Livy, *Ab Urbe Condita*).

dissimilis, -e UNLIKE
doctus, -a, -um LEARNED IN

expers, -ertis DEPRIVED OF, LACKING, FREE FROM

- Ipse adulescentulus ... non expers fuit *illius periculi* HE HIMSELF, AS A YOUNG BOY, ... WAS NOT FREE FROM THAT DANGER (Nepos, *Vitae*).

✧ Note that a typical mistake is to translate **expers, -ertis** by EXPERT.

immemor, -oris FORGETFUL OF
imperitus, -a, -um UNSKILLED IN
inanis, -e EMPTY OF

memor, -oris MINDFUL OF

- Erit *tanti criminis* illa memor SHE WILL BE MINDFUL OF SUCH A BIG FAULT (Propertius, *Elegiae*).

particeps, -cipis SHARING IN
patiens, -entis TOLERANT OF
peritus, -a, -um SKILLED IN
plenus, -a, -um FULL OF

scitus, -a, -um SKILLED IN

- Est enim scitus *pugnandi* HE IS INDEED SKILLED IN FIGHTING (Quintilianus, *Institutio Oratoria*).

✧ Note that **pugnandi** is a gerund, but in any case it is a genitive.

similis, -e SIMILAR TO

studiosus, -a, -um FOND OF

- Agri enim *culturae* ab initio fui studiosus FROM THE BEGINNING I WAS FOND OF AGRICULTURE (Terentius Varro, *Res Rusticae*).

✧ It would be worth noting that the corresponding verb **studeo** rules dative, while this adjective rules genitive.

> **Note**
>
> Some of them can also be followed by an ablative, and **similis** and **dissimilis** can also be followed by a dative.

b) Adjectives followed by a dative [276]

amicus, -a, -um FRIENDLY TO, FRIEND OF

- A. Ligurius ... mortuus est, bonus homo et *nobis* amicus A. LIGURIUS HAS DIED, A GOOD MAN AND A FRIEND OF US (Cicero, *Epistulae ad Familiares*).

✧ It can also be followed by a genitive:

- Quintum iam mensem socius et amicus *populi Romani* armis obsessus teneor IT IS OVER FOUR MONTHS NOW THAT I, AN ALLY AND A FRIEND OF THE ROMAN PEOPLE, HAVE BEEN HELD, BESIEGED BY WEAPONS (Sallust, *Bellum Iugurthinum*).

carus, -a, -um DEAR TO
dissimilis, -e UNLIKE
gratus, -a, -um PLEASING TO

inimicus HOSTILE TO, ENEMY TO

✧ This adjective has the meaning of *personal enemy*:

- Vident omnes qua de causa *huic* inimicus venias EVERYBODY SEES WHY YOU COME AS AN ENEMY TO THIS MAN (Cicero, *Pro Roscio Amerino*).

✧ The meaning of ENEMY in military sense is given by the adjective hostis, -e.

proximus, -a, -um NEAR TO
similis, -e SIMILAR TO

Note

Similis and dissimilis can also be followed by a genitive.

c) Adjectives followed by an ablative [277]

contentus, -a, -um CONTENT WITH
dignus, -a, -um WORTHY OF

fretus, -a, -um RELYING UPON

- Fretus *numero* copiarum suarum confligere cupiebat RELYING UPON THE NUMBER OF HIS TROOPS, HE WANTED TO FIGHT (Nepos, *Vitae*).

indignus, -a, -um UNWORTHY OF

orbus, -a, -um DEPRIVED OF

- Itaque orbus *iis rebus omnibus* ... THEREFORE, DEPRIVED OF ALL THESE THINGS ... (Cicero, *Epistulae ad Familiares*).

praeditus, -a, -um ENDOWED WITH

- Opportune adest homo summa *fide et omni virtute* praeditus CONVENIENTLY, WE HAVE HERE A MAN ENDOWED WITH THE GREATEST GOOD FAITH AND WITH EVERY VIRTUE (Cicero, *Pro Cluentio*).

Note

Some of them can also be followed by a genitive.

SYNTAX OF CLAUSES

a) Simple clauses

1. Describing real actions
2. Expressing potential actions
3. Expressing commands and prohibitions
4. Expressing wishes
5. Asking questions
6. Impersonal verbs

b) Subordinate clauses

1. The concept of *consecutio temporum*
2. Causal clauses
3. Purpose clauses
4. Temporal clauses
5. Concessive clauses
6. Result clauses
7. Conditional clauses
8. Relative clauses
9. Comparative clauses
10. Fear clauses
11. Indefinite clauses
12. Proviso clauses
13. **Quominus** and **quin** clauses
14. Summary of the uses of **cum**
15. Summary of the uses of **ut**
16. Completive **quod** clauses

c) Infinitive clauses

1. General principles
2. Which tense of infinitive?
3. Where there is no change of subject
4. Historical infinitive
5. Exclamatory infinitive

d) Participle clauses

1. General principles
2. The participle is impersonal
3. The temporal correlation
4. Participle as a verb
5. Participle as a noun
7. The ablative absolute

e) Indirect speech

1. General remarks
2. Indirect statement clauses
3. Indirect command clauses
4. Indirect question clauses
5. Subordinate clauses in indirect speech
6. A special technique: *Oratio Obliqua*

f) Uses of the gerund and gerundive

1. Definition and forms
2. Uses of the gerund
3. Gerundive replacing the gerund
4. Exceptions to the replacement

g) The periphrastic conjugation and the supine

1. The active periphrastic
2. The passive periphrastic
3. The supine in **-um**
4. The supine in **-u**

h) Combination of negatives

1. Negatives cancelling or reinforcing each other?
2. Other combinations of negatives side by side

a) Simple clauses

1. Describing real actions [278]

a/ In order to describe real actions, it is necessary to use the *indicative* mood, in the appropriate tense:

- Ubi *sunt* milites? WHERE ARE THE SOLDIERS?
- Heri multa templa *vidi* YESTERDAY I SAW MANY TEMPLES.
- Cras domi *manebo* TOMORROW I WILL STAY AT HOME.

b/ It is worth remembering at this stage the difference in aspect between the imperfect and the perfect tenses: the imperfect indicates a *continuous* action or process, while the perfect conveys the idea of a *punctual* action, as shown in the following examples.

- Litteras *scribebam* I WAS WRITING A LETTER.
- Fortunam temptare Galba *nolebat* GALBA DID NOT WANT TO TEMPT FORTUNE (Caesar, *De Bello Gallico*).

- Litteras *scripsi* I WROTE A LETTER.
- Nostri celeriter arma *ceperunt* OUR MEN QUICKLY TOOK UP ARMS (Caesar, *De Bello Gallico*).

Another point that is worth remembering is the possibility of translating the perfect tense using the construction *have + past participle* :

- Litteras *scripsi* I WROTE A LETTER / I HAVE WRITTEN A LETTER.

c/ In some cases, the presence of an adverb will help us to decide which option sounds more natural in English; for instance, **Heri litteras scripsi** should be translated as YESTERDAY I WROTE A LETTER (YESTERDAY I HAVE WRITTEN A LETTER would not be right in English).

2. Expressing potential actions [279]

a) Future potentiality

1/ To express future potentiality in Latin, it is necessary to use the *subjunctive* in the present tense. Let's see some examples:

- Talem librum *scribam* I WOULD/COULD WRITE SUCH A BOOK.
- *Dicam* hoc scelus esse I WOULD SAY THAT THIS IS A CRIME.
- Ubi *invenias* ducem meliorem quam Caesarem? WHERE WOULD/COULD YOU FIND A BETTER GENERAL THAN CAESAR?
- Quis non *admiretur* splendorem puchritudinemque virtutis? WHO WOULD NOT ADMIRE THE SPLENDOUR AND BEAUTY OF VIRTUE? (Cicero, *De Officiis*).
- Quid de P. Licini Crassi ... *loquar*? WHAT MIGHT I SAY ABOUT P. LICINIUS CRASSUS? (Cicero, *De Senectute*).

2/ This construction actually corresponds to the apodosis of a conditional period, specifically of an eventual conditional (see section on Conditionals), but without the protasis: [280]

- Talem librum *scribam* (si quis me poscat) I WOULD/COULD WRITE SUCH A BOOK (IF ANYBODY WERE TO ASK ME TO).

3/ In some cases, it is also possible to use the *perfect subjunctive* tense in order to express future potentiality:

- Ego hoc *dixerim* I WOULD/COULD SAY THIS.
- ... Aristoteles, quem excepto Platone haud scio an recte *dixerim* principem philosophorum ... ARISTOTLE, WHOM, WITH THE EXCEPTION OF PLATO, I DO NOT KNOW WHETHER I COULD RIGHTLY CALL THE FIRST OF THE PHILOSOPHERS (Cicero, *De Finibus*).

b) Present potentiality [281]

The difference between future and present potentiality is minimal in Latin and, therefore, these two constructions are easy to confuse with each other.

To express potentiality in the present, it is necessary to use the *imperfect subjunctive*:

- Talem librum *scriberem* I WOULD/COULD WRITE SUCH A BOOK.
- Omnia tibi *dicerem* I WOULD/COULD TELL YOU EVERYTHING.
- *Cuperem* vultum videre tuum cum haec legeres (Cicero, *Epistulae ad Atticum*). I WOULD LIKE TO SEE YOUR FACE WHEN YOU READ THIS

Note that we have translated in the same way both the sentence **Talem librum scriberem** and the sentence **Talem librum scribam** reported in the section on *future potentiality*. The difference lies in the interpretation given to the potentiality: while in the example featured in the previous section we wanted to express a possibility in the future (and therefore we used the present subjunctive), in this case we consider an event that theoretically could be happening now, an action that is not prevented by present impediments.

There is a small difference between these two cases but it will hardly affect the translation; some grammars do not distinguish the two constructions, introducing just one model that features the same tenses to express either present or future potentiality.

c) Potentiality in the past [282]

1/ The best way to express potentiality in the past is to use the *pluperfect subjunctive* :

- Talem librum *scripsissem* I WOULD HAVE WRITTEN SUCH A BOOK.
- *Vicisset* iuvenis senem, *vicisset* sceleratus pium? WOULD A YOUNG MAN HAVE DEFEATED AN ELDERLY PERSON? WOULD A WICKED MAN HAVE DEFEATED A PIOUS PERSON? (Quintilianus, *Declamationes Minores*).

This is nothing else than the apodosis of a conditional period of unfulfilled condition in the past (see the corresponding chapter *b) Subordinate clauses*, section 7, on *Conditionals*).

2/ Nonetheless, it is very common to find the *imperfect subjunctive* employed to express potentiality in the past, especially with verbs like **credo** and **dico** (*verba dicendi*):

- *Crederes* eum malum ducem esse YOU WOULD HAVE BELIEVED THAT HE IS A BAD GENERAL.
- Quis *crederet* hoc? WHO WOULD HAVE BELIEVED THIS?
- Quis umquam *crederet* mulierum adversarium Verrem futurum [esse]? WHO WOULD HAVE BELIEVED THAT VERRES WAS GOING TO BE AN OPPONENT OF WOMEN? (Cicero, *In Verrem*).

Remember that the imperfect subjunctive is frequently used to express present potentiality as well.

3. Expressing commands and prohibitions [283]

a) Commands

1/ The most common form used to express a command in Latin is the *present imperative*:

- *Dic* mihi tuum nomen TELL ME YOUR NAME.
- *Lege* hunc librum READ THIS BOOK.
- *Tace*, Lucretia, inquit KEEP SILENT, LUCRETIA, HE SAID (Livy, *Ab Urbe Condita*).
- Me manibus impiis *eripite* SET ME FREE FROM THESE CRUEL HANDS (Sallust, *Bellum Iugurthinum*).

An imperative can be preceded by **age** (imperative of **ago**), meaning COME ON:

- Sed *age responde* BUT COME ON, ANSWER (Plautus, *Amphitruo*).
- *Age dic!* COME ON, TELL! (Cicero, *In Verrem*).

The use of future imperative is very rare, but it can be found in some legal documents and ordinances:

- Duces Romani exercitus audaces *sunto* GENERALS OF THE ROMAN ARMY MUST BE BRAVE.

2/ In order to express a command in the 3rd person, it is necessary to use the present subjunctive, called in this case the *iussive subjunctive*, as the 3rd person imperative is attested only in archaic Latin: [284]

- *Veniat* LET HIM COME.
- *Legat* LET HIM READ.
- Pacem vult M. Antonius? Arma *deponat* M. ANTHONY WANTS PEACE? THEN LET HIM PUT DOWN ARMS (Cicero, *Philippicae*).
- *Sit* adulescentia liberior LET THE YOUNG BE MORE FREE (Cicero, *Pro Caelio*).

3/ Sometimes the iussive subjunctive can substitute the imperative for the 2nd person as well, and in this case it may be preceded by **ut**: [285]

- *[Ut] taceas* KEEP SILENT.
- *Taceas*, me *spectes* SHUT UP, LOOK AT ME (Plautus, *Asinaria*).

This is the abbreviated version of the expression **Fac ut taceas**, without the first imperative **fac**, which has been elided:

- *Fac* modo *ut venias* JUST COME! (Cicero, *Epistulae ad Atticum*).
  ✧ It would have been normal to find only **Ut venias**.

4/ A specific form of orders are what we call *exhortations*, or orders we give to ourselves, equivalent to the English *LET'S + infinitive*. In order to express exhortations we should use the present subjunctive, which is called in this case *hortatory subjunctive* :

- *Eamus* Romam — LET'S GO TO ROME.
- *Mittamus* litteras ad Caesarem — LET'S SEND A LETTER TO CAESAR.
- *Abeamus* a fabulis — LET'S GET AWAY FROM MYTHS (Cicero, *De Divinatione*).

To sum up: you can use the imperative to give orders and choose the 2nd person, or employ the present subjunctive for orders expressed in the 1st, 2nd or 3rd person, singular or plural.

b) Prohibitions [286]

1/ In Latin, to express orders involving prohibitions (*verba prohibendi*), the imperative form is not commonly used but it is substituted by the imperative of **nolo** NOT TO WANT followed by the infinitive of the verb:

- Quinte, *noli* hoc *facere* — QUINTUS, DO NOT DO THIS ✧ Literally, QUINTUS, DO NOT WANT TO DO THIS.
- Milites, *nolite pugnare* — SOLDIERS, DO NOT FIGHT ✧ Literally, SOLDIERS, DO NOT WANT TO FIGHT.
- *Nolite* Cn. Fannio dicenti *credere* — DO NOT TRUST WHAT C. FANNIUS SAYS (Cicero, *In Verrem*).

2/ In the previous section we have seen how to use the subjunctive to give orders; we can use it as well to express prohibitions directed to 1st, 2nd or 3rd person, singular or plural, adding the negative **ne** before the verb. Moreover remember that it is more common to use the perfect subjunctive, rather than the present, in relation to the 2nd person.

- *Ne eamus* Romam — LET'S NOT GO TO ROME.
- *Ne* hoc *dixeris* — DO NOT SAY THIS. ✧ Observe: 2nd person – perfect subjunctive.
- *Ne veniat* — DO NOT LET HIM COME.
- Mihi [possessionem] *ne adimat* — DO NOT LET HIM TAKE [MY POSSESSIONS] AWAY FROM ME (Cicero, *In Verrem*).
- Iuventus ... *ne* quem vi *terreat* — DO NOT LET YOUTH SCARE ANYONE WITH VIOLENCE (Cicero, *Pro Caelio*).

3/ Sometimes we can find **cave** instead of **ne**; **cave** is the imperative form of the verb **caveo** TO BEWARE, which in this construction rules the subjunctive: [287]

- *Cave* hoc *dixeris* DO NOT SAY THIS.
  ✧ Literally we are saying BEWARE THAT YOU SAY THIS, implying that the consequences would be bad.
- *Cave* in ista tam frigida, tam ieiuna calumnia *delitiscas* BEWARE THAT YOU TAKE SHELTER IN THESE LIES, SO COLD AND MEAGRE (Cicero, *Pro Caecina*).
- Quorum *cave* tu quemquam peregrinum *appelles* BEWARE THAT YOU CALL FOREIGNER ANY OF THOSE MEN (Cicero, *Pro Sulla*).

4. Expressing wishes [288]

a) For the future

The forms IF ONLY.../ WOULD THAT.../ I WISH..., when used to express a wish for the future, are translated into Latin by means of the *present subjunctive*, usually preceded by the word **utinam** (sometimes simply **ut**), with the negative **ne** if it is a negative desire:

- Utinam *veniat* Caesar — WOULD THAT CAESAR WILL COME!
- Utinam *ne vincant* hostes — IF ONLY THE ENEMY WOULD NOT WIN!
- Utinam *ne vincamur* — I WISH WE MAY NOT BE DEFEATED!
- De qua utinam aliquando tecum *loquar* — I WISH I MAY SOMETIME TALK WITH YOU ABOUT THIS! (Cicero, *Ad Atticum*).

b) For the present [289]

In order to express desires about the present situation, or about something still capable of fulfilment, you can use the *imperfect subjunctive* :

- Utinam *veniret* Caesar nunc — WOULD THAT CAESAR WERE COMING NOW!
- Utinam *ne viderem* hoc — I WISH I WERE NOT SEEING THIS!
- Utinam *viveret* Caesar — IF ONLY CAESAR WERE STILL ALIVE!
- Utinam Romae nemo *esset* dives — IF ONLY THERE WERE NO RICH MAN IN ROME! (Propertius, *Elegiae*).
- Utinam *exstarent* illa carmina — IF ONLY THOSE POEMS WERE STILL HERE! (Cicero, *Brutus*).

c) For the past [290]

To express a wish for the past (therefore incapable of fulfilment), use the *pluperfect subjunctive*:

- Utinam Caesar *venisset* — IF ONLY CAESAR HAD COME!
- Utinam *ne* hoc *vidissem* — IF ONLY I HAD NOT SEEN THIS!
- Utinam Brutus *ne necatus esset* — WOULD THAT BRUTUS HAD NOT BEEN KILLED!
- Utinam *potuissem* obire — IF ONLY I COULD HAVE DIED! (Cicero, *Tusculanae Disputationes*).

5. Asking questions [291]

a) Yes/no questions

1/ When a *yes/no* question is introduced and we do not know whether the answer will be affirmative or negative, we can either invert the order of the words or we can attach the particle -**ne** to the end of the first word, as an opening question mark:

- Caesar venit — CAESAR IS COMING.
- Venit Caesar? — IS CAESAR COMING?
- Venit*ne* Caesar? — IS CAESAR COMING?

- **Exheredare filium voluit. ... Exheredavit*ne* ?** HE WANTED TO DISINHERIT HIS SON. ... DID HE DISINHERIT HIM? (Cicero, *Pro Sex. Roscio*).
- **Potest*ne* in tam diversis mentibus pax aut amicitia esse?** IS IT POSSIBLE FOR PEACE OR FRIENDSHIP TO STAND BETWEEN SUCH DIFFERENT MINDS? (Sallust, *Bellum Iugurthinum*).

2/ If we suppose that the answer will be *yes*, then we put at the beginning of the phrase the particle **nonne**, which is nothing else than the negative **non** followed by the aforementioned ending **-ne**:

- ***Nonne* venit Caesar?** ISN'T CAESAR COMING? / CAESAR IS COMING, ISN'T HE?
- ***Nonne* omnis ille terror ... ex Autroni improbitate pendebat?** DIDN'T ALL THAT STATE OF FEAR ... ARISE FROM THE VILLAINY OF AUTRONIUS? (Cicero, *Pro Sulla*).

3/ If we suppose that the answer will be *no*, we put **num** at the beginning:

- ***Num* venit Caesar?** IS CAESAR COMING? / CAESAR ISN'T COMING, IS HE?
- ***Num* igitur peccamus?** ARE WE ACTING WRONGLY? (Cicero, *Ad Atticum*).

b) Double questions [292]

1/ Double questions like DO YOU WANT THIS OR THAT? are introduced by **utrum** WHICH ONE OF THE TWO and completed by **an** OR:

- ***Utrum* venis nobiscum *an* hic manes?** DO YOU COME WITH US OR DO YOU STAY HERE?
- ***Utrum* quid agatur non vides, *an* apud quos agatur?** DO YOU NOT SEE WHAT IS BEING DEALT WITH, OR DO YOU NOT SEE AMONG WHOM? (Cicero, *Pro Sex. Roscio*).

✧ Observe that usually the **utrum** is not translated into English.

2/ Instead of **utrum** we can use **-ne**, or even nothing:

- **Venis*ne* nobiscum *an* hic manes? / Venis nobiscum *an* hic manes?** ARE YOU COMING WITH US OR ARE YOU STAYING HERE?
- **Ipse percussit *an* aliis occidendum dedit?** DID HE HIT HIM HIMSELF, OR DID HE ENTRUST TO OTHER PEOPLE THE JOB OF KILLING HIM? (Cicero, *Pro Sex. Roscio*).

3/ If the second choice is just a simple *or not*, it is expressed by **an non**:

- **Venisne nobiscum *an non* ?** DO YOU COME WITH US OR NOT?
- **Sed isne est quem quaero *an non* ?** BUT IS HE THE ONE I AM LOOKING FOR OR NOT? (Terentius Afer, *Phormio*).

c) Partial questions [293]

Sometimes we may ask about only one aspect of the sentence (a place, somebody's identity, etc.), and this is done by means of interrogative adverbs or adjectives.

1/ *Adverbial questions* use an interrogative adverb as the interrogative element:

- ***Ubi* est pater?** WHERE IS MY FATHER?
- ***Quo* eunt nunc?** WHERE DO THEY GO NOW?
- ***Ubi* erant ceteri creditores?** WHERE WERE THE REST OF THE CREDITORS? (Cicero, *Pro Quinctio*).
- ***Unde* eam esse aiunt?** FROM WHERE DO THEY SAY SHE IS? (Plautus, *Bacchides*).

2/ *Adjectival/pronominal questions* use an interrogative adjective/pronoun as the interrogative element, in the necessary case:

- *Cui* puero pecuniam dedisti? — TO WHICH BOY DID YOU GIVE THE MONEY?
- *Quis* venit heri? — WHO CAME YESTERDAY?
- – Eum vendidi — I SOLD HIM.
  – *Cui* homini? — TO WHAT MAN? (Plautus, *Captivi*).
- *Quis* huic rei testis est? — WHO IS A WITNESS OF THIS AFFAIR? (Cicero, *Pro Quinctio*).

Both these types of questions are dealt with more extensively in the corresponding sections on adverbs and adjectives/pronouns.

d) Deliberative questions [294]

In deliberative questions we use the *subjunctive mood.* In these questions, usually in 1st person, the speaker uses the subjunctive to express some degree of uncertainty about what should be done, as if asking for instructions or suggestions.

Compare and contrast the following examples to clarify the difference:

- Quid *facimus* ? — WHAT ARE WE DOING NOW? — ✧ Present indicative: normal question.
- Quid *faciamus* ? — WHAT ARE WE TO DO? — ✧ Present subjunctive: deliberative question.

It is interesting to note that a deliberative question is simply the interrogative form of an exhortative subjunctive:

- Quid *faciamus* ? — WHAT ARE WE TO DO = LET'S DO WHAT?
  ✧ The second translation, really "forced", shows clearly the role of the exhortative subjunctive.
- Sed quid *faciamus* ? — BUT WHAT ARE WE TO DO? (Cicero, *Epistulae ad Atticum*).
- Quid *agam*, iudices? — WHAT AM I TO DO, JUDGES? (Cicero, *Contra Verrem*).
- Quem *implorem* ? — WHOM AM I GOING TO IMPLORE? (Cicero, *Pro Flacco*).

6. Impersonal verbs [295]

In English, impersonal verbs normally use the pronoun IT to indicate their subject: *IT* IS NECESSARY TO GO THERE, *IT* IS NOT POSSIBLE TO DO THIS, etc., but in Latin the subject is not expressed at all. As in most languages, the verb will always be in 3rd person singular.

Impersonal verbs can be divided into four main groups:

a) Verbs of propriety
b) Verbs of negative feeling (*verba affectuum*)
c) Verbs of interest
d) Verbs describing meteorological phenomena

After analysing these four groups, we will also study two frequent constructions related to the impersonal construction.

a) Verbs of propriety [296]

1/ The three main impersonal verbs of propriety are these:

licet, licere, licuit IT IS PERMITTED, IT IS POSSIBLE
oportet, oportere, oportuit IT IS NECESSARY
necesse est IT IS NECESSARY ✧ This is an impersonal expression rather than an impersonal verb, it is obvious that **est** is not an impersonal verb.

a/ They can present more than one construction; note that the following translations are in a "forced" English form, for the sake of showing the little differences between meanings:

Accusative + infinitive:

- **Necesse est *me* librum *legere*** IT IS NECESSARY THAT I READ THE BOOK.
- **Licet *me* librum *legere*** IT IS PERMITTED THAT I READ THE BOOK.
  ✧ Grammatically speaking, the infinitive clause **me librum legere** is the actual subject of **licet**, a common phenomenon with impersonal verbs.
- ***Meam orationem gratissimam esse* oportet** MY SPEECH HAS TO BE VERY PLEASANT (Cicero, *Pro Sex. Roscio*).

Dative + infinitive:

- **Necesse est *mihi* librum *legere*** IT IS NECESSARY FOR ME TO READ THE BOOK.
- **Licet *mihi* librum *legere*** IT IS PERMITTED TO ME TO READ THE BOOK.
- **Etenim eos una cenasse dixit, qui aut absunt, aut *quibus* necesse est idem *dicere*** INDEED, HE CLAIMED THAT THEY DINED TOGETHER, [PEOPLE] WHO EITHER ARE NOT HERE OR MUST TELL THE SAME STORY (Cicero, *Pro Caelio*).
- **Id *Sex. Roscio facere* non licet?** CAN'T SEX. ROSCIUS DO THIS? (Cicero, *Pro Sex. Roscio*).

Ut + subjunctive:

- **Necesse est *ut* librum *legam*** IT IS NECESSARY THAT I READ THE BOOK.
- **Licet *ut* librum *legam*** IT IS PERMITTED THAT I READ THE BOOK.
- **Necesse est *ut legas*** IT IS NECESSARY THAT YOU READ IT (Valerius Probus, *Fragmenta*).

✧ The **ut** is usually omitted:

- **Rationem tantae familiaritatis ... *reddas* atque *exponas* necesse est** YOU MUST ANSWER AND EXPLAIN THE REASON FOR SUCH A DEEP INTIMACY (Cicero, *Pro Caelio*).
- ***Dicas* licet** YOU ARE ALLOWED TO SPEAK (Cicero, *Pro Sex. Roscio*).
- **Ego crimen oportet *diluam*** I MUST CLARIFY THE ACCUSATION (Cicero, *Pro Sex. Roscio*).

b/ These impersonal verbs can be used without a direct object that indicates the person who should perform the action, as in the following cases. Note that the translation should emphasise the general implication of the verb: [297]

- ***Licet* abire** IT IS PERMITTED TO LEAVE / ONE CAN LEAVE / PEOPLE CAN LEAVE / WE CAN LEAVE etc.
- **Quod genus operis sine ullo periculo, sine suspicione hostium facere *licebat*** IT WAS POSSIBLE TO PERFORM THIS TASK WITHOUT ANY DANGER AND WITHOUT AROUSING SUSPICION IN THE ENEMY (Caesar, *De Bello Gallico*).
- **Id quod *necesse erat* accidere, totius exercitus perturbatio facta est** AS WOULD NECESSARILY HAPPEN, THERE WAS A GREAT CONFUSION THROUGHOUT THE ARMY (Caesar, *De Bello Gallico*).

c/ In some cases, these verbs have a subject:

- *Quicquid* vero non licet, certe non oportet   WHATEVER IS ACTUALLY NOT ALLOWED, SURELY IS NOT APPROPRIATE (Cicero, *Pro Balbo*).   ✧ **Quicquid** is the real subject of **licet** (and of **oportet**).

2/ There are some other impersonal verbs in addition to the previous ones, although they do not appear as frequently as the former ones: [298]

libet   IT PLEASES
decet   IT IS CONVENIENT
dedecet   IT IS NOT CONVENIENT
praestat   IT IS BETTER   ✧ It is just the verb **praesto** used impersonally.

They use the same constructions as above:

- Ex quibus neminem *mihi libet* nominare   IT DOES NOT PLEASE ME TO SAY THE NAME OF ANY OF THEM (Cicero, *Pro Caelio*).

3/ There is also the idiomatic expression **Opus est** THERE IS NEED FOR, and the case used to express what is needed can be nominative, genitive or ablative:

- Nihil *vi*, nihil *secessione* opus est: necesse est suomet ipsi more praecipites eant   THERE IS NO NEED FOR VIOLENCE AND SEDITION: IT IS NECESSARY THAT THEY FALL OUT OF POWER BECAUSE OF THEIR OWN ATTITUDE (Sallust, *Bellum Iugurthinum*).

4/ Other impersonal expressions are followed by *ut + subjunctive*, like these ones (the translations are extremely literal, even if they produce wrong English, for the sake of showing the sense):

mos est ut   IT IS CUSTOMARY THAT...
aequum est ut   IT IS FAIR THAT...
restat ut   IT JUST REMAINS THAT...

- Apud omnis Graecos *hic mos est, ut* honorem hominibus habitum in monumentis eius modi non nulla religione deorum consecrari *arbitrentur*   THERE IS THIS CUSTOM AMONG ALL THE GREEKS, THAT THE HONOUR BESTOWED UPON MEN BY MONUMENTS OF THIS KIND ARE CONSIDERED TO BE CONSECRATED UNDER SOME PROTECTION OF THE GODS (Cicero, *In Verrem*).
- *Restat ut* omnes unum *velint*   IT JUST REMAINS THAT ALL WANT ONE THING   (Cicero, *Pro Marcello*).

b) Verbs of negative feeling (*verba affectuum*) [299]

There are five frequently used impersonal verbs that express negative feelings. We offer a literal translation just for the same of showing the meaning in 3rd person. Obviously, in English it would never be expressed this way.

miseret, miserere, miseruit IT PITIES
piget, pigere, piguit IT DISGUSTS
taedet, taedere, taeduit IT TIRES, BORES
paenitet, paenitere, paenituit IT REPENTS, DISPLEASES
pudet, pudere, puduit IT SHAMES, MAKES ASHAMED

✧ Observe the lack of supine in all of them.

➪ The *person* affected by the feeling must be in accusative.
➪ The *reason* of the feeling can be expressed
- in genitive
- with an infinitive
- with a subordinate clause.

- **Miseret** *me mortis* **Caesaris** I FEEL SORRY FOR CAESAR'S DEATH.
  ✧ Literally, IT PITIES ME OF THE DEATH OF CAESAR.
- *Me* **taedet** *ut semper eadem dicas* IT BORES ME THAT YOU ALWAYS SAY THE SAME THINGS.
- *Me* **pudet** *mentiri* I AM ASHAMED OF LYING
  ✧ Literally, LYING ASHAMES ME.
- *Me* **quoque** *erroris mei* **paenitet** I ALSO REPENT FROM MY MISTAKE (Cicero, *Pro Caelio*).
- **Neque** *eos*, **qui ea fecere, pudet aut paenitet** AND THOSE, WHO DID THESE THINGS, DO NEITHER FEEL SHAME NOR SORROW (Sallust, *Bellum Iugurthinum*).

c) Verbs of interest [300]

There are two verbs, **intersum** and **refero**, that do exist as personal verbs. Nevertheless, if they are used impersonally, i.e. **interest** and **refert**, they acquire a special meaning: IT IS OF INTEREST / IT IS IN SOMEONE'S INTEREST. As usual, we offer a rather literal translation in order to show the structure, even if it sounds unnatural in English.

1/ The structure of these sentences is as follows:

➪ The *person* for whom the matter is of interest, if mentioned, must be in genitive.
➪ The *event* (or thing) that is of interest can be expressed by an infinitive clause, an indirect question, an **ut** clause, etc.

- *Caesaris* **interest** *te venire* IT IS IN CAESAR'S INTERESTS THE FACT THAT YOU COME.
  ✧ Literally, IT IS IN THE INTEREST OF CAESAR THAT YOU COME.
- *Caesaris* **interest** *ut venias* (same meaning as above).
- **Semper ... quantum interesset** *P. Clodi se perire* ... **cogitabat** HE WAS ALWAYS THINKING OF HOW MUCH HIS DEATH WOULD BE IN P. CLODIUS' INTEREST (Cicero, *Pro Milone*).
- **Tribuni plebis permagni interest** *qui sint* IT IS OF THE GREATEST IMPORTANCE WHO THE TRIBUNES OF THE PLEBS ARE (Cicero, *Pro Plancio*).
  ✧ In this last example, there is no mention of the persons for whom this is important: it is left in a general sense.

2/ If the person is expressed by means of a personal pronoun, then it is expressed in the ablative fem. sing. form of the corresponding possessive adjective: **mea**, **tua**, etc.: [301]

- *Mea* interest te venire IT IS IN MY INTEREST THE FACT THAT YOU COME.
  ✧ Literally, IT IS OF INTEREST FOR ME THAT YOU COME.
- *Tua* refert oppidum tutum esse IT IS IN YOUR INTEREST THE FACT THAT THE CITADEL IS SAFE.
  ✧ Literally, IT IS OF YOUR INTEREST THAT THE CITADEL IS SAFE.
- Si, quod *mea* minus interest, id te magis forte delectat, ... IF WHAT I AM LESS INTERESTED IN PLEASES YOU MORE, ... (Cicero, *Pro Plancio*).

3/ What is of interest can even be expressed by means of a neuter pronoun:

- *Hoc* Caesaris interest THIS IS INTERESTING FOR CAESAR. ✧ Literally, THIS IS OF INTEREST FOR CAESAR.

✧ Note that in this case **interest** cannot be considered an impersonal verb, as **hoc** would clearly be its subject.

d) Verbs describing meteorological phenomena [302]

1/ As in most languages, verbs that describe natural phenomena are used only in the 3rd person singular:

pluit IT RAINS
tonat IT THUNDERS
nivit IT SNOWS
grandinat IT HAILS

- In Hyrcanis montibus a meridiano latere non *pluit* IN THE HYRCAN MOUNTAINS, ON THE SOUTH SIDE, IT DOES NOT RAIN (Plinius Secundus, *Naturalis Historia*).

2/ In mythological and poetical texts we can find expressions in which the meteorological verb has a symbolic subject:

- Caelum *tonat* THE HEAVEN THUNDERS (Vergil, *Aeneis*).
- Iuppiter omni arce *tonat* IUPPITER THUNDERS AROUND THE WHOLE CITADEL (Statius, *Thebais*).

Or we can find expressions of "what" it rains:

- In Aventino lapidibus *pluit* ON THE AVENTINE HILL IT RAINS STONES (Livy, *Ab Urbe Condita*).
  ✧ Literally, IT RAINS WITH STONES.

e) The impersonal passive [303]

1/ Some transitive verbs can be used in an impersonal way in the passive voice (translations have been adapted to produce correct English, for instance adding the word PEOPLE to allow the verb to have a subject):

- Romae ... de proelio facto et oppugnatione Cirtae audiebatur AT ROME ... PEOPLE WERE HEARING ABOUT THE BATTLE THAT HAD TAKEN PLACE AND THE SIEGE OF CIRTA (Sallust, *Bellum Iugurthinum*).
- Diu atque acriter pugnatum est THE BATTLE WAS LONG AND CRUEL (Caesar, *De Bello Gallico*).

2/ The same impersonal use of the passive forms is possible as well with some intransitive verbs (i.e., verbs that do not have a direct object):

- **Romam itur** PEOPLE GO TO ROME
  ✧ Equivalent to the French *On va*, or the German *Man geht*.
- **Ubi eo ventum est, Caesar...** WHEN THEY ARRIVED THERE, CAESAR… (Caesar, *De Bello Gallico*).
- **Rhodanus ... nonnullis locis transitur** THE RHONE … CAN BE CROSSED ON FOOT IN SOME PLACES (Caesar, *De Bello Gallico*).

f) Impersonal passive and personal construction [304]

1/ As stated above, sometimes verbs that are not impersonal, like **dico**, are used impersonally:

- ***Dicitur / Fertur* Romanos venisse** IT IS SAID THAT THE ROMANS HAVE COME.

Nonetheless in Latin it is much more frequent to use the so called *personal construction* with the same meaning as the previous form:

- **Romani *dicuntur / feruntur* venisse** IT IS SAID THAT THE ROMANS HAVE COME.
  ✧ Literally, THE ROMANS ARE SAID TO HAVE COME.
- **Magnum ibi numerum versuum ediscere *dicuntur*** IT IS SAID THAT THEY HAD LEARNT BY HEART A LARGE NUMBER OF VERSES (Caesar, *De Bello Gallico*).

2/ The verb **videor** can be used in this way as well:

- ***Videtur* amicos Caesaris proditores** (Acc.) **esse** IT SEEMS THAT CAESAR'S FRIENDS ARE TRAITORS ...

... or, much more frequently, with the personal construction:

- **Amici Caesaris *videntur* proditores** (Nom.) **esse** (same meaning as above).
- **Id mihi duabus de causis instituisse *videntur*** IT SEEMS TO ME THAT THEY HAVE ESTABLISHED THIS BECAUSE OF TWO REASONS (Caesar, *De Bello Gallico*).

It is interesting to note that this construction is attested in 1st person too:

- ***Videor* mihi iecisse fundamenta defensionis** I THINK THAT I HAVE SET THE BASICS OF MY DEFENCE (Cicero, *Pro Caelio*).

b) Subordinate clauses

1. The concept of *consecutio temporum* [305]

a) Main concept

A lot of subordinate clauses follow a series of rules with respect to what verbal tense they must use in the clause; in these cases, the choice of tense for the subordinate will depend on the tense of the main verb.

Observe this double example in English:

> I GIVE YOU MONEY SO THAT YOU MAY BUY BOOKS.
> I GAVE YOU MONEY SO THAT YOU MIGHT BUY BOOKS.

The change from GIVE to GAVE in the main clause has made us change the verb from MAY to MIGHT in the subordinate clause.

Something similar happens in Latin, and this change of the tense of the verb in the subordinate clause depending on the tense in the main clause is called ***consecutio temporum***. We will see some examples in Latin further down.

b) How it works (a first idea) [306]

1/ In Latin there are a lot of subordinate clauses that have their verb in the subjunctive mood, and the rules of the *consecutio temporum* establish that there must be some relationship between the verb of the main clause (usually in indicative) and the verb of the subordinate clause (in the subjunctive). The general double rule is this:

- ⇨ If the verb in the main clause is primary, the subjunctive verb of the subordinate must be primary. In this case, the group formed by the two clauses is called *primary sequence*.
- ⇨ If the verb of the main clause is secondary, the subjunctive verb of the subordinate clause must be secondary. In this case, the group formed by the two clauses is called *secondary sequence*.

2/ Let's see the two former sentences in Latin, even before knowing what "primary" and "secondary" mean:

- Tibi pecuniam *do* ut libros *emas* I GIVE YOU MONEY SO THAT YOU MAY BUY BOOKS.
  ✧ Both verbs **do** (indicative) and **emas** (subjunctive) are in a *primary tense*.

- Tibi pecuniam *dedi* ut libros *emeres* I GAVE YOU MONEY SO THAT YOU MIGHT BUY BOOKS.
  ✧ Both verbs **dedi** (indicative) and **emeres** (subjunctive) are in a *secondary tense*.

c) Primary and secondary tenses [307]

What has been said before leads us to the question: what tenses are primary and what tenses are secondary? Making use of the table we have used to introduce the tenses, the distribution is as follows:

Indicative

Present-stem	**Perfect-stem**
Present *primary*	Perfect *primary* AND *secondary*
Imperfect *secondary*	Pluperfect *secondary*
Future *primary*	Fut. perfect *primary*

Subjunctive

Present-stem	**Perfect-stem**
Present *primary*	Perfect *primary*
Imperfect *secondary*	Pluperfect *secondary*

For memory purposes, the rules are very simple:

- ⇨ For both moods, the two tenses at the top row are *primary.*
  - ✧ But see the problem of the perfect indicative.
- ⇨ For both moods, the two tenses of the second row are *secondary.*
- ⇨ Both futures (only indicative) are primary.

d) How it works (a deeper idea) [308]

1/ Let's see a new example, the translation of the two sentences

HE WORKS A LOT IN ORDER TO GET A LOT OF MONEY and HE WORKED A LOT IN ORDER TO GET A LOT OF MONEY.

As we will see further ahead in the corresponding section, in Latin language purpose (in order to...) is not expressed by an infinitive but by **ut** + subjunctive.

The translation of both main clauses will be

HE WORKS A LOT...	**Multum laborat...**	✧ **laborat**	is present,	a *primary* tense.
HE WORKED A LOT...	**Multum laborabat...**	✧ **laborabat**	is imperfect,	a *secondary* tense.

The translation of the subordinate clauses (a purpose clause, in this example) must follow the rules of the *consecutio temporum.* Purpose clauses, in Latin, can only be either in present subjunctive or in imperfect subjunctive (this will be seen further ahead, in the corresponding section), so the choice is simple:

- ⇨ **Multum laborat...** must be followed by ... **ut multam pecuniam *accipiat*,** because **accipiat** is a *primary* tense (present subjunctive) like **laborat**.
- ⇨ **Multum laborabat...** must be followed by ... **ut multam pecuniam *acciperet*,** because **acciperet** is a *secondary* tense (imperf. subjunctive) like **laborabat**.

2/ This example is very simple, as the final result in the first sentence has been present in both clauses (indicative in the main clause, subjunctive in the subordinate clause) and in the second sentence imperfect in both clauses (indicative in the main clause, subjunctive in the subordinate clause). It will not always be so simple (the same tense in both clauses: in indicative in the main one and in the subjunctive in the subordinate one), but it has been useful to set the basics.

e) The problem of the perfect indicative [309]

1/ With respect to the perfect tense of the indicative, if we translate it as a complete action in the past, it is *secondary*, but if we translate it as an action already completed but completed inside the current unit of time, it is *primary*; an example will make it clear:

- **Heri multa *feci*** YESTERDAY I DID MANY THINGS *(secondary).*
  - ✧ We are no longer inside the unit of time of yesterday, so **feci** is here *seconday*, and therefore we translate it by I DID.
- **Hodie multa *feci*** TODAY I HAVE DONE MANY THINGS *(primary).*
  - ✧ We are still inside the unit of time of today, so **feci** is here *primary*, and therefore we translate it by I HAVE DONE.

Another example of the double meaning of the perfect indicative:

- **Heri Caesar multa *scripsit*** YESTERDAY CAESAR WROTE A LOT *(secondary).*
  - ✧ We are no longer inside the unit of time of yesterday, so **scripsit** is *secondary*, and therefore we translate it by WROTE.
- **Hoc anno Caesar multa *scripsit*** THIS YEAR CAESAR HAS WRITTEN A LOT *(primary).*
  - ✧ We are still inside the unit of time of this year, so **scripsit** is *primary*, and therefore we translate it by HAS WRITTEN.

2/ So, depending on whether the perfect tense of the main clause is considered primary (with the sense of I HAVE WRITTEN) or secondary (with the sense of I WROTE), the tense of any subordinate clause it may have, if it must be in the subjunctive, can correspondingly be either primary or secondary. Let's add a purpose clause to the former example (avoiding the expressions **heri** and **hoc anno**, to make both options possible): [310]

> Caesar multa scripsit ut omnia *sciamus.*
> Caesar multa scripsit ut omnia *sciremus.*

➪ In the first sentence we find **sciamus**, which is a present subjunctive, a *primary* tense. So, it means that the **scripsit** of the main clause must be considered a *primary* tense and therefore the translation should be

> CAESAR HAS WRITTEN MANY THINGS SO THAT WE MAY KNOW EVERYTHING.

➪ In the second sentence we find **sciremus**, which is an imperfect subjunctive, a *secondary* tense. So, it means that the **scripsit** of the main clause must be considered a *secondary* tense and therefore the translation should be

> CAESAR WROTE MANY THINGS SO THAT WE MIGHT KNOW EVERYTHING.

We can see that in some cases it will be the subordinate that will tell us how the perfect tense of the main clause must be translated, but it must be said that in Latin texts a perfect tense has almost always a sense of *secondary* tense (I WROTE, I CAME) and just in a small percentage of cases it has a sense of *primary* tense (I HAVE WRITTEN, I HAVE COME).

2. Causal clauses [311]

a) Which conjunctions and mood?

1/ Causal clauses may be introduced by several conjunctions; the two most common ones are **quod** and **quia**, and the verb should be in the indicative:

- ***Quia*** **diei extremum** ***erat*****, proelium non inceptum [est]** AS IT WAS ALMOST THE END OF THE DAY, THE BATTLE DID NOT START (Sallust, *Bellum Iugurthinum*).
- **Quem locum Marius,** ***quod*** **ibi regis thesauri** ***erant*****, summa vi capere intendit** MARIUS TRIED TO TAKE THIS PLACE WITH ALL OF HIS FORCES, BECAUSE THE KING'S TREASURES WERE THERE (Sallust, *Bellum Iugurthinum*).

But if the reason is given as an alleged one, the verb will be in the subjunctive:

- **Pompeius hoc fecit** ***quod/quia*** **Romam ire** ***vellet*** HE DID THIS BECAUSE HE WANTED TO GO TO ROME.
  ✧ The subjunctive means that this is the reason that Pompeius gave, but the writer may have some doubts about it.

2/ It is very common to express two reasons for an action in the same sentence, an unreal one which must be ruled out and the real one, and in these double sentences it is very frequent to find ***quod*** *(sometimes* ***quo****) + subjunctive* to express the unreal one followed by ***quia*** *+ indicative* to express the real one:

- ***Nec*** **haec idcirco omitto** ***quod*** **non gravissima** ***sint, sed quia*** **nunc sine teste** ***dico*** AND I OMIT THESE MATTERS NOT BECAUSE THEY ARE NOT REALLY SERIOUS, BUT BECAUSE NOW I AM DECLARING WITHOUT ANY WITNESS (Cicero, *De Provinciis Consularibus*).

This construction of **non quod** (**nec ... quod** in our example) followed by **sed quia** is very common.

b) Other possible constructions [312]

1/ Other ways of expressing cause are by means of **quoniam** or **quando** (almost always followed by indicative), and usually they introduce a cause that the reader (or listener) already knows:

- ***Quoniam*** **nos tanti viri res admonuit, idoneum visum est de natura cultuque eius paucis dicere** AS THIS MATTER HAS REMINDED US OF SUCH A GREAT MAN, IT SEEMS APPROPRIATE TO SAY A FEW WORDS ABOUT HIS NATURE AND EDUCATION (Sallust, *Bellum Iugurthinum*).
- **Id omitto,** ***quando*** **vobis ita placet** I OMIT THIS, AS TO DO SO PLEASES YOU (Sallust, *Bellum Iugurthinum*).

2/ It is very normal to find a harbinger in the main clause, indicating that a causal clause is going to follow; some usual ones are: **ea re, propter hanc causam, eo, idcirco,** etc., all of them translatable by BECAUSE OF THIS; when one of them is used, it is normal to find the causal clause separated by a comma (to avoid two BECAUSE in the same sentence):

- **Ea re veni, quia Caesarem videre volebam** BECAUSE OF THIS I CAME, BECAUSE I WANTED TO SEE CAESAR.
- **Iuventus nomen indidit Scorto mihi, eo quia invocatus soleo esse in convivio** YOUNG PEOPLE HAVE GIVEN ME THE NAME OF "PROSTITUTE" BECAUSE OF THIS, BECAUSE I USUALLY ATTEND THE BANQUET UNINVITED (Plautus, *Captivi*).

3/ **Cum** can also be used to introduce a causal clause with the present and perfect tenses of the subjunctive. Given the fact that **cum** can have several meanings with the subjunctive, it is better to have a whole glance of all of them in *Point 14 Summary of the uses of* ***cum*** rather than presenting here its use in that meaning with only these two tenses.

3. Purpose clauses [313]

a) Normal construction

1/ Purpose clauses are introduced by **ut**, and they have their verb in the subjunctive, and only either present or imperfect subjunctive are used. As expected, the *consecutio temporum* will be observed: if the verb of the main clause is primary, the purpose clause will use the present subjunctive; if it is secondary, the imperfect subjunctive:

- Venio *ut* mihi librum *des* I COME SO THAT YOU MAY GIVE ME THE BOOK.
- Veni *ut* mihi librum *dares* I CAME SO THAT YOU MIGHT GIVE ME THE BOOK.
- Maiores nostri ab aratro adduxerunt Cincinnatum illum, *ut* dictator *esset* OUR ANCESTORS REMOVED CINCINNATUS FROM THE PLOUGH SO THAT HE MIGHT BE DICTATOR (Cicero, *De Finibus Bonorum et Malorum*).
- Lentulus ... T. Volturcium ... mittit, *ut* Allobroges ... societatem *confirmarent* LENTULUS SENT T. VOLTURCIUM SO THAT THE ALLOBROGES MIGHT CONFIRM THE AGREEMENT (Sallust, *Catilinae Coniuratio*).

  ✧ The verb **mittit** is here a historic present, in fact it is to be considered a past (secondary tense), this is why we find **confirmarent**, a secondary tense, in the subordinate clause.

2/ An important difference with English is that if the subject of the main sentence and of the purpose clause is the same person, in English we use just an infinitive, but in Latin we must use *ut + subjunctive* :

- Lego *ut* multum *discam* I READ IN ORDER TO LEARN A LOT ✧ Literally, I READ SO THAT I MAY LEARN A LOT.
- Venio *ut* te *videam* I COME TO SEE YOU ✧ Literally, I COME SO THAT I MAY SEE YOU.

b) Construction with a comparative [314]

If there is a comparative adjective in the purpose clause, instead of **ut** we will use **quo**:

- Multum laborare debes *quo melius* vivas YOU MUST WORK A LOT IN ORDER TO LIVE BETTER.
- Ei pecuniam dedi *quo citius* Romam iret I GAVE HIM MONEY SO THAT HE MIGHT GO TO ROME MORE QUICKLY.
- *Quo melius* de sene iudicare possitis, narrabo me iuvenem SO THAT YOU CAN JUDGE ME BETTER AS AN ELDERLY MAN, I WILL RECOUNT MY LIFE AS A YOUNG MAN (Seneca senior, *Controversiae*).
- Facessant igitur omnes qui docere nihil possunt, *quo melius* sapientiusque vivamus THEREFORE, LET ALL THOSE WHO CAN NOT TEACH ANYTHING DEPART, SO THAT WE MAY LIVE BETTER AND MORE WISELY (Cicero, *Hortensius*).

c) Negative purpose clause [315]

1/ Instead of using the expected **ut ... non**, Latin replaces **ut** by **ne** to get a negative sense:

- Curro *ne* hostes me *necent* I RUN SO THAT THE ENEMY MAY NOT KILL ME.
- Metellus conspectum Mari fugerat, *ne videret* ea, quae ... METELLUS HAD AVOIDED THE MEETING WITH MARIUS, IN ORDER NOT TO SEE THE THINGS THAT ... (Sallust, *Bellum Iugurthinum*).

It should be mentioned that, given the Latin practice of attaching the negative meaning to a conjunction rather than using a negative adverb or pronoun, we will find these combinations:

- **Quam celerrime veni *ne quis* te occideret** I CAME AS QUICKLY AS POSSIBLE SO THAT NOBODY MIGHT KILL YOU.
  ✧ Literally, ... SO THAT NOT ANYBODY MIGHT KILL YOU.
  ✧ Instead of saying **ut nemo**, the negative sense has been shifted to **ut**, that has become **ne**, and has been removed from **nemo** NOBODY, that has become **quis** ANYBODY.
- **Praesidium in vestibulo relinquit *ne quis* adire curiam iniussu suo neve inde egredi possit** HE LEFT A GARRISON IN THE ENTRANCE IN ORDER THAT NO ONE COULD GO INTO THE SENATE WITHOUT HIS ORDERS OR GO OUT OF IT (Livy, *Ab Urbe Condita*).
  ✧ Again, instead of **ut nemo**, we find **ne quis**.

2/ The same can be observed here:

- **Multum laboro ne umquam pecunia caream** I WORK A LOT SO THAT I MAY NEVER LACK MONEY.
  ✧ Literally, ...SO THAT NOT EVER..., and remember that **careo** rules an ablative.

Although the natural tencency would have been to write **... ut numquam...**, we must move the negative meaning from **numquam** NEVER (which then changes to **umquam** EVER) to **ut** (which then becomes **ne**).

d) Other possibilities

It would be worth mentioning that purpose can be expressed in Latin also by means of other constructions which will be studied in their corresponding sections: gerund, gerundive, supine, relative + subjunctive, etc., but the construction that is usually called a *purpose clause* is the construction we have introduced here.

4. Temporal clauses **[316]**

a) Main temporal clauses

Temporal clauses will usually have their verb in indicative, unless some meaning of intention or purpose accompanies the whole meaning (we will see this further ahead).

1/ The most usual temporal clause is that introducing the idea of WHEN, and this is achieved by means of the conjunctions **cum**, **ut** and **ubi** (remember that **ubi** can also have local meaning WHERE):

- **Dux, *ut* hoc *vidit*, quam celerrime e castris discessit** WHEN THE GENERAL SAW THIS, HE WENT OUT OF THE CAMP AS QUICKLY AS POSSIBLE.
- ***Ut veni* Athenas, ...** WHEN I CAME TO ATHENS, ... (Cicero, *Epistulae ad Familiares*).
- **Caesar, *ubi* ex captivis *cognovit* quo in loco hostium copiae consedissent, ad hostes contendit** WHEN CAESAR LEARNT FROM THE PRISONERS WHERE THE TROOPS OF THE ENEMY HAD SETTLED, HE WENT TOWARDS THEM (Caesar, *De Bello Gallico*).
- **Erravit Cornelius Nepos, *cum scripsit* Ciceronem tres et viginti annos natum causam pro Sexto Roscio dixisse** C. NEPOS WAS WRONG WHEN HE SAID THAT CICERO HAD MADE HIS DEFENCE SPEECH FOR R. AMERINUS WHEN HE WAS TWENTY-THREE YEARS OLD (A. Gellius, *Noctes Atticae*).

2/ There are several other conjunctions that introduce other temporal meanings (note that some of them may have more than one meaning): [317]

⇨ **cum primum** AS SOON AS

- **Itaque, *cum primum* audivi, ...** THEREFORE, AS SOON AS I HEARD THIS, ... (Cicero, *Epistulae ad Familiares*).

⇨ **simul ac / simul atque** AS SOON AS

This combination of the adverb **simul** and **ac/atque** produces the same meaning as **cum primum**:

- ***Simul ac* legiones accepi ..., scripsi ad te** AS SOON AS I TOOK COMMAND OF THE LEGIONS, I WROTE TO YOU (Cicero, *Epistulae ad Familiares*).

⇨ **donec / dum** WHILE, AS LONG AS, UNTIL

- ***Donec* eris sospes, multos numerabis amicos** AS LONG AS YOU ARE FORTUNATE, YOU WILL HAVE MANY FRIENDS (Ovid, *Tristia*).
- ***Dum* Carthaginienses incolumes fuere, iure omnia saeva patiebamur** WHILE THE CARTHAGINIANS WERE UNBEATABLE, WE SUFFERED, WITH RIGHT, ALL CRUELTIES (Sallust, *Bellum Iugurthinum*).
- **Milites expectaverunt *dum* dux regressus est** THE SOLDIERS WAITED UNTIL THE GENERAL CAME BACK.

⇨ **antequam / priusquam** BEFORE ✧ Do not confuse with the adverb **ante** BEFORE, PREVIOUSLY.

- **Caesar hoc scripsit *antequam* Nero natus est** CAESAR WROTE THIS BEFORE NERO WAS BORN.

It is normal to find the conjunction split into two, with **ante** in the main sentence and **quam** starting the temporal clause:

- **Caesar *ante* hoc scripsit *quam* Nero natus est** (same meaning).
- **Denique aliquanto *ante* in provinciam iste proficiscitur *quam* opus effectum est** FINALLY, HE GOES TO HIS PROVINCE SOME TIME BEFORE THE WORK IS COMPLETED (Cicero, *In Verrem*).
- **Prius multo *ante* aedis stabam *quam* illo adveneram** I HAD BEEN STANDING IN FRONT OF THE HOUSE MUCH BEFORE GOING THERE (Plautus, *Amphitruo*).

⇨ **postquam** AFTER ✧ Do not confuse with the adverb **postea** AFTERWARDS.

- ***Postquam* id animadvertit, copias suas Caesar in proximum collem subducit** AFTER HE REALISED IT, CAESAR MOVED HIS TROOPS TO A NEARBY HILL (Caesar, *De Bello Gallico*).

As with **antequam** and **priusquam**, it is normal to find **postquam** split into two, with **post** in the main sentence and **quam** starting the temporal clause:

- **Cicero *post* necatus est *quam* Marcus Romam intravit** CICERO WAS KILLED AFTER MARCUS ENTERED ROME.

And it is very common that after **post** we find a *numeral in accusative* indicating the amount of time elapsed between two events:

- **Venerunt post *diem quadragensimum et sextum* quam a vobis discesserant** THEY CAME ON THE 46TH DAY AFTER DEPARTING FROM YOU (Cicero, *Epistulae ad Familiares*).

b) A curious use of the present indicative in past time [318]

We have seen that **dum** has three possible meanings. When it carries the meaning of WHILE and we mention in the main sentence an event that takes place in the middle of a larger event, we will use the present tense, even if we are making reference to a past event:

- *Dum cenamus,* Caesar repente hoc dixit WHILE WE WERE HAVING DINNER, CAESAR SAID THIS SUDDENLY.
  ✧ Literally, WHILE WE *ARE* HAVING DINNER, ...
- *Dum* haec Romae *geruntur,* qui ... exercitui praeerant ... plurima et flagitiosissima facinora fecere
  WHILE THESE AFFAIRS HAPPENED AT ROME, THOSE WHO WERE IN COMMAND OF THE ARMY COMMITTED MANY SHAMEFUL DEEDS (Sallust, *Bellum Iugurthinum*).
  ✧ Literally, WHILE THESE AFFAIRS *HAPPEN* AT ROME, ...

c) Repeated action [319]

In order to express the repetition of an action, in the sense of EVERY TIME THAT..., Latin uses the conjunction **cum**, but with a curious combination of tenses:

1/ Repeated action in the present

While in English we would use present indicative in both clauses, Latin uses perfect tense in the subordinate one (and present in the main one):

- Cum Romam *venerunt*, dona filiis *ferunt* EVERY TIME THEY COME TO ROME, THEY BRING PRESENTS TO THE CHILDREN.
  ✧ Literally, EVERY TIME THEY *HAVE COME*...

2/ Repeated action in the past

In this case, both verbs go "one step down" in the table of tenses: pluperfect in the subordinate clause and imperfect in the main clause:

- Cum Romam *venerant*, dona filiis *ferebant* EVERY TIME THEY CAME TO ROME, THEY BROUGHT PRESENTS TO THE CHILDREN.
  ✧ Literally, EVERY TIME THEY *HAD COME*...

d) Temporal clauses in the subjunctive [320]

1/ In all the temporal clauses we have seen, the event mentioned in the temporal clause is mentioned just as an event that does take place:

- Milites expectaverunt dum dux *regressus est* THE SOLDIERS WAITED UNTIL THE GENERAL CAME BACK.

The general *did come back*, we see just a narrative of events. We do not see any purpose or intention in the soldiers.

But if the temporal clause had been in the subjunctive,

Milites expectaverunt dum dux *regrederetur*

then it would indicate purpose or intention in the soldiers, as if the soldiers were saying "WE WILL REMAIN HERE UNTIL THE GENERAL RETURNS, WE REFUSE TO LEAVE BEFORE HE RETURNS," and the sentence should be translated as

THE SOLDIERS WAITED UNTIL THE GENERAL *WOULD RETURN*. ✧ Even if nobody knew *if* and *when* he would return.

Let's see this in an example from Caesar:

- **Caesar ex eo tempore, *dum* ad flumen Varum *veniatur*, se frumentum daturum [esse] pollicetur** CAESAR PROMISES THAT HE WILL SUPPLY CORN FROM THEN ON UNTIL WHENEVER HE REACHES THE RIVER VAR (Caesar, *Bellum Civile*).

The fact that **veniatur** (an impersonal passive, by the way) is in the subjunctive indicates that who knows when they will reach that river. Using WHENEVER is a way of indicating this indefinition.

2/ We can see the same with **priusquam**: [321]

- **Caesar copias instruxit priusquam Pompeius *venit*** CAESAR ARRANGED HIS TROOPS BEFORE POMPEIUS CAME.

Nothing indicates any intention in Caesar, we are just told that one fact (Caesar arranging his troops) took place before another one (Pompeius' arrival).

But if we write

Caesar copias instruxit priusquam Pompeius *veniret*

the meaning is that Caesar made an effort of arranging his troops making sure that he had arranged them *before Pompeius might come*, and we should translate it as

CAESAR ARRANGED HIS TROOPS BEFORE POMPEIUS *MIGHT COME* ✧ And who knows *if* and *when* Pompeius would come.

Another example:

- **Conantibus, priusquam id effici *posset*, adesse Romanos nuntiatur** TO THOSE WHO WERE TRYING [IT], BEFORE IT COULD BE MADE, IT WAS ANNOUNCED THAT THE ROMANS WERE THERE (Caesar, *De Bello Gallico*).

The use of the subjunctive in **posset** indicates that somebody took care to cast that information around before any attempt could take place.

3/ Apart from these uses of the subjunctive in order to indicate some kind of purpose within the temporal clause, the conjunction **cum**, which we have seen above in its use with the indicative, can also be used with the imperfect and the pluperfect subjunctive in temporal sense, in the so-called *Historic **Cum***. This is presented in the *Point 14 Summary of the uses of **cum***. Rather than presenting here only that temporal use of **cum** with the subjunctive, we consider that it is better to see all of them together as a whole in Point 14.

5. Concessive clauses [322]

Concessive clauses are expressed in the indicative if the objection is considered a real fact, and in the subjunctive if it is considered just a supposition. With respect to the main clause, it is very frequent that it carries inside it the adverb **tamen** NEVERTHELESS.

a) Real objection: indicative

The conjunctions used to introduce it are: **quamquam, etsi, tametsi, etiamsi**:

- *Quamquam* **Caesar** *venit*, **tamen hostes nos vicerunt** ALTHOUGH CAESAR CAME, NEVERTHELESS THE ENEMY CONQUERED US.
- *Quamquam* **merito** *sum* **iratus Metello, tamen haec quae vera sunt dicam** ALTHOUGH I AM RIGHTLY ANGRY WITH METELLUS, NEVERTHELESS I WILL SAY THESE THINGS THAT ARE TRUE (Cicero, *In Verrem*).
- *Etsi* **pecuniam mihi** *dedisti*, **hoc emere non potui** ALTHOUGH YOU GAVE ME THE MONEY, I WAS NOT ABLE TO BUY THIS.
- **Ego te hoc, soror,** *tametsi es* **maior, moneo** I ADVISE YOU, MY SISTER, ALTHOUGH YOU ARE OLDER (Plautus, *Stichus*).

b) Possible objection: subjunctive [323]

1/ The conjunctions used are **quamvis, etiamsi** (note that **etiamsi** can also be used for real objections, see above), **cum** and **ut**, and it is also possible to use the verbal form **licet**:

- *Quamvis* **dives** *sis*, **non te amo** ALTHOUGH YOU MAY BE RICH, I DO NOT LOVE YOU.
- *Licet* **dux** *iubeat*, **pugnare nolo** ALTHOUGH THE GENERAL MAY ORDER IT, I DO NOT WANT TO FIGHT.
- *Quamvis* **res mihi non** *placeat*, **tamen contra hominum auctoritatem pugnare non potero** ALTHOUGH IT MAY NOT PLEASE ME, NEVERTHELESS I WILL NOT BE ABLE TO FIGHT AGAINST THE AUTHORITY OF MEN (Cicero, *In Verrem*).
- *Licet* **iste** *dicat* **emisse se, sicuti solet dicere, credite hoc mihi, iudices** ALTHOUGH THIS MAN MAY SAY THAT HE BOUGHT [THEM], AS HE USUALLY SAYS, BELIEVE ME, JUDGES (Cicero, *In Verrem*).

Observe that by *possible objection* we do not mean a possibility in the future; in the first example, the subject probably knows very well that the other person is rich; what is meant by *possible objection* is the sense of *even if.*

2/ **Cum** can also be used with any tense of the subjunctive to express a concessive meaning. This is presented in the *Point 14 Summary of the uses of* **cum**. As we have said above in the section of *Temporal clauses*, rather than presenting here only that meaning of **cum** with the subjunctive we consider that it is better to see all of them together as a whole in Point 14.

6. Result clauses [324]

a) Basic principles

Result clauses (also called *consecutive clauses*) are introduced in Latin by the conjunction **ut** (the negative is **ut non**) and they have their verb in subjunctive; the translation in English may be either THAT or SO THAT.

1/ It is frequent that we find a signal word in the main sentence (usually an adverb or an adjective) that tells us that a result clause is going to follow; in the following examples, the signal word is the quantitative adverb **tantum** SO MUCH, and we translate **ut** by THAT:

- *Tantum* laborat *ut* multam pecuniam habeat HE WORKS SO MUCH THAT HE HAS A LOT OF MONEY.
- *Tantum* potentia antecesserant, *ut* magnam partem clientium ab Haeduis ad se traducerent THEY SURPASSED [THEM] SO MUCH IN POWER THAT THEY TRANSFERRED FROM THE AEDUI TO THEMSELVES A LARGE PORTION OF THEIR DEPENDENTS (Caesar, *De Bello Gallico*).
- Inter duas acies *tantum* erat relictum spatii, *ut* satis esset ad concursum utriusque exercitus BETWEEN BOTH FRONT LINES THERE WAS SO MUCH SPACE LEFT THAT IT WAS ENOUGH FOR THE ENCOUNTER OF EITHER ARMY (Caesar, *Bellum Civile*).

2/ It may be that there is no signal word in the main sentence, as in the following example (**multum** A LOT is an adverb, but it does not play any role of telling us that some result is going to be expressed); in this case, we translate the **ut** by SO THAT.

- *Multum* laborat, *ut* multam pecuniam habeat HE WORKS A LOT, SO THAT HE HAS A LOT OF MONEY.

3/ The tense of the subjunctive will be the same one that the sentence would have used if expressed as a statement in indicative instead of as a result clause; in our first example, the statement would have been HE HAS A LOT OF MONEY, which would need a present indicative, **Multam pecuniam habet**; therefore, for this example we will use the present subjunctive **habeat**.

4/ We can also find *impersonal expressions* followed by a result clause (observe also the lack of signal word in the impersonal expression): **[325]**

- Eadem nocte accidit *ut esset* luna plena ON THE SAME NIGHT IT HAPPENED THAT THERE WAS A FULL MOON (Caesar, *De Bello Gallico*).
- Fit, *ut* impetus *fiat* in vacuam rem publicam IT HAPPENS THAT AN ATTACK TAKES PLACE AGAINST A DEFENCELESS STATE (Sallust, *Catilinae Coniuratio*).
- Accidit *ut* subito ille *interiret* IT HAPPENED THAT SUDDENLY HE DIED (Cicero, *Epistulae ad Atticum*).
- Fieri non potest ut ... eum tu in tua provincia non cognoveris IT CAN NOT BE THAT YOU HAD NOT GOT TO KNOW HIM IN YOUR PROVINCE (Cicero, *In Verrem*).

  ✧ Observe the **ut ... non**: the way of expressing a negative clause of result, instead of the usual **ne** in for instance purpose clauses.

Sometimes these **ut** clauses following an impersonal expression are considered *completive clauses*, but although they may look similar to the completive clauses presented in *Point 15 Summary of the uses of* **ut** they are in fact result clauses (for instance, a completive clause would have **ne** as negative instead of **ut non**).

b) Possible confusions **[326]**

As purpose clauses are also introduced by **ut** and they have also their verb in subjunctive, in some cases a sentence may have an ambiguous meaning, especially if there is no signal word in the main sentence; for instance, in the previous example

Multum laborat, *ut* multam pecuniam habeat

it could be argued that the **ut** is introducing a purpose clause and that the translation should be HE WORKS A LOT IN ORDER TO HAVE A LOT OF MONEY. Usually the context will clarify whether it is a *purpose* or a *result* clause.

If there is a signal word, a harbinger, there will be no confusion; in our first examples, the **tantum** SO MUCH is telling us clearly that a result clause will follow.

c) Negative results [327]

If we want to express a negative result (negative in the sense of a *negative sentence*, not in the sense that the consequences are bad), we just add **non** before the verb or use the necessary negative adverb, pronoun, etc.):

- **Tantum laborat *ut* domum ire *non* possit** HE WORKS SO MUCH THAT HE CAN NOT GO HOME.
- **Tantum laborat *ut* domum ire *numquam* possit** HE WORKS SO MUCH THAT HE CAN NEVER GO HOME.
- **Hic tantum potuit *ut nemo* illo invito nec bona ... nec vitam retinere posset** HE HAD SO MUCH POWER THAT NOBODY COULD, WITHOUT HIS CONSENT, KEEP EITHER HIS PROPERTY OR HIS LIFE (Cicero, *In Verrem*).
- **Tantum animi habuit ad audaciam *ut* dicere in contione *non* dubitaret ...** HE HAD SO MUCH [OF] AUDACITY THAT HE DID NOT HESITATE TO SAY IN THE ASSEMBLY ... (Cicero, *In Verrem*).
- **In hoc tantum fuit odium multitudinis, *ut nemo* ausus sit eum liber sepelire** THE HATRED OF THE PEOPLE AGAINST HIM WAS SO MUCH THAT NOBODY OPENLY DARED TO BURY HIM (Nepos, *Vitae*).

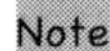

Do not replace **ut** by **ne** to make a negative clause of result; this replacement takes place in *purpose clauses*, but not in *result clauses* (so, it also helps to distinguish a result clause from a purpose clause if it is negative).

In some cases, **ut non** may be replaced by **quin**:

- **Nunquam venies *quin* te videam** YOU WILL NEVER COME WITHOUT ME SEEING YOU.

7. Conditional clauses [328]

The way of classifying the several types of conditional clauses and which name to give to each type has always been a point in which there has never been absolute agreement; we will offer here what is usually accepted as the standard classification.

A conditional clause is a clause in which a condition is expressed, like IF YOU COME TO ROME, ... and it is called *protasis*. The main clause on which it depends, for instance ..., I WILL SHOW YOU THE CIRCUS, is called *apodosis*. Both together form what is called a *conditional period*: IF YOU COME TO ROME, I WILL SHOW YOU THE CIRCUS.

Conditional periods are classified according to the verbal tense they use both in protasis and apodosis (in most cases, both protasis and apodosis use the same tense).

a) Open conditionals [329]

1/ In these periods, the verbal tense used is the *indicative*, and tenses should be translated correspondingly:

- **Si hoc *dicis*, stultus *es*** IF YOU SAY THIS, YOU ARE FOOLISH.
- **Si Caesar hoc *dixit*, stultus *fuit*** IF CAESAR SAID THIS, HE WAS FOOLISH.

- Has ego, si *vis*, tibi *dabo* — IF YOU WANT, I WILL GIVE THESE TO YOU (Plautus, *Asinaria*).
- Si *vincimus*, omnia nobis tuta *erunt* (Sallust, *Catilinae Coniuratio*). — IF WE WIN, WE WILL HAVE EVERYTHING FOR SURE
- *Abeo*, si *iubes* — I LEAVE, IF YOU ORDER IT (Plautus, *Amphitruo*).
- Quis ego *sum* saltem, si non *sum* Sosia? — BUT WHO AM I, IF I AM NOT SOSIAS? (Plautus, *Amphitruo*).

2/ There is an exception; observe this sentence:

- Si hoc mihi *dabis*, laetus *ero* IF YOU GIVE ME THIS, I WILL BE HAPPY.
  ✧ Observe that, theoretically, it says IF YOU WILL GIVE ME THIS, as Latin uses the same tense in protasis and apodosis, but we must translate the future tense in the protasis by a *present*.

It can even be the case that Latin uses the *future perfect* in the protasis and the *simple future* in the apodosis:

- Si hoc mihi *dederis*, laetus *ero* IF YOU GIVE ME THIS, I WILL BE HAPPY (same meaning as before).
  ✧ Theoretically, it says IF YOU WILL HAVE GIVEN ME THIS: Latin uses this resource to emphasize that the condition in the protasis will have been accomplished before the action of the apodosis takes place. But again we must translate it in English by a present.

- Praeterea si quid meque vobisque dignum *petiveris*, haud repulsus *abibis* MOREOVER, IF YOU REQUEST ANYTHING WORTHY OF ME AND OF YOU, YOU WILL NOT GO AWAY REJECTED (Sallust, *Bellum Iugurthinum*).
  ✧ Theoretically, it says IF YOU WILL HAVE REQUESTED. As before, translate by a present.

3/ We can find an *imperative* in the main clause, instead of an indicative: [330]

- *Dic* si quid vis SAY, IF YOU WANT [TO SAY] ANYTHING (Plautus, *Amphitruo*).

And we should include here the use of a *iussive subjunctive* instead of an imperative (here we should pay attention to the "imperative" sense of the iussive subjunctive, not to the potential use that we will find in the next section):

- Quod si comitia placet in senatu haberi, *petamus* BUT IF WE WANT AN ELECTION TO BE HELD IN THE SENATE, LET'S SEEK [VOTES] (Cicero, *Philippicae*).

b) Remote conditionals [331]

They are used to indicate a possibility in the future. *Present subjunctive* is used in both sides, and the way of translating it into English is by means of SHOULD ... WOULD :

- Si hoc mihi *dicas*, laetus *sim* IF YOU SHOULD TELL ME THIS, I WOULD BE HAPPY.
  ✧ We could also say IF YOU WERE TO TELL ME THIS, ...
- *Possis*, ... si *videas*, cognoscere? WOULD YOU BE ABLE TO RECOGNISE [HIM], IF YOU SHOULD SEE [HIM]? (Plautus, *Asinaria*).

Note

They use present, but they refer to the future.

c) Unfulfilled conditions in the present [332]

They are used to indicate that the condition is unfulfilled now, in the present; maybe it will be fulfilled further ahead, but now it is unfulfilled. *Imperfect subjunctive* is used for both sides:

- Si dux *adesset*, milites laeti *essent* IF THE GENERAL WERE HERE, THE SOLDIERS WOULD BE HAPPY.
- Si pecunia *haberem*, hanc domum *emerem* IF I HAD MONEY, I WOULD BUY THIS HOUSE.
- Plura *dicerem*, Quirites, si timidis virtutem verba *adderent* I WOULD SAY MORE, CITIZENS, IF WORDS ADDED COURAGE TO THE FAINT-HEARTED (Sallust, *Bellum Iugurthinum*).
- Ego si somnum capere *possem*, tam longis te epistulis non *obtunderem* IF I WERE ABLE TO SLEEP, I WOULD NOT PESTER YOU WITH SUCH LONG LETTERS (Cicero, *Epistulae ad Atticum*).
- Quod si ipsa res publica *iudicaret* ..., Antonione an Bruto legiones populi Romani *adiudicaret*? BUT IF THE STATE ITSELF WERE TO JUDGE, WOULD IT AWARD LEGIONS OF THE ROMAN PEOPLE TO ANTONIUS OR TO BRUTUS? (Cicero, *Philippicae*).
- Si ipse *viveret* C. Caesar, acrius, credo, acta sua *defenderet* quam ... IF C. CAESAR HIMSELF WERE ALIVE, HE WOULD DEFEND HIS DEEDS MORE VIGOROUSLY, I THINK, THAN ... (Cicero, *Philippicae*).

  ✧ Although in this case it is obvious that the protasis can not take place (Caesar is already dead), the imaginary possibility must be expressed.

They use imperfect, but they refer to the present.

d) Unfulfilled conditions in the past [333]

They are used to indicate that the condition was not fulfilled and can not be fulfilled any more (a practical way of naming this type is by calling them *the "too late" type*). *Pluperfect subjunctive* is used for both sides:

- Si hoc mihi *dixisses*, ego quam celerrime *venissem* IF YOU HAD TOLD ME THIS, I WOULD HAVE COME AS QUICKLY AS POSSIBLE. ✧ Too late, nothing can be done now.
- Si *debuisset*, Sexte, *petisses* IF HE HAD OWED [YOU MONEY], SEXTUS, YOU WOULD HAVE ASKED FOR IT (Cicero, *Pro Quinctio*).
- Si *venisses* ad exercitum, a tribunis militaribus *visus esses* IF YOU HAD COME TO THE ARMY, YOU WOULD HAVE BEEN SEEN BY THE MILITARY TRIBUNES (Cicero, *De Inventione*).
- Argenti viginti minas, si *adesset*, *accepisset* IF HE HAD BEEN PRESENT, HE WOULD HAVE GOT TWENTY MINAE (Plautus, *Asinaria*).

e) Combined periods [334]

Conditional periods do not always follow the rules indicated above, as the several nuances that language can express must be reflected also in grammar. We will examine here some of the most common alterations of the former rules.

1/ It is normal to find a type of conditional period that uses *pluperfect subjunctive* in the protasis and *imperfect subjunctive* in the apodosis: the protasis will refer to the past and the apodosis to the present; observe these examples:

- Si in proelio *vicissem*, felix *essem* IF I HAD WON (at a point in the past) IN THE BATTLE, I WOULD (now) BE HAPPY.

  ✧ Observe the combination of tenses, as there is also a combination of present (unfulfilled) reality and of past (unfulfilled) condition.

- Si *dixisset* haec solum, omni supplicio *esset* dignus IF HE HAD SAID ONLY THIS, HE WOULD BE WORTHY OF ALL PUNISHMENT (Cicero, *Pro Sestio*).

2/ Another usual combination is the one formed by a *future perfect indicative* in the protasis and a *present indicative* in the apodosis:

- Romani si rem *obtinuerint*, finem laborum omnium *exspectant* THE ROMANS, IF THEY GAIN THE DAY, EXPECT THE END OF ALL OF THEIR TOILS (Caesar, *De Bello Gallico*).
  ✧ The use of the future perfect is to put emphasis on the fact that first the protasis must be accomplished, but we should translate it by a present.

3/ The presence of some internal subordinate inside the apodosis produces some unexpected combinations. For instance: **[335]**

- At, si ita *esset*, hac lege accusatum fuisse *oportuit* qua accusatur Habitus BUT, IF IT WERE SO, IT WOULD HAVE BEEN NECESSARY THAT HE HAD BEEN ACCUSED UNDER THE SAME LAW UNDER WHICH HABITUS HAS BEEN ACCUSED (Cicero, *Pro Cluentio*).

Observe the *imperfect subjunctive* in the protasis and the *perfect indicative* in the apodosis: literally, the apodosis says ... IT WAS NECESSARY THAT HE HAD BEEN ACCUSED..., but the potential meaning (the sense that in fact he was not accused) is to be taken from the internal infinitive clause in the apodosis and the fact that the protasis is an unfulfilled condition. This makes putting the verb **oportuit** in subjunctive unnecessary.

4/ Another case of the combination *subjunctive* (protasis) / *indicative* (apodosis) takes place when an impersonal verb (or impersonal verbal expression) is used in the apodosis:

- **Quod si quis illud iudicium appellet, tamen hoc confiteatur necesse est, nullo modo ...** BUT IF ANYBODY WERE TO CALL THAT A TRIAL, THEN IT IS NECESSARY THAT HE ADMITS THIS, THAT IN NO WAY ... (Cicero, *Pro Cluentio*).

We could have expected **necesse sit**, meaning IT WOULD BE NECESSARY, but the general sense allows us to use the indicative.

8. Relative clauses **[336]**

a) Introduction

1/ Relative clauses give us additional information about somebody or something mentioned in the main clause; for instance, in the sentence THE MAN (WHOM) YOU SAW YESTERDAY IS A TEACHER, there are two parts:

➪ The main clause:	THE MAN IS A TEACHER	This is the main information.
➪ The relative clause:	(WHOM) YOU SAW YESTERDAY	This is additional information, and in this case this additional information delimits who that man is: *the one you saw yesterday*, not another one.

⌑ Observe that in English it is very common to avoid the relative pronoun in this kind of delimitative relative sentences, but it Latin it must be mentioned; in the example above, in Latin we will not be able to avoid WHOM.

Another example:

I LOVE ITALY, WHICH IS A VERY NICE COUNTRY.

⇨ Main clause: I LOVE ITALY
⇨ Relative clause: WHICH IS A VERY NICE COUNTRY

In this case, the relative clause gives us additional information about Italy, but it does not restrict its meaning; so, comparing with the former example, we can see that sometimes a relative clause *delimits* the meaning and in other cases it just *adds more information*. Observe also that sometimes the relative clause may be in the middle of the main sentence, or at the end, or even at the beginning.

2/ The relative itself (it can have several forms in English: THAT, WHICH, WHO, WHOSE, WHOM, etc.) is the word that links to the main clause: WHOM and WHICH in the previous examples.

Remember that, when it has a restrictive, delimitative meaning, in English it is normal to avoid it: THE STORY *THAT* YOU HAVE TOLD ME HAS SURPRISED ME = THE STORY YOU HAVE TOLD ME HAS SURPRISED ME.

3/ The word about which the relative sentence tells us something is called the *antecedent*; in the former examples, THE MAN is the antecedent of *WHOM* YOU SAW YESTERDAY, and ITALY is the antecedent of *WHICH* IS A VERY NICE COUNTRY. [337]

Another example, this time with whole analysis:

THE CITY (THAT) CAESAR DESTROYED WAS WEALTHY.

⇨ Main clause: THE CITY WAS WEALTHY
⇨ Relative clause: (THAT) CAESAR DESTROYED
⇨ Antecedent: THE CITY
⇨ Relative: THAT ✧ Remember that in English a restrictive relative can be left unmentioned.

b) Simple relative sentences [338]

1/ Antecedent-relative relationship

a/ The most important point is the relationship between the relative and the antecedent. The different forms of the relative in Latin have been presented in the corresponding section of pronouns, and which one we choose will depend on the antecedent. Relative and antecedent must agree in gender and number, but not necessarily in case. Observe this example:

I SEE THE MAN TO WHOM YOU GAVE A BOOK YESTERDAY.

⇨ Main clause: I SEE THE MAN
⇨ Relative clause: TO WHOM YOU GAVE A BOOK YESTERDAY
⇨ Antecedent: THE MAN
⇨ Relative: TO WHOM

THE MAN is masculine and singular, so TO WHOM will have to be masculine and singular.

With respect to the case,

⇨ THE MAN performs the role of *direct object* in the main clause, so it will have to be in *Acc.*: **hominem**
⇨ TO WHOM performs the role of *indirect object* in the relative clause, so it will have to be in *Dat.*: **cui**

Therefore, the whole sentence will be

Video *hominem cui* heri librum dedisti.

b/ In the case that we have some difficulty in seeing the syntactical function of the relative, a good system is to replace it by the antecedent and re-order the clause to make it make sense, then we will see it easily: [339]

TO WHOM YOU GAVE A BOOK YESTERDAY > TO THE MAN YOU GAVE A BOOK YESTERDAY > YOU GAVE A BOOK TO THE MAN YESTERDAY

Now it is clear that TO WHOM plays the role of indirect object and therefore it must be in dative.

✧ In this example we have seen, antecedent and relative are in different cases because each one performs a different function in its own clause.

Important: When trying to find out the function of the relative in order to decide in which case it must be, you must forget about the function that the antecedent plays in its own sentence: they belong to different sentences; in the former example, to find out the function (and therefore the case) of TO WHOM, we have not taken the role of THE MAN into account, we have ignored it because we must ignore it.

Of course, if they happen to perform the same function each one in its sentence, they will be in the same case:

- I SEE THE MAN WHOM YOU LOVE Video *hominem quem* amas.

⇨ THE MAN is *direct object* in the main clause.
⇨ WHOM is also *direct object* in the relative clause.

So, in this case they coincide just because each one happens to have the same function in its sentence.

c/ Let's see some original examples:

- Sed in ea coniuratione fuit Q. *Curius, ..., quem* censores senatu probri gratia moverant BUT IN THAT CONSPIRACY WAS Q. CURIUS, WHOM THE CENSORS HAD EXPELLED IGNOMINIOUSLY OUT OF THE SENATE (Sallust, *Catilinae Coniuratio*).
  ✧ **Curius** is *subject* in the main clause, and **quem** is *direct object* in the relative clause.

- *Nemone* fuit *cui* deberet Quinctius? WAS THERE NOBODY WHOM QUINCTIUS OWED [MONEY]? (Cicero, *Pro Quinctio*).
  ✧ **Nemo** (the **-ne** is just a question mark) is the *subject* of the main clause, and **cui** is the *indirect object* of the relative clause (in Latin, the person to whom you owe something is in dative).

- ... in *eis rebus quas* L. Sulla gessit ... IN THOSE THINGS THAT L. SULLA DID (Cicero, *Pro Roscio Amerino*).
  ✧ **Rebus** is *part of a prepositional phrase* in the main clause, and **quas** (**rebus** is feminine) is *direct object* in the relative clause.

- Ea tempestate in exercitu nostro fuere *conplures novi atque nobiles, quibus* divitiae bono honestoque potiores erant AT THAT TIME THERE WERE IN OUR ARMY MANY NEW AND NOBLE MEN, FOR WHOM RICHES WERE BETTER THAN GOODNESS AND HONESTY (Sallust, *Bellum Iugurthinum*).
  ✧ The relative **quibus** is clearly a *dative of reference* in the relative clause, while the antecedent is the long *subject* of the main clause.

And a double example:

- **Edepol me *uxori* exoptatum credo adventurum domum, *quae* me amat, *quam* contra amo** BY POLLUX, I THINK I WILL GO HOME MUCH DESIRED BY MY WIFE, WHO LOVES ME, WHOM IN TURN I LOVE (Plautus, *Amphitruo*).
  - ✧ **Uxori**, the antecedent, is in dative in the main clause because of the syntactical function it performs, and it has two relatives depending on it: **quae**, which is *subject* in the first relative clause, and **quam**, which is *direct object* in the second relative clause.

2/ The genitive [340]

The use of the relative in genitive has a more difficult translation in English; observe this example:

Video hominem *cuius* librum legisti.

The main clause is really clear: **Video hominem** I SEE THE MAN. The relative **cuius** is in genitive, so that is must have the role of a possessive object. So, we should translate the relative **cuius** by OF WHOM or, more frequently, WHOSE. So, the translation should be

I SEE THE MAN WHOSE BOOK YOU HAVE READ / I SEE THE MAN THE BOOK OF WHOM YOU HAVE READ.

Let's see some examples from Cicero:

- **Dicebam huic Q. Roscio, *cuius* soror est cum P. Quinctio, ...** I WAS TELLING THIS Q. ROSCIUS, WHOSE SISTER IS WITH (IS THE WIFE OF) P. QUINCTIUS, ... (Cicero, *Pro Quinctio*).
- **Inventus est nemo *cuius* non haec et sententia esset et oratio** NO ONE WAS FOUND WHOSE OPINION AND SPEECH WERE NOT THIS (Cicero, *In Verrem*).
  - ✧ **Cuius** depends on **sententia** and **oratio**.
- **Sine infamia illud dederis, ut is absolvatur *cuius* ego causa laboro** WITHOUT DISGRACE YOU WILL HAVE GRANTED THIS, THAT HE, FOR WHOSE CAUSE I AM WORKING, WILL BE ACQUITTED (Cicero, *In Q. Caecilium*).
  - ✧ **Causa** is an ablative.

3/ Its use with prepositions [341]

We can use prepositions with a relative in the same way as we would use them with any noun; observe this example:

THE CITY IN WHICH I LIVE IS NICE.

The main clause, THE CITY IS NICE, will be easily translated as **Urbs pulchra est.**

The relative clause, IN WHICH I LIVE, should offer no difficulty: I LIVE = **habito**. With respect to the relative IN WHICH, if the sentence were I LIVE IN THE CITY, we would translate IN THE CITY by **in urbe** (**in** + ablative), so we must do the same with the relative: IN WHICH = **in qua**: **qua** because it must be feminine singular, as **urbs** is feminine singular, and because in this relative clause we need it in ablative after **in**.

The final result will be

Urbs *in qua* habito pulchra est.

Let's see some examples a little more difficult:

- **Omnes ad eam domum *in qua* iste deversabatur profecti sunt** ALL SET OUT TO THAT HOUSE IN WHICH THIS MAN WAS LODGED (Cicero, *In Verrem*).
- **Itaque ad te litteras statim misi, *per quas* ... gratias tibi egi** SO, I SENT YOU A LETTER BY MEANS OF WHICH I THANKED YOU (Cicero, *Epistulae ad Familiares*).
  - ✧ Remember that LETTER **litterae** is plural.
- **Estne quisquam omnium mortalium *de quo* melius existimes tu?** IS THERE ANYONE AMONG ALL MORTALS ABOUT WHOM YOU THINK BETTER? (Cicero, *Pro Roscio Comoedo*).

c) Special uses of the relative [342]

Relative clauses are not always as simple as described, as there are several special constructions; we will refer here to the most usual ones.

1/ Connective relative

Also called *demonstrative relative* (because it is usually translated by a demonstrative), it is a relative that opens a new sentence after a full stop. It refers to an antecedent which is in the former sentence, but the full stop prevents the usual continuity between a main clause and a relative sentence. Observe this double example:

- **Video duces qui heri venerunt** I SEE THE GENERALS WHO CAME YESTERDAY.
- **Video duces. Qui heri venerunt** *Literal* translation: I SEE THE GENERALS. WHO CAME YESTERDAY.

In the second example, the first sentence is simple: I SEE THE GENERALS. But we can not translate the second sentence, which is a new sentence and not a subordinate clause, by WHO CAME YESTERDAY, this does not make any sense. It is clear that this **Qui** means THE GENERALS, so that what is usually done is translate the relative by the equivalent form of **hic, haec, hoc** or of **is, ea, id**: I SEE THE GENERALS. THESE (or THEY) CAME YESTERDAY.

⌑ In other words: the connective relative is a relative that replaces the expected form of the demonstrative **hic, haec, hoc** (this is why some grammars call this a *demonstrative relative*) or of the anaphoric **is, ea, id**.

Let's see some examples:

- ***Quibus rebus* Micipsa tametsi initio laetus fuerat, ...** ALTHOUGH AT THE BEGINNING MICIPSA HAD BEEN HAPPY WITH THESE THINGS, ... (Sallust, *Bellum Iugurthinum*).
  - ✧ In this sentence **Eis rebus** has been replaced by **Quibus rebus**.

It should be noted that this need of putting the relative as the first word of the new clause makes it appear before it should; for instance, in the former example, the **Quibus rebus** belongs to the concessive clause introduced by **tametsi**.

- **... Caeparium Terracinensem. *Qui* in Apuliam ad concitanda servitia proficisci parabat ...** CEPARIUS FROM TERRACINA. THIS ONE WAS PREPARING TO DEPART TO APULIA TO RAISE THE SLAVES (Sallust, *Catilinae Coniuratio*).
- ***Quem* iste *conlegam* nisi habuisset, lapidibus coopertus esset in foro** IF THIS MAN HAD NOT HAD HIM FOR A COLLEAGUE, HE WOULD HAVE BEEN STONED IN THE FORUM (Cicero, *In Verrem*).
  - ✧ Again, the words **Quem iste conlegam** belong to the conditional clause introduced by **nisi**, but the practice of placing the connective relative as soon as possible after the full stop makes them appear previously.

2/ Relative of characteristic (generic relative) [343]

a/ A relative clause may have its verb in subjunctive, and this has the effect of describing the antecedent with respect to the group to which it belongs. A double example will make it clear:

Cicero non est qui hoc *dicit*.

This is a normal relative sentence, with its verb in *indicative*, and it means something as simple as CICERO IS NOT THE ONE WHO SAYS THIS, in the assumption that somebody is saying something but it is not Cicero, it is somebody else. But if we put the verb of the relative in *subjunctive*,

Cicero non est qui hoc *dicat*

the sentence will mean CICERO IS NOT THE KIND OF PERSON WHO MAY SAY THIS.

So, we describe the antecedent with respect to the group to which it belongs: CICERO DOES NOT BELONG TO THE GROUP OF PEOPLE WHO WOULD SAY THIS.

b/ It may also be that the antecedent is not somebody identified but rather somebody indefinite (and not even expressed), like for instance in the sentence

Sunt *qui dicant* Ciceronem malum oratorem esse.

In this case, the translation should be THERE ARE THE KIND OF PEOPLE WHO MAY SAY THAT CICERO IS A BAD ORATOR.

✧ We could leave it as THERE ARE PEOPLE WHO SAY THAT CICERO IS A BAD ORATOR.

- **Sunt *qui dicant*, Quirites, a me eiectum esse Catilinam** THERE ARE PEOPLE WHO SAY, CITIZENS, THAT CATILINA HAS BEEN EXPELLED BY ME (Cicero, *In Catilinam*).

Another example of indefinite antecedent (in this case, the antecedent is mentioned through **nemo**):

- ***Nemo* est *qui* Ciceronem non *amet*** THERE IS NO ONE WHO DOES NOT LOVE CICERO.
  ✧ In the sense of THERE IS NOT THIS KIND OF PERSON WHO WOULD NOT LOVE CICERO.
  ✧ Catilina would have loved this example of relative of characteristic ...
- ***Nemo* est *qui* ullam spem salutis reliquam esse *arbitretur*** THERE IS NO ONE WHO THINKS THAT THERE IS ANY HOPE FOR SALVATION LEFT (Cicero, *In Verrem*).

c/ The relative of characteristic can even be used to replace **ut** in a *clause of result*: [344]

- ***Nemo* est tam crudelis *ut* Caesarem necare *velit* = *Nemo* est tam crudelis *qui* Caesarem necare *velit***
  THERE IS NOBODY SO CRUEL THAT HE WANTS TO KILL CAESAR.
  ✧ In the sense of THERE IS NOT THE KIND OF PERSON SO CRUEL WHO WOULD LIKE TO KILL CAESAR.
  ✧ ... and Cassius would have loved this other example.
- ***Nemo* est tam stultus *qui* non *intellegat* ...** THERE IS NOBODY SO FOOLISH THAT HE DOES NOT UNDERSTAND ... (Cicero, *Philippicae*).
  ✧ We could have found **ut non intellegat**, but in this kind of sentences starting with **Nemo est tam** ... it is much more common to find the relative rather than **ut**.

In case it is a negative clause of result, like in the last example, **qui non / quae non / quod non** can be replaced by **quin**:

- **Nemo est tam fortis, quin rei novitate perturbetur** THERE IS NOBODY SO STRONG THAT HE IS NOT DISTURBED BY THE NEWS (Caesar, *De Bello Gallico*).

3/ Relative of purpose [345]

The so-called *relative of purpose* with the verb in subjunctive is in fact a derivation of the relative of characteristic. A relative clause with its verb in subjunctive may have the meaning of purpose; observe this example:

- **Catilina misit homines *qui* Ciceronem *necarent*** CATILINA SENT MEN IN ORDER TO KILL CICERO .
  ✧ This is in fact a "rearranged" translation of CATILINA SENT THE KIND OF MEN WHO WOULD KILL CICERO.

If we replace the relative by **ut**, we will have a perfect *purpose clause* :

- **Catilina misit homines *ut* Ciceronem *necarent*** (same meaning).

Observe that in all these examples the relative could be replaced by **ut** and this would produce perfect *purpose clauses* :

- **Tibi mitto libros *quos legas*** I AM SENDING YOU SOME BOOKS WHICH YOU MAY READ = I AM SENDING YOU SOME BOOKS TO READ = I AM SENDING YOU SOME BOOKS SO THAT YOU MAY READ THEM.
- **Legatos ad eum mittunt nobilissimos civitatis ... *qui dicerent* sibi esse in animo sine ullo maleficio iter per provinciam facere** THEY SEND AMBASSADORS TO HIM TO SAY THAT THEY WERE PLANNING TO CROSS THE PROVINCE WITHOUT CAUSING ANY HARM (Caesar, *De Bello Gallico*).
- **Apponit ... quendam *qui dicat* se Diodorum Melitensem rei capitalis reum velle facere** HE APPOINTS SOMEBODY TO SAY THAT HE WANTS TO INSTITUTE A PROSECUTION AGAINST DIODORUS OF MELITA (Cicero, *In Verrem*).

¤ Both the relative of characteristic and of purpose are in fact lateral uses of the *potential meaning of the subjunctive* when used on its own (**Hoc dicam** I WOULD/COULD SAY THIS, etc.).

4/ Lack of antecedent [346]

If the antecedent is any generic form of **is, ea, id** in the role of nominative, it is very normal that it is elided. In general lines, it would be the same as if the English sentence

THOSE WHOM I SAW YESTERDAY HAVE WON THE CHAMPIONSHIP became WHOM I SAW YESTERDAY HAVE WON THE CHAMPIONSHIP.

Observe the following example (there is a possessive dative in the relative clause, which we have translated literally, but this is independent of the presence or absence of antecedent):

- **Semper in civitate, *quibus* opes nullae sunt, bonis invident** IN A STATE, THOSE FOR WHOM THERE IS NO WEALTH ALWAYS ENVY THE WELL-OFF MEN (Sallust, *Catilinae Coniuratio*).

With the antecedent (unnecessary in Latin), the sentence would have been **Semper in civitate *ei*, quibus...** with **ei** meaning THOSE, but there is no need to put the demonstrative **ei** in Latin (although we must write THOSE in English); observe this example:

- *Qui* de scelere suspicari eius nihil potuerunt, socium offici metuere non debuerunt THOSE WHO COULD NOT SUSPECT ANYTHING ABOUT HIS WICKEDNESS OUGHT NOT TO HAVE FEARED HIS PARTNER IN HIS DUTIES (Cicero, *Pro Roscio Amerino*).
  ✧ As before, the demonstrative Ei THOSE is omitted in Latin (the sentence would have been *Ei*, qui de ...).

5/ Inclusion of the antecedent in the relative clause [347]

We may find that the antecedent is repeated inside the relative clause (and in the same case as the relative, no matter in what case the antecedent is in the main clause). This resource adds emphasis by making clear what the relative refers to:

- Lex Porcia aliaeque leges paratae sunt, *quibus legibus* exilium damnatis permissum est THE PORCIAN LAW AND OTHER LAWS WERE PROVIDED, BY WHICH LAWS EXILE WAS ALLOWED TO CONDEMNED PEOPLE (Sallust, *Catilinae Coniuratio*).
  ✧ The forced English translation BY WHICH LAWS is in fact a literal translation of this repetition.

- Huc adcedebat munificentia animi atque ingeni sollertia, *quibus rebus* sibi multos ex Romanis familiari amicitia coniunxerat TO THIS WAS ADDED THE MAGNIFICENCE OF HIS SPIRIT AND THE ABILITY OF HIS TALENT, BY WHICH QUALITIES HE HAD JOINED TO HIS SIDE MANY OF THE ROMANS BY MEANS OF A INTIMATE FRIENDSHIP (Sallust, *Bellum Iugurthinum*).
  ✧ Rebus means the munificentia and the sollertia. In this case, more than repeating the antecedent, what Sallust has made has been put side by side with the relative a word that summarises the two antecedents munificentia and sollertia.

9. Comparative clauses [348]

a) First type

1/ The first type of comparatives would include what has already been seen in the corresponding chapter of correlatives, with the use of talis ... qualis, etc.:

- Amicos non habeo *quales* tu habes I HAVEN'T GOT FRIENDS SUCH AS YOU HAVE.
  ✧ Meaning OF THE SAME KIND AS YOU HAVE.

Apart from what has been said in that chapter, there are other adverbs used in pairs to produce some type of comparison; for instance, quotiens ... totiens AS MANY TIMES AS ... SO MANY TIMES :

- *Quotiens* enim dicimus, *totiens* de nobis iudicatur AS MANY TIMES AS WE SPEAK, SO MANY TIMES PEOPLE JUDGE US (Cicero, *De Oratore*).
  ✧ A more free translation could be PEOPLE JUDGE US EVERY TIME WE SPEAK, the above translation was somewhat forced to translate both terms.

2/ It is worth remembering the adverbial use of the neuters tantum ... quantum:

- *Tantum* possem in te dicere *quantum* in litteris invenissem I WOULD BE ABLE TO SAY AGAINST YOU AS MUCH AS I HAD FOUND IN THESE LETTERS (Cicero, *In Verrem*).

b) Second type [349]

The second type is the one that deals with the simultaneous intensification of some kind of activities, in the sense THE MORE ... THE MORE... The usual ways to express this are:

⇨ **quo** + comparative ... **eo** + comparative
⇨ **quanto** + comparative ... **tanto** + comparative

- *Quo* **minus petebat gloriam,** *eo* **magis illum adsequebatur** THE LESS HE SOUGHT GLORY, THE MORE HE ACHIEVED IT (Sallust, *Catilinae Coniuratio*).
- *Quanto* **vita illorum praeclarior,** *tanto* **horum socordia flagitiosior** THE MORE ILLUSTRIOUS THE LIFE OF THOSE IS, THE MORE IGNOMINIOUS THE DULLNESS OF THESE IS (Sallust, *Bellum Iugurthinum*).

Notes

1/ **eo** and **tanto** are sometimes omitted.

2/ The two parts of the comparison can be reverted (**tanto ... quanto** instead of **quanto ... tanto**, etc.).

c) Third type [350]

1/ The third type deals with the comparison of two events that happen in the same way; the comparative clause is introduced by **ut, sicut(i), quomodo** or **tamquam** IN THE SAME WAY AS, and it is frequent to find a counterbalancing word in the main clause, which is usually **ita** or **sic**, both meaning SO:

- *Sicuti* **mari portibusque Caesarem prohibebat,** *ita* **ipse omni terra earum regionum prohibebatur** IN THE SAME WAY AS HE PREVENTED CAESAR FROM HAVING ACCESS TO SEA AND HARBOURS, SO HE HIMSELF WAS PREVENTED FROM GOING ASHORE IN THE WHOLE REGION (Caesar, *Bellum Civile*).

In fact, the use of only **ut** in some expressions is nothing else than an elliptic use:

- **Te amo** *ut* **fratrem** I LOVE YOU LIKE A BROTHER.

This sentence is just a shorter way of saying this other one:

- **Sic te amo** *ut* **fratrem** *amo* I LOVE YOU SO IN THE SAME WAY AS I LOVE A BROTHER.

2/ Inside this third type we must include the comparisons based on a supposition, usually introduced in English by AS IF; being a supposition, the comparative clause will have its verb in *subjunctive*, and they are introduced by any of these conjunctions: **quasi, tamquam, tamquam si, ut si, velut si** (observe that, with the exception of **tamquam**, all of them have **si** as component, whether as an independent word or not):

- **Semper loquitur** *quasi* **dux** *sit* HE IS ALWAYS SPEAKING AS IF HE WERE A GENERAL.
- **Descenderunt ut istum,** *tamquam si esset* **consul, salutarent** THEY CAME DOWN IN ORDER TO SALUTE THIS ONE, AS IF HE WERE CONSUL (Cicero, *Philippicae*).

✧ Note that in this kind of sentences it is very common not to find any anticipatory adverb in the main sentence.

3/ It is also worth mentioning the combination of a main sentence introduced by a comparative expression (**magis**, for instance) with **quam si** introducing the comparative clause, in order to achieve the meaning MORE… THAN IF :

- Magis laboras *quam si* servus *esses* YOU WORK MORE THAN IF YOU WERE A SLAVE.
- Quamvis multi sint, magis tamen ero solus *quam si* unus *esses* EVEN IF THEY ARE MANY, NEVERTHELESS I WILL BE MORE ALONE THAN IF ONLY YOU WERE HERE (Cicero, *Epistulae ad Atticum*).

d) Fourth type [351]

The fourth type is used to express THE SAME AS, and this is achieved by the use of the identity pronoun **idem, eadem, idem** in the main clause and **atque/ac** or a relative pronoun introducing the comparative clause:

- Postulavit deinde *eadem, quae* legatis in mandatis dederat THEN HE DEMANDED THE SAME HE HAD TOLD THE AMBASSADORS IN HIS INSTRUCTIONS (Caesar, *De Bello Gallico*).
- Gallorum *eadem atque* Belgarum oppugnatio est haec THE BESIEGING TACTIC OF THE GAULS, THE SAME AS THAT OF THE BELGAE, IS THIS ONE (Caesar, *De Bello Gallico*).

  ✧ In this example, the comparative clause does not have its own verb.

10. Fear clauses [352]

The main verbs that will be followed by a fear clause are **timeo, metuo** and the deponent **vereor** (a lot of times **vereor** has more a meaning of TO BE AFRAID OF in the sense of TO FEEL RESPECT FOR, but it can also be used in the normal meaning of TO FEAR).

a/ Fear clauses are introduced by **ne**, but this **ne** must be translated by THAT, without carrying any negative sense (in other subordinates, **ne** has a negative sense); the verb must be in *subjunctive*, and we will follow the rules of the *consecutio temporum*:

- Timeo *ne* pater *veniat* I FEAR THAT MY FATHER MAY COME.
- Timebam *ne* pater *veniret* I FEARED THAT MY FATHER MIGHT COME.
- Timeo *ne* male facta antiqua mea *sint* inventa omnia I FEAR THAT ALL MY PREVIOUS BAD DEEDS MAY HAVE BEEN FOUND OUT (Plautus, *Truculentus*).
- Timeo *ne* C. Verres ... omnia quae fecit impune *fecerit* I FEAR THAT C. VERRES MAY HAVE DONE ALL HE HAS DONE WITH IMPUNITY (Cicero, *In Verrem*).

b/ If we fear that something may *not* happen, the conjunction to be used is **ut**, which we must translate by THAT … NOT (in some cases we can find **ne … non** instead of **ut**):

- Timeo *ut* nostri milites *vincant* / Timeo *ne* nostri milites *non vincant* I AM AFRAID THAT OUR SOLDIERS MAY NOT WIN.
- Omnis labores te excipere video; timeo *ut sustineas* I SEE THAT YOU ARE TAKING ON ALL THE TASKS; I FEAR THAT YOU MAY NOT ENDURE (Cicero, *Epistulae ad Familiares*).
- Vereor *ut* Dolabella ipse satis nobis prodesse *possit* I FEAR THAT DOLABELLA HIMSELF MAY NOT BE OF ANY USE TO US (Cicero, *Epistulae ad Familiares*).

c/ We should insist on the *consecutio temporum*: [353]

- *Metuerunt* ne hostes urbem *delevissent* THEY WERE AFRAID THAT THE ENEMY MIGHT HAVE DESTROYED THE CITY.

If this sentence had the main verb in primary tense, the verb of the subordinate would also have been in primary tense:

- *Metuunt* ne hostes urbem *deleverint* THEY ARE AFRAID THAT THE ENEMY MAY HAVE DESTROYED THE CITY.

Points to be taken into account:

1/ Although the main sentence may be negative, this does not affect the choice of ut or ne for the subordinate:

- *Non* timeo *ne* pater veniat I DO NOT FEAR THAT MY FATHER MAY COME.
  ✧ ...ne pater veniat remains unchanged, because we want to say ... THAT MY FATHER MAY COME; whether the main sentence is Timeo I FEAR or Non timeo I DO NOT FEAR is indifferent.
- *Non* timeo *ne* quis inveniatur I AM NOT AFRAID THAT SOMEBODY MAY BE FOUND (Petronius, *Satyrica*).

2/ We should not forget that these verbs can also rule a normal direct object:

- Timebat *iram* senatus HE FEARED THE ANGER OF THE SENATE (Sallust, *Bellum Iugurthinum*).
- Nemo *tribunos aut plebem* timebat NOBODY FEARED THE TRIBUNES OR THE PLEBS (Livy, *Ab Urbe Condita*).

11. Indefinite clauses [354]

a) Indefinite clauses of repeated action

When we want to express temporal sentences that imply a repeated action, like for instance EVERY TIME THEY COME TO ROME, THEY BRING PRESENTS TO THE CHILDREN, we make use of a special combination of indicative tenses.

1/ Repeated action in the present EVERY TIME THEY COME TO ROME, THEY BRING PRESENTS FOR THE CHILDREN

➪ The verb of the main clause will be in *present indicative*, as expected: ..., dona pueris ferunt.
➪ The subordinate clause will be introduced by cum, and it will have the verb in *perfect indicative*.

The whole sentence will be: Cum Romam *venerunt*, dona pueris *ferunt*.

Observe that, word by word, it means WHEN THEY HAVE COME TO ROME, THEY BRING PRESENTS FOR THE CHILDREN.

- Cum *dixi* ficus, *rides* quasi barbara verba et dici ficos, Laetiliane, *iubes* EVERY TIME I SAY "FICUS", YOU LAUGH AS IF AT A WRONG EXPRESSION AND YOU, LAETILIANUS, SAY THAT IT MUST BE SAID "FICOS" (Martial, *Epigrammata*).
  ✧ Martial is discussing with Laetilianus about the spelling of a word, as this word ficus can be declined through the 2nd or the 4th declension (there is some sarcasm about a double meaning of this word, but it is not necessary to comment on it here).

2/ Repeated action in the past EVERY TIME THEY CAME TO ROME, THEY BROUGHT PRESENTS TO THE CHILDREN [355]

⇨ The verb of the main clause will be in *imperfect indicative*, as expected: ..., **dona pueris ferebant**.
⇨ The verb of the subordinate clause will be in *pluperfect indicative*.

The whole sentence will be: **Cum Romam *venerant*, dona pueris *ferebant*.**

Observe that, word by word, it means WHEN THEY HAD COME TO ROME, THEY BROUGHT (WERE BRINGING) PRESENTS FOR THE CHILDREN.

- **Cato ille noster, cum *venerat* ..., visere *solebat* ...** OUR GLORIOUS CATO, EVERY TIME HE CAME, HE OBSERVED ... (Cicero, *De Republica*).

3/ Repeated action in the future EVERY TIME THEY COME TO ROME, THEY WILL BRING PRESENTS FOR THE CHILDREN [356]

⇨ The verb of the main clause will be in *future*, as expected: ..., **dona pueris ferent**.
⇨ The subordinate clause will have the verb in *future perfect*.

The whole sentence will be: **Cum Romam venerint, dona pueris ferent.**

Observe that, word by word, it means WHEN THEY WILL HAVE COME TO ROME, THEY WILL BRING PRESENTS FOR THE CHILDREN.

¤ In other words: The verb of the main clause will be in the same tense as in English, while the verb of the subordinate clause will be the tense that will be found immediately at its right side in the verbal table, taking as a model the usual table of distribution of tenses.

b) Indefinite clauses of single action ("ever" clauses) [357]

1/ When the notion of indefinite falls on a specific part of the sentence (WHOEVER, WHEREVER...) rather than somebody executing the same action several times, we make use either of the indefinite relative pronoun **quicumque** (in any necessary case, gender and number) or of an indefinite relative adverb (**ubicumque, quandocumque**, etc.). The verb of the "EVER" clause will usually be in the *indicative*:

- ***Ubicumque* res *postulabat*, praesidium inpositum (est)** WHEREVER THE SITUATION REQUIRED IT, A GARRISON WAS SET (Sallustius, *Bellum Iugurthinum*).
- ***Quicumque* hoc *fecit*, supplicio dignus est** WHOEVER HAS DONE THIS, DESERVES TO BE PUNISHED (Cicero, *In Verrem*).

2/ In "EVER" clauses referring to the future, it is very common that also the indefinite clause has its verb in future, while English would use a present tense:

- **Cetera, *quotienscumque voletis*, et hoc loco et aliis parata vobis erunt** THE REST WILL BE READY FOR YOU BOTH IN THIS PLACE AND IN OTHER PLACES HOWEVER OFTEN YOU WANT (Cicero, *Tusculanae Disputationes*).

  ✧ Literally, ... HOWEVER OFTEN YOU WILL WANT.
- Romulus, after killing Remus: **Sic deinde, *quicumque* alius *transiliet* moenia mea** AND THUS FROM NOW ON, WHICHEVER OTHER ONE JUMPS ACROSS MY WALLS (Livy, *Ab Urbe Condita*).

  ✧ Literally, ... WILL JUMP ACROSS MY WALLS.

12. Proviso clauses [358]

Proviso clauses are sometimes considered a sub-group of the conditional clauses, with some temporal sense also, and they introduce the idea of AS LONG AS, PROVIDED THAT. The verb must be in *subjunctive*, and the main conjunctions that introduce them are **dum**, **modo** and **dummodo**, and the negative to be used is **ne**:

- ... querentibus et Hippocratem atque Epicydem abire seu Locros seu quo alio mallent, *dummodo* Sicilia *cederent* ... REQUESTING THAT BOTH HIPPOCRATES AND EPICYDES SHOULD DEPART TO LOCRI OR TO WHEREVER THEY WOULD PREFER, AS LONG AS THEY WITHDREW FROM SICILY (Livy, *Ab Urbe Condita*).
- *Dummodo sit* dives, barbarus ipse placet AS LONG AS HE IS RICH, A STRANGER HIMSELF IS WELCOME (Ovid, *Ars Amatoria*).
- *Dum ne* ob male facta *peream*, parvi aestumo AS LONG AS I DO NOT PERISH BECAUSE OF MY BAD DEEDS, I DO NOT CARE (Plautus, *Captivi*).

13. *Quominus* and *quin* clauses [359]

Quominus and **quin** are usually studied together, as in some case they can alternate without any alteration of meaning. The best way is to divide their study into expressions of *doubting* (and similar) and of *preventing* (and similar).

Please refer to *Point 6 Result clauses* to see an additional usage of **quin**.

a) Expressions of doubting

A sentence in which the main verb expresses doubt can be either positive or negative with respect to this main verb:

I DOUBT THAT ... or I DO NOT DOUBT THAT ...

1/ If the sentence is positive, the subordinate will follow the same structure as an *indirect question*; some examples will make this clear:

- Dubito *utrum Caesar venire velit necne* I DOUBT WHETHER CAESAR WANTS TO COME OR NOT.
- Dubitas *quis optimus senator sit?* DO YOU DOUBT WHO THE BEST SENATOR IS?
- Itaque de Ciceronibus nostris dubito *quid agam* THEREFORE I AM NOT SURE WHAT I SHOULD DO ABOUT OUR "CICEROS" (Cicero, *Epistulae ad Atticum*).
- Antea dubitabam *venturaene essent* PREVIOUSLY, I DOUBTED WHETHER THEY WOULD COME (Cicero, *Epistulae ad Familiares*).

Observe in all these examples that the subordinate clause has the usual structure of an indirect question with the verb in subjunctive; in fact, instead of **Dubito** we could have written **Volo scire** or any other expression that introduces an indirect question.

2/ If the sentence is negative, the subordinate is usually introduced by **quin** + subjunctive:

- Non dubito *quin* Caesar *venturus sit* I DO NOT DOUBT THAT CAESAR WILL COME.
- Non dubito *quin* vobis satis *fecerim*, iudices I DO NOT DOUBT THAT I HAVE DONE ENOUGH FOR YOU, JUDGES (Cicero, *In Verrem*).

- **Non dubium est *quin* Quintus totam veritatem *dixerit*** THERE IS NO DOUBT THAT QUINTUS HAS SPOKEN ALL THE TRUTH.

  ✧ Observe in this last example that **non dubium est** is an expression that has the same force as a verb of doubting.
- **Non dubium est, *quin* M. Tullius omnium *sit* eloquentissimus** THERE IS NO DOUBT THAT M. TULLIUS IS THE MOST ELOQUENT OF ALL (A. Gellius, *Noctes Atticae*).

But it can be that, rather than introducing a statement, it introduces an indirect question, even if the main sentence is negative; then, obviously it will be followed by an indirect question instead of by a **quin** clause:

- **Non dubium est *utrum iudices an iuris consulti vituperandi sint*** THERE IS NO DOUBT WHETHER THE JUDGES OR THE LAWYERS MUST BE BLAMED (Cicero, *Pro Caecina*).

3/ Observe this apparent contradiction: **[360]**

- **Num ergo dubium est *quin* ei *obtulerint* hanc praedam Chrysogono?** IS THERE ANY DOUBT THAT THEY OFFERED THIS BOOTY TO CHRYSOGONUS? (Cicero, *Pro Roscio Amerino*).

There is no negative word with the expression **dubium est**, and even so the subordinate is introduced by **quin**, as if the main sentence were negative. The explanation is that even if the main sentence is positive it is a question after which a negative answer is expected, so that, if not grammatically, at least in its background it can be considered negative (and therefore a **quin** clause follows).

4/ Let's remember that the verb **dubito** can be used also in the sense of TO HESITATE, and then it is followed by an infinitive, whether the main clause is negative or not:

- **Ea nubere illi dubitabat** SHE HESITATED TO MARRY HIM (Sallust, *Catilinae Coniuratio*).
- **Latro in hac controversia non dubitabat facere primam quaestionem** THE BRIGAND, IN THIS DISPUTE, DID NOT HESITATE TO ASK THE FIRST QUESTION (Seneca senior, *Controversiae*).

b) Expressions of preventing **[361]**

By expressions of preventing we mean not only verbs of preventing with this direct meaning, like **deterreo** TO DETER, TO DISSUADE, **obsto** TO HINDER, **impedio** TO PREVENT, but also other adjacent idiomatic expressions.

1/ If the sentence is positive, the subordinate can be introduced by either **quominus** or **ne** (either of them with the verb in *subjunctive*):

- **Te deterreo *quominus/ne* Romam *abeas*** I DETER YOU FROM DEPARTING TO ROME.
- **Tum vir optimus Sex. Naevius hominem multis verbis deterret *ne auctionetur*** THEN SEXTUS NAEVIUS, AN EXCELLENT MAN, BY MAKING A LONG SPEECH, DISSUADES THE MAN FROM HOLDING AN AUCTION (Cicero, *Pro Quinctio*).
- **Antea deterrere te *ne* popularis *esses* non poteramus** BEFORE, WE COULD NOT DETER YOU FROM BECOMING A POPULAR MAN (Cicero, *Philippicae*).
- **Deterrere eum voluit ... *quominus* medicamentum *biberet*** HE TRIED TO DISSUADE HIM FROM DRINKING THE MEDICINE (Curtius Rufus, *Historiae Alexandri Magni*).

2/ But if the sentence is negative, the subordinate will be introduced by either **quominus** (so, **quominus** can be used after positive and negative main clauses) or **quin**: [362]

- Non te deterreo *quominus/ quin* hoc *facias* I DO NOT PREVENT YOU FROM DOING THIS.
- Me homo nemo deterrebit, *quin* ea *sit* in his aedibus NO MAN WILL PREVENT ME FROM HAVING HER IN THIS HOUSE (Plautus, *Miles Gloriosus*).
  ✧ Literally, ... PREVENT ME THAT SHE MAY BE IN THIS HOUSE.

3/ Let's see some examples with related verbs:

- Omnia ... confessus est neque recusavit *quominus* legis poenam *subiret* HE CONFESSED EVERYTHING AND DID NOT REFUSE TO RECEIVE THE PUNISHMENT OF THE LAW (Nepos, *Vitae*).
  ✧ In this example, the sense of preventing is in the verb **recuso** TO REFUSE, in its sense of trying to prevent something from happening (in this case, a punishment).
- *Quominus* ad ultimam senectutem *perveniant*, non prohibentur THEY ARE NOT PREVENTED FROM REACHING THE LAST STAGE OF OLD AGE (Celsus, *De Medicina*).
  ✧ Celsus is writing about the lack of effect of some medicines.
  ✧ **Prohibeo** not only means TO FORBID but also TO PREVENT.

14. Summary of the uses of *cum* [363]

After finding this conjunction used in several subordinate clauses, it would be worth making a summary of its uses (apart from its use as a preposition, WITH).

a) With indicative

1/ Its meaning is always WHEN or WHENEVER / EVERY TIME THAT

We have seen that **cum** + indicative means WHEN (and EVERY TIME THAT if used in that combination of tenses to express repeated action):

- *Cum* de iure et legitimis hominum controversiis *loquimur*, ... WHENEVER WE SPEAK ABOUT LAW AND DISPUTES AMONG MEN, ... (Cicero, *Pro Caecina*).

2/ The inverted **cum** [364]

Cum + indicative has a special construction (apart from that one in which it will mean EVERY TIME THAT ...); in this special construction it will still mean WHEN, but it will have some characteristics. Observe these examples:

- Nondum Hannibal e castris exierat *cum* pugnantium clamorem *audivit* HANNIBAL HAD NOT GONE OUT OF THE CAMP YET WHEN HE HEARD SHOUTS OF PEOPLE FIGHTING (Livy, *Ab Urbe Condita*).
- Domi cenabamus cum repente audimus Caesarem necatum esse WE WERE HAVING DINNER AT HOME, WHEN SUDDENLY WE HEARD THAT CAESAR HAD BEEN KILLED.
  ✧ Observe that the use of the *historic present* in the main sentence is usual in this construction.

Observe these characteristics:

- ⇨ The **cum** clause comes second (usually it comes first).
- ⇨ The main information is in the **cum** clause rather than in the main one (that we were having dinner is really irrelevant).
- ⇨ As said, the **cum** clause is in the indicative.

If the sentence has these three characteristics, it is called an *inverted* ***cum*** (***cum inversum***). See this example from Livy:

- **Iam montani ... conveniebant, cum repente conspiciunt alios ...** THE MOUNTAINEERS WERE ALREADY GATHERING, WHEN SUDDENLY THEY SEE OTHERS ... (Livy, *Ab Urbe Condita*).
  - ✧ The choice of translating the verb in the **cum** clause by a present tense they see (so, keeping the Latin tense) or by a past tense they saw may be a matter of personal taste.

b) With subjunctive [365]

With the subjunctive, the uses and meanings of **cum** may produce some confusion. The best way to schematise the meanings of **cum** in subjunctive is by means of this table that we will clarify after presenting it:

Present	*Perfect*
– Concessive – Causal	– Concessive – Causal
Imperfect	***Pluperfect***
– Concessive – Historic **cum**	– Concessive – Historic **cum**

1/ **Cum** can have *concessive* meaning in any of the four tenses of the subjunctive:

- ***Cum*** **dives** ***sis*****, tamen non te amo** ALTHOUGH YOU MAY BE RICH, NEVERTHELESS I DO NOT LOVE YOU.
- **Saepe officium est sapientis desciscere a vita,** ***cum sit*** **beatissimus** OFTEN THE DUTY OF A WISE MAN IS TO LEAVE LIFE, ALTHOUGH HE MAY BE VERY HAPPY (Cicero, *De Finibus*).

2/ With any of the two tenses above, it may also have *causal* meaning:

- ***Cum*** **dives** ***sis*****, te amo** AS YOU ARE RICH, I LOVE YOU.
- **Nimis abes diu, praesertim** ***cum sis*** **in propinquis locis** YOU HAVE BEEN ABSENT FOR TOO LONG, ESPECIALLY AS YOU ARE IN PLACES NEARBY (Cicero, *Epistulae ad Atticum*).

3/ And with any of the two tenses below it may be a *Historic* ***cum***. This kind of subordinate clause has a meaning that can be described like *causal and temporal* at the same time:

- ***Cum*** **Caesar** ***venisset*****, milites Gallos vicerunt** WHEN/BECAUSE CAESAR HAD COME, THE SOLDIERS DEFEATED THE GAULS.

It is called *Historic* ***cum*** because it is mainly used in the description of past events; usually the sense will be more temporal than causal, but sometimes a causal sense can be detected; a usual way of translating this double sense is by using AS : AS CAESAR HAD COME, ...

More examples of *Historic* **cum**:

- **Ea *cum* Ciceroni *nuntiarentur*, ... rem ad senatum refert** WHEN THESE AFFAIRS WERE ANNOUNCED TO CICERO, ... HE REPORTED IT TO THE SENATE (Sallust, *Catilinae Coniuratio*).
  - ✧ In this example, the sense is clearly temporal rather than causal, so we can use WHEN instead of AS, but either would suit.
- **Eo *cum venisset*, ea quae fore suspicatus erat facta [esse] cognovit** AS HE ARRIVED THERE, HE GOT TO KNOW THAT THOSE DEEDS THAT HE HAD SUSPECTED THAT WOULD HAPPEN HAD HAPPENED (Caesar, *De Bello Gallico*).
  - ✧ Although here the main meaning of **cum** is WHEN, one could argue that Caesar got to know those events because he had come.
- **Caesar *cum* in Asiam *venisset*, reperiebat T. Ampium conatum esse ...** AS CAESAR ARRIVED IN ASIA, HE FOUND OUT THAT T. AMPIUS HAD TRIED ... (Caesar, *Bellum Civile*).
  - ✧ The same as in the sentence above: both causal and temporal meaning make sense.
- ***Cum* haec *agerem*, repente ad me venit Heraclius** WHEN I WAS DEALING WITH THESE MATTERS, SUDDENLY HERACLIUS CAME TO ME (Cicero, *In Verrem*).
  - ✧ Clear temporal sense: Heraclius comes not *because* I am dealing with this, but *when* I am dealing with this.

15. Summary of the uses of *ut* [366]

As we have done with **cum**, it would be worth making a summary of the uses of **ut**.

a) With indicative

1/ Temporal

- **Homo, *ut* haec *audivit*, ...** THE MAN, WHEN HE HEARD THIS, ... (Cicero, *In Verrem*).
- **Eorum *ut* quisque primus *venerat*, sub muro consistebat** WHEN EACH ONE OF THEM FIRST CAME, HE STOOD BENEATH THE WALL (Caesar, *De Bello Gallico*).

Although **cum** can also be used in the meaning of WHEN with an indicative, it is more common to find **ut**.

2/ Comparative

This use, apart from comparative, could also be called *modal*, as in fact it is telling us *in what way* something is done.

- **Certum scio esse ita *ut dicis*** I KNOW THAT IT IS CERTAIN, AS YOU SAY (Lucilius, *Saturae*).
- **Faciam ita *ut vis*** I WILL DO SO AS YOU WANT (Plautus, *Amphitruo*).
- **Pompeius ... aciem instruebat, semper, *ut videbatur*, expectans, si ...** POMPEIUS ARRANGED THE BATTLE-ARRAY, ALWAYS EXPECTANT, AS IT SEEMED, IN CASE ... (Caesar, *Bellum Civile*).

Inside this use of **ut** as comparative we should include sentences like

- **Tibi pareo ut consuli** I OBEY YOU AS CONSUL / I OBEY YOU IN YOUR ROLE OF CONSUL.

This is nothing else than **Tibi pareo ut consuli *pareo*** but with the last verb omitted. Look further down, in the section of uses of **ut** + subjunctive, for another kind of similar clauses.

3/ Translating both temporal and comparative

Some grammars say that *ut + indicative* should be always translated by AS, because it comprehends both meanings, *temporal* and *comparative* (observe that the examples of its use with temporal meaning could have been translated by AS). In any case, it seems reasonable to distinguish the two different meanings, even if translated by the same English word.

b) With subjunctive [367]

1/ Result (consecutive)

- Tantum labore suo frumenti exarabant *ut* populo Romano totique Italiae suppeditare *possent* WITH THEIR WORK THEY PRODUCED SO MUCH CORN THAT THEY COULD SUPPLY THE ROMAN PEOPLE AND ALL OF ITALY (Cicero, *In Verrem*).

2/ Comparative

A similar case to what we have seen above in the uses with the indicative. Observe this sentence:

- Paulus Octaviam amat *ut* sororem PAUL LOVES OCTAVIA LIKE A SISTER.

This is nothing else than an abbreviation of

- Paulus Octaviam amat *ut* sororem *amaret* (si ea soror esset) PAUL LOVES OCTAVIA AS HE WOULD LOVE A SISTER (IF SHE WERE HIS SISTER).

This is a case more complicated than the simple **Tibi pareo ut consuli** that we have seen above. See why:

In the case **Paulus Octaviam amat ut sororem**, it is understood that Octavia is not a sister of Paul, and this is why, if the sentence were complete, it would use the *potential subjunctive*. This is why we have included the use of **ut** in comparative sense both in the section of indicative and in the section of subjunctive, although in fact, as the verb is usually omitted, neither an indicative nor a subjunctive will be seen.

- ... quem veretur *ut* deum ... amat verum *ut* sodalem, *ut* fratrem ... WHOM HE REVERES LIKE A GOD ... BUT LOVES LIKE A COMRADE, LIKE A BROTHER (Cicero, *Pro Plancio*).

3/ Purpose

- Edictum et litteras ad consulem misit *ut* is exercitus idibus Martiis Arimini *adesset* in castris HE SENT AN ORDER AND A LETTER TO THE CONSUL SO THAT THIS ARMY WOULD BE IN THE CAMP AT ARIMINUM BY THE IDES OF MARCH (Livy, *Ab Urbe Condita*).

4/ Concessive

- Nihil enim est profecto homini prudentia dulcius, quam, *ut* cetera *auferat*, adfert certe senectus ACTUALLY THERE IS NOTHING SWEETER FOR A MAN THAN PRUDENCE, WHICH OLD AGE BRINGS ON, ALTHOUGH IT DEPRIVES OF THE REST OF THINGS (Cicero, *Tusculanae Disputationes*).

5/ Completive

Some verbs of ordering or desiring require a THAT clause, introduced in Latin by **ut** + subjunctive:

- **Allobrogibus imperavit *ut* iis frumenti copiam *facerent*** HE ORDERED THE ALLOBROGES TO PROVIDE THEM (WITH) A SUPPLY OF CORN (Caesar, *De Bello Gallico*).

  ✧ From a strictly grammatical point of view, the **ut** clause is the direct object of **imperavit**: this is what he ordered.

- **Volo *ut* mihi *respondeas*** I WANT YOU TO ANSWER TO ME (Cicero, *In Vatinium*).
- **Optamus *ut* quam primum te in Italia *videamus*** (Cicero, *Epistulae ad Familiares*). WE WISH TO SEE YOU IN ITALY AS SOON AS POSSIBLE
- **Di faciant *ut* id *bibatis* quod vos numquam transeat** MAY THE GODS GRANT THAT YOU DRINK WHAT WILL NEVER PASS THROUGH YOU (Plautus, *Persa*).
- **... nisi ... caveant *ne* possessione urbis *pellantur*** ... UNLESS THEY TAKE CARE THAT THEY ARE NOT EXPELLED FROM THE ESTATE OF THE CITY (Livy, *Ab Urbe Condita*).

Observe the **ne** in this last example: although sometimes this kind of completive clauses may seem to be result clauses, they are not: a result clause would not have **ne** as negative, it would have **ut non**.

16. Completive *quod* clauses [368]

There are a series of completive clauses introduced by **quod**. The literal sense of this **quod** is THE FACT THAT, but we will have to adapt the translation to produce a sentence acceptable in English.

- **Multum eos adiuvabat, *quod Liger ex nivibus creverat*** IT WAS OF MUCH HELP TO THEM THAT THE LOIRE HAD INCREASED [ITS LEVEL OF WATER] BECAUSE OF THE SNOW (Caesar, *De Bello Gallico*).
- ***Quod sapiens est* negare non possum** I CAN NOT DENY THAT HE IS WISE.
- **Opportunissime res accidit, *quod postridie ... Germani ... ad eum in castra venerunt*** SOMETHING HAPPENED VERY OPPORTUNELY, THAT ON THE FOLLOWING DAY THE GERMANS CAME TO HIM TO THE CAMP (Caesar, *De Bello Gallico*).
- **Hoc enim uno praestamus vel maxime feris, *quod conloquimur inter nos*** ONLY IN ONE THING WE ARE AHEAD OF BEASTS, THAT WE SPEAK AMONG OURSELVES (Cicero, *De Oratore*).

Although these kinds of **quod** clauses have been included in this section of subordinate clauses, as a general rule they are not considered subordinate clauses but *completive*, as they are part of the main clause (subject, object, or additional information on either).

Observe these functions with respect to the former examples:

- ➪ First example: The **quod** clause plays the role of *subject* (the fact that the Loire had increased its level of water is what had helped them).
- ➪ Second example: The **quod** clause plays the role of *direct object* (that he is wise is what I can not deny).
- ➪ Third example: The **quod** clause is an *explanation of the subject* ***res*** (it tells us what the **res** is).
- ➪ Fourth example: The **quod** clause is an *explanation of the circumstantial object* ***hoc uno*** (it tells us what the **hoc uno** is).

c) Infinitive clauses

1. General principles [369]

a) The use of the infinitive

1/ An infinitive is a verbal noun; as CHAIR indicates an object, TO WRITE indicates an action. So, it is usually defined as a *verbal noun*.

We must be aware that in English sometimes we use the form ending in -ING to indicate an action:

TO READ BOOKS IS CONVENIENT FOR CHILDREN / *READING* BOOKS IS CONVENIENT FOR CHILDREN.

The READING in the second example denotes the action, and in Latin it will be expressed by an infinitive. We must not confuse this with a *gerund*, which answers the question How? :

READING BOOKS, YOU WILL LEARN A LOT. ✧ In this example, READING is a gerund.

2/ The use of the infinitive in Latin is quite parallel to its use in English; for instance,

- **Volo *edere*** I WANT TO EAT.
- **Volo *scire*** I WANT TO KNOW (Plautus, *Aulularia*).
- ***Edere* bonum est** EATING IS GOOD.
- **Non enim *vivere* bonum est, sed bene *vivere*** CERTAINLY, IT IS NOT LIVING THAT IS GOOD, BUT LIVING WELL (Seneca iunior, *Epistulae Morales ad Lucilium*).

Observe that we use the infinitive as we could use any noun; we have said I WANT *TO EAT* as we could have said I WANT *A BOOK*. **Edere** in the first sentence is *direct object* of **volo**, and in the second one it is the *subject* of **est**; so, it can perform different functions.

3/ There are several verbs that can use an infinitive. Observe how we can add an infinitive after any of these verbs, for instance:

volo TO WANT
nolo NOT TO WANT
malo TO PREFER
praefero TO PREFER

- **Nolo cetera ... *recitare*** I DO NOT WANT TO RECITE THE OTHER MATTERS (Cicero, *Pro Plancio*).
- **Malo enim plus *dare* quam ...** I PREFER TO GIVE MORE THAN ... (Cicero, *In Verrem*).

b) Infinitive clauses [370]

When we say *infinitive clauses*, we do not mean the simple use we have seen above, but a more complicated construction that has a good parallel in English.

1/ To say I WANT TO EAT, we have just translated each element: **Volo edere**. Observe that the person who will perform the action expressed by the infinitive is the same as the subject of the main verb: *I* WANT, and it is *me* who will eat. But if we want to say I WANT THE CHILD TO EAT, in this case the person who will perform the action of the infinitive is not the subject of the main verb (I), but somebody else (THE CHILD).

In this case, we will say that THE CHILD is the subject of the infinitive (it is *him* who will eat), and we will express it in accusative (this is why usually an infinitive clause is also called *accusative + infinitive construction*):

Volo *puerum edere*.

✧ It could be humorously argued that the sentence means I WANT TO EAT A CHILD; it is normal that in some cases confusion may arise, and the context should clarify which one of both meanings must be considered.

2/ An infinitive is a verbal noun, but at the same time it goes on being a verb, which means that it can have the same [371]
objects it has when used normally as a verb; so, we can add a direct object, for instance, to the former example:

I WANT THE CHILD TO EAT THE DINNER.

All we have to do is put this direct object in the same case we would put it if the infinitive were used as a verb, which in this case is in accusative (because THE DINNER is the direct object of the verb TO EAT):

Volo *puerum cenam edere*.

Note that in this example we end up having two accusatives: one, **puerum**, because we must put in accusative the subject of the infinitive, and the other one, **cenam**, for obvious reasons: it is a direct object. Usually, the sense will help us to see which one is the subject and which one is the direct object (I WANT THE DINNER TO EAT THE CHILD would not make any sense unless you like *Alice in Wonderland*).

- *Meminisse* ego *hanc rem vos* volo I WANT YOU TO REMEMBER THIS THING (Plautus, *Cistellaria*).
  ✧ **Vos** is the accusative *subject* of the infinitive, and **hanc rem** is the accusative *direct object* of the infinitive **meminisse**.

An infinitive can have all kinds of objects, also prepositional objects:

- *Te* cupio *perire* mecum I WANT YOU TO PERISH WITH ME (Plautus, *Epidicus*).

3/ We may find some cases where either could be the subject or the direct object; for instance:

Volo *Caesarem Pompeium* vincere.

Do I want Caesar to defeat Pompeius or Pompeius to defeat Caesar? In these cases, the general practice is that the first one is the subject of the infinitive and the second one the direct object (it is the general practice, but not a golden rule: there may be exceptions).

c) Indirect statement [372]

The most frequent use of the infinitive clauses is in the *indirect statement*. In the cases seen above, in which we have been using verbs that express desire, we have seen constructions parallel in English and in Latin:

- Volo *pueros* libros *legere* I WANT THE CHILDREN TO READ BOOKS.

But in indirect statement we find that in English the statement starts with the word THAT:

⇨ Direct statement: CAESAR IS WRITING A LETTER.
⇨ Indirect statement: I SAY THAT CAESAR IS WRITING A LETTER.

In this case, what Latin does is transforming the THAT clause, i.e. the information we are reproducing, into an *accusative + infinitive construction:*

Dico *Caesarem* epistulam *scribere*.

More examples:

- Dux dicit *milites* in urbe *esse* THE GENERAL SAYS THAT THE SOLDIERS ARE IN THE CITY.
- Dico *eum esse* apud me I SAY THAT HE IS AT MY PLACE (Plautus, *Captivi*).

In the chapter on *Indirect Speech* this is dealt with in more amplitude.

d) An unexpected agreement [373]

We may find that some impersonal verbs are followed by an infinitive and that this infinitive may have a subject in accusative or dative, depending on the construction (see the section on *Impersonal Verbs*). If the subject of the infinitive is in dative and moreover the infinitive has a predicative object, it will usually be in dative (therefore agreeing with its subject) rather than in accusative:

- *Quieto tibi* licet esse YOU CAN REMAIN CALM (Plautus, *Epidicus*).

Observe the several options:

- *Quietum* licet esse IT IS POSSIBLE TO REMAIN CALM.
  ✧ **Quietum** in accusative, following the usual rule that the predicative object of an infinitive must be in accusative.
- *Quietum te* licet esse YOU CAN REMAIN CALM.
  ✧ **Licet** can rule an accusative (**te**), and **quietum** agrees with it.
- *Quieto tibi* licet esse YOU CAN REMAIN CALM.
  ✧ **Licet** can also rule a dative (**tibi**), and in this case **quieto** agrees with it.

There are in fact small differences between the use of accusative or dative, please see the section on *Impersonal Verbs* for more details.

2. Which tense of infinitive? [374]

a) With verbs other than of indirect statement

1/ As we know, there are six infinitives in Latin, and we will use in each case the one that corresponds to what must be expressed; for instance, if we want to say

I WANT TO DESTROY THIS BRIDGE

it is quite obvious that we will translate TO DESTROY by the present active infinitive **delere**, which is the one that corresponds to the usual English infinitive (*to read, to write, to run, to sleep,* etc.), and we will write

Volo hunc pontem *delere*.
✧ Observe that **hunc pontem** is the *direct object* of **delere**.

Supposing that we wanted to say I WANT THIS BRIDGE TO BE DESTROYED, we see that TO BE DESTROYED has a passive meaning, so we would use the present passive infinitive **deleri**:

Volo hunc pontem *deleri*.
✧ Observe that now **hunc pontem** is the *subject* of **deleri**: the subject must be in accusative.

2/ It may be that we need to express another tense rather than the present; for instance, if we want to say

I WANT THIS BRIDGE TO HAVE BEEN DESTROYED BEFORE NIGHT

we will have to make use of the passive past tense (TO HAVE BEEN DESTROYED, past action), and the final result will be

Volo hunc pontem ante noctem *deletum esse*.

Nevertheless, this use of tenses other than the usual present is more normal in infinitive clauses introduced by verbs of indirect statement.

b) With verbs of indirect statement [375]

This will be more widely dealt with in the corresponding chapter on indirect speech (indirect statement is just a part of indirect speech), but we give here some basic guidelines.

1/ In the case of reproducing a former direct statement, the infinitive must be in the same tense (and voice) as it was in the direct statement. For instance:

⇨ Direct statement: Caesar Gallos vicit — CAESAR DEFEATED THE GAULS.
⇨ Indirect statement: Dico *Caesarem* Gallos *vicisse* — I SAY THAT CAESAR DEFEATED THE GAULS.
✧ The indirect statement uses the *perfect infinitive* because the **vicit** in the direct statement was a perfect tense.

More examples:

⇨ Direct statement: **Caesar Gallos vincet** CAESAR WILL DEFEAT THE GAULS.
⇨ Indirect statement: **Dico *Caesarem* Gallos *victurum esse*** I SAY THAT CAESAR WILL DEFEAT THE GAULS.
✧ The indirect statement uses the *future infinitive* because **vincet** in the direct statement was a future tense.

- ***Metellum* in Capitolium *venisse* dixit** HE SAID THAT METELLUS HAD COME TO THE CAPITOLIUM (Gellius, *Noctes Atticae*).
  ✧ In some cases the translation into English can be flexible. For instance, in this example we could have said CAME instead of HAD COME.

2/ Now let's see two examples worked backwards:

a/ First example

- **... tribus istis clarissimis philosophis, *quos* Romam *venisse* dixisti** ... THESE THREE VERY FAMOUS PHILOSOPHERS, WHOM YOU SAID HAD COME TO ROME (Cicero, *De Oratore*).
  ⇨ It seems that somebody said at some point something like this:
  - **Clarissimi philosophi Romam *venerunt*** THREE VERY FAMOUS PHILOSOPHERS HAVE COME TO ROME.

  ⇨ As the direct statement uses a perfect tense (**venerunt**), in the indirect statement we must use a *perfect infinitive*.

b/ Second example

- **P. Clodium meo consilio interfectum esse dixisti** YOU SAID THAT P. CLODIUS HAD BEEN KILLED BY MY CONTRIVANCE (Cicero, *Philippicae*).
  ⇨ The direct statement said by the person Cicero is addressing was probably something like this:
  - **P. Clodius tuo consilio *interfectus est*** P. CLODIUS HAS BEEN KILLED BY YOUR CONTRIVANCE.

  ⇨ **Interfectus est** is passive and perfect, so the infinitive in the indirect statement must be *passive and perfect*.

3. Where there is no change of subject [376]

a/ If the subject of the infinitive happens to be the same as that of the main verb and the infinitive has a predicative object, it is not necessary to add an accusative as subject of the infinitive; in this case, the predicative object, if any, will be in nominative:

- ***Bonus* volo iam ex hoc die esse** I WANT TO BE A GOOD PERSON NOW FROM THIS DAY ON (Plautus, *Persa*).
  ✧ The subject of **esse** is the same as the subject of **volo** (I), so there is no need to put the accusative **me** as subject of **esse** (in the same way as if we want to say I WANT TO EAT we will just say **Volo edere**, we do not need to say **Volo me edere**), and the predicative object **bonus** will be in *nominative*.

b/ But if the subject is mentioned, even if it is the same subject as the main verb, it must be in *accusative*, and the predicative object also:

- **Cupio ... *me* esse *clementem*** I WANT TO BE MERCIFUL (Cicero, *In Catilinam*).
  ✧ In other words: If Cicero had skipped the **me**, the predicative object would have been in nominative (there would have been no **me** with which to agree in case), and the sentence would have been **Cupio esse clemens**.

Another example using the 3rd person:

- **Clamabat ille miser *se civem* esse Romanum** THAT POOR MAN WAS SHOUTING THAT HE WAS A ROMAN CITIZEN (Cicero, *In Verrem*).

  ✧ **Se** is the same person as the subject of **clamabat**; as there is a **se** as subject of **esse**, the predicative object **civem** must be in accusative, like **se**.

4. Historical infinitive [377]

It is normal that in the course of a long narrative of continuous short events (for instance, the recount of a battle, with its non-stop stream of actions) the verbs that would be in past tense (usually imperfect tense) appear in *infinitive*, although usually the very last one of the events appears in imperfect.

Let's see a very long example and a short one:

- **Interea Catilina cum expeditis in prima acie *vorsari*, laborantibus *succurrere*, integros pro sauciis *arcessere*, omnia *providere*, multum ipse *pugnare*, saepe hostem *ferire*: strenui militis et boni imperatoris officia simul exequebatur** MEANWHILE CATILINA WAS GOING UP AND DOWN WITH HIS LIGHT TROOPS IN THE FIRST LINE, HE WAS HELPING THOSE WHO WERE STRUGGLING, REPLACING THE WOUNDED SOLDIERS WITH FRESH ONES, HE WAS PROVIDING EVERYTHING, HE HIMSELF WAS CHARGING, WOUNDING THE ENEMY OFTEN: HE WAS PERFORMING ATTHE SAME TIME THE DUTIES OF A BRAVE SOLDIER AND OF A GOOD GENERAL (Sallust, *Catilinae Coniuratio*).

  ✧ Observe that **exequebatur**, the very last one, is in *imperfect tense*.

- **Ego *instare* ut mihi responderet quis esset** (Cicero, *In Verrem*).

5. Exclamatory infinitive [378]

Usually accompanied by a subject in accusative, it expresses indignation, surprise, etc.:

- ***Me* hoc *videre*!** THAT I HAVE TO SEE THIS!
- ***Te* ... in tantas aerumnas propter me *incidisse*!** THAT YOU HAVE FALLEN INTO SUCH CALAMITIES BECAUSE OF ME! (Cicero, *Epistulae ad Familiares*).
- **Siculosne milites ... eo cibo *esse usos* !** THAT THE SOLDIERS OF SICILY HAVE GOT TO MAKE USE OF THAT FOOD! (Cicero, *In Verrem*).

  ✧ Cicero is complaining that, when Verres was governor of Sicily, the soldiers were compelled to eat anything but healthy food, when in fact Sicily was the main corn supplier for the whole of Italy.

  ✧ The addition of **-ne** (something usually used as an opening question mark) is normal in these exclamative sentences..

d) Participle clauses

1. General principles [379]

a/ If we have defined an infinitive as a verbal noun, we can define a participle as a *verbal adjective*. A participle tells us that the noun with which it agrees is executing (or will execute, or has received) the action expressed by it.

Observe this simple example:

- **Video puerum *altum*** I SEE A TALL BOY.

If we replace the adjective **altum** by a participle, let's say the present participle of **scribo**, we will have this sentence:

Video puerum *scribentem*.

The participle **scribentem** is an adjective (so, it agrees in gender, number and case with **puerum** as **altum** did), and therefore it is qualifying **puerum**; the way to translate a participle may be not as direct as expected: a Latin participle is only one word, but maybe we will need some kind of periphrasis to express the same in English. A relative clause is a very useful resource, and this example would mean

I SEE A BOY *THAT WRITES*.

- **Pilum in hostes inmittit atque *unum* ex multitudine *procurrentem* traicit** HE THROWS A SPEAR AGAINST THE ENEMY AND PIERCES ONE OF THE CROWD WHO WAS RUNNING UP (Caesar, *De Bello Gallico*).
  ✧ The case agreement makes it clear that who was running up was *one of the crowd*, not the crowd itself.

b/ The present participle can sometimes be translated by the English -ING form, if the context allows it: [380]

- **Video *puerum currentem*** I SEE THE BOY THAT RUNS / I SEE THE RUNNING BOY / I SEE THE BOY RUNNING.
  ✧ The case agreement of **currentem** with **puerum** makes it clear that the one who is running is *the boy*, not me; so, a translation like RUNNING, I SEE THE BOY would be wrong.
- ***Exeuntem filium* video *meum*** I SEE MY SON GOING OUT (Plautus, *Mercator*).

Note

Do not confuse this use of the -ING form (THE WRITING BOY, THE READING GIRL, THE ASTONISHING EVENT, etc.) with its use as a gerund (I HAVE ACHIEVED THIS *STUDYING* A LOT) or even replacing an infinitive (TO STUDY / *STUDYING* IS GOOD); this is a coincidence of three meanings of the -ING form in English.

c/ The passive perfect participle can be translated more easily by only one word, as it corresponds to the equivalent English participle:

- **Video pontem *deletum*** I SEE A DESTROYED BRIDGE.

d/ The future participles will need again a periphrasis to be translated:

- **Video puerum *scripturum*** I SEE A BOY THAT IS ABOUT TO WRITE.

2. The participle is impersonal [381]

We have seen that the participle, although it is a verbal form, is simply an adjective, therefore corresponds directly to the noun with which it agrees, whichever person it is. See these examples, in which the participle is in the nominative case, therefore providing information about the subject, whichever person it is (I, YOU, HE, etc.):

- Per urbem *ambulans*, amicum vidi — TAKING A WALK THROUGH THE CITY, I SAW MY FRIEND.
- Per urbem *ambulans*, amicum vidisti — TAKING A WALK THROUGH THE CITY, YOU SAW YOUR FRIEND.
- Per urbem *ambulans*, amicum vidit — TAKING A WALK THROUGH THE CITY, HE SAW HIS FRIEND.

In the following examples, the participle is in the *accusative* case, therefore providing information about the *direct object*, whichever person it is (I, YOU, HE, etc.):

- *Manilium* nos etiam vidimus ... *ambulantem* (Cicero, *De Oratore*). — WE ALSO SAW MANILIUS [WHEN HE WAS] TAKING A WALK
- *Eum* nos etiam vidimus *ambulantem* — WE ALSO SAW HIM [WHEN HE WAS] TAKING A WALK.
- *Te* nos etiam vidimus *ambulantem* — WE ALSO SAW YOU [WHEN YOU WERE] TAKING A WALK.

3. The temporal correlation [382]

a) Use of the present participle

1/ The use of the present participle indicates that the action takes place at the same time as the main verb (whether the main verb is present, past or future). Therefore, "present" means *simultaneous*, rather than *now*. For instance, let's see this sentence where the main verb is in the imperfect, but a present participle has been used:

- Multas litteras mittebam ad Caesarem in Gallia *pugnantem* — I USED TO SEND MANY LETTERS TO CAESAR WHEN HE WAS FIGHTING IN GAUL.

The participle is translated into English using the imperfect tense, but since it is in the present tense it signifies that the action expressed by the participle was taking place *at the same time* as the action of the main verb. Both actions take place simultaneously. More examples:

- Undique suis *laborantibus* succurrebant — THEY HELPED THEIR COMPANIONS WHO WERE STRUGGLING ON ALL SIDES (Caesar, *Bellum Civile*).
- Hic Quinctium simul *pugnantem* hortantemque suos, ... hasta transfigit — THIS MAN PIERCED WITH A SPEAR QUINCTIUS, WHO WAS AT THE SAME TIME FIGHTING AND ENCOURAGING HIS MEN (Livy, *Ab Urbe Condita*).

2/ In some cases, the action expressed by the participle is an action that takes place habitually (not only at one point in time), in which case the participle can be translated by the present tense even in a sentence where the main verb is in a past tense:

- Ego semper admirabar magistros bene *docentes* — I ALWAYS USED TO ADMIRE THE TEACHERS THAT TEACH / TAUGHT WELL.
- Petrus loquebatur semper de hominibus patriam *defendentibus* — PETER WAS ALWAYS TALKING ABOUT THE PEOPLE WHO DEFEND/DEFENDED THE HOMELAND.

b) Use of the future participle [383]

Aside from the other uses that will be studied subsequently, the future participle has the following two functions:

1/ The person / thing etc. to whom / which the participle refers is expected to perform the action *in the future*. Compare the following pairs:

- **Video hominem *scribentem*** I SEE A MAN WHO IS WRITING.
- **Video hominem *scripturum*** I SEE A MAN WHO WILL WRITE / WHO IS ABOUT TO WRITE.

- ***Pugnantes* milites cotidie exercent** THE SOLDIERS THAT FIGHT PRACTICE EVERY DAY.
- ***Pugnaturi* milites cotidie exercent** THE SOLDIERS THAT WILL FIGHT / THAT ARE ABOUT TO FIGHT PRACTICE EVERY DAY.

Note that *in the future* means the future time with respect to the moment in which the action of the main verb takes place. For instance:

- **Do arma mulieribus *pugnaturis*** I GIVE THE WEAPONS TO THE WOMEN WHO WILL FIGHT / WHO ARE ABOUT TO FIGHT.
- **Dedi arma mulieribus *pugnaturis*** I GAVE THE WEAPONS TO THE WOMEN WHO WOULD FIGHT / WHO WERE ABOUT TO FIGHT.

In the last sentence, if a future participle has been used, it means that the action of fighting was to take place *after* somebody had given the women the weapons; therefore, the English translation must be adapted to express this temporal relation.

Another example:

- **Nunc video puerum *scripturum*** NOW I SEE A BOY THAT IS ABOUT TO WRITE.
- **Heri vidi puerum *scripturum*** YESTERDAY I SAW A BOY THAT WAS ABOUT TO WRITE.

Scripturum is a future participle, which means that the action of the participle will take place after the action of the main verb, so the boy is not writing yet when we see him, but later, and we have to adapt the translation of the participle. Observe the translation of the second example: maybe the boy wrote something ten years ago, but in the very moment in which I saw him he had not written it yet; in that moment, when I saw him, he still had to write it, so the action of writing was future *then*, no matter if it is a past action with respect to now.

A more complicated example:

- **Nunc video hominem *moriturum*** NOW I SEE A MAN WHO IS GOING TO DIE.
- **Cras videbo hominem *moriturum*** TOMORROW I WILL SEE A MAN WHO WILL (BE GOING TO) DIE.

Moriturum is a future participle, so it means that this action will take place after the action of the main verb; if the main verb is already a future action, then the action of the participle means "still more future", and the translation must reflect it somehow.

A couple of original examples:

- **Cui consuli in Hispaniam *ituro* haec prodigia acciderunt** TO THIS CONSUL, WHEN HE WAS ABOUT TO GO TO HISPANIA, THESE PORTENTS HAPPENED (Valerius Maximus, *Facta et Dicta Memorabilia*).

  ✧ In this example, the future participle accompanies a noun (**consuli**).

- ... ut alienos equos *pugnaturis* distribuat ... SO THAT HE MAY DISTRIBUTE OTHER PEOPLE'S HORSES TO THOSE GOING TO FIGHT (Curtius Rufus, *Historiae Alexandri Magni*).
  ✧ In this example, the future participle does not accompany any noun, so we must add the term THOSE to the translation in order to make it make sense.

2/ The other use is when the future participle has a *purpose meaning* (IN ORDER TO): **[384]**

- Galli multitudine ingenti ad Clusium venerunt legionem Romanam castraque *oppugnaturi* THE GAULS CAME TO CLUSIUM IN A LARGE NUMBER IN ORDER TO FIGHT THE ROMAN LEGION AND THE CAMP (Livy, *Ab Urbe Condita*).
- Ipse per agrum Campanum mare inferum petit, *oppugnaturus* Neapolim HE HIMSELF GOES THROUGH THE FIELD OF CAMPANIA TOWARDS THE LOWER SEA IN ORDER TO BESIEGE NAPLES (Livy, *Ab Urbe Condita*).

In the following example, the future participle is in the passive voice, which always compels us to make some hard adaptation of the translation, sometimes really far away from the literal translation:

- Postquam oppressam metu civitatem vidit, advocat consilium de *oppugnandis* Argis AFTER HE SAW THE CITY OPPRESSED BY FEAR, HE CALLED THE COUNCIL [IN ORDER TO DEBATE] ABOUT THE BESIEGING OF ARGOS (Livy, *Ab Urbe Condita*).
  ✧ Literally, it says ... ABOUT ARGOS THAT MUST BE BESIEGED.

3/ A very important use of the future participle is found in the so-called periphrastic conjugation (also called Periphrastic Construction). This is dealt with in another chapter.

c) Use of the perfect (or past) participle **[385]**

1/ The perfect participle is used frequently, especially to indicate an action that has taken place *before* the action mentioned by the main verb, and let's remember that there is only perfect *passive* participle, there is no perfect active participle (except in the case of the deponent verbs, dealt with in the corresponding chapter). Obviously, here we will have a look at the use of the perfect participle when used on its own, not to its use when forming the passive voice of some tenses that make use of this participle in order to form it.

- Reliquias eum esse duorum exercituum ante paucos dies *deletorum* succurrebat IT CAME TO HIS MIND THAT THESE WERE THE REMNANTS OF THE TWO ARMIES WIPED OUT A FEW DAYS BEFORE (Livy, *Ab Urbe Condita*).
  ✧ Idiomatic expression: me succurrit IT COMES TO MY MIND.
- Undecim volumina epistularum, ... ad Atticum *missarum* ELEVEN VOLUMES OF LETTERS, SENT TO ATTICUS (Nepos, *Vitae*).

It is very usual that the participle appears on its own, with a fitting noun to be supplied:

- De ... *necatis* plura dicenda sunt ABOUT THE KILLED ONES MORE DETAILS MUST BE MENTIONED (Cicero, *Pro Rabirio*).

2/ When a perfect participle is used, the entirety of the sentence does not necessarily have to refer to past events. Indeed, it may concern the future:

- Tibi dabo *scriptum* librum I WILL WRITE THE BOOK AND I WILL GIVE IT TO YOU.
  ✧ Literally, I WILL GIVE YOU THE WRITTEN BOOK.

Maybe I have not written it yet, but whenever I may have written it I will give it to you; it is obvious that the event of the participle will already belong to the past (the book will have already been written) whenever the event of the main verb (I will give the book to you) may take place.

3/ We find an important use of the perfect participle in the construction of the *ablative absolute*, dealt with further down.

4. Participle as a verb [386]

a) It can have objects

1/ We should insist on the fact that a participle is an adjective, but at the same time it goes on being a verb (like the infinitive is a noun but at the same time is also a verb), and as a verb it may have the same kind of objects it may have when used as the verb of a sentence.

So, if we retake the simple example of the beginning above, **Video puerum scribentem** I SEE A BOY THAT WRITES, we can make the participle a direct object:

- **Video puerum scribentem** ***librum*** I SEE A BOY THAT WRITES A BOOK.

We can make it have also an indirect object, or a prepositional object:

- **Video puerum scribentem librum** ***tibi*** I SEE A BOY THAT WRITES A BOOK FOR YOU.
- **Carmen** ***in Iunonem reginam*** **canentes ibant** (Livy, *Ab Urbe Condita*). THEY WALKED SINGING A SONG IN HONOUR OF GODDESS IUNO

2/ As a general rule, the participle and any object depending on it is what is usually called a *participial clause.* A participle alone, as in **Video puerum** ***scribentem***, is in fact a participial clause without any object, but we use the expression *participial clause* usually when we have a participle and at least some object depending on it.

Some examples by Cicero:

- ***Quibuscum*** **me, iudices,** ***pugnantem more meo pristino*** **non videbitis** YOU WILL NOT SEE ME, O JUDGES, FIGHTING WITH THESE MEN IN MY FORMER FASHION (Cicero, *Pro Plancio*).
  - ✧ This participle has two objects depending on it: **Quibuscum** and **more meo pristino**. The participial clause would be the participle and anything that depends on it: **Quibuscum ... pugnantem more meo pristino.**
  - ✧ It is not unusual that part of the participial clause appears before the participle itself; in fact, in this case it happens because **Quibuscum** is a connecting relative and a connecting relative must appear at the very beginning of the sentence.
- ***Redeuntem a cena*** **senem saepe videbam** I OFTEN SAW THE OLD MAN COMING BACK FROM DINNER (Cicero, *Cato Maior de Senectute*).
  - ✧ In this example, **a cena** depends on **redeuntem**.
- **Quid aut de Codro dubitare possumus aut de ceteris qui** ***pugnantes pro patriae libertate*** **ceciderunt?** WHAT DOUBT MAY WE HAVE ABOUT CODRUS OR ABOUT THE OTHERS WHO FELL FIGHTING FOR THE FREEDOM OF THEIR COUNTRY? (Cicero, *De Natura Deorum*).
  - ✧ **Pro patriae libertate** depends on the participle **pugnantes**.

b) Replacing the infinitive [387]

In some cases in which we would normally use the infinitive, for instance in

- Video te *scribere* I SEE THAT YOU WRITE

we can use the participle (making it agree with the necessary object):

- Video te *scribentem* I SEE YOU WRITING.

The difference is that in the second sentence we emphasise the physical perception, I DO SEE YOU IN THE VERY MOMENT WHEN YOU ARE WRITING.

c) It can be translated by a subordinate clause [388]

1/ Sometimes translating the participle in the simple ways we have seen up to now may produce an unnatural sentence; observe this example:

Caesar *victum* Sextum Romam misit.

We could translate it as CAESAR SENT THE *DEFEATED* SEXTUS TO ROME, but this does not sound natural, we should rather translate it as CAESAR SENT SEXTUS TO ROME AFTER DEFEATING HIM. The participle is a past participle, so it is obvious that Sextus was first defeated and, later, Caesar sent him to Rome (we assume that the person who defeated him was Caesar). So, we have transformed the participle into a *temporal clause* (observe that we have to change the structure upside down: the participle was a passive one, but there is no sign of the passive voice in the new translation, etc.).

Let's see another example:

Urbem *captam* Caesari dux dabit.

Option 1: The direct meaning is THE GENERAL WILL GIVE TO CAESAR THE CAPTURED CITY, and this will be a perfect translation if the general has already captured it and he is deciding what to do with it.

Option 2: But supposing that the battle has not taken place yet (so, the city has not been captured yet) and that these are just the plans that the general has if he captures it, we could translate the participle by a *conditional clause* : IF HE CAPTURES THE CITY, THE GENERAL WILL GIVE IT TO CAESAR (observe again that we have got to introduce strong changes in the structure).

An example form Cicero:

- Non multo ante urbem *captam* exaudita vox est a luco Vestae NOT LONG BEFORE THE CITY WAS CAPTURED A VOICE WAS HEARD COMING FROM THE SACRED WOOD OF VESTA (Cicero, *De Divinatione*).
  ✧ In this case, we have transformed the prepositional object into a temporal subordinate clause.

2/ A future participle can be translated by a *purpose clause* : [389]

- Mei amici venerunt *visuri* urbem MY FRIENDS CAME (IN ORDER) TO SEE THE CITY.
  ✧ In fact there would be no way of giving a direct translation; anything like MY FRIENDS CAME THAT WOULD SEE THE CITY would not make any sense.

Also if it is passive:

- **Tibi dabo librum *legendum*** I WILL GIVE YOU A BOOK TO READ / I WILL GIVE YOU A BOOK SO THAT YOU MAY READ IT.
  ✧ The direct translation I WILL GIVE YOU A BOOK THAT MUST BE READ would sound unnatural, unless we mean a book that is worth reading.
- **Dabo meum testamentum *legendum* cui voluerit** I WILL GIVE MY LAST WILL TO READ TO WHOMEVER WANTS / I WILL GIVE MY LAST WILL TO WHOMEVER WANTS, SO THAT HE MAY READ IT (Cicero, *Epistulae ad Atticum*).

3/ Sometimes we must even use the resource of forming an abstract noun of the action expressed in the participle and then making the necessary changes to reflect the sense; observe this example: [390]

Semper de Caesare necato loquitur.

Literally, it means HE IS ALWAYS TALKING ABOUT CAESAR MURDERED, but a more natural translation could be HE IS ALWAYS TALKING ABOUT THE MURDER OF CAESAR.

And let's remember the famous title: **Ab urbe *condita*** (Livy's book title). Literally, it means FROM THE FOUNDED CITY, but a more natural translation would be FROM THE FOUNDATION OF THE CITY.

An example from Sallust:

- **Ante Carthaginem *deletam* populus et senatus Romanus placide modesteque inter se rem publicam tractabant** BEFORE THE DESTRUCTION OF CARTHAGE, THE SENATE AND THE ROMAN PEOPLE RULED THE REPUBLIC WITH CALM AND MODERATION AMONG THEM (Sallust, *Bellum Iugurthinum*).

5. Participle as a noun [391]

a) Use and meaning

1/ We know that any adjective can be used on its own, without any noun, and adopting therefore the role of noun:

- ***Boni* Romam non produnt** GOOD PEOPLE DO NOT BETRAY ROME.
  ✧ No need to say **Boni cives** GOOD CITIZENS, for instance.

Being an adjective, a participle can do the same:

- **Necesse est [homines] patriam *defendentes* laudare** PEOPLE WHO DEFEND THEIR HOMELAND MUST BE PRAISED.
  ✧ We can easily get rid of **homines** and the sentence will keep its meaning.
- **Miseris et *laborantibus* negare nihil possumus** WE CAN DENY NOTHING TO THE POOR PEOPLE AND TO THOSE WHO STRUGGLE (Cicero, *Pro Plancio*).

2/ In any case, sometimes we must keep the noun to avoid losing precision:

- **Necesse est *milites* patriam *defendentes* laudare** SOLDIERS WHO DEFEND THEIR HOMELAND MUST BE PRAISED.
  ✧ We can get rid of **milites**, but then we lose the precision that we mean SOLDIERS, not just people in general.

3/ Sometimes we can use English nouns to translate participles (if used on their own):

- *Legentes* semper in bibliotheca sunt — READERS ARE ALWAYS IN THE LIBRARY.
  ✧ No need to translate **Legentes** by THOSE WHO READ.
- *Gesta* Augusti narrare volo — I WANT TO NARRATE THE EXPLOITS OF AUGUSTUS.
  ✧ No need to translate **Gesta** by THE DONE THINGS.
- Quam facile irati verbo mutantur *amantes* (Propertius, *Elegiae*). — HOW EASILY LOVERS CHANGE BECAUSE OF AN ANGRY WORD!

b) Also as nouns they can have objects [392]

As expected, these substantivised participles can also have objects (as they continue being verbs):

- *Currentes* per bibliothecam molestiam legentibus afferunt — THOSE WHO RUN THROUGH THE LIBRARY DISTURB THE READERS.
  ✧ Observe that in this case the translation by THOSE WHO RUN for the first participle makes more sense than THE RUNNERS; for the second participle, we could have left THOSE WHO READ.
- Carmina *scribentes* semper domi sunt — WRITERS OF POEMS ARE ALWAYS AT HOME.
  ✧ Observe how the translation of **scribentes** by WRITERS compels us to translate **Carmina** preceded by OF. If we had kept the translation as THOSE WHO WRITE, this would not have been necessary.

6. The ablative absolute [393]

a) Normal use

1/ There is a special construction in Latin that consists of a participle and a noun, both of them in ablative and grammatically disconnected from the rest of the sentence; it is called an *ablative absolute* (from **absolutus** DISCONNECTED), and it informs us of the circumstances adjacent to the action expressed in the main sentence. Almost always the ablative absolute will be the equivalent of a *temporal* or a *causal* clause:

Duce necato, milites fugerunt.

The main sentence **milites fugerunt** is really simple: THE SOLDIERS FLED. With respect to **Duce necato** (the noun GENERAL and the passive past participle KILLED), it is telling us that there is (or was) a general and that he has been killed; the participle is past, so this action has taken place before the action of the main sentence.

The most direct way of translating it would be: KILLED THE GENERAL, ...

✧ Note: KILLED in *participial* sense as in WRITTEN, not in perfect tense sense as in WROTE.

From here on, we can make use of several possibilities:

THE GENERAL HAVING BEEN KILLED, ...
AFTER THE GENERAL HAD BEEN KILLED, ...
WHEN THE GENERAL HAD BEEN KILLED, ...
AS THE GENERAL HAD BEEN KILLED, ...

We can even make use of a noun derived from the verbal meaning of the participle:

AFTER THE GENERAL'S *DEATH*, ...

Let's see a couple of examples from Caesar, in which the final translation makes use of the device of making the subject of the main sentence also the subject of the ablative absolute:

- *Cognito* Caesaris *adventu*, Ariovistus legatos ad eum mittit AFTER HEARING OF CAESAR'S ARRIVAL, ARIOVISTUS SENDS AMBASSADORS TO HIM (Caesar, *De Bello Gallico*).
  - ✧ Literally, CAESAR'S ARRIVAL HAVING BEEN KNOWN, ARIOVISTUS SENDS AMBASSADORS TO HIM.
- *Hoc responso dato* discessit HAVING GIVEN THIS ANSWER, HE DEPARTED (Caesar, *De Bello Gallico*).
  - ✧ Literally, THIS ANSWER HAVING BEEN GIVEN, HE DEPARTED.

2/ Let's suppose now the same sentence as before, but with the main verb in future tense: [394]

Duce necato, milites *fugent*.

Now the main sentence means THE SOLDIERS WILL FLEE. The participle goes on being past, which means that its action (that the general has died) must have taken place before the action of the main verb (the soldiers fleeing). Not all of the former possible translations would be valid now; some possible translations would be (observe that some of the translations are a whole subordinate clause):

THE GENERAL HAVING BEEN KILLED,	THE SOLDIERS WILL FLEE.
AFTER THE GENERAL HAS BEEN KILLED,	THE SOLDIERS WILL FLEE.
AS THE GENERAL HAS BEEN KILLED,	THE SOLDIERS WILL FLEE.
WHEN THE GENERAL HAS BEEN KILLED,	THE SOLDIERS WILL FLEE.
AFTER THE GENERAL'S DEATH,	THE SOLDIERS WILL FLEE.

✧ Observe that some of them suppose that the general has already died, other suppose that he will probably die at some point in the future; context should help to choose.

3/ Let's see now an example with a present participle: [395]

Puero legente, in horto ludebamus.

The main sentence means WE WERE PLAYING IN THE GARDEN. With respect to **Puero legente**, this construction tells us of the existence of a boy and of his action of reading; the participle is present, so the action of reading must take place at the same time as the action of the main clause.

A possible translation would be: WHILE THE BOY WAS READING, WE WERE PLAYING IN THE GARDEN (observe the verb WAS: it makes clear that both actions, *the boy reading* and *us playing in the garden*, take place at the same time).

As any participle, participles that form an ablative absolute can also have their own objects (they continue being verbs):

- *Puero* librum tibi *scribente*, in horto ludebamus WHILE THE BOY WAS WRITING A BOOK FOR YOU, WE WERE PLAYING IN THE GARDEN.

4/ Now let's see the same example but with the main verb in present tense:

Puero legente, in horto *ludimus*.

The main sentence now means *we are playing in the garden*, so that in order to make clear that both actions happen at the same time (because the participle is in present tense) the ablative absolute should now be translated as *While the boy is reading*. Observe that the ablative absolute is the same one in both examples, present tense in both, but (as happens with any participle, whether ablative absolute or not) we must adapt the translation to make both actions keep their temporal relationship.

An example from Livy:

- Forte *potantibus* his apud Sex. Tarquinium, ... incidit de uxoribus mentio BY CHANCE, WHILE THEY WERE HAVING DRINKS AT THE TENT OF SEXTUS TARQUINIUS, ... THEY STARTED TALKING ABOUT THEIR WIVES (Livy, *Ab Urbe Condita*).

5/ The use of a future participle in an ablative absolute is not common, but we offer an example: [396]

Patre ituro Romam, servi omnia parant.

The main sentence means THE SLAVES PREPARE EVERYTHING. The ablative absolute tells us of a father and of his going to Rome; the participle is future, which means that his going to Rome must happen after the action of the main verb (the slaves preparing everything). To reflect this temporal relationship, we can translate it so:

AS THE FATHER IS ABOUT TO GO TO ROME, THE SLAVES PREPARE EVERYTHING.
WHEN THE FATHER IS ABOUT TO GO TO ROME, THE SLAVES PREPARE EVERYTHING.
WITH THE FATHER ABOUT TO GO TO ROME, THE SLAVES PREPARE EVERYTHING.
BEFORE THE FATHER GOES TO ROME, THE SLAVES PREPARE EVERYTHING.

✧ Note that in none of the possible translations of ituro have we used the English future tense, but the expression of this action taking place after the main one is achieved by other means: *to be about to...*, *before...*, etc.

6/ Important: The noun of the ablative absolute can not be part of the main sentence; for instance, if we want to say [397]

YESTERDAY I SAW QUINTUS WHILE HE WAS WORKING IN THE FIELD

it would be wrong to translate it as

Quinto in agro *laborante* heri vidi

because QUINTUS is the direct object of I SAW in the English sentence, it is part of the main clause, it is not "disconnected" from it and so it can not be part of an ablative absolute. This Latin sentence would mean WHILE QUINTUS WAS WORKING IN THE FIELD, I SAW... (I saw what / whom?). The right sentence would be

Quintum in agro *laborantem* heri vidi.

The sentence

- *Quinto* in agro *laborante* Petrum heri vidi YESTERDAY I SAW PETER WHILE QUINTUS WAS WORKING IN THE FIELD

would be right, as now QUINTUS has nothing to do with I SAW.

Note

The noun in ablative can be referred to as the "subject" of the participle; it seems strange to call something that is in ablative a subject, but from a functional point of view it would be the subject if the ablative absolute were a whole sentence: QUINTUS WAS WORKING IN THE FIELD, THE BOY IS READING, etc.).

b) The type *Cicerone consule* [398]

1/ Let's suppose that we want to translate in Latin

WHILE CICERO WAS CONSUL, THE CITIZENS WERE HAPPY.

The main sentence would be something as simple as **cives laeti erant**. We can translate WHILE CICERO WAS CONSUL by means of an ablative absolute, all we need to say is CICERO in ablative, CONSUL in ablative, and the present participle of **sum** in ablative (so, we will be saying something like CICERO BEING CONSUL, ...):

Cicerone consule ...

Problem: The verb **sum** does not have a present participle. The solution is really simple: leave the translation as it is, with only the subject and the predicative object in ablative and without any participle (we can not put a participle that does not exist). The final sentence would then look like

***Cicerone consule*, cives laeti erant.**

Cicerone consule can be translated in several ways:

WITH CICERO AS CONSUL,...
CICERO BEING CONSUL, ...
WHEN CICERO WAS CONSUL, ...
DURING THE CONSULSHIP OF CICERO, ...

✧ Observe in the last translation the use of a noun, CONSULSHIP, and the corresponding adaptation of the rest of the translation.

A couple of examples from Cicero:

- **Fuit adsiduus mecum *praetore me*** HE WAS ALWAYS AT MY SIDE WHEN I WAS PRAETOR (Cicero, *Pro Caelio*).
- ***Te praetore* Siculi milites palmarum stirpibus ... alebantur** WHEN YOU WERE PRAETOR, SOLDIERS IN SICILY WERE FED WITH PALM-TREE ROOTS (Cicero, *In Verrem*).

2/ This system was widely used by writers to specify the year during the late period of the Republic, in which two [399]
consuls were in office simultaneously: rather than saying the number of the year, they said the name of the two consuls in office on that year:

***Marco et Antonio consulibus*, respublica magno in periculo erat.**
✧ Observe that **consulibus** must be in plural, agreeing with two subjects.

Possible translations:

WHEN M. AND A. WERE CONSULS, THE STATE WAS IN GREAT DANGER.
IN THE YEAR WHEN M. AND A. WERE CONSULS, THE STATE WAS IN GREAT DANGER.
DURING THE CONSULSHIP OF M. AND A., THE STATE WAS IN GREAT DANGER.

An example of this in Caesar:

- Is *M. Messalla et M. Pisone consulibus* ... coniurationem nobilitatis fecit HE, DURING THE CONSULSHIP OF M. MESSALLA AND M. PISO, ... FORMED A CONSPIRACY OF THE NOBILITY (Caesar, *De Bello Gallico*).

> **Note**
>
> In some books, the name *ablative absolute* is reserved for only this specific type of ablative absolute without participle (because of the lack of a present participle for **sum**), and the other ablative absolute uses we have seen (those in which there is a participle, like **puero legente**) are then called *participle absolute*.

c) Reasons for its abundance [400]

It will be observed that Latin makes a wide use of the ablative absolute with the passive past participle, and this has a simple explanation. The use of a time clause to express an event previous to that of the main verb is very common in any language; let's suppose that we want to translate this sentence into Latin:

AFTER WRITING THE BOOK, CAESAR WENT INTO THE SENATE.

As we know, the table of participles is this one (taking the verb **scribo** as a paradigm):

	Present	*Past*	*Future*
Active	**scribens, -ntis** WRITING, THAT WRITES	non-existent	**scripturus, -a, -um** THAT IS ABOUT TO WRITE
Passive	non-existent	**scriptus, -a, -um** THAT HAS BEEN WRITTEN	**scribendus, -a, -um** THAT MUST BE WRITTEN

We could translate AFTER WRITING THE BOOK by means of a time clause, **Postquam librum scripsit**, but if we want to make use of a participle we find that there is not an active past participle that would mean HAVING WRITTEN and that would agree with CAESAR. So, the only solution (if we want to use a participle) is to restructure the whole sentence this way:

- *Libro scripto*, Caesar in Senatum ivit Literally: THE BOOK HAVING BEEN WRITTEN, CAESAR WENT INTO THE SENATE.

In the new construction, **libro** THE BOOK has nothing to do with what is the main sentence, so we use an ablative absolute. Of course, when translating from Latin we should avoid these rough translations in the style of THE BOOK HAVING BEEN WRITTEN. Let's see an example:

- *Ponte deleto*, milites cenam parare coeperunt.
  - ➪ Literal translation: THE BRIDGE HAVING BEEN DESTROYED, THE SOLDIERS STARTED TO PREPARE DINNER.
  - ➪ More natural translation: AFTER DESTROYING THE BRIDGE, THE SOLDIERS STARTED TO PREPARE DINNER.

Observe again how the lack of an active past participle that would have meant HAVING DESTROYED THE BRIDGE and that would have agreed with **milites** compels Latin to rephrase the structure if we want to use a participle. The lack of an active past participle is what makes Latin have so many ablative absolutes.

d) Common expressions [401]

The use of the ablative absolute was so common that some uses of it became fixed idioms. Some examples of these expressions are:

proelio facto	AFTER THE BATTLE	✧ Literally,	THE BATTLE HAVING BEEN DONE
me puero	WHEN I WAS A CHILD	✧ Literally,	ME BEING A CHILD
his nuntiatis	AFTER THIS HAD BEEN ANNOUNCED	✧ Literally,	THESE THINGS HAVING BEEN ANNOUNCED
me absente	WHILE I WAS ABSENT	✧ Literally,	ME BEING ABSENT

Let's see some examples:

- In aedis meas *me absente* neminem volo intro mitti I DO NOT WANT ANYBODY TO BE SENT INTO MY HOUSE WHILE I AM ABSENT (Plautus, *Aulularia*).
- Itaque Pharsalico *proelio facto* a Pompeio discessit THEREFORE, AFTER THE BATTLE OF PHARSALIA HAD TAKEN PLACE, HE DEPARTED FROM POMPEIUS (Cicero, *Pro Rege Deiotaro*).
- *His rebus* in Italiam Caesari *nuntiatis*, ... in Transalpinam Galliam profectus est WHEN THIS NEWS WAS BROUGHT TO ITALY TO CAESAR, HE DEPARTED TO TRANSALPINE GAUL (Caesar, *De Bello Gallico*).

e) Indirect speech

1. General remarks [402]

a) Concept of indirect speech

1/ Indirect speech is the reproduction of somebody's words, the reproduction of a former direct speech; for instance:

- Direct speech: I WANT TO GO HOME.
- Indirect speech: HE / SHE SAYS THAT HE / SHE WANTS TO GO HOME
  I SAY THAT I WANT TO GO HOME
  I SAID THAT I WANTED TO GO HOME
  etc.

As we can see, the introducer of the indirect speech does not have to be the same person as the one who made the direct speech: I myself can reproduce what I said, or somebody else can reproduce what I said, or I can reproduce somebody else's words, etc.

2/ Nevertheless, as a general rule, it is admitted that indirect speech does not always mean that somebody has said some words and that later somebody else (or the same person) reproduces them, because in the concept of *indirect speech* we include also the reproduction of somebody's thought.

If somebody says I SAID THAT OUR SOLDIERS WOULD WIN TODAY ... ✧ Indirect speech
... it is obvious that at some point somebody had said OUR SOLDIERS WILL WIN TODAY. ✧ Direct speech

But I can say I *THOUGHT* THAT OUR SOLDIERS WOULD WIN TODAY.

This is also indirect speech, but there is no verb of *saying*; I am not reproducing any former direct speech because none was made. In fact I am just reproducing somebody's thought (my own, in this example), which, in case it had been orally expressed, would indeed have been OUR SOLDIERS WILL WIN TODAY.

b) Parts of indirect speech [403]

1/ **Indirect statement clauses:** The examples we have been using up to now are reproductions of somebody's words, thought, etc. We reproduce a former statement (or an imaginary former statement). They will usually be introduced by expressions of the kind I THINK THAT..., HE SAID THAT..., etc. Strictly speaking, the indirect statement, obviously, is just what comes from the THAT on, and I THINK / HE SAID etc. is in fact the main clause.

2/ **Indirect question clauses:** As their name indicates, it is the reproduction of a former question; see this example:

- Direct question: WHERE IS CAESAR?
- Indirect question: HE ASKED WHERE CAESAR WAS.

Strictly speaking, HE ASKED is the main clause, and WHERE CAESAR WAS is the indirect question.

As in the indirect statement, we can find a sentence that includes an indirect question and maybe this question was in fact never asked in a direct way; for instance, I can say TELL ME WHERE CAESAR IS, or TELL ME WHETHER YOU HAVE WON, and maybe nobody has asked previously WHERE IS CAESAR? or HAVE YOU WON?

3/ **Indirect command clauses:** The reproduction of somebody's orders; for instance:

⇨ Direct command: DO NOT KILL THE PRISONERS!
⇨ Indirect command: HE ORDERED THEM NOT TO KILL THE PRISONERS

As expected, NOT TO KILL THE PRISONERS is the indirect command, and HE ORDERED THEM is the main clause.

2. Indirect statement clauses [404]

a) Main concept

1/ As seen in the examples, it is the reproduction of a former statement or of somebody's thought. The way Latin expresses an indirect statement is by means of the *accusative + infinitive* construction: the subject of the original statement must be put in accusative and the verb must be put in infinitive.

The most important point is that the tense of the original statement must be kept. For example, let's suppose that somebody says **Urbs deleta est** THE CITY HAS BEEN DESTROYED.

Supposing, for instance, that somebody (let's say Caesar) wants to inform us about it, the steps to put this direct statement in the indirect statement form CAESAR SAYS THAT THE CITY HAS BEEN DESTROYED will be:

⇨ **Urbs** must be written in *accusative*: **urbem**.

⇨ **deleta est** is a past tense in passive voice, so we will have to use the *passive past infinitive* for the indirect statement. The passive past infinitive for the verb **deleo** is **deletum, -am, -um + esse**; as the participial part of this compound infinitive must agree with the accusative **urbem**, we will choose the option **deletam esse**.

The final result will be **Caesar dicit *urbem deletam esse.***

Another example:

Supposing that the direct statement had been **Galli urbem delebunt** THE GAULS WILL DESTROY THE CITY, the steps to follow to reach the indirect statement CAESAR SAYS THAT THE GAULS WILL DESTROY THE CITY would be:

⇨ **Galli** moves into *accusative*: **Gallos**.

⇨ **Delebunt**, a future active indicative, moves into *future active infinitive*; the future active infinitive of the verb **deleo** is **deleturum, -am, -um + esse**; as it must agree with **Gallos**, we will choose the option **deleturos esse**.

The final result will be **Caesar dicit *Gallos urbem deleturos esse.***

Let's see a simple original example:

- ***Civis Romanos necatos esse* arguo** I ASSERT THAT ROMAN CITIZENS HAVE BEEN KILLED (Cicero, *In Verrem*).

And now a double example:

- ... **unde audissent** ***imperatores Romanos in Asia captos [esse] ab Antiocho rege et exercitum deletum esse*** ... FROM WHERE THEY HEARD THAT THE ROMAN COMMANDERS IN ASIA HAD BEEN CAPTURED BY THE KING ANTIOCHUS AND THAT THE ARMY HAD BEEN DESTROYED (Livy, *Ab Urbe Condita*).
  ✧ The omission of **esse** when using a compound infinitive is very common.

2/ Remember also that an indirect statement does not always need to come from a direct one, especially if it reflects some thought: **[405]**

- **Neque ego** ***umquam fuisse tale monstrum in terris ullum*** **puto** AND I DO NOT THINK THAT THERE HAS EVER BEEN SUCH A MONSTER ON THE EARTH (Cicero, *Pro Caelio*).

Cicero is expressing what he thinks; the presence of an indirect statement (THAT THERE HAS EVER BEEN SUCH A MONSTER ON THE EARTH) does not mean that somebody at some point expressed orally the direct statement **Numquam fuit tale monstrum in terris ullum** THERE HAS NEVER BEEN SUCH A MONSTER ON THE EARTH.

A final example:

- **Cuius causa** ***scriptam esse legem*** **putatis?** BECAUSE OF WHOM DO YOU THINK THAT THE LAW WAS WRITTEN? (Fabius Quintilianus, *Declamationes Minores*).

b) Translation **[406]**

We must remember that the translation of the infinitive into English must be adapted to its relationship with the introductory verb. For instance, let's see the example **Dux urbem delebit** THE GENERAL WILL DESTROY THE CITY introduced by different tenses:

- **Caesar** ***dicit*** **ducem urbem deleturum esse** CAESAR SAYS THAT THE GENERAL WILL DESTROY THE CITY.
- **Caesar** ***dixit*** **ducem urbem deleturum esse** CAESAR SAID THAT THE GENERAL WOULD DESTROY THE CITY.

Observe that we have got to adapt the translation of the Latin future infinitive. It has not changed in Latin, but the sense of *future with respect to the main verb* must be reflected in the translation.

Let's see an example from Sallust:

- **Iturum [esse] se** ***dixit*** HE SAID THAT HE WOULD GO (Sallust, *Catilinae Coniuratio*).
  ✧ The omission of **esse** when using a compound infinitive is very common.

More examples, with a past infinitive:

- **Cives** ***dicunt*** **Pompeium victum esse** THE CITIZENS SAY THAT POMPEIUS HAS BEEN DEFEATED.
- **Cives** ***dixerunt*** **Pompeium victum esse** THE CITIZENS SAID THAT POMPEIUS HAD BEEN DEFEATED.
  ✧ Observe again how we have to change the English tense to make clear the condition of *past with respect to the main verb*: in the moment they said it, Pompeius had already been defeated.
- **Catilina ubi eos, quos paulo ante memoravi, convenisse** ***videt*** ... CATILINA, WHEN HE SEES THAT THOSE I HAVE MENTIONED ABOVE HAVE / HAD GATHERED ... (Sallust, *Catilinae Coniuratio*).
  ✧ The infinitive clause has a relative clause inside. This is quite normal.

c) Negative statement [407]

Dico must not be used with the negative non in the reproduced statement; if we wish to express I SAY THAT ... NOT..., we must replace dico by nego I DENY:

⇨ Direct statement:	Caesar non venit	CAESAR HAS NOT COME.
⇨ *Wrong* indirect statement:	Dico Caesarem non venisse	I SAY THAT CAESAR HAS NOT COME.
⇨ *Right* indirect statement:	Nego Caesarem venisse	I SAY THAT CAESAR HAS NOT COME. ✧ Literally, I DENY THAT CAESAR HAS COME.

¤ But Non dico Caesarem venisse would be a perfectly right sentence, as in this case what we are denying is the introductory verb and what we are saying is I DO NOT SAY THAT CAESAR HAS COME, in the sense of "I AM SAYING SOMETHING ELSE, BUT NOT THIS".

A couple of examples from Sallust and Cicero:

- Ille animo feroci *negat* se totiens fusum Numidam pertimescere HE, WITH FIERCE SPIRIT, SAYS THAT HE DOES NOT FEAR THE NUMIDIAN, SO MANY TIMES DEFEATED (Sallust, *Bellum Iugurthinum*).
- *Negavit* umquam se bibisse iucundius HE SAID THAT HE HAD NEVER DRUNK SO HAPPILY (Cicero, *Tusculanae Disputationes*).

d) Verbs that can be followed by an indirect statement [408]

This list is not exhaustive, but the most frequent verbs that can introduce an indirect statement are:

affirmo, -are, -avi, -atum	TO DECLARE	nego, -are, -avi, -atum	TO DENY
arbitror, -ari, arbitratus sum	TO THINK	nescio, -ire, -ivi (no supine)	NOT TO KNOW
audio, -ire, -ivi, -itum	TO HEAR	nuntio, -are, -avi, -atum	TO ANNOUNCE
cognosco, -ere, cognovi, cognitum	TO ASCERTAIN	puto, -are, -avi, -atum	TO THINK
credo, -ere, credidi, creditum	TO BELIEVE	reor, reri, ratus sum	TO THINK
dico, -ere, dixi, dictum	TO SAY	scio, -ire, -ivi, -itum	TO KNOW
existimo, -are, -avi, -atum	TO THINK	sentio, -ire, -ivi, -itum	TO PERCEIVE
intellego, -ere, intellexi, intellectum	TO UNDERSTAND	video, -ere, vidi, visum	TO SEE

3. Indirect command clauses [409]

[The terms *command* and *order* are used indistinctly here.]

a) Indirect commands

1/ They are expressed by means of ut + subjunctive; if the introductory verb is a primary tense, we will use the present subjunctive; if it is a secondary tense, the imperfect subjunctive.

In other words: they will have the same structure as purpose clauses. Let's see an example:

⇨ Direct order:	Veni!	COME!
⇨ Indirect order (intr. verb in *primary* tense):	Mihi imperat *ut veniam*	HE ORDERS ME TO COME.
⇨ Indirect order (intr. verb in *secondary* tense):	Mihi imperavit *ut venirem*	HE ORDERED ME TO COME.

Observe that in both cases we have translated the **ut** + subjunctive by an English infinitive, but the Latin form is a subjunctive, and moreover different in each sentence, depending on the introductory verb.

Two original examples:

- **Allobrogibus imperavit *ut* iis frumenti copiam *facerent*** HE ORDERED THE ALLOBROGES TO PRODUCE TO THEM A SUPPLY OF CORN (Caesar, *De Bello Gallico*).
- **... suisque imperavit *ne* quod omnino telum in hostes *reicerent*** ... AND HE ORDERED HIS MEN NOT TO THROW BACK ANY WEAPON AT ALL AGAINST THE ENEMY (Caesar, *De Bello Gallico*).
  ✧ It could be argued that this is in fact an *indirect prohibition*, dealt with further down, but as the introductory verb is **impero** we classify it here under *Indirect commands*.

2/ There is an exception: the verb **iubeo** TO ORDER is followed by an *accusative + infinitive* structure; observe this example: [410]

⇨ Direct order:	**Lege hunc librum!**	READ THIS BOOK!
⇨ Indirect order (intr. verb in *primary* tense):	***Me* hunc librum *legere* iubet**	HE ORDERS ME TO READ THIS BOOK.
⇨ Indirect order (intr. verb in *secondary* tense):	***Me* hunc librum *legere* iussit**	HE ORDERED ME TO READ THIS BOOK.

We can see that in this construction it is indifferent whether the introductory verb is in primary or secondary tense: after **iubeo**, an *accusative + infinitive* will be used.

Two examples from Cicero:

- ***Prendi hominem* iussit** HE ORDERED THE MAN TO BE ARRESTED (Cicero, *Pro Rege Deiotaro*).
- **Domum ad se *venire* iussit *centuriones*** HE ORDERED THE CENTURIONS TO COME TO HIM TO HIS HOUSE (Cicero, *Philippicae*).

3/ The verb **impero** can sometimes be found also ruling an infinitive rather than an **ut** clause: [411]

- **Imperavit frumentum et alia, quae bello usui forent, *comportare*** HE ORDERED TO GATHER CORN AND OTHER ASSETS THAT COULD BE OF SOME USE FOR WAR (Sallust, *Bellum Iugurthinum*).
  ✧ To make it more complicated, there is no accusative performing the role of subject of the infinitive.

4/ The most common verbs that are used to introduce indirect orders are:

hortor, -ari, hortatus sum	TO URGE
impero, -are, -avi, -atum (+ Dat.)	TO ORDER
moneo, -ere, monui, monitum	TO ADVISE
oro, -are, -avi, -atum	TO ENTREAT
persuadeo, -ere, persuasi, persuasum (+ Dat.)	TO PERSUADE
rogo, -are, -avi, -atum	TO ASK

Observe that this list includes verbs that do not have a direct sense of ordering: this concept of *indirect command* includes also sentences introduced by verbs of *advising*, *persuading*, etc.

b) Indirect prohibitions [412]

1/ A first method of expressing an indirect prohibition is using the same verbs that can be used to introduce indirect commands, but followed by **ne** instead of by **ut** (obviously, **ne** is translated with a negative meaning). But in fact the construction we get is not a real indirect prohibition, this is just a request *not to do something*, rather than a prohibition to do something. It would go on being an indirect command. For instance:

⇨ Direct command: **Noli me ingratum existimare** DO NOT CONSIDER ME AN UNGRATEFUL PERSON.
⇨ Indirect command: **Rogo *ne* me ingratum *existimes*** (Seneca iunior, *De Beneficiis*). I ASK YOU NOT TO CONSIDER ME AN UNGRATEFUL PERSON

2/ But this is not the same as I FORBID YOU TO CONSIDER ME AN UNGRATEFUL PERSON. The real way of expressing an indirect prohibition is by means of the verbs **prohibeo** and **veto**. Let's start with **prohibeo**. [413]

If Seneca had wanted to express a real indirect prohibition, he could have said:

- **Te *prohibeo* ne me ingratum existimes** I FORBID YOU TO CONSIDER ME AN UNGRATEFUL PERSON.

Observe that **prohibeo** is followed by **ne**, but with the verb **prohibeo** the negative sense of **ne** must not be translated. In fact, it is the same phenomenon as with *fear clauses* in the style of **Timeo ne ...**

But possibly Seneca did not mean to give such a strict order, so he used the construction we have seen above, with the verb **rogo**. Let's see an easier example, this time meaning a real prohibition:

⇨ Direct prohibition: **Noli legere hunc librum!** DO NOT READ THIS BOOK!
⇨ Indirect prohibition (intr. verb in *primary* tense): **Me prohibet *ne* hunc librum *legam*** HE FORBIDS ME TO READ THIS BOOK.
⇨ Indirect prohibition (intr. verb in *secondary* tense): **Me prohibuit *ne* hunc librum *legerem*** HE FORBADE ME TO READ THIS BOOK.

An original example from Cicero:

- **Quem in locum prohibui *ne venires*** I FORBADE YOU TO COME TO THIS PLACE (Cicero, *Pro Caecina*).
  ✧ In this case, Cicero really meant a prohibition to do something rather than a request not to do it.

3/ Verbs of forbidding can also be introduced by **quominus**, and if they are negative they can be introduced also by **quin**. [414]
As this is part of the complicated uses of **quominus** and **quin**, to avoid repetition here please refer to the corresponding Section 13 in the chapter on Subordinate Clauses.

4/ With respect to the verb **veto** TO FORBID, it is followed by an infinitive (as happened with the verb **iubeo** for indirect commands):

- **Me vetat hunc librum *legere*** HE FORBIDS ME TO READ THIS BOOK.
- **Me vetuit hunc librum *legere*** HE FORBADE ME TO READ THIS BOOK.
- **Ille me vetuit domum *venire*** HE FORBADE ME TO COME HOME (Plautus, *Epidicus*).
- **Hic me ... vetuit *contemnere* Musas** HE FORBADE ME TO DESPISE THE MUSES (Propertius, *Elegiae*).

Note

To order somebody not to do something must be translated by **veto**, not by **iubeo** and a negative: **Me hunc librum non legere iubet** would be a wrong translation for HE ORDERS ME NOT TO READ THIS BOOK.

4. Indirect question clauses [415]

An indirect question can be introduced in several ways, depending on whether the original question was a *yes/no* question (DO YOU WANT TO COME WITH US?), an adverbial question (WHERE IS THAT BOOK?), etc. But, whichever kind of indirect question we have, the most important rule of an indirect question is that its verb must be in *subjunctive*.

They can be introduced by several verbs, not only by verbs with a meaning of asking, and even by some combined expression; some of them are:

rogo, -are, -avi, -atum	TO ASK	**nescio, -ire, nescivi** (no supine)	NOT TO KNOW
interrogo, -are, -avi, -atum	TO ASK	**scire volo**	TO WANT TO KNOW
quaero, -ere, quaesivi, quaesitum	TO ASK	**videre volo**	TO WANT TO SEE
miror, -ari, miratus sum	TO WONDER	**incertum est**	IT IS UNCERTAIN

Note that some of these verbs, like **rogo**, that can also be used to introduce an indirect order, and in each case the corresponding construction must be used (in fact, the same as in English with the verb TO ASK: *I ask you to remain here* or *I ask you whether he has returned*).

a) Adverbial or pronominal questions [416]

After the introductory verb, we must reproduce the direct question but with the verb in *subjunctive*.

1/ If the introductory verb is in *primary* tense, we keep the same tense as we had in the original question, but of course in subjunctive:

⇨ Direct question: **Quem librum legis?** WHICH BOOK ARE YOU READING?
⇨ Indirect question: **Rogo quem librum *legas*** I ASK WHICH BOOK YOU ARE READING.

- **Quaerito quid fieri *possit*** ASK WHAT CAN BE DONE (Porcius Cato, *De Agri Cultura*).
  ✧ **Quaerito** is a future imperative, not a very common form.

The direct question would probably have been **Quid fieri potest?** WHAT CAN BE DONE? and **potest** has moved from present indicative to present subjunctive in order to become an indirect question.

2/ If we reproduce a future indicative, it's obvious that we can not move it to future subjunctive, as it does not exist. In this case, we will use the *future participle* with the verb **sum** in subjunctive: [417]

⇨ Direct question: **Quem librum leges?** WHICH BOOK WILL YOU READ?
⇨ Indirect question: **Rogo quem librum *lecturus sis*** I ASK WHICH BOOK YOU WILL READ.

In fact, we are respecting the former rule: a future indicative has been "rephrased" to the equivalent periphrastic construction (**Quem librum lecturus es?**) and the verb **sum** has been moved to the present subjunctive.

- **Nescis quid ego *acturus sim*** YOU DO NOT KNOW WHAT I WILL DO (Plautus, *Bacchides*).

The direct question would probably have been **Quid ages?** WHAT WILL YOU DO? and the future indicative has moved to the periphrasis **acturus sim**, where **sim** is in subjunctive and the future participle conveys the sense of future.

3/ Exception: an original imperfect moves to perfect, it does not remain imperfect:

⇨ Direct question: **Quem librum legebas?** WHICH BOOK WERE YOU READING?
⇨ Indirect question: **Rogo quem librum *legeris*** I ASK WHICH BOOK YOU WERE READING.

4/ If the indirect question is introduced by a verb in a secondary tense, the tense of the verb of the original direct question must be changed not only to the subjunctive but also to another tense. The rules for this change are as follows: **[418]**

❑ *Present moves to imperfect:*

⇨ Direct question: **Quem librum legis?** WHICH BOOK ARE YOU READING?
⇨ Indirect question: **Rogavi quem librum *legeres*** I ASKED WHICH BOOK YOU WERE READING.

The present **legis** has moved to imperfect **legeres**.

- **Quis *esset* aut quid *vellet* quaesivit** HE ASKED WHO HE WAS OR WHAT HE WANTED (Caesar, *Bellum Civile*).

The original question had probably been **Quis es aut quid vis?** WHO ARE YOU AND WHAT DO YOU WANT?

Both verbs are in the present indicative. In order to make it an indirect question, they move to subjunctive, and moreover, as the introductory verb is in a secondary tense, they move one step backwards: from present to imperfect.

❑ *Imperfect or perfect move to pluperfect:*

⇨ Direct question: **Quem librum legisti?** WHICH BOOK HAVE YOU READ?
⇨ Indirect question: **Rogavi quem librum *legisses*** I ASKED WHICH BOOK YOU HAD READ.

The perfect **legisti** has moved to pluperfect **legisses**.

- **Quaesivi quem ad modum *revertissent*** I ASKED IN WHAT CONDITION THEY HAD RETURNED (Cicero, *In Verrem*).

The original sentence was probably **Quo modo reverterunt?** IN WHAT CONDITION DID THEY RETURN?

Note

As a general rule, **quo modo** becomes **quem ad modum** in an indirect question.

❑ *Future moves to periphrastic future with verb* **sum** *in imperfect:*

⇨ Direct question: **Quem librum leges?** WHICH BOOK WILL YOU READ?
⇨ Indirect question: **Rogavi quem librum *lecturus esses*** I ASKED WHICH BOOK YOU HAD READ.

The same phenomenon as before: we transform the future tense into the equivalent periphrastic expression, and the present indicative of **sum** moves into subjunctive, and one step backwards in time: **esses** (imperfect) instead of **sis** (present).

- **Quaesivi ... quem ad modum illum agrum *esset distributurus*** I ASKED IN WHAT WAY HE WOULD DISTRIBUTE THAT LAND (Cicero, *De Lege Agraria*).

The original sentence was probably **Quo modo hunc agrum distribues?** IN WHAT WAY WILL YOU DISTRIBUTE THIS LAND?

5/ As already mentioned above, two interrogative words that experience modifications when used in an indirect question are **cur** WHY and **quomodo** HOW: **cur** becomes **quam ob rem** (which can be written as a single word) and **quomodo** (or **quo modo**) becomes **quem ad modum**: [419]

⇨ Direct question: **Cur et quomodo hoc fecisti?** WHY AND HOW HAVE YOU DONE THIS?
⇨ Indirect question: **Scire volo *quam ob rem* et *quem ad modum* hoc feceris** I WANT TO KNOW WHY AND HOW YOU HAVE DONE THIS.

- **Nunc ... *quam ob rem* venerim dicam** NOW I WILL SAY WHY I HAVE COME (Plautus, *Amphitruo*).

b) Double questions [420]

In the case of double-choice questions (DO YOU WANT TO COME WITH US OR NOT? DO YOU PREFER WINE OR WATER?), the same rules of change of tense are followed, but the indirect question must be introduced by some specific conjunctions; as in English the question IS CAESAR HERE?, if asked indirectly, must be introduced by IF or WHETHER, HE ASKS *IF* CAESAR IS HERE, the same happens in Latin.

1/ In a *yes/no* question, the English IF is translated by **num** (it is obvious that in this case **num** will not have any meaning of expectancy of a negative answer as when used in a direct question):

⇨ Direct question: **Hunc librum legisti?** HAVE YOU READ THIS BOOK?
⇨ Indirect question: **Rogo *num* hunc librum *legeris*** I ASK IF YOU HAVE READ THIS BOOK.

- **Rogavit *num* mortuum *ferrent*** HE ASKED IF THEY WERE CARRYING A CORPSE (Gellius, *Noctes Atticae*).

2/ When two options are offered, the English WHETHER is translated by **utrum** (and the OR is translated by **an**): [421]

⇨ Direct question: **Vis nobiscum venire *an* hic manere?** DO YOU WANT TO COME WITH US OR TO REMAIN HERE?

⇨ Indirect question: **Rogo *utrum* velis nobiscum venire *an* hic manere** I ASK WHETHER YOU WANT TO COME WITH US OR TO REMAIN HERE.

- **Nunc quaero *utrum* vestras iniurias *an* rei publicae persequamini** NOW I ASK WHETHER YOU ARE TRYING TO AVENGE YOUR OFFENCES OR [THOSE] OF THE STATE (Cicero, *Pro Ligario*).

If the second option is just the usual form of **annon** OR NOT, **annon** changes to **necne** in an indirect question:

⇨ Direct question: **Vis nobiscum venire annon?** DO YOU WANT TO COME WITH US OR NOT?
⇨ Indirect question: **Rogo *utrum* velis nobiscum venire *necne*** I ASK WHETHER YOU WANT TO COME WITH US OR NOT.

- **Hoc primum quaero, venerit ea res in hoc iudicium *necne*** FIRST I ASK THIS, WHETHER THIS MATTER HAS COME TO COURT OR NOT (Cicero, *Pro Tullio*).
  - ✧ Observe that in this case the **utrum** is elided: the presence of **necne** makes it clear that there is a double choice, and the marker for the first choice can be considered unnecessary.

3/ Apart from all this, we should remember that it is normal to place **utrum** at the beginning of the direct question: **Utrum vis nobiscum venire an hic manere?** DO YOU WANT TO COME WITH US OR TO REMAIN HERE? Of course, in this case the presence of **utrum** in the indirect question is automatic.

5. Subordinate clauses in indirect speech [422]

The verb of a subordinate clause that depends on a former main clause that now has become indirect speech must be in *subjunctive*. Let's examine the three possible cases.

a) Subordinate clauses in indirect statements

1/ We know that when we pass a sentence from direct into indirect statement it must be rewritten as an infinitive clause. Observe this sentence:

- **Librum legi dum pater Romae erat** I READ THE BOOK WHILE MY FATHER WAS AT ROME.

In indirect statements, such as those introduced by the verb **dico**, an infinitive with an accusative subject must be used in the main sentence:

Dico me librum legisse... I SAY THAT I READ THE BOOK...

With respect to the subordinate clause ...WHILE MY FATHER WAS AT ROME that depended on the main one (which has now become an infinitive clause), it must have its verb in *subjunctive*, and the final result would be

- **Dico me librum legisse dum pater Romae *esset*** I SAY THAT I READ THE BOOK WHILE MY FATHER WAS AT ROME.

2/ Let's see an example from Cicero:

- **Dixit se istum publice laudare, quod sibi ita *mandatum esset*** HE SAID THAT HE PRAISED THIS MAN IN PUBLIC BECAUSE IT HAD BEEN ORDERED TO HIM THUS (Cicero, *In Verrem*).

Probably, the direct statement had been **Ego istum publice laudo, quod mihi ita mandatum est** I PRAISE THIS MAN IN PUBLIC BECAUSE IT HAS BEEN ORDERED TO ME THUS.

In Cicero's sentence, the verb **mandatum esset** is in subjunctive because now it depends on the infinitive **laudare** (the former **laudo** that now, having become an indirect statement, has moved to an infinitive).

b) Subordinate clauses in indirect questions [423]

Apart from the main rule stated above (the verb of a subordinate clause that depends on a clause in indirect statement has to be in subjunctive), an indirect question must have its verb in subjunctive, and as a general rule any subordinate clause that depends on a sentence with a verb in subjunctive will also have its own verb in subjunctive, so that in fact the verb will be in subjunctive for two reasons.

- **Quaesivi quid *dubitaret* proficisci eo quo iam pridem *pararet*** I ASKED WHY HE HESITATED TO GO WHERE HE LONG AGO WAS PREPARING TO GO (Cicero, *In Catilinam*).

The direct question would probably have been **Quid dubitas proficisci eo quo iam pridem paras?** WHY DO YOU HESITATE TO GO WHERE YOU ARE LONG PREPARING TO GO?

In Cicero's sentence, the verb **pararet** is in subjunctive because now in depends on **dubitaret** (the former **dubitat** that now, having become an indirect question, is in subjunctive).

c) Subordinate clauses in indirect commands [424]

1/ As above, the verb must be in subjunctive, no matter whether the indirect command is expressed by means of an infinitive clause or by means of an **ut** clause. Observe this direct command:

- **Da mihi librum quem heri tibi dedi** GIVE ME THE BOOK THAT I GAVE YOU YESTERDAY.

If expressed as an indirect command, it will become

- **Imperavit ut sibi librum *daret* quem pridie ei *dedisset*** HE ORDERED HIM TO GIVE HIM THE BOOK THAT HE HAD GIVEN HIM THE DAY BEFORE.
  ✧ Example with infinitive clause.
- **Iussit eum sibi librum *dare* quem pridie ei *dedisset*** (same meaning).
  ✧ Example with **ut** clause.

2/ Sometimes it is possible to find examples in which the verb is in *indicative*, like these two: [425]

- **Flaccum praetorem scrinium cum litteris, quas a legatis *acceperat*, eodem adferre iubet** HE ORDERS FLACCUS, THE PRAETOR, TO BRING THE BOX WITH THE LETTERS THAT HE HAD RECEIVED FROM THE LEGATES (Sallust, *Catilinae Coniuratio*).
- **Imperat lictoribus ut Sopatrum de porticu, in qua ipse *sedebat*, praecipitem in forum deiciant** HE ORDERS THE LICTORS TO THROW SOPATER DOWN FROM THE PORTICO ON WHICH HE HIMSELF WAS SITTING (Cicero, *In Verrem*).

The explanation is very simple: the verb is in indicative because the information given in the relative clause is not part of what had been the direct speech but additional information supplied by the author. It is obvious, for instance, that Verres did not say THROW SOPATER DOWN FROM THE PORTICO ON WHICH I AM SITTING but just THROW SOPATER DOWN FROM THE PORTICO: the relative clause **in qua ipse sedebat** has been added by Cicero as additional information for the audience.

In the first example, possibly the consul had ordered something like GIVE ME THE BOX WITH THE LETTERS. If he had ordered GIVE ME THE BOX WITH THE LETTERS THAT YOU HAVE RECEIVED FROM THE LEGATES, the verb would have been **accepisset**, in subjunctive. In this case, the relative clause **quas a legatis acceperat**, explaining that the letters were those which had been received from the legates, is additional information supplied by Sallust.

6. A special technique: *Oratio Obliqua*

a) Introduction [426]

We have seen how to express statements, questions and commands in reported speech, but these were examples of reporting one statement, one question or one command. Nevertheless, a lot of times reported speech does not limit itself to reporting only one statement, only one question or only one command, but *a long string of sentences* expressed in a continuous way, a string in which there may be a combination of the three elements, and most probably with several of each of them (maybe, for instance, a paragraph with five or six consecutive statements with a question in the middle , etc.).

In this circumstance, most languages, and Latin among them, do not reproduce each sentence introducing it with the usual verb of saying, as this would produce a very burdensome accumulation of these introductory expressions, an accumulation like HE SAID THAT..., AND HE SAID THAT..., AND HE ORDERED..., AND HE ASKED..., AND HE SAID THAT..., AND HE ASKED, AND HE SAID THAT... etc.

What is done in these cases is that the whole narrative is introduced *only in its very first sentence* by one of these expressions, and the other introductory expressions are skipped (and sometimes even the very first sentence lacks this introductory expression): each of the sentences that are being reproduced are written one after another, producing a continuous reproduction of somebody's words, whether statements or questions or commands, without any introductory AND HE SAID THAT..., AND HE ASKED WHETHER...., etc. This technique is called *Oratio Obliqua*.

Nevertheless, the rules of transforming a direct speech into indirect will not be the same as when we transformed single sentences, especially with respect of the reproduction of questions. First we will examine what happens to each one of the three kinds of sentences (statements, questions and commands) and later we will see an example of a combination of all of them in a single paragraph. We will pay special attention to the difference between reproducing a sentence using the rules of normal reported speech and reproducing the same kind of sentence in the middle of the reproduction of a long list of sentences.

As a general rule, Oratio Obliqua is supposed to be always in *secondary sequence*. Therefore, the choice of tenses in the subjunctive will be made according to this.

b) What happens to statements? [427]

This is the simplest case: we follow the same rule as for the reproduction of a single statement in reported speech: we put it in *accusative and infinitive*. The only difference is that we will not have the introductory expression HE SAID THAT...

- ⇨ Direct statement: • **Caesar hostes vicit** CAESAR DEFEATED THE ENEMIES.
- ⇨ Indirect statement: • **Dixit *Caesarem* hostes *vicisse*** HE SAID THAT CAESAR HAD DEFEATED THE ENEMIES.
- ⇨ Oratio Obliqua: • ***Caesarem* hostes *vicisse*** HE SAID THAT CAESAR HAD DEFEATED THE ENEMIES.
  - ✧ Observe the absence of the introductory **Dixit** (unless this sentence were the very first one opening the whole paragraph).

Now let's see an original example taken from the famous interview between Caesar and Ariovistus. Obviously, we do not have the direct statement, but we can deduce it:

- ⇨ Oratio Obliqua: • **Non *sese* Gallis sed *Gallos* sibi bellum *intulisse*** HE HAD NOT BROUGHT WAR TO THE GAULS BUT THE GAULS TO HIM (Caesar, *De Bello Gallico*).
  - ✧ Again, observe the absence of **Dixit**.
- ⇨ Direct statement: • **Non ego Gallis sed Galli mihi bellum intulerunt** I DID NOT BRING WAR TO THE GAULS, BUT THE GAULS TO ME.

Another example from the same text:

⇨ Oratio Obliqua: • ***Provinciam suam hanc esse Galliam***, **sicut *illam nostram*** THIS [PART OF] GAUL WAS HIS PROVINCE, JUST AS THAT ONE WAS OURS (Caesar, *De Bello Gallico*).

✧ And, as usual, observe the absence of **Dixit**.

⇨ Direct statement: • **Provincia mea haec est Gallia, sicut illa vestra** THIS [PART OF] GAUL IS MY PROVINCE, JUST AS THAT ONE IS YOURS.

c) What happens to questions? [428]

1/ This is probably the point in which Reported Speech and Oratio Obliqua differ most:

In Reported Speech:

- *All* questions become indirect questions in subjunctive.
- *There is no difference* with respect to whether an answer is expected or not.
- They *lose* their question mark.

In Oratio Obliqua:

- *Some* questions become indirect questions in subjunctive, while *others* become accusative + infinitive clauses.
- *There is difference* with respect to whether an answer is expected or not.
- They *keep* their question mark.

2/ As we can see, the most complicated point is when a direct question becomes an indirect question in subjunctive and when it becomes an accusative + infinitive clause. It depends on whether an answer is expected or not. [429]

⇨ If an answer is expected, it will become an *indirect question in subjunctive.*
⇨ If no answer is expected (rhetorical questions), it will become an *accusative + infinitive construction.*

As a general rule, questions formulated in 2nd person will become indirect questions in subjunctive, as usually an answer is expected from somebody to whom we are asking something.

With respect to questions formulated in 1st or 3rd person, they may have both constructions, because for instance we can ask a deliberative question, like **Quid faciamus?** WHAT ARE WE TO DO? (an answer is expected, no matter whether it is finally given or not) or a rhetorical question, like **Huic stulto praemium dare debeo?** DO I HAVE TO GIVE A PRIZE TO THIS FOOLISH MAN? (although the tone of the question is clearly pointing to a negative answer, no real answer is expected).

Let's see this in a triple example, with a question in the 2nd person:

⇨ Direct question: • **Quem librum legis?** WHAT BOOK ARE YOU READING?
⇨ Indirect question: • **Quaesivit quem librum *legeret*** HE ASKED WHAT BOOK HE WAS READING.
⇨ Oratio Obliqua: • **Quem librum *legeret?*** WHAT BOOK WAS HE READING?

It was a normal question with an answer expected, so it has become an indirect question in subjunctive, but observe the two key points in its result as Oratio Obliqua:

- Lack of introductory verb like **Quaesivit**.
- The question mark remains.

3/ Original example from Caesar: **[430]**

- ➪ Oratio Obliqua: • **Cur in suas possessiones *veniret?*** (Caesar, *De Bello Gallico*). WHY DID HE COME INTO HIS DOMINION?
- ➪ Direct statement: • **Cur in meas possessiones venis?** WHY DO YOU COME INTO MY DOMINION?

An answer is expected (as almost always happens with 2nd person questions), so it becomes an indirect question in subjunctive.

Another triple example, this time a question in the 1st person:

- ➪ Direct question: • **Quid dicam nunc?** WHAT AM I TO SAY NOW?
- ➪ Indirect question: • **Dubitavit quid diceret tunc** HE DOUBTED WHAT HE WAS TO SAY THEN.
- ➪ Oratio Obliqua: • **Quid *diceret tunc?* / Quid *se dicere tunc?*** WHAT WAS HE TO SAY THEN?

– If the direct question was considered a deliberative question (i.e., I am trying to reach an answer), it becomes an *indirect question in subjunctive.*

– If the direct question was considered a rhetorical question (i.e., I know that I will not be able to say anything), it becomes an *accusative + infinitive construction.* The result is really unusual: an accusative + infinitive construction playing the role of a question, and even with its own question mark. Observe, by the way, that we have got to add **se** in order to provide a subject (in accusative) for the infinitive.

4/ This time an example with a question in the 3rd person: **[431]**

- ➪ Direct question: • **Quis hoc uno die perficere potest?** WHO CAN DO THIS IN ONE DAY?
- ➪ Indirect question: • **Quaesivit quis illud uno die perficere *posset*** HE ASKED WHO COULD DO THAT IN ONE DAY.
- ➪ Oratio Obliqua: • ***Quis* illud uno die perficere *posset?* / *Quem* illud uno die perficere *posse?*** WHO COULD DO THAT IN ONE DAY?

– If the direct question was considered a normal question (i.e., we really want to know the identity of the person capable of doing it in one day, for instance in order to hire his/her services), it becomes an *indirect question in subjunctive.*

– If the direct question was considered a rhetorical question (i.e., it is clear that nobody can do that in one day), it becomes an *accusative + infinitive construction.*

d) What happens to commands? [432]

Commands (and prohibitions) become an imperfect subjunctive clause:

- ⇨ Direct commands:
  - **Veni mecum** COME WITH ME.
  - **Noli dormire** DO NOT SLEEP.
- ⇨ Indirect commands:
  - **Illi imperavit *ut* secum *veniret*** HE ORDERED HIM TO COME WITH HIM.
  - **Vetuit *illum dormire*** HE FORBADE HIM TO SLEEP.
- ⇨ Oratio Obliqua:
  - **Secum *veniret*** HE WAS TO COME WITH HIM
  - ***Ne dormiret*** HE WAS NOT TO SLEEP.

  ✧ Observe that for a command we do not write the **ut**, but for a prohibition we must write the **ne**.

An example from Caesar (for the sake of practice, we also add a statement, as it happens to be the following sentence):

- ⇨ Oratio Obliqua:
  - **Uterque cum equitatu *veniret:* alia ratione sese non esse venturum** EITHER SHOULD COME WITH THE CAVALRY: OTHERWISE, HE WOULD NOT COME (Caesar, *De Bello Gallico*).
- ⇨ Direct command:
  - **Uterque cum equitatu *veniat:* alia ratione non veniam** LET EITHER COME WITH THE CAVALRY; OTHERWISE, I WILL NOT COME.

e) What happens to pronouns and adverbs? [433]

1/ If a direct statement like I HAVE NOW DEFEATED MY ENEMIES HERE is written in Oratio Obliqua, the result will be HE HAD THEN DEFEATED HIS ENEMIES THERE. The changes are obvious:

I	has become	HE	MY	has become	HIS
NOW	has become	THEN	HERE	has become	THERE

A basic table of correspondences of pronouns would be this one:

ego	becomes	**se**	**nos**	becomes	**se**
tu	becomes	**ille, illa, illud**	**vos**	becomes	**illi, -ae, -a**
3rd sing.	becomes	**is, ea, id**	3rd plural	becomes	**ei, eae, ea**

2/ A special note should be made about the 1st person:

Maybe a 1st person pronoun is not mentioned in the direct statement, but we must write **se** in the Oratio Obliqua:

- ⇨ Direct statement:
  - **Hostes vici** I HAVE DEFEATED THE ENEMIES.
- ⇨ Oratio Obliqua:
  - ***Se* hostes *vicisse*** HE HAD DEFEATED THE ENEMIES.

  ✧ **Se** is replacing an imaginary **ego** in the direct statement.

3/ A basic table of correspondence to adverbs would be this one:

heri	becomes	**pridie**	**nunc**	becomes	**tunc**
hodie	becomes	**illo die**	**hic**	becomes	**ibi**
cras	becomes	**postero die**			

f) A final collective example [434]

Let's see a paragraph with a combination of the three types of sentences (statements, questions and commands) transformed into Oratio Obliqua. Observe these three points:

- The change of structures.
- The change of pronouns and adverbs.
- The absence of introductory forms of the kind Dixit..., Quaesivit..., etc.

⇨ Direct speech: • Ego semper tibi pecuniam dedi. Cur nunc hoc dicis? Cras tibi plus pecuniae dabo. Num de me dubitas? Noli dubitare, crede mihi.
I HAVE ALWAYS GIVEN YOU MONEY. WHY DO YOU SAY THIS NOW? TOMORROW I WILL GIVE YOU MORE MONEY. DO YOU DOUBT ABOUT ME? DO NOT DOUBT, BELIEVE IN ME.

⇨ Oratio Obliqua: • *Se* semper *illi* pecuniam *dedisse.* Cur *tunc illud diceret? Postero die illi* plus pecuniae *se daturum esse.* Num de *se dubitare? Ne dubitaret, sibi crederet.*
HE HAD ALWAYS GIVEN HIM MONEY. WHY WAS HE SAYING THAT THEN? ON THE FOLLOWING DAY HE WOULD GIVE HIM MORE MONEY. DID HE DOUBT ABOUT HIM? HE SHOULD NOT DOUBT, HE SHOULD BELIEVE IN HIM.

Observations about the two questions: [435]

1/ Cur nunc hoc dicis?

It can be considered a question for which an answer is expected, so it has become an *indirect question in subjunctive.*

2/ Num de me dubitas?

It can be considered a rhetorical question, so it has become an *infinitive + accusative construction.*

f) Uses of the gerund and gerundive

1. Definition and forms [436]

a/ We have been using the infinitive as subject (for instance, ***Legere* bonum est** READING / TO READ IS GOOD) or as direct object (for instance, **Volo *legere*** I WANT TO READ).

But if we want to say for instance I HAVE WRITTEN A BOOK ABOUT THE ART OF READING
we will write **Librum scripsi de arte ...**

How should we translate OF READING? This sounds like we need the genitive of the infinitive, but how can an infinitive be declined?

The *gerund* can be defined as the declension of the present active infinitive (only of the *present active* one: **amare**, **habere**, etc.). This declension has these four characteristics (we have already seen some examples of the gerund in the chapter on the verbal conjugation):

- It has only four cases: accusative, genitive, dative and ablative.
- Its declension endings are those that correspond to a neuter noun of the 2nd declension.
  ✧ Remember that an infinitive is a neuter noun.
- The accusative is *almost* always preceded by the preposition **ad**.
- It has only singular.

For instance, the gerund of **scribo** would be:

[**Nom**. scribere]
Acc. ad scribendum
Gen. scribendi
Dat. scribendo
Abl. scribendo

The inclusion of the infinitive as nominative in the above table is of course symbolic, just as an indication that the gerund corresponds to the declension of the infinitive.

b/ With respect to the gerundive, it is just the *future passive participle*, also called gerundive because of the similarities it has with the gerund: [437]

scribendus, -a, -um

The forms of the gerund (**-ndum, -ndi, -ndo**) coincide with some masculine and neuter singular forms of the gerundive.

c/ The difference between them is obvious: the gerund is a neuter *noun* and it declines only through four cases (Acc., Gen., Dat. and Abl.) and only in singular, while the gerundive is a *participle* (and therefore an adjective) and it declines thoroughly in all cases, genders and numbers, like **bonus, -a, -um**.

2. Uses of the gerund [438]

a) Accusative

We have seen that, for the role of direct object, we use the infinitive as such:

- Volo *legere* I WANT TO READ.

Then, if as direct object we do not use the gerund in accusative (usually we need a noun in the accusative if it is to perform the role of direct object, but it is not so if it is an infinitive), what do we use the accusative of the gerund for?

The use of the accusative of the gerund has nothing to do with direct objects (let's remember that it is usually preceded by the preposition ad). In fact it is the only case of the gerund which is not used for the usual function of that case, and the meaning it has is one of purpose:

- Venio *ad ludendum* — I COME TO PLAY.
- Milites *ad pugnandum* venient — THE SOLDIERS WILL COME TO FIGHT.
- Studium *ad pugnandum* virtusque deerat (Caesar, *Bellum Civile*). — THE DESIRE FOR FIGHTING AND BRAVERY WAS ABSENT
- Exercitus Romanorum *ad pugnandum* concitatus est (Iulius Frontinus, *Strategemata*). — THE ROMAN ARMY WAS INCITED TO FIGHT
- Scio te ... *ad occidendum* me venisse (Petronius, *Satyrica*). — I KNOW THAT YOU HAVE COME TO KILL ME

It must be remembered that purpose can also be expressed by ut + subjunctive:

- Venio *ut ludam* I COME TO PLAY

and moreover there are more methods of expressing purpose, which we will see further ahead.

b) Genitive [439]

The use of the gerund in the genitive is identical to the use of any noun in the genitive:

- Librum scripsi de arte *legendi* I HAVE WRITTEN A BOOK ABOUT THE ART OF READING.
- Cupidus sum *bibendi* I AM DESIROUS OF DRINKING.
- Bomilcar, ... cupidus incepta *patrandi* ..., litteras ad eum per homines fidelis mittit BOMILCAR, DESIROUS OF CARRYING OUT WHAT HAD ALREADY BEGUN, SENDS HIM A LETTER BY MEANS OF FAITHFUL MEN (Sallust, *Bellum Iugurthinum*).

Its use after the ablatives causa or gratia is very common, and the construction as a whole will express *purpose*:

- Domum iniit *dormiendi causa/gratia* — HE WENT INTO THE HOUSE FOR THE SAKE OF SLEEPING.
- Si *praedandi causa* ad eos venissent, ... (Caesar, *De Bello Gallico*). — IF THEY HAD COME TO THEM FOR THE SAKE OF PLUNDERING, ...

c) Dative [440]

Its use in dative is not very frequent; we may find it for instance depending on expressions that must be followed by a dative, like these:

- Operam do *legendo* I GIVE ATTENTION TO READING.
- Hic locus idoneus est *pugnando* THIS PLACE IS ADEQUATE FOR FIGHTING.
- *Solvendo* enim non erat HE WAS NOT ABLE TO PAY (Cicero, *Epistulae ad Atticum*).
  ✧ Solvendo sum means TO BE ABLE TO PAY.

d) Ablative [441]

If used without a preposition, it corresponds to the English gerund: it is the equivalent to the -ING form which answers to the question How? (do not confuse them with the -ING forms of the kind of THE RUNNING MAN or RUNNING IS GOOD). For instance,

- Hoc obtinui *laborando* I HAVE OBTAINED THIS BY WORKING.
- *Legendo* multa disces BY READING YOU WILL LEARN MANY THINGS.
- Hominis autem mens *discendo* alitur et *cogitando* (Cicero, *De Officiis*). THE HUMAN MIND IS NOURISHED BY LEARNING AND THINKING

It can be used with the preposition in with the same meaning:

- *In legendo* multa disces BY READING YOU WILL LEARN MANY THINGS.
- Quis est tam *in scribendo* impiger quam ego? (Cicero, *Epistulae ad Familiares*). WHO IS SO ACTIVE AS I IN WRITING?

Other prepositions will give to the gerund the same meaning they would give to a noun:

- Librum scripsi *de pugnando* I HAVE WRITTEN A BOOK ABOUT FIGHTING.
- Nihil *de resistendo* cogitabat HE DID NOT THINK ANYTHING ABOUT RESISTING (Caesar, *Bellum Civile*).

3. Gerundive replacing the gerund [442]

a/ The gerundive is the *future passive participle* (amandus, -a, -um, for instance). As such, we can find it used as any other participle; for instance:

- Heri captivos *necandos* vidi YESTERDAY I SAW PRISONERS THAT WERE ABOUT TO BE KILLED.

Its use for the *passive periphrastic conjugation* (see the corresponding chapter) is also very common, but its most common use is as a replacement for the gerund.

b/ We have seen in the former chapter several uses of the gerund, like for instance

- Cupidus sum *scribendi* I AM DESIROUS OF WRITING.

In those examples, the gerund did not have any object. Let's suppose that we want to add a direct object to the former gerund, for instance the noun **epistulam** LETTER:

- **Cupidus sum *scribendi epistulam*** I AM DESIROUS OF WRITING A LETTER.

Although this sentence is grammatically right, Latin has a tendency to avoid using a gerund with a direct object. The way to avoid it is to rephrase the sentence by means of the gerundive, and the steps to follow are these:

⇨ What would be the direct object of the gerund is put in the case in which the gerund was.
⇨ The gerund becomes a gerundive agreeing (as any adjective) with the former object.

So, our former example would now be:

- **Cupidus sum *epistulae scribendae*** I AM DESIROUS OF WRITING A LETTER.
  ✧ Literal translation: I AM DESIROUS OF THE LETTER THAT HAS TO BE WRITTEN.

Another example:

Construction with *gerund + direct object* (acceptable, but not common):

- **Venio *ad videndum hos libros*** I COME TO SEE THESE BOOKS.

Construction with *gerundive* (preferred):

- **Venio *ad hos libros videndos*** (same meaning)
  ✧ Literal translation: I COME TO THESE BOOKS THAT MUST BE SEEN.

Let's see more complex examples:

- **Quam putamus fuisse causam *conscribendae legis huiusce* ?** WHAT DO WE THINK WAS THE REASON FOR SETTING THIS LAW? (Quintilianus, *Declamationes Minores*).
  ✧ What would have been ... **causam conscribendi hanc legem**, in order to avoid the gerund **conscribendi** having an object, has been changed into a gerundive construction.

- **Ipse in citeriorem Galliam *ad conventus agendos* profectus est** HE HIMSELF SET OUT FOR CISALPINE GAUL TO HOLD THE MEETINGS (Caesar, *De Bello Gallico*).
  ✧ What would have been ... **ad agendum conventus** has been changed into ... **ad conventos agendos**.

- ***Ad eas res conficiendas* Orgetorix deligitur** ORGETORIX WAS CHOSEN TO FULFIL THESE OBJECTIVES (Caesar, *De Bello Gallico*).
  ✧ What would have been **Ad conficiendum eas res...** has been changed into a gerundive construction.

c/ In some cases, it may happen that the replacement does not produce any visual change; observe this sentence: **[443]**

- **Venio *ad videndum amicum*** I COME TO SEE A FRIEND OF MINE.

If we want to avoid **videndum** having a direct object (**amicum**) and we make the replacement, we will find that the result is the same: **Venio ad amicum videndum** (just the word order may be different), because **amicum** is put in accusative but it was already in accusative, and **videndum** must be in accusative (it already was) and masculine singular (which looks like the neuter gerund **videndum**).

4. Exceptions to the replacement [444]

There are two cases in which this replacement does not take place.

a) Neuter adjectives or pronouns

If the direct object is a *neuter adjective* or *pronoun*, then we will leave the structure *gerund + direct object* without changing it into a gerundive structure in order to avoid a confusion. For example:

- Cupidus sum *videndi multa* I AM DESIROUS OF SEEING MANY THINGS.

If we change it into a gerundive construction, we will have

Cupidus sum *multorum videndorum*.

This sentence could come either from (1) Cupidus sum videndi multos or from (2) Cupidus sum videndi multa, and it would be unclear whether it means I AM DESIROUS OF SEEING MANY PEOPLE (option 1) or I AM DESIROUS OF SEEING MANY THINGS (option 2).

b) Cacophonic reasons

The last example connects directly with the second reason. Let's depart from a similar example:

- Cupidus sum *scribendi multos libros* I AM DESIROUS OF WRITING MANY BOOKS.

If we change it into the gerundive structure, we will have

Cupidus sum *multorum librorum scribendorum*

and Latin tries to avoid these combinations of consecutive -orum or -arum; so we would leave it as it is, accepting a gerund with a direct object.

- Mihi de memet ipso tam *multa dicendi* necessitas quaedam imposita est ab illo THE NEED OF SPEAKING SO MUCH ABOUT MYSELF HAS BEEN IMPOSED BY HIM (Cicero, *Pro Sulla*).

But, curiously, Cicero himself seems to skip this rule from time to time:

- ... si sunt ad rem militarem apti et cupidi *bellorum gerendorum* ... IF THEY ARE APT FOR MILITARY LIFE AND EAGER FOR WAGING WARS (Cicero, *De Officiis*).
  - ✧ We could have expected ... cupidi *gerendi bella*, but for some reason Cicero in this case prefered the other option in spite of the -orum ... -orum effect.

g) The periphrastic conjugation and the supine

1. The active periphrastic [445]

a/ The active periphrastic conjugation is nothing else than the use of the *active future participle in the role of predicative object* with the verb **sum**; in other words, let's imagine the sentence

- **Petrus altus est** PETER IS TALL.

If we replace **altus** by an active future participle, let's say **scripturus**, we will have

Petrus *scripturus est*.

Altus is very easily translated by TALL, but we know that the translation of a future participle on its own (**scripturus** would mean THAT IS ABOUT TO WRITE) does not make much sense, so we will have to rephrase the resulting translation.

Word by word, it says PETER IS THAT IS ABOUT TO WRITE; instead of telling us is that Peter is tall, or clever, or whatever, it tells us that he is about to execute a specific action, the one expressed by the future participle. Obviously, the translation should be rephrased into PETER IS ABOUT TO WRITE.

More examples:

- **Heri mea soror *lectura erat* hunc librum** YESTERDAY MY SISTER WAS ABOUT TO READ THIS BOOK.
- **Nunc *itura sum* Romam** I AM ABOUT TO GO TO ROME.
- **Quod vero Flavius tibi *daturus est*?** (Cicero, *Pro Roscio Comoedo*). [THE AMOUNT] THAT INDEED FLAVIUS IS GOING TO GIVE YOU?
- **Castra *posituri erant*** THEY WERE ABOUT TO PITCH A CAMP (Livy, *Ab Urbe Condita*).
- **Eiusdem iuris esse debent, qui sub eodem rege *victuri sunt*** THOSE WHO ARE GOING TO LIVE UNDER THE SAME KING MUST HAVE THE SAME LAW (Curtius Rufus, *Historiae Alexandri Magni*).

b/ Another possible translation is TO HAVE THE INTENTION OF; for instance:

- **Nunc *audituri sumus* hunc poetam** NOW WE HAVE THE INTENTION OF LISTENING TO THIS POET.

NOW WE ARE ABOUT TO LISTEN TO THIS POET would also be perfectly suitable. Sometimes the context will tell us which option is better.

2. The passive periphrastic [446]

The passive periphrastic conjugation follows the same parameters as the active one, but obviously the future participle will be passive; so, it will imply the use of a *passive future participle in the role of predicative object* with the verb **sum**; moreover, as it is normal in the passive future participle, there will be a sense of obligation, the sentence tells us that the subject must undergo some action. The double translation of the first example will show us the way to rephrase the literal translation:

- Carthago *delenda est* CARTHAGE IS THAT MUST BE DESTROYED ✧ Simplified, CARTHAGE MUST BE DESTROYED.
- Tres libri *scribendi sunt* THREE BOOKS MUST BE WRITTEN.
- Caesar *necandus erat* CAESAR HAD TO BE MURDERED.
- Ego autem si omnia quae *dicenda sunt* libere dixero, ... BUT IF I SAY FREELY EVERYTHING THAT MUST BE SAID, ... (Cicero, *Pro Roscio Amerino*).
- Impetus *faciendus erat* AN ATTACK HAD TO BE MADE (Livy, *Ab Urbe Condita*).
- Eius modi civis *laudandus ac diligendus est* A CITIZEN OF THIS KIND MUST BE PRAISED AND ESTEEMED (Cicero, *In Verrem*).
- A iudicibus *condemnandus est* HE MUST BE CONDEMNED BY THE JUDGES (Cicero, *Pro Plancio*).

Triple note for both active and passive periphrastic

a/ The use of a future participle is not enough to make it a periphrastic conjugation; for instance,

- Heri quinque captivos *necandos* vidi YESTERDAY I SAW FIVE PRISONERS THAT ARE (WERE) ABOUT TO BE KILLED

is not an example of periphrastic conjugation, as the participle is not performing any role of predicative object (in this example, it is just giving some information about the direct object).

b/ Being in nominative is not enough either:

- *Necandi* captivi fugerunt THE PRISONERS THAT WERE ABOUT TO BE KILLED FLED.

Necandi gives us information about the subject, but it is not a predicative object with the verb **sum** (which is not even in the sentence).

c/ But observe this example:

- Captivi *necandi sunt* THE PRISONERS MUST BE KILLED.

This is a periphrastic conjugation (passive, in this example); now **necandi** does perform the role of predicative object with the verb **sum**.

3. The supine in -um [447]

The supine, also used for the formation of some participles, is on its own a *verbal noun*, but it is not used in the same way as the infinitive or the gerund (both verbal nouns also), as its use is very restricted to a couple of possibilities.

The first one of its two possible forms is the supine in accusative, with the ending -**um**. It is used with *verbs of movement* and it has a meaning of purpose; as a general rule, it will not have any object (only some scarce cases can be found in which it has a direct object):

- Venio *lectum* I COME TO READ.
- Milites *praedatum* ierunt THE SOLDIERS WENT TO PLUNDER.
- *Cubitum* eo I GO TO SLEEP.
- Postquam rediit a cena domum, abimus omnes *cubitum* AFTER HE CAME BACK HOME FROM THE DINNER, ALL OF US WENT TO SLEEP (Plautus, *Mostellaria*).
- Illi *oppugnatum* venturi erant? WERE THOSE GOING TO COME TO FIGHT? (Cicero, *Pro Tullio*).
- Legatos ad Iugurtham de iniuriis *questum* misit HE SENT AMBASSADORS TO IUGURTHA TO COMPLAIN ABOUT THE OFFENCES (Sallust, *Bellum Iugurthinum*).

4. The supine in -u [448]

This form is supposed to be dative, and it is used after a reduced group of adjectives; in English, the translation after these adjectives will depend on the usual way of expressing a concept after each one of them:

- Hoc est facile *dictu* THIS IS EASY TO SAY.
- Hic liber dignus *lectu* est THIS BOOK IS WORTH READING.
- Grave est hoc *dictu* THIS IS UNPLEASANT TO SAY (Cicero, *Pro Sulla*).
- Quaerunt quid optimum *factu* sit THEY ASK WHAT IS THE BEST THING TO DO (Cicero, *In Verrem*).
  ✧ In this last example, the supine is inside an indirect question.

A double example:

- O rem non modo *visu* foedam sed etiam *auditu*! O, WHAT A HORRIBLE THING NOT ONLY TO SEE BUT ALSO TO HEAR! (Cicero, *Philippicae*).

h) Combination of negatives

1. Tendencies in the use of negatives [449]

a/ Apart from the combination of negatives that we will see in the following points, it is worth mentioning that Latin has a peculiar tendency to advance the sense of negativity as much as possible in the sentence. For instance:

- **Qui sic purgatus erit, diutina valetudine utetur, *neque ullus* morbus veniet** WHO IS CLEANSED IN THIS WAY WILL ENJOY LASTING HEALTH, AND NO OTHER ILLNESS WILL FALL UPON (Porcius Cato, *De Agricultura*).

Observe that we could have expected **..., atque *nullus morbus* veniet** ..., AND NO OTHER ILLNESS WILL FALL UPON

but the negative sense of **nullus** is applied to **atque** (and, obviously, **atque** AND becomes **neque** NOR and **nullus** NO ONE becomes **ullus** ANY):

..., *neque ullus* morbus veniet ..., which literally means NOR ANY ILLNESS WILL FALL UPON.

b/ The same can happen with an adverb:

- **Memini *neque umquam* obliviscar noctis illius cum ...** I REMEMBER AND I WILL NEVER FORGET THAT NIGHT WHEN ... (Cicero, *Pro Plancio*).

We could have expected **Memini *atque numquam* obliviscar** I REMEMBER AND I WILL NEVER FORGET

but the negative sense of **numquam** is applied to **atque** (and, obviously, **atque** AND becomes **neque** NOR and **numquam** NEVER becomes **umquam** EVER):

Memini *neque umquam* obliviscar ..., which literally means I REMEMBER NOR I WILL EVER FORGET.

2. Negatives cancelling or reinforcing each other? [450]

The combination of the main negative **non** with another negative word may have two different results, depending on the position of the main negative adverb **non**:

a/ If **non** *follows* another negative word, it *cancels* the negative meaning of this word and makes it positive. The first translation that we offer, a literal translation, will make clear why:

- ***Nemo non* venit** — NOBODY DID NOT COME = EVERYBODY CAME.
- ***Nihil non* feci** — NOTHING HAVE I NOT DONE = I HAVE DONE EVERYTHING.
- ***Numquam* meos amicos *non* amabo** — NEVER WILL I NOT LOVE MY FRIENDS = I WILL ALWAYS LOVE MY FRIENDS.
- **Eripere vitam *nemo non* homini potest** (Seneca iunior, *Phoenissae*). — THERE IS NO ONE THAT CAN NOT TAKE AWAY THE LIFE FROM A MAN

- **Aperte enim adulantem *nemo non* videt** THERE IS NO ONE, TO BE SURE, THAT DOES NOT SEE AN OPEN FLATTERER (Cicero, *Laelius de Amicitia*).
- ***Nihil non* facere debuisti secundum meam voluntatem** THERE IS NOTHING YOU DID NOT HAVE TO DO / YOU HAD TO DO EVERYTHING ACCORDING TO MY DESIRE (Quintilianus, *Declamationes Minores*).

In fact, the effect we achieve is much stronger. For instance, saying **Nemo non venit** has a much stronger effect than saying **Omnes venerunt** ALL CAME. By saying **Nemo non venit** we are making very clear that *there was not a single person who did not come:* in Latin, the double negative produces an affirmative sense much stronger than an affirmative sentence itself.

b/ But if **non** *precedes* a negative word, it *reduces partially* the negative meaning of this word: **[451]**

- ***Non nemo* venit** NOT NOBODY CAME = SOMEBODY CAME.
- ***Non* feci *nihil*** I HAVE NOT DONE NOTHING = I HAVE DONE SOMETHING.
- ***Non nihil* commoveor** I AM A LITTLE MOVED (Cicero, *Pro Quinctio*).
- ***Non numquam* in Germaniam ibo** I WILL NOT NEVER GO TO GERMANY = I WILL GO TO GERMANY SOMETIME.
- **Quod fortasse *non nemo* vestrum audierit, ...** WHAT MAYBE SOME OF YOU WILL HAVE HEARD, ... (Cicero, *In Verrem*).
- **In ipsa, inquam, curia *non nemo* hostis est** IN THE SENATE ITSELF, I SAY, THERE IS SOME ENEMY (Cicero, *Pro Murena*).
- ***Non nihil* enim me levant tuae litterae hoc tempore** YOUR LETTER ALLEVIATES ME A LITTLE IN THIS PERIOD (Cicero, *Epistulae ad Atticum*).

While the cancellation in a/ looked logical, this combination in which the main negative **non** precedes the other negative may be a little more difficult to grasp, but the explanation is quite simple. Observe the first example from above:

Non nemo venit [IT IS] NOT [THE CASE THAT] NOBODY CAME, which means that *at least somebody came*.

ALIA

a) Peculiarities and idioms

1. General remarks
2. Non-verbal expressions
3. Verbal expressions

b) Words that are easily confused

1. Non-verbal forms
2. Verbal forms

a) Peculiarities and idioms

1. General remarks [452]

Latin has some peculiarities and idioms that may present some difficulty to the student. Some involve a verb, while others do not.

In the case of those that are not linked to a definite verb, a participle, an infinitive or even a personal verbal form may still be found, but note that the peculiarity or idiom does not depend on this or that verb. Here, they have been grouped under *Non-verbal expressions*, and then subdivided according to several concepts.

Some expressions could have been placed under more than one heading; for instance, **re bene gesta** could have been placed under *Nouns involved* (with respect to the noun **res**) or under *Adjectives or participles involved* (with respect to the participle **gesta**).

In the case of those that are linked to a specific verb, they have been grouped under *Verbal expressions* and classified by alphabetical order of that verb (compound verbs will be found also inside the group of the verb of which they are a compound). We have alternated both orders of *verb + object*, as this variety is typical of Latin; therefore, for example, you can find either **iram condere** or **careo morte**. Moreover, some will be introduced just by mentioning the words that form the idiom, and others will be introduced by a whole sentence.

2. Non-verbal expressions [453]

a) Nouns involved

❑ dies, -ei DAY

diem de die DAY AFTER DAY

- Cum is *diem de die* differret dum Hippocrates atque Himilco admoverent castra ... AS HE WAS DELAYING THE ACTION UNTIL HIPPOCRATES AND HIMILCO MIGHT MOVE THEIR CAMP ... (Livy, *Ab Urbe Condita*).

❑ domus, -us HOUSE

1/ domi militiaeque IN PEACE AND IN WAR

- Igitur *domi militiaeque* boni mores colebantur THEREFORE GOOD CUSTOMS WERE PRACTISED IN PEACE AND IN WAR (Sallust, *Catilinae Coniuraio*).

2/ Unde domo? FROM WHICH COUNTRY?

- Quo tenditis? inquit. Qui genus? *Unde domo?* WHERE ARE YOU GOING? WHAT PEOPLE ARE YOU? FROM WHICH COUNTRY? (Vergil, *Aeneis*).

❑ locus, -i PLACE

1/ nullum locum praetermittere NOT TO MISS ANY OPPORTUNITY

- *Nullum locum praetermitto* monendi I DO NOT MISS ANY OPPORTUNITY FOR ADVISING (Cicero, *Epistulae ad Familiares*).

2/ suo loco WHEN THE RIGHT MOMENT ARRIVES

- ... de qua planius paulo post *suo loco* dicemus, nunc breviter ... ... ABOUT WHICH A LITTLE LATER WE WILL SPEAK MORE CLEARLY WHEN THE RIGHT MOMENT ARRIVES, NOW JUST BRIEFLY ... (Anon., *Rhetorica ad Herennium*).

3/ obsidum loco AS HOSTAGES / IN THE PLACE OF HOSTAGES

- Reliquos *obsidum loco* secum ducere decreverat HE HAD DECIDED TO TAKE THE REMAINING ONES WITH HIM AS HOSTAGES (Caesar, *De Bello Gallico*).

4/ ad id locorum UP TO THEN

- Tamen is *ad id locorum* talis vir ... consulatum adpetere non audebat NEVERTHELESS HE, UP TO THEN SUCH A MAN, DID NOT DARE TO STRIVE FOR THE CONSULATE (Sallust, *Bellum Iugurthinum*).

5/ interea loci MEANWHILE

- Te *interea loci* cognovi MEANWHILE I BECAME ACQUAINTED WITH YOU (Terentius Afer, *Eunuchus*).

6/ post id locorum / postea loci AFTERWARDS

- Neque post id locorum Iugurthae dies aut nox ulla quieta fuit AFTERWARDS IUGURTHA DID NOT HAVE ANY DAY OR NIGHT IN CALM (Sallust, *Bellum Iugurthinum*).

❑ ludus, -i GAME, SCHOOL

1/ There are two ways of saying to mock someone:

aliquem/alicui ludos facere

- Quo modo *me ludos fecisti* de illa conducticia fidicina? WHY DID YOU MOCK ME ABOUT THAT HIRED LYRE-PLAYER? (Plautus, *Epidicus*).

2/ Let's remember that ludus may also mean SCHOOL:

ludus litterarum or ludus litterarius ELEMENTARY SCHOOL (where children learnt the basics of writing and reading)

- Relinque istum *ludum litterarium* philosophorum LEAVE THAT ELEMENTARY SCHOOL OF PHILOSOPHERS (Seneca iunior, *Epistulae Morales ad Lucilium*).

❑ **opus est / usus est** IT IS NECESSARY

1/ These two impersonal expressions, both of them meaning IT IS NECESSARY, are usually followed by a past participle in ablative instead of by an infinitive:

- Tibi ut opus est *facto*, fac DO AS IT IS NECESSARY FOR YOU TO DO (Cicero, *De Finibus Bonorum et Malorum*).
- Tacere nequeo misera quod *tacito* usus est I CAN'T KEEP SILENT, POOR ME, WHAT NEED IS THERE TO BE SILENT (Plautus, *Cistellaria*).

2/ But we can find it also followed by an infinitive clause (which sounds more normal to our ears):

- Quid me tibi *adesse* opus est? WHY DO I HAVE TO HELP YOU (Plautus, *Bacchides*).

❑ **poena, -ae** PUNISHMENT

1/ poenas do

Although the first impression is that it means to impose a punishment, in fact it means *to pay a penalty, to be punished:*

- Praedones multi saepe *poenas dant* MANY PIRATES OFTEN ARE PUNISHED (Cicero, *De Natura Deorum*).

2/ The idiom that means TO IMPOSE A PENALTY is **poenas peto** (but there are many verbs that can be used instead of **peto**: **expeto, sumo, capio, reposco**, etc.):

- Forsitan *poenas petet* irata Iuno MAYBE THE ANGRY JUNO WILL IMPOSE A PUNISHMENT (Seneca iunior, *Hercules Oetaeus*).

3/ And the maximum punishment:

capitis poena DEATH PENALTY

- *Capitis poenam* iis qui non paruerint constituit HE ESTABLISHED THE DEATH PENALTY FOR THOSE WHO WOULD NOT OBEY (Caesar, *De Bello Gallico*).

❑ **res, rei** THING

As with **dies**, the noun **res** combines in many idioms:

1/ re vera IN FACT

- Dat praeterea potestatem verbo praetoriam, *re vera* regiam AFTERWARDS HE CONCEDES THEORETICALLY PRAETORIAN POWER, BUT IN FACT ROYAL POWER (Cicero, *De Lege Agraria*).

2/ non ab re est IT IS NOT DESPICABLE

- Id quoque notasse *non ab re est* IT IS NOT DESPICABLE TO HAVE NOTED IT (Pliny, *Historia Naturalis*).
  ✧ Notasse = notavisse

3/ res publica THE STATE

- A quo periculo prohibete *rem publicam* KEEP THE STATE AWAY FROM THIS DANGER (Cicero, *Pro Lege Manilia*).

4/ rerum potior TO SEIZE POWER

- Dominationem tamen exspectant, *rerum potiri* volunt THEY EXPECT TO HAVE CONTROL, THEY WANT TO SEIZE POWER (Cicero, *In Catilinam*).

5/ res gestae EXPLOITS, ACHIEVEMENTS

- Thucydides enim *rerum gestarum* pronuntiator sincerus et grandis etiam fuit THUCYDIDES WAS A SINCERE AND ALSO GREAT NARRATOR OF EXPLOITS (Cicero, *Brutus*).

6/ res familiaris THE HOUSEHOLD

- *Res familiaris* sua quemque delectat EVERYBODY LIKES HIS OWN HOUSEHOLD (Cicero, *Post Reditum ad Populum*).

7/ res rustica AGRICULTURE

- Totae autem *res rusticae* eius modi sunt ALL ASPECTS OF AGRICULTURE ARE OF THIS KIND (Cicero, *In Verrem*).
  ✧ Literally, ALL AGRICULTURES ARE...

8/ res militaris THE ART OF WAR, MILITARY AFFAIRS

- Demus igitur imperium Caesari sine quo *res militaris* administrari ... non potest LET'S GIVE THE COMMANDMENT TO CAESAR, WITHOUT WHICH MILITARY AFFAIRS CAN NOT BE DEALT WITH (Cicero, *Philippicae*).

9/ res manifesta EVIDENCE

- *Res manifestas* quaeris YOU DEMAND EVIDENCE (Cicero, *In Verrem*).

❑ senatus, -us SENATE

1/ senatu movere TO EXPEL OUT OF THE SENATE
✧ Not in a physical sense but in the sense of removing from somebody the rank of senator.

2/ senatus frequens THE WHOLE OF THE SENATE
✧ In the sense of a session in which most of its members are present, not in the sense of a totally unanimous decision:

- Decrevit *senatus frequens* de meo reditu THE WHOLE OF THE SENATE DECIDED ABOUT MY RETURN (Cicero, *Pro Sestio*).

3/ senatus datus est means that somebody was given the opportunity of speaking to the senate:

- Ubi est Romam ventum, in Capitolio eis *senatus datus est* WHEN HE CAME TO ROME, HE WAS GIVEN THE OPPORTUNITY OF SPEAKING TO THE SENATE (Livy, *Ab Urbe Condita*).

❑ tempus, -oris TIME

1/ id temporis AT THAT TIME

- ... quos ego iam ... ad me *id temporis* venturos esse praedixeram ... WHOM I HAD ALREADY PREDICTED WOULD COME TO ME AT THAT TIME (Cicero, *In Catilinam*).

2/ The sense of **tempus** as CHANCE, OPPORTUNITY is very frequent:

tempore capto TAKING ADVANTAGE OF THE OPPORTUNITY

- Cum ad Flaccum in castra venissent ut inde *tempore capto* abirent, ... WHEN THEY HAD GONE TO FLACCUS TO HIS CAMP IN ORDER TO DEPART FROM THERE AT THE RIGHT MOMENT, ... (Livy, *Ab Urbe Condita*).

tempus habes YOU HAVE A GOOD OPPORTUNITY

- *Tempus habes* tale quale nemo habuit umquam YOU HAVE AN OPPORTUNITY SUCH AS NOBODY EVER HAD (Cicero, *Philippicae*).

3/ ex quo tempore FROM THE TIME WHEN

- *Ex quo tempore* tu me diligere coepisti ... FROM THE TIME WHEN YOU BEGAN TO ESTEEM ME ... (Cicero, *Epistulae ad Familiares*).

4/ ad tempus AT THE APPOINTED TIME

- Accurrunt tamen *ad tempus* tutores THE DEFENDERS COME RUNNING AT THE APPOINTED TIME (Cicero, *In Verrem*).

5/ ad hoc tempus UP TO NOW / THEN

- Nero princeps iusserat colosseum se pingi CXX pedum linteo, incognitum *ad hoc tempus* NERO, THE RULER, HAD ORDERED A COLOSSAL IMAGE OF HIM TO BE PAINTED IN A CLOTH OF 120 FEET, SOMETHING UNKNOWN UP TO THEN (Pliny, *Historia Naturalis*).

  ✧ Literally, it says ... HAD ORDERED THAT HE HIMSELF BE PAINTED...; **pingi** is a passive infinitive.

❑ via, -ae WAY

se in viam dare TO SET OFF

- *In viam* quod *te des* hoc tempore nihil est YOU SHOULD NOT SET OFF IN THIS TIME OF THE YEAR (Cicero, *Epistulae ad Familiares*).

b) Adjectives or participles involved [454]

❑ captus, -a, -um CAPTURED

The participle **captus** offers us several idioms, all of them with the background meaning of AFFECTED:

1/ mente captus, animi captus SILLY, FOOLISH

- Quis potest esse .. tam *mente captus* qui neget ...? WHO CAN BE SO FOOLISH WHO MAY DENY ...? (Cicero, *In Catilinam*).

2/ oculis captus BLIND

- ... si *oculis captus* sit, ut Tiresisas fuit, ... IF HE IS AS BLIND AS WAS TIRESIAS ... (Cicero, *De Divinatione*).

3/ membris omnibus captus DISABLED (in physical sense)

- Cum denique Q. Scaevola ... *membris omnibus captus* ac debilis ... WHEN FINALLY Q. SCAEVOLA, DISABLED AND WEAK ... (Cicero, *Pro Rabirio*).

❑ certus, -a, -um CERTAIN, AWARE

1/ certiorem facere TO INFORM SOMEBODY

- ... perveniunt atque eum de rebus gestis *certiorem faciunt* ... THEY ARRIVE AND INFORM HIM ABOUT WHAT HAD BEEN DONE (Caesar, *De Bello Gallico*).

2/ pro certo negare TO DENY CATEGORICALLY

- Omnia quae recta non erunt *pro certo negato* EVERYTHING THAT IS NOT RIGHT, DENY IT CATEGORICALLY (Cicero, *Epistulae ad Atticum*).

  ✧ An example of future imperative, something difficult to find except in Cicero.

3/ pro certo scire TO KNOW AS SOMETHING SURE

- Quid rei esset nemo satis *pro certo scire* WHAT THE AFFAIR WAS, NOBODY KNEW FOR CERTAIN (Livy, *Ab Urbe Condita*).

4/ mihi certum est I HAVE DECIDED

- *Mihi certum est* ... illius uti confessione et testimoniis I HAVE DECIDED TO MAKE USE OF HIS CONFESSION AND OF THE WITNESSES (Cicero, *Pro Caecina*).

❑ coeptus, -a, -um BEGUN

The participle of **coepi** forms several temporal fixed expressions as ablative absolutes:

1/ coepta luce AT THE BEGINNING OF THE DAY

- *Coepta luce* missae in latera legiones ... locum deseruere AT THE BEGINNING OF THE DAY THE LEGIONS THAT HAD BEEN SENT TO THE FLANKS ABANDONED THE PLACE (Tacitus, *Annales*).

2/ coepta hieme AT THE BEGINNING OF THE WINTER

❑ dictus, -a, -um SAID

Its neuter dictum, -i is used as a noun:

dicta dare TO PRONOUNCE WORDS

- Haec ubi *dicta dedit*, ... WHEN HE HAD SAID THESE WORDS, ... (Vergil, *Aeneis*).

❑ gestus, -a, -um DONE, MADE

1/ re bene gesta AFTER THE VICTORY HAD BEEN ACHIEVED

- omnibus locis *re bene gesta*, ... triumphans in urbem rediit AFTER VICTORY HAD BEEN ACHIEVED EVERYWHERE, HE CAME BACK INTO THE CITY AMONG CELEBRATIONS (Livy, *Ab Urbe Condita*).

2/ re male gesta AFTER SUFFERING A DEFEAT

- Ita *re male gesta* Cn. Pompeius filius naves inde avertit THUS, AFTER SUFFERING A DEFEAT, C. POMPEIUS, THE SON, DIVERTED HIS SHIPS FROM THERE (Anon., *Bellum Africum*).

3/ res gestae EXPLOITS, ACHIEVEMENTS

- *Tuae res gestae* ita notae sunt ut ... YOUR EXPLOITS ARE SO WELL-KNOWN THAT ... (Cicero, *Epistulae ad Familiares*).

❑ laborantes, -ium (several meanings)

It may have the sense of STRUGGLING: milites laborantes SOLDIERS THAT ARE STRUGGLING FOR THEIR LIFE.

- Tertium aciem *laborantibus nostris* subsidio misit HE SENT THE THIRD LINE TO HELP OUR SOLDIERS THAT WERE STRUGGLING (Caesar, *De Bello Gallico*).

❑ magnus, -a, -um LARGE, BIG

1/ magna loqui TO SPEAK PROUDLY

- Cur non arma capit, dat, quod vaga turba sequatur? Non erat hoc nimium numquam nisi *magna loquenti* WHY DOES HE NOT TAKE UP ARMS, SO THAT THE HESITANT CROWD MAY FOLLOW HIM? THIS WOULD NOT BE TOO MUCH FOR ONE WHO SPEAKS PROUDLY (Ovid, *Metamorphoses*).

2/ magno emere TO BUY AT A HIGH PRICE

- Si *magno emerat*, ... IF HE HAD BOUGHT IT AT A HIGH PRICE, ... (Cicero, *In Verrem*).

3/ magni aestimare / facere TO HAVE IN HIGH ESTEEM

- ... quod tu scis, quod ego *magni aestimo* ... WHAT YOU KNOW, WHAT I HAVE IN HIGH ESTEEM (Cicero, *Epistulae ad Atticum*).

4/ magna voce ALOUD, LOUDLY

- *Magna voce* dicere solebat ... HE USED TO SAY ALOUD ... (Cicero, *Tusculanae Disputationes*).

❑ **natus, -a, -um** BORN

1/ **post homines natos** SINCE MANKIND WAS CREATED

- ... **optimus multo** ***post homines natos*** **gladiator** ... THE BEST GLADIATOR, BY MUCH, SINCE MANKIND EXISTS (Lucilius, *Saturae*).

2/ **natus** may also mean SON, and **nata** may mean DAUGHTER.

❑ **pugnans, -antis** (several meanings)

pugnantia loquor TO SAY CONTRADICTORY THINGS:

- ***Pugnantia*** **te** ***loqui*** **non vides?** DO YOU NOT SEE THAT YOU ARE SAYING CONTRADICTORY THINGS? (Cicero, *Tusculanae Disputationes*).

c) Cases of unexpected agreement [455]

1/ When a predicative object is an adjective, we may find that the subject and predicative object do not agree in gender as one would expect. First let's take a look at what would be the expected case:

- **Victoria pulchra est** VICTORY IS BEAUTIFUL.

But if it is written **Victoria** ***pulchrum*** **est** the meaning will be VICTORY IS SOMETHING BEAUTIFUL.

In this case, although **victoria** is feminine, the predicative object **pulchrum** is in neuter, and rather than just qualifying **victoria** it is telling us *what* **victoria** is.

2/ A similar phenomenon is the use of a masculine or feminine demonstrative form instead of the expected neuter:

- **Eius belli** ***haec*** **fuit causa** THIS WAS THE REASON FOR THIS WAR (Caesar, *De Bello Gallico*).

We could have found ... **hoc fuit causa**, THIS WAS THE REASON ..., with **hoc** meaning THIS in a general sense (some circumstance, some event, etc.), but it is made to agree in gender with **causa**.

d) The personal construction of the infinitive [456]

With verbs of *reporting*, instead of the impersonal construction of the infinitive, such as

Dicitur Caesarem venisse IT IS SAID THAT CAESAR HAS COME

where **dicitur** is used impersonally (although, grammatically speaking, the infinitive clause **Caesarem venisse** is the subject), we can find the personal construction of the infinitive:

- ***Caesar dicitur*** **venisse** IT IS SAID THAT CAESAR HAS COME
  - ✧ Literally, CAESAR IS SAID TO HAVE COME.
  - ✧ Observe that now the verb **dicitur** has a personal subject (**Caesar**).

Let's see a double example in which moreover there is a predicative object:

⇨ Impersonal construction: Dicitur Graecos gratos esse IT IS SAID THAT THE GREEKS ARE GRATEFUL.

⇨ Personal construction: *Graeci dicuntur* grati esse IT IS SAID THAT THE GREEKS ARE GRATEFUL.

✧ Literally, THE GREEKS ARE SAID TO BE GRATEFUL.

✧ Observe that now the predicative object **grati** is in nominative, as now it refers to the subject of the main verb.

Some examples of personal construction

- *Dicitur* eo tempore glorians apud suos *Pompeius* dixisse ... IT IS SAID THAT AT THAT TIME POMPEIUS, BOASTING AMONG HIS MEN, SAID ... (Caesar, *Bellum Civile*).
- *C. Verres* per triennium ... fana spoliasse *dicitur* IT IS SAID THAT VERRES PLUNDERED THE TEMPLES FOR THREE YEARS (Cicero, *In Q. Caecilium*).
- *Hi* centum pagos habere *dicuntur* THESE ARE SAID TO HAVE ONE-HUNDRED DISTRICTS (Caesar, *De Bello Gallico*).
- *Septem* fuisse *dicuntur* uno tempore, qui sapientes et haberentur et vocarentur IT IS SAID THAT THEY WERE SEVEN AT THE SAME TIME, WHO WERE BOTH CONSIDERED AND CALLED WISE (Cicero, *De Oratore*).

e) The uses of et [457]

1/ The usual meaning of AND:

Not much to comment here, as this is the most well-known meaning of **et**:

- In Graecia Lacedaemonii *et* Athenienses coepere urbis atque nationes subigere IN GREECE SPARTANS AND ATHENIANS STARTED TO SUBDUE CITIES AND NATIONS (Sallust, *Catilinae Coniuratio*).

2/ The meaning of ALSO:

- Non solum meum patrem, *et* me necare conati sunt THEY TRIED TO KILL NOT ONLY MY FATHER, BUT ALSO ME.

3/ The meaning BOTH ... AND:

When repeated, they must be translated by BOTH ... AND:

- L. Catilina, nobili genere natus, fuit magna vi *et* animi *et* corporis L. CATILINA, BORN FROM NOBLE ORIGIN, WAS A MAN OF GREAT STRENGTH BOTH OF SOUL AND OF BODY (Sallust, *Catilinae Coniuratio*).

f) Quod si [458]

This combination means BUT IF. The meaning BUT is not one of the usual meanings of **quod**, although in this case we must accept that this combination produces this meaning:

- *Quod si* ille suas proferet tabulas, proferet suas quoque Roscius BUT IF HE SHOWS HIS ACCOUNTS, ROSCIUS WILL SHOW HIS ALSO (Cicero, *Pro Roscio Comoedo*).

g) Futurum esse / fore ut [459]

1/ We have seen in the section on infinitive clauses that future infinitives can be used like in this example:

⇨ Direct statement: **Octavia libros Caesari dabit** OCTAVIA WILL GIVE THE BOOKS TO CAESAR.
⇨ Indirect statement: **Puto Octaviam libros Caesari *daturam esse*** I THINK THAT OCTAVIA WILL GIVE THE BOOKS TO CAESAR.

The problem would come if the verb is in the passive voice, like in this example:

⇨ Direct statement: **Pons delebitur a Caesare** THE BRIDGE WILL BE DESTROYED BY CAESAR.
⇨ Indirect statement: **Puto pontem *deletum iri* a Caesare** I THINK THAT THE BRIDGE WILL BE DESTROYED BY CAESAR.

Although this is grammatically right, the passive future infinitive is not much used for reported speech, and in exchange this kind of statements about a future action are usually expressed in another way: by means of **futurum esse**, the future infinitive of **sum** in its neuter singular form, followed by a result clause (obviously, introduced by **ut**).

- The sense of future is in the infinitive **futurum esse** (or **fore**).
- The action to be performed is expressed in the **ut** clause.

The final result would be **Puto *fore ut* pons a Caesare deleatur**.
✧ Literally: I THINK THAT IT WILL BE THAT THE BRIDGE BE DESTROYED BY CAESAR.

- **Sperant *fore ut* patris litteris nuntiisque filius ab illo furore revocetur** THEY HOPE THAT THE SON MAY BE CALLED OFF FROM THAT INSANITY BY MEANS OF LETTERS AND MESSENGERS FROM HIS FATHER (Cicero, *In Verrem*).

2/ This device is also used in the active voice, in case we need a future active infinitive of a verb that has no supine (and that therefore can not have a future active infinitive):

⇨ Direct statement: **Marcus Caesarem timebit** MARCUS WILL FEAR CAESAR.
⇨ Indirect statement: **Puto Marcum Caesarem** + *future inf. of* ***timeo*** I THINK THAT MARCUS WILL FEAR CAESAR.

The verb **timeo** has no supine, so it does not have a future infinitive. The only option we have is to use the aforementioned construction with **fore (futurum esse) ut**:

Puto *fore ut* Marcus Caesarem timeat I THINK THAT MARCUS WILL FEAR CAESAR.
✧ Literally: I THINK THAT IT WILL BE THAT MARCUS FEAR CAESAR.

3/ So, the usage of **fore ut** is a matter either of avoiding the unusual passive future infinitive or of solving the problem of the absence of a future active infinitive. For example, the deponent verb **ulciscor** TO AVENGE has no future infinitive; most deponent verbs can have a future infinitive, like **conaturum, -am, -um esse**, but not all of them have it, and **ulturum, -am, -um esse** (derived from its perfect form **ultus sum**) is not found:

- **Clamabant *fore ut* ipsi se di immortales ulciscerentur** THEY WERE SHOUTING THAT THE IMMORTAL GODS THEMSELVES WOULD AVENGE THEM (Cicero, *In Verrem*).

3. Verbal expressions [460]

As specified at the beginning of the chapter, the verbal expressions are listed alphabetically, grouping together the expressions based on the same verb; some additional explanation has been added when it has been considered necessary.

The list of verbal expressions can be endless, so we have included only those which students are more liable to come across.

❑ admitto

equo admisso AT FULL GALLOP

- Considius *equo admisso* ad eum accurrit CONSIDIUS RUNS TO HIM AT FULL GALLOP (Caesar, *De Bello Gallico*).

❑ aestimo

1/ As part of the genitive of value, we can find a strange construction to mean that we value something at very little: instead of using the genitive **minimi**, we use the genitive **assis** OF AN AS (minimum monetary unit, like a penny) or the genitive **flocci** OF A LOCK OF WOOL:

- Rumores senum severiorum omnes *unius aestimemus assis* LET'S VALUE ALL THE GOSSIP OF THE ELDERLY PEOPLE, RATHER AUSTERE, AT ONE AS (Catullus, *Carmina*).
- Rumorem, famam *flocci fecit* HE GAVE NO IMPORTANCE TO GOSSIP AND FAME (Sex. Pompeius Festus, *De Verborum Significatione*).

2/ In this idiom it is common to find the phenomenon of the unnecessary negative (a **non** that must not be translated):

- *Non* ego te flocci facio I GIVE NO IMPORTANCE TO YOU (Plautus, *Curculio*).
  ✧ Without the **Non**, it would go on meaning the same.

Of course, if we want to translate this **Non**, then we must remove the negative meaning from **flocci**: I DO NOT GIVE ANY IMPORTANCE TO YOU. We have changed from NO IMPORTANCE to ANY IMPORTANCE.

❑ ago

1/ vitam ago TO SPEND ONE'S LIFE

2/ gratias ago TO SAY THANKS

- Maximas tibi omnes *gratias agimus* WE ALL ARE VERY GRATEFUL TO YOU (Cicero, *Pro Marcello*).

3/ animam agere TO DIE

- Hortensius, cum has litteras scripsi, *animam agebat* HORTENSIUS, WHILE I WROTE THIS LETTER, WAS DYING (Cicero, *Epistulae ad Familiares*).

4/ causam agere TO DEFEND A JUDICIAL CASE

- Cicero ipse etiam *causam egit* ad populum CICERO HIMSELF DEFENDED THE CASE IN FRONT OF THE PEOPLE (Asconius Pedianus, *Pro Milone*).

❑ amo

amabo te PLEASE

- Dic, *amabo te*, ubi est Diniarchus? TELL ME, PLEASE, WHERE IS DINIARCHUS? (Plautus, *Truculentus*).

❑ arcesso

This verb, that has the meaning of TO SUMMON, may have the meaning of TO ACCUSE, in the sense of *calling to court*, and the accusation is in genitive:

pecuniae captae arcessere TO ACCUSE OF BRIBERY

- ... quos *pecuniae captae arcessebat*, ... WHOM HE ACCUSED OF BRIBERY, ... (Sallust, *Bellum Iugurthinum*).

❑ audio

1/ male audire TO HAVE A BAD REPUTATION

- Nullo in loco male audit misericordia MERCY HAS BAD FAME NOWHERE (Publilius Syrus, *Sententiae*).

2/ male loqui TO SPEAK IN BAD TERMS ABOUT SOMEBODY

- At etiam, furcifer, *male loqui* mi audes? AND YOU, RASCAL, DO YOU DARE TO SPEAK IN BAD TERMS ABOUT ME? (Plautus, *Captivi*).

  ✧ Observe that the person about whom we speak in bad terms must be in *dative* (and here **mi** = **mihi**).

❑ capio

1/ portum capere TO ARRIVE IN HARBOUR

- Hae naves euro ... *portum capere* prohibebantur THESE SHIPS WERE PREVENTED FROM ARRIVING IN HARBOUR BY THE EURUS
  (Anon., *Bellum Alexandrinum*).

  ✧ The Eurus was a kind of wind (but Eurosceptics may like this example about the bad effects of the Euro...).

2/ tempus capere TO MAKE USE OF THE OPPORTUNITY

- Commode *tempus* ad te *cepit* adeundi HE SUITABLY MADE USE OF THE OPPORTUNITY OF APPROACHING YOU (Cicero, *Epistulae ad Familiares*).

❑ careo

carere morte TO BE IMMORTAL

- Carmina *morte carent* POEMS ARE IMMORTAL (Ovid, *Amores*).

❑ cogo

Si res cogat, ... IF IT IS NECESSARY ✧ Literally, IF THE SITUATION COMPELS, ...

- ... bello quoque *si res cogat* ... ALSO BY MEANS OF WAR, IF THE SITUATION MAKES IT NECESSARY (Livy, *Ab Urbe Condita*).

❑ condo

1/ iram condere TO HIDE YOUR ANGER

- Adeo *iram condiderat* TO SUCH AN EXTENT HE HAD HIDDEN HIS ANGER (Tacitus, *Annales*).

2/ in carcerem condere TO IMPRISON

- Hominibus acceptis et *in carcerem conditis* ... AFTER THE MEN HAD BEEN TAKEN AND IMPRISONED ... (Livy, *Ab Urbe Condita*).

❑ deleo

bellum delere TO PUT A COMPLETE END TO THE WAR

- Non modo praesentia, verum etiam *futura bella delevit* NOT ONLY DID HE PUT AN END TO THE CURRENT WARS, BUT EVEN TO THE FUTURE ONES (Cicero, *Laelius de Amicitia*).

❑ do

1/ vela dare TO SET SAIL

- Hanc quoque deserimus sedem paucisque relictis *vela damus* WE LEAVE ALSO THIS SETTLEMENT AND, AFTER LEAVING BEHIND A FEW PEOPLE, WE SET SAIL (Vergil, *Aeneis*).

2/ poenas dare TO SUFFER THF PUNISHMENT

- Praedones multi saepe *poenas dant* OFTEN MANY PIRATES SUFFER PUNISHMENT (Cicero, *De Natura Deorum*).

❑ duco

1/ uxorem ducere TO GET MARRIED

Related to this meaning, we have these idioms:

ducere ex plebe TO MARRY A WOMAN FROM THE PLEBS ✧ Observe the absence of direct object.

- ... nec *ducendo ex plebe* neque vestras filias sororesque ecnubere sinendo ... ... NEITHER MARRYING WOMEN FROM THE PLEBS NOR ALLOWING YOUR DAUGHTERS AND SISTERS TO MARRY ... (Livy, *Ab Urbe Condita*).

ex latere uxorem ducere TO GET MARRIED WITH A COUSIN

2/ fossam ducere TO DIG A DITCH

- *Duxit fossam* latitudine pedum C HE DUG A DITCH ONE HUNDRED FEET WIDE (Plinius Secundus, *Naturalis Historia*).

❑ egredior

Apart from the normal meaning of TO GO OUT, this verb can also mean TO EXCEED, and we can find this meaning in these idioms:

1/ modum egredi TO EXCEED THE LIMIT

- Sed copia quoque *modum egressa* vitiosa est BUT ALSO EXCESS (literally, ABUNDANCE THAT HAS EXCEEDED THE LIMIT) IS A FAULT (Quintilianus, *Institutio Oratoria*).

2/ decem annos egressus AT THE AGE OF TEN YEARS

❑ exigo

1/ With expressions of time (accusatives of extension), it has the meaning of TO SPEND:

- Noctem domi *exegi* I SPENT THE NIGHT AT HOME.

2/ secum aliquid exigere TO MEDITATE ABOUT SOMETHING WITH YOURSELF

- Dum *talia secum exigit* Hippomenes, ... WHILE HIPPOMENES MEDITATES ABOUT SUCH MATTERS WITH HIMSELF, ... (Ovid, *Metamorphoses*).

❑ experior

experior extrema omnia TO MAKE USE OF THE VERY LAST RESOURCES

- Constituit bellum facere et *extrema omnia experiri* HE DECIDED TO WAGE WAR AND MAKE USE OF THE VERY LAST RESOURCES (Sallust, *Catilinae Coniuratio*).

❑ facio

1/ potestatem facere TO AUTHORISE

- Caesar iis, quos in castris retinuerat, discedendi *potestatem fecit* CAESAR GAVE PERMISSION TO LEAVE TO THOSE WHOM HE HAD RETAINED IN THE CAMP (Caesar, *De Bello Gallico*).

2/ ab/cum aliquo facere TO SUPPORT SOMEONE

- Si ratio *mecum facit*, ... IF I AM RIGHT, ... (Cicero, *De Divinatione*).
  ✧ Literally, IF REASON SUPPORTS ME, ...

3/ naufragium facere TO SUFFER SHIPWRECK

- Inprobe Neptunum accusat, qui iterum *naufragium facit* HE WHO SUFFERS SHIPWRECK A SECOND TIME ACCUSES NEPTUNE IMPROPERLY (Publilius Syrus, *Sententiae*).

❑ gero

1/ bellum gero TO WAGE WAR

- Magna cum hominum multitudine *bellum gerere* conantur THEY TRY TO WAGE WAR WITH A LARGE MULTITUDE OF MEN (Caesar, *De Bello Gallico*).

2/ When used reflexively, it means TO BEHAVE:

- *Se* bene *gessit* HE BEHAVED WELL.
- Ita *se gessit*, ut ea facere ei liceret HE BEHAVED THUS, AS IF IT WERE ALLOWED TO HIM TO DO THAT (Cicero, *Tusculanae Disputationes*).

❑ habeo

1/ Ludibrio aliquem habeo TO MOCK SOMEBODY

- *Ludibrio*, pater, *habeor* I AM BEING MOCKED, FATHER (Plautus, *Menaechmi*).

2/ orationem habere TO MAKE A SPEECH
oratione habita, ... AFTER THE SPEECH, ...
verba habere TO SAY A FEW WORDS.

- M. Porcius Cato ... sententiam huiusce modi *orationem habuit* M. PORCIUS CATO MADE A SPEECH IN THIS WAY (Sallust, *Catilinae Coniuratio*).

3/ vitam/aetatem habere TO SPEND YOUR LIFE

- Qui ... in obscuro *vitam habent*, ... THOSE WHO SPEND THEIR LIFE IN AN IGNOBLE WAY ... (Sallust, *Catilinae Coniuratio*).

4/ bene se habere TO FEEL WELL

- Imperator, inquit, *bene se habet* THE EMPEROR, HE SAID, FEELS WELL (Seneca senior, *Suasoriae*).

5/ res sic se habet THIS IS THE STATE OF AFFAIRS

- *Sic* enim *res se habet* THIS IS THE STATE OF AFFAIRS (Cicero, *De Natura Deorum*).

6/ persuasum habeo TO BE PERSUADED

- Romanos ... culmina Alpium occupare conari ... *persuasum habebant* THEY WERE PERSUADED THAT THE ROMANS WERE TRYING TO OCCUPY THE SUMMITS OF THE ALPS (Caesar, *De Bello Gallico*).

❑ iaceo

pretia iacent PRICES ARE VERY LOW

- Accepit enim agrum temporibus eis cum *iacerent pretia* praediorum HE TOOK POSSESSION OF A FIELD IN THOSE TIMES WHEN THE PRICES OF FARMS WERE VERY LOW (Cicero, *Pro Roscio Comoedo*).

❑ lego

1/ vestigia legere TO FOLLOW THE TRACK

- ..., qui sparsa ducis *vestigia legit* ..., WHO FOLLOWED THE SCATTERED TRACKS OF THE GENERAL (Lucan, *Bellum Civile*).

2/ In its more basic meaning of TO PICK UP, it may also mean TO STEAL:

sacra legere TO STEAL SACRED OBJECTS

- Sacrilegus dicitur, qui *sacra legit* HE WHO STEALS SACRED OBJECTS IS CALLED SACRILEGIOUS (Servius Honoratus, *In Vergilii Bucolicon Librum*).

❑ mitto

1/ vocem pro aliquo mittere TO SPEAK IN SOMEBODY'S DEFENCE

- Haec ergo cum viderem, ... *vocem pro me* ac pro re publica neminem *mittere*, ... SO, WHEN I SAW THESE THINGS, THAT NOBODY SPOKE IN MY DEFENCE OR IN DEFENCE OF THE STATE, ... (Cicero, *Pro Sestio*).

2/ manu mittere TO GIVE FREEDOM

- Omnes illos in testamento meo *manu mitto* IN MY WILL, I GIVE FREEDOM TO ALL THOSE (Petronius, *Satyrica*).

❑ morior

moriar si ... MAY I DIE IF ...

- *Moriar si* quicquam fieri potest elegantius MAY I DIE IF ANYTHING CAN BE DONE WITH MORE ELEGANCE (Cicero, *Epistulae ad Atticum*).

❑ moveo

1/ gradum moveo TO WALK A STEP

- *Move* formicinum *gradum* MAKE AN ANT'S STEP! (Plautus, *Menaechmi*).

2/ castra movere TO DISMANTLE THE CAMP

- Duodecimo die *castra movet* ON THE TWELFTH DAY HE DISMANTLES THE CAMP (Caesar, *De Bello Gallico*).

3/ lacrimas movere TO MAKE CRY

- Ego fortasse illi *lacrimas movebo* MAYBE I WILL MAKE HIM CRY (Seneca iunior, *Epistulae Morales ad Lucilium*).
  ✧ Observe that the person affected must be in dative.

❑ muto

mutari in peius TO GET WORSE

- Bona facile *mutantur in peius* GOOD THINGS GET WORSE EASILY (Quintilianus, *Institutio Oratoria*).

❑ narro

male/bene narrare TO BRING GOOD/BAD NEWS

- *Male narras* de Nepotis filio YOU BRING BAD NEWS ABOUT NEPOS' SON (Cicero, *Epistulae ad Atticum*).

❑ nubo

As this verb is used when talking about a woman (in nominative) marrying a man (in dative), we can find this funny idiom:

- Uxori *nubere* nolo meae I DO NOT WANT TO BE UNDER MY WIFE'S CONTROL (Martial, *Epigrammata*).
  ✧ The grammatical interchange of functions produces this image of a woman and a man exchanging the familiar roles: the woman has become the husband and the man has become the wife.

❑ oportet

Preceded by **atque**, very frequently it has the meaning of WHEN IT IS CONVENIENT:

- ... alio tempore atque *oportuerit* ... AT A MOMENT WHEN IT WAS CONVENIENT (Caesar, *De Bello Gallico*).

❑ pello

1/ sitim pello TO PUT AN END TO YOUR THIRST

- ... nec *sitim pellit* ... AND HE DOES NOT PUT AN END TO HIS THIRST (Horace, *Carmina*).

2/ famem pello TO PUT AN END TO YOUR HUNGER

❑ peto

1/ ima petere TO SINK

- *Ima petunt* pisces FISH SINK (Ovid, *Metamorphoses*).

2/ altum petere TO GO OUT TO DEEP SEA

- Lustrata classe ... *altum petit* AFTER THE FLEET HAD BEEN PURIFIED HE PUT OUT TO SEA (Livy, *Ab Urbe Condita*).

3/ poenas ab aliquo petere TO SEEK REVENGE ON SOMEBODY

- ... etiam si *poenas a populo Romano* ob aliquod delictum *expetiverunt* ... EVEN IF THEY SOUGHT REVENGE ON THE ROMAN PEOPLE BECAUSE OF SOME CRIME (Cicero, *Pro Marcello*).

❑ profiteor

1/ Although this verb usually means TO CONFESS, it can also have the meaning of *working in a specific specialisation* :

- *Medicinam* profiteor I WORK AS A PHYSICIAN.
- Ii, qui *rationalem medicinam* profitentur, ... THOSE WHO PRACTISE RATIONAL MEDICINE ... (Celsus, *De Medicina*).

2/ It may also mean TO OFFER:

- *Operam* profiteor I OFFER MY SUPPORT.

❑ recipio

se recipere TO GO, TO WITHDRAW

- Germani ... trans Rhenum *sese receperunt* THE GERMANS WITHDREW ACROSS THE RHINE (Caesar, *De Bello Gallico*).

❑ revertor

ad sanitatem reverti TO RETURN TO A SOUND MIND

- Caesar ... eum *ad sanitatem reverti* arbitrabatur CAESAR THOUGHT THAT HE WAS RETURNING TO A SOUND MIND (Caesar, *De Bello Gallico*).

❑ rogo

1/ legem rogare TO PROPOSE A LAW

- Q. Papirius, qui *hanc legem rogavit*, ... Q. PAPIRIUS, WHO PROPOSED THIS LAW, ... (Cicero, *De Domo Sua*).

2/ Uti rogas AS YOU PROPOSE (an affirmative vote)

- Tabellae ministrabantur ita ut nulla daretur *'uti rogas'* VOTING TABLETS WERE DISTRIBUTED SO THAT NO ONE TABLET OF "AS YOU PROPOSE" MIGHT BE GIVEN (Cicero, *Epistulae ad Atticum*).

❑ sto

1/ magno pretio stare TO COST A LOT

- *Quinque talentis stat* IT COSTS FIVE TALENTS.
- Polybius scribit *centum talentis* eam rem Achaeis *stetisse* POLYBIUS WRITES THAT THIS COST ONE-HUNDRED TALENTS TO THE ACHAEANS (Livy, *Ab Urbe Condita*).

2/ Mihi sententia stat hoc facere I HAVE DECIDED TO DO THIS.

- Hannibal, postquam *ipsi sententia stetit pergere*, ... HANNIBAL, AFTER HE DECIDED TO PROCEED, ... (Livy, *Ab Urbe Condita*).

❑ studeo

1/ nobis rebus studere TO DESIRE A REVOLUTION

- Cupiditate regni adductus *novis rebus studebat* MOVED BY THE DESIRE OF POWER, HE DESIRED A REVOLUTION (Caesar, *De Bello Gallico*).

  ✧ Let's remember that **studeo** rules dative.

2/ It may also mean TO SUPPORT (for instance, in elections):

- Hegesaretos ... *Pompeianis rebus studebat* HEGESARETOS SUPPORTED POMPEIUS' SIDE (Caesar, *Bellum Civile*).

❑ sum

1/ opus est TO BE NECESSARY

This construction is followed by a dative of the person who needs something:

Opus est mihi ... I NEED ...

and the thing needed can be either in *nominative* or in *ablative*:

- *Opus est mihi* amicus / *Opus est mihi* amico I NEED A FRIEND.
- Quid *opus est mihi* liberis? WHAT NEED DO I HAVE OF CHILDREN? (Plautus, *Miles Gloriosus*).

In a few cases, we can find the needed thing in genitive:

- Opus est mihi *amici* (same meaning).

2/ fructui est TO BE AN ASSET

This is one of the usual constructions of double dative, but with a very strong idiomatic meaning:

- Nihil est quod tibi maiori *fructui* gloriaeque *esse* possit THERE IS NOTHING THAT COULD BE A GREATER ASSET AND GLORY TO YOU (Cicero, *Epistulae ad Familiares*).

3/ cum imperio esse TO BE IN COMMAND

- Ipse autem Caesar ... *erat cum imperio* CAESAR HIMSELF WAS IN COMMAND (Cicero, *Pro Sestio*).

❑ supero

It may have the meaning of TO OUTLIVE:

- Marcus Caesari vita *superavit* MARCUS LIVED LONGER THAN CAESAR.
  ✧ Vita must be in *ablative*, and the person who has been outlived must be in *dative*.

❑ tollo

1/ signa tollere TO GET IN MOTION (an army as subject)

- Altera ex duabus legionibus ... *signa sustulit* seseque Hispalim recepit ONE OF THE TWO LEGIONS GOT IN MOTION AND WENT TO HISPALIS (Caesar, *Bellum Civile*).

2/ in crucem tollere TO CRUCIFY

- Pastorem ... *in crucem sustulit* HE CRUCIFIED A SHEPHERD (Quintilianus, *Institutio Oratoria*).

3/ aliquem tollere TO KILL SOMEONE

- *Sustulit* hic *matrem, sustulit* ille *patrem* THIS ONE KILLED HIS MOTHER, THAT ONE KILLED HIS FATHER (Suetonius, *De Vita Caesarum*).

❑ **valeo**

It may mean TO HAVE INFLUENCE:

- **Apud Gallos Vercingetorix multum valebat** VERCINGETORIX HAD A GREAT INFLUENCE AMONG THE GAULS.

❑ **venio**

1/ in consuetudinem venire TO BECOME NORMAL PRACTICE

- **Quod quoniam iam *in consuetudinem venit*** ... AS THIS HAS BECOME NORMAL PRACTICE ... (Cicero, *Pro Caecina*).

2/ in odium Caesari venire TO BECOME AN OBJECT OF HATRED FOR CAESAR

✧ Observe that **Caesari** is in *dative*, not in genitive.

- **Tu non vides ... nomen *huic populo in odium venisse* regium?** DO NOT YOU SEE THAT THE ROYAL NAME HAS BECOME AN OBJECT OF HATRED FOR THIS COUNTRY? (Cicero, *De Republica*).

❑ **verto**

sententiam vertere TO CHANGE YOUR MIND

- **Maxime tamen sententiam vertisse dicitur Ti. Gracchus** IT IS SAID THAT NEVERTHELESS T. GRACCHUS CHANGED HIS MIND COMPLETELY (Livy, *Ab Urbe Condita*).

❑ **voco**

This verb may have the meaning of *making somebody end up in this or that situation* :

in discrimen vocare TO PUT IN DANGER

- **Eum ... *in discrimen* omnium fortunarum *vocavisti* ?** DID YOU PUT HIM IN DANGER OF ALL HIS FORTUNES? (Cicero, *Pro Flacco*).

b) Words that are easily confused

In Latin, we encounter words that seem to be almost identical, and which therefore may lead to confusion in meaning. These words differ only very slightly, perhaps in one letter or maybe even they look equal letter by letter (there may be a difference in the length of some vowels, but this is not reflected in texts).

1. Non-verbal forms [461]

- We include participles, although they are obviously verbal adjectives.
- In the cases in which the dictionary entry forms coincide, we have written the word just once.

❑ aetas, -atis and aestas, -atis

a/ aetas, -atis means AGE, PERIOD.
b/ aestas, -atis means SUMMER.

❑ forte

a/ It can be the neuter of the adjective **fortis, -e** STRONG.
b/ It can also be the adverb that means BY CHANCE.

❑ liber

a/ It can be the noun **liber, libri** BOOK.

b/ It can also be the masculine of the adjective **liber, -a, -um**, and we should remember also that in plural **liberi, -orum** is used to mean CHILDREN:

- Cum *meos liberos* et uxorem me absente ... defendisses, ... AS YOU DEFENDED MY CHILDREN AND MY WIFE WHILE I WAS ABSENT, ... (Cicero, *Pro Plancio*).

❑ natus

a/ **natus, -us** is a noun of the 4th declension, and it means BIRTH. It is much used in the ablative, in the sense of WITH RESPECT TO BIRTH:

- De istis rebus ... maiores *natu* consulemus LET'S CONSULT THOSE OLDER BY BIRTH / BY AGE ABOUT THESE MATTERS (Livy, *Ab Urbe Condita*).

b/ **natus, -a, -um** is the past participle of the verb **nascor, -i, natus sum** TO BE BORN. Moreover, it is used also in the sense of SON (**natus**) and DAUGHTER (**nata**).

❑ **nusquam** and **numquam**

a/ **nusquam** is an adverb that means NOWHERE:

- **Tu censeo Luceriam venias; *nusquam* eris tutius** I SUGGEST THAT YOU COME TO LUCERIA; NOWHERE WILL YOU BE MORE IN SAFETY (Cicero, *Epistulae ad Atticum*).

b/ **numquam** means NEVER:

- ***Numquam* te antea vidimus** WE HAVE NEVER SEEN YOU BEFORE (Cicero, *Divinatio in Q. Caecilium*).

❑ **populus, -i**

a/ It can be the noun **populus, -i,** masculine, PEOPLE.
b/ It can be the noun **populus, -i,** feminine, POPLAR-TREE. It is worth remembering that nouns of trees are usually feminine.

❑ **relictus** and **reliquus**

a/ **relictus** is the past passive participle of the verb **relinquo, -ere, reliqui, relictum** TO LEAVE BEHIND, TO ABANDON, therefore it means ABANDONED, LEFT BEHIND.
b/ **reliquus** is an adjective that means REMAINING.

The problem with these two words is that **reliquus** has a much greater resemblance to the verb **relinquo**, but the form that comes from this verb happens to be the other one, **relictus**.

❑ **victus, -a, -um**

a/ Past passive participle of **vinco, -ere, vici, victum** TO CONQUER.
b/ Past passive participle of **vivo, -ere, vixi, victum** TO LIVE ✧ This verb is scarcely used in the passive.

❑ **vir** and **vis**

a/ **vir, -i,** 2nd declension MAN
b/ **vis, --** 3rd declension and irregular STRENGTH ✧ The genitive **vis** belongs to late Latin.

A usual mistake when translating a text of military content is to translate a sentence like **Urbem oppugnavit omnibus viribus** by HE BESIEGED THE CITY WITH ALL HIS MEN instead of ... WITH ALL HIS FORCES, for the simple reason that the first translation sounds logical.

❑ **quidam** and **quidem**

a/ **quidam** is the masculine of the indefinite pronoun **quidam, quaedam, quoddam** A CERTAIN.
b/ **quidem** is an adverb that means INDEED (and let's remember that the combination **ne ... quidem** means NOT EVEN).

2. Verbal forms [462]

❑ fugio and fugo

a/ fugio, -ere, fugi (no supine) TO FLEE ✧ It is an intransitive verb.
b/ fugo, -are, -avi, -atum TO PUT TO FLIGHT ✧ It is a transitive verb.

❑ cado, caedo and occido

a/ cado, -ere, cecidi, casum TO FALL (therefore, also TO DIE) ✧ It is an intransitive verb.
b/ caedo, -ere, cecidi, caesum TO MAKE FALL (therefore also TO KILL) ✧ It is a transitive verb.

These two verbs have a compound each, with the same meaning, not only sharing the perfect but also the present tense:

c/ occido, -ere, occidi, occasum TO FALL, TO DIE ✧ Intransitive verb
d/ occido, -ere, occidi, occisum TO MAKE FALL, TO KILL ✧ Transitive verb

❑ pareo, paro, pario and parco

a/ pareo, -ere, parui (no supine) has two meanings:

– TO APPEAR, TO BE EVIDENT ✧ In this meaning, it is intransitive.
– TO OBEY ✧ In this meaning, the person one obeys is in dative.

b/ paro, -are, -avi, -atum TO PREPARE ✧ It is therefore transitive.
c/ pario, -ere, peperi, partum TO GIVE BIRTH ✧ It is transitive.
d/ parco, -ere, peperci, parsum TO SPARE ✧ Usually its object is in *dative*.

❑ redeo and reddo

1/ redeo, -ire, -ii, -itum TO GO BACK, TO COME BACK ✧ It is intransitive.
2/ reddo, -ere, reddidi, redditum TO GIVE BACK ✧ It is transitive.

❑ servio and servo

a/ servio, -ire, -ivi, -itum TO SERVE ✧ Usually it has its object (the person whom one serves) in dative.
b/ servo, -are, -avi, -atum TO SAVE ✧ It has its object in accusative.

❑ sto and sisto

1/ sto, stare, steti, statum TO STAND ✧ It is intransitive.
2/ sisto, -ere, stiti, statum TO CAUSE TO STAND ✧ It is transitive.

❑ video and viso

1/ video, -ere, vidi, visum TO SEE
2/ viso, -ere, visi, visum TO GO TO SEE and TO BEHOLD

The similarity in meaning between these two verbs sometimes makes students think that the perfect tense of the frequent verb video is visi instead of vidi, and the fact that its supine features also an "s", visum (as the supine of viso), adds to this confusion.

Index of grammatical terms

This index contains the English terms and expressions that have been used in the presentation of Latin grammar.

In some cases, the same item can be found under two or more different entries; for instance, *Personal construction of the infinitive* can be found under *Infinitive* and under *Personal construction.* This will help students to find the requested item more easily. Also, in some cases it makes more sense to name the grammatical item in the singular or in the plural, independently from whether the main entry is in singular or plural; for instance, under the entry of *Prepositions* (it is customary to use the plural when introducing this concept) we find the sub-entry *Lack of prep.*, obviously *Lack of preposition*, while further down we find the sub-entry *Preps. of one case*, obviously *Prepositions of one case.* The presence or absence of a final *-s* will make it clear.

The numbers make reference to the numbered paragraphs, not to the pages.

Ablative [5], [7]
- Abl. absolute [393-401]
- Abl. of cause [239]
- Abl. of characteristic [238]
- Abl. of intensity [240]
- Abl. of manner [240]
- Abl. of price [239]
- Abl. of respect [239]
- Abl. of separation [237]
- Abl. with adjectives [241], [277]
- Abl. with verbs [241], [274]
- Adverbial abl. [241]
- Agent abl. [242]
- Gerund in abl. [441]
- Instrumental abl. [238]
- Use of abl. [237-242]

Accentuation [3]

Accusative [5], [7]
- Acc. exclamative [227]
- Acc. of extension [226]
- Acc. of respect [227]
- Adverbial acc. [228]
- Double acc. [225]
- Gerund in acc. [438]
- Internal acc. [224]
- Use of acc. [224-228]

Active voice [133-134]

Addressed object [6], [223]

Adjectives
- Adjs. with ablative [277]
- Adjs. with dative [276]
- Adjs. with genitive [275]
- Adj. with supine [448]
- Position of the adj. [36]
- Use of adjs. as a noun [37]
- 1st class of adjs. [30-31]
- 2nd class of adjs. [32-35]
  - Adjs. of 1 Nom. [34-35]
  - Adjs. of 2 Nom. [32]
  - Adjs. of 3 Nom. [33]

Adverbs in Oratio Obliqua [433]

Affirmative adverbs [114]

Agreement [455]

Alphabet [1]

Anaphoric pronoun [64]

Antecedent [337-339]
- Lack of antec. [346]
- Inclusion of antec. [347]

Apodosis [328]

Article
- Lack of definite art. [10]

Cacophonic effects [444]

Cardinals [38-39]

Case
- Concept of case [5]
- Functions and cases [7]
- Use of cases [218]

Causal clauses [311-312]

Circumstantial object [6]

Commands [283-285]

Comparative [43-44]
- Comp. by means of adverbs [52]
- Comp. of equality [52]
- Comp. of inferiority [51]
- Irregular comps. [46-47]
- Syntax of comp. [48-49]

Comparative clauses [348-351]

Completive quod clauses [368]

Completive ut clauses [367]

Compound
- Comp. verbs [217-218]
- Comps. of eo [208]
- Comps. of fero [210]
- comps. of sum [200-203]

Concessive clauses [322-323]
- Subjunctive in conc. clauses [323]

Conditional clauses [328-335]
- Combined periods of cond. cl. [334-335]
- Open cond. cl. [329-330]
- Remote cond. cl. [331]
- Unfulfilled cond. cl. [332-333]

Conjugation
- 1st conj. [140-149]
- 2nd conj. [150-157]
- 3rd conj. [158-165]
- 4th conj. [166-173]
- The mixed conj. [174-181]

Consecutio temporum [305-310]

Consonant stems [18-20], [24]

Constructions
- Different possible consts. [271]
- Peculiar consts. [215-216]
- Personal const. [304]

Correlative adjectives [125-129]

Correlative adverbs [118-124]

Dative [5], [7]
- Agent dat. [236]
- Dat. of purpose [235]
- Dat. with adjectives [236], [276]
- Dat. with verbs [236], [273]
- Double dat. [235]
- Gerund in dat. [440]

Possessive dat. [234]
Use of dat. [233-236]
Declension
Concept of decl. [8]
General structure of decls. [11]
1st decl. [12-13]
2nd decl. [14-17]
3rd decl. [18-25]
4th decl. [26-27]
5th decl. [28]
Defective verbs [213-214]
Demonstrative pronouns
Accidence of dem. prons. [55-58]
Syntax of dem. prons. [59-60]
Deponent verbs [192-196]
Passive dep. verbs [198]
Distributives [42]
Direct object [6], [224]
Endings, concept of [4]
Fear clauses [352-353]
Feminine [9]
Future tense [131]
Formation of fut. tense [134-135]
Future perfect tense [131]
Formation of fut. perf. tense [134-135]
Gender
Concept of gender [9]
Genitive [5], [7]
Gen. of characteristic [231]
Gen. of value [231]
Gen. partitive [232]
Gen. partitive with numbers [39]
Gen. partitive with plus [47]
Gen. with adjectives [232], [275]
Gen. with quantitative adverbs [232]
Gen. with verbs [232], [272]
Gerund in gen. [439]
Judicial gen. [231]
Infinitive + gen. [230]
Objective gen. [230]
Possessive gen. [229-230]
Subjective gen. [230]
Use of gen. [229-232]
Gerund [132], [136], [436-444]
Gerundive [132], [436-437], [442-444]
-i stems [21-25]
Identity pronouns
Accidence of ident. prons. [65]
Syntax of ident. prons. [66]
Idiomatic expressions [452]
Idiom. exprs. without verbs [453-454]
Idiom. exprs. with verbs [460]
Imparisyllabic [18]
Imperative [132], [136]
Imperfect tense [131]
Formation of imperf. tense [134-135]
Impersonal passive [303]
Impersonal verbs [295-304]
Imp. verbs with result clauses [325]
Indefinite adverbs [112-113]
Indefinite clauses [354-357]
Indefinite pronouns [76-93]
Indicative [132], [134]
Indirect commands [403], [409-414]
Ind. comms. in Oratio Obliqua [432]
Subord. clauses in ind. comms. [424-425]
Indirect object [6], [233]
Indirect prohibitions [412-414]
Indirect questions [403], [415-421]
Ind. qus. in Oratio Obliqua [428-431]
Subord. clauses in ind. qus. [423]
Indirect speech [402-435]
Subord. clauses in ind. sp. [422-425]
Indirect statement [372], [375], [403], [404-408]
Ind. stat. in Oratio Obliqua [427]
Subord. clauses in ind. stat. [422]
Infinitive [132], [136], [369]
Exclamative inf. [378]
Historic inf. [377]
Personal construction of the inf. [456]
Infinitive clauses [369-378]
Interrogative adverbs [111]
Interrogative pronouns/adjectives [70-74]
Irregular verbs [204-214]
Iussive subjunctive [285]
Letters of Greek origin [1]
Locative [267]
Masculine [9]
Modal adverbs [101-102]
Comp. and superl. of mod. advs. [103-104]
Moods [132]
Formation of moods [136]
Multiplicatives [41]
Negative adverbs [115]
Negative pronouns [94-99]
Negative statement [407]
Negatives in combination [449-451]
Neuter [9]
Nominative [5], [7]
Use of nom. [222]
Numerals [38-42]
Compound nums. [39]
Oratio Obliqua [426-435]
Ordinals [40]
Parisyllabic [21]
Participle [132], [136]
Future part. [383-384]
Part. is impersonal [381]
Part as noun [391-392]
Part. as verb [386-390]
Perfect part. [385-386]
Present part. [382]
Participle clauses [379-401]
Passive
Impersonal pasive [303-304]
Passive deponent verbs [198]
Passive voice [133], [135], [182-191]
Perfect tense [131]
Formation of perf. tense [134-135]
Problem with perf. tense [309-310]
Periphrastic conjugation [445-446]
Personal construction [304]
Pers. const. of the infinitive [456]
Personal pronouns [61-62]
Place
Adverbs of place [108-110]
Expressions of place [266-270]
Pluperfect tense [131]
Formation of plup. tense [134-135]
Possessive object [6]
Possessive pronouns [63]
Potential actions [279-282]
Pot. actions in the future [279-280]
Pot. actions in the past [282]
Pot. actions in the present [281]
Predicative object [6], [222]
Prepositional adverbs [116-117]
Prepositions [243-261]
General observations on prep. [243]
Preps. in compound verbs [218]
Preps. of one case [244-258]
Preps. of two cases [259-261]
Preps. with ablative [253-258]
Preps. with accusative [244-252]
Use of prep. [6], [271]
Present tense [131]
Curious use of pr. tense [318]
Formation of pr. tense [134-135]
Prohibitions [286-287]
Prohs. in Oratio Obliqua [432]

Pronouns in Oratio Obliqua [433]
Pronunciation [2]
Protasis [328]
Proviso clauses [358]
Purpose clauses [313-315]
  Purp. cls. by means of supine [447]
Quantitative adverbs [105]
Questions
  Deliberative questions [294]
  Double questions [292], [420]
  Partial questions [293]
  Yes/no questions [291]
Quin/Quominus clauses [359-362]
Real actions [278]
Reflexive pronouns
  Accidence of refl. prons. [67]
  Indirect refl. pron. [69]
  Syntax of refl. prons. [68]
Relative
  Connective rel. [342]
  Rel. clauses [336-347]
  Rel. of characteristic [343-344]
  Rel of purpose [345]
  Rel. with prepositions [341]
Relative pronoun [75]
  Indefinite relat. pron. [76]
Repeated action [319]
Result clauses [324-327]
Semi-deponent verbs [197]
Subject [6], [222]
Subjunctive [132], [136]
  Iussive subj. [285]
  Subj. in concessive clauses [323]
  Subj. in indirect questions [415]
  Subj. in temporal clauses [320-321]
Superlative [43], [45-46]
  Irregular superls. [46]
  Superl. by means of adverbs [52]
  Superl. with quam [53]
  Syntax of superl. [50], [54]
Supine [132], [136]
  Supine in -um [447]
  Supine in -u [448]
Syntactical function
  Concept of synt. function [4]
  Main synt. functions [6]
  Synt. functs. and cases [7]
Temporal clauses [316-321]
  Temp. clauses in subjunctive [320-321]
Tenses [121]
  Formation of tenses [134-135]
  Primary and secondary tenses [307]
Time
  Adverbs of time [106-107]
  Expressions of time [262-265]
Verbs
  Impersonal verbs [295-304]
  Main characteristics [130]
  Principal parts of verbs [138-139]
  Types of verbs [137]
  Verbs that rule ablative [274]
  Verbs that rule dative [273]
  Verbs that rule genitive [272]
Vocative [5], [7]
  Use of voc. [223]
Voices [133]
Wishes
  Wishes for the future [288]
  Wishes for the past [290]
  Wishes for the present [289]

Index of Latin words

This index contains the Latin *grammatical words*, i.e. words associated to some grammatical function (like for instance **ut** is associated to *purpose clauses*) or that have to be presented in the study of the grammar even if they are not associated to any definite grammatical function (like for instance the numeral **tres**). It does not contain either the vocabulary used in the examples (all the examples, in any case, are translated) or the vocabulary of the lists of frequent terms that follow a given parameter.

With respect to the verbal forms, including all the main parts of each verb introduced in the grammar would have been excessive, but some of them, given their importance, have been included.

The numbers make reference to the numbered paragraphs, not to the pages.

a / ab /abs [253]
abeo [208]
abhinc [265]
absum [200-201]
ad [244]
adeo [208]
adeptus [195]
adsum [200]
aedes / -is [25]
aestas [461]
aetas [461]
age [283]
aio [214]
alicui [112]
alicunde [112]
aliqua [112]
aliquando [112]
aliquantum [105]
aliquantus [127]
aliquis [77]
aliquo [112]
aliquot [129]
aliquotiens [124]
alius [88-89]
alter [91]
an [421]
animal [24]
annon [421]
ante [245]
antequam [317]
apud [246]
arma [17]
Athenae [13]
audeo [197]
aufero [210]
auxilia / -um [17]
bene [102]
bini [42]
bis [41]
bonus [46]
cado [462]
caedo [462]
captus [454]
castra / -um [17]
cave [287]
celeberrimus [45]
centiens [41]
certus [454]
circa [116]
circum [247]
circumeo [208]
citra [116]
clam [117]
coepi [213]
coeptus [454]
comitatus [195]
complector [198]
confero [210]
confido [197]
contra [116]
copia / -ae [13]
coram [117]
cum (conj.) [316-317], [319] [363-365]
cum (prep.) [254]
cur [111]
de [255]
dea [12]
decet [298]
dedecet [298]
Delphi [17]
desum [200]
deus [14]
dicitur [304], [456]
dictus [454]
dies [453]
difficillimus [45]
diffido [197]
dissimillimus [45]
ditior [46]
ditissimus [46]
diu [107]
dives [46]
divitiae [13]
divus [14]
do [140]
domus [26], [267], [453]
donec [317]
dum [317-318], [320], [358]
dummodo [358]
duo [38]
duplex [41]
e / ex [256]
edo [211]
effero [210]
ego [61]
eo (adverb) [120]
eo (verb) [207]
erga [248]
et [457]
etiamsi [322]
etsi [322]
exeo [208]
extra [116]
exulo [198]
facillimus [45]
fasti [17]
fatur [214]
fero [209]
fertur [304]
festinatim [102]
fido [197]
filia [14]
filius [14]
fines / -is [25]
fio [212]
fluctuo [198]
fore [459]
forte [102], [461]
fugio [462]
fugo [462]
futurum [459]
frater [24]
gaudeo [197]
gestus [454]
grandinat [302]
haud [115]
hic, haec, hoc [56]
humus [267]
iam [264]
ibi [118-119]
idem, eadem, idem [65-66] [351]
ille, illa, illud [58]
impedimenta / -um [17]
impero [411]
in [259]
inde [121]
ineo [208]
inferi [17]

infero [210]
infra [116]
inquam [213]
insidiae [13]
insum [200]
inter [249]
interest [300-301]
intersum [200]
intra [116]
ipse [65-66], [69]
is, ea, id [62-64]
iste, ista, istud [57]
itur [303]
iubeo [410]
iuxta [116]
laborantes [454]
liber [461]
liberi [17], [461]
libet [298]
licet [296]
littera / -ae [13]
loca / -us [14], [453]
longe [110]
ludus [453]
magis [105]
magnopere [105]
magnus [46], [454]
maior [46]
malo [206]
malus [46]
manus [26]
mater [24]
mater familias [12]
maximus [46]
me [61]
medius [36]
melior [46]
memini [213]
mens [24]
meus [63]
milia [39]
mille [39]
minimus [46]
minus [51], [105]
minor [46]
miseret [299]
modo [358]
moenia [25]
mons [24]
mors [24]
multum [228]
natus [454], [461]
ne [286], [315], [352-353] [412]
-ne [291-292]
necne [421]
necesse [296]
nemo [99], [450-451]
neque [449]
neuter [95]
nihil [96-98], [228] [450-451]
nimis [105]
nivit [302]
nolo [205], [286]
non [115], [450-451]
nonne [291]
nos [61]
noster [63]
novi [213]
nullus [94], [99] [449-450]
num [78], [291], [420]
numquam [450-451], [461]
nuper [107]
nuptiae [13]
nusquam [461]
ob [250]
obeo [208]
obsum [200]
occido [462]
odi [213]
offero [210]
opes / ops [25]
oportet [296]
optimus [46]
opus [453]
paenitet [299]
palam [117]
parco [462]
pareo [462]
pario [462]
paro [462]
parum [105]
parvus [46]
pater [24]
pater familias [12]
peior [46]
penes [250]
per [251]
pereo [208]
pessimus [46]
piget [299]
pluit [302]
plures [47]
plurimum [105]
plus [47], [105]
poena [453]
pollicitus [195]
populus [461]
possum [202]
post [252]
postquam [317]
prae [257]
praeeo [208]
praefero [210]
praestat [298]
praesum [200]
praeter [252]
primum [228]
priusquam [317], [321]
pro [257]
profero [210]
prohibeo [413]
prope [110], [116]
propinquus [46]
propior [46]
propter [117]
prosum [203]
proximus [46]
pudet [299]
pugnans [454]
pulcherrimus [45]
qua [111]
quadruplex [41]
quaeso [214]
qualis [73], [125], [348]
qualiscumque [127]
quam [48], [51-53]
quamdiu [111]
quamobrem [111]
quamquam [322]
quamvis [323]
quando [111], [312]
quantum [111], [348]
quantus [72], [126]
quantuscumque [127]
quare [111]
queo [214]
quemadmodum [111]
qui, quae, quod [75], [78] [338-347]
quia [311]
quicumque [76], [127]
quidam [80], [461]
quidem [115], [461]
quilibet [83]
quin [327], [359-362]
quique [54]
quisquam [84]
quisque [81-82]
quis, quid [70-71], [78]
quispiam [79]
quisquis [76]
quo [111], [314]
quocumque [120]
quod [311], [368], [458]
quominus [361-362]
quomodo [111], [350]
quoniam [312]
quot [72], [129]
quotcumque [129]
quotiens [124]
quotienscumque [124]
ratus [195]
reddo [462]
redeo [208], [462]
refero [210]
refert [300-301]
relictus [461]
reliquus [461]
res [28], [453]
rus [267]
saepe [107]
satis [105]
se [67-69]
secundum [117], [228]
semel [41]
senatus [453]
senex [24]
servio [462]
servo [462]
si [328-335]
sicut [350]
simillimus [45]
simul [317]
sine [116], [258]
singuli [42]
sisto [462]
soleo [197]

solus [86]
sors / sortes [25]
sto [216], [462]
sub [260]
subito [101]
subter [261]
suffero [210]
sum [199]
super [261]
superi [17]
supersum [200]
supra [116]
suus [63]
taedet [299]
talis [125], [348]
tam [52]
tametsi [322]
tamquam [350]
tantum [324], [348]
tantus [126]
te [61]
tempus [453]
tenus [258]
ter [41]
Tiberis [25]
tonat [302]
tot [129]
totidem [129]
totiens [124]
totus [87]
trans [252]
transeo [208]
tres [38]
trini [42]
triplex [41]
tu [61]
tum [123]
turris [25]
tuus [63]
ubi [111], [316]
ullus [84], [90], [449]
ultra [116]
umquam [449]
unde [111]
unus [38], [85]
urbs [24]
usus [195], [453]
ut [285], [313], [316], [324] [327], [350], [352-353] [366-367], [409], [459]
uter [74], [92]
uterque [93]
utinam [288-290]
utrum [292], [421]
valde [105]
vapulo [198]
veneo [198]
veritus [195]
vester [63]
veterrimus [46]
veto [414]
vetus [46]
vetustior [46]
via [453]
victus [461]
video [462]
videor [304]
vigilia / -ae [13]
vir [15], [461]
vis [25], [241], [461]
viso [462]
volo [204]
vos [61]

Made in the USA
Middletown, DE
04 June 2024